VIRTUALLY PERFECT

VIRTUALLY PERFECT

Driving Innovative and Lean Products through Product Lifecycle Management

DR. MICHAEL GRIEVES

SPACE COAST PRESS
Cocoa Beach, Florida

www.plmvirtuallyperfect.com

Space Coast Press, LLC
Cocoa Beach, Florida

Printed in the United States of America.

ISBN 9780982138007

To my wife, Diane,
of ∞ wonderful years

CONTENTS

PREFACE

Second books are harder to write than first books, especially if they are written on the same topic. The second book needs to stand on its own and needs not to be repetitive. However, the second book needs to be consistent and extend the ideas of the first book. In writing this second book on Product Lifecycle Management (PLM), I hope to cover some new and interesting material, while reminding the reader of the material from my first book.

The good news about my first book, *Product Lifecycle Management: Driving the Next Generation of Lean Thinking*, is that it was well received. While falling short of the success of the Harry Potter novels, the book has been successful in capturing the attention of those interested in the topic of PLM. It is gratifying to find that my book graces the bookshelves of many people involved with product creation, building, support, and disposal in most major companies. I have been pleasantly surprised to be asked questions to indicate that a fair amount of them have actually read it!

On the topic of Harry Potter, I had organized a meeting a while back at NASA in order to have a PLM application provider do a presentation and demonstration of their latest software. It went over well with all of the participants, except one. This was an individual whose sole qualification for being there was that she had a PhD. What little theoretical knowledge she possessed was clearly not sufficient for her to understand the state of Product Lifecycle Management.

Her complaint to me was that my advocation that NASA build a digital rocket along with the physical rocket was based on "magic." I dismissed this at the time, but on further reflection, thought maybe she had a point from her perspective. As Arthur Clarke, the famous science-fiction author noted, "Any sufficiently advanced technology is indistinguishable from magic." For a lot of people, the rapid advances in Product Lifecycle Management may certainly look to them like magic. However, it is the rapid advances in computing, communications, and software that are making possible what would have been impossible a few years ago.

The ability to create and organize information about products that mirrors their physical nature has only been recently possible. While we long have had abstracted and simplified information about products, the rich representations of both product form and their functions has only occurred recently. This may look like magic to some, but it is the product of a tremendous technology trajectory, and it is still only the beginning.

Because of this book, I've had the opportunity to visit some of the best companies in the world in their respective product categories. I have gotten to see some of the most amazing products that have literally change our world. I have discussed with these manufacturers both how they have created and built a product in the past and how PLM is changing and will change how they will build the successor products in the future.

My first book has been translated into a number of languages, and I have been allowed the opportunity to give talks related to PLM in United States, Asia, and Europe. In the classes I have taught for both universities and industry, I have had professionals from every continent, except Antarctica.

While I am pleased with the impact that my book has had on industry, I am equally pleased that my book is being used at the university level. Institutions such as Purdue University, Virginia Tech, and Shanghai Jiao Tong University have all used my book to educate students in this new way of thinking about products and its associated information. My belief is that students who learn about this new way of doing things and bring these ideas to their workplace will have a competitive advantage over their peers who are being educated in the obsolete, siloed way of the past.

The better news about my book from my perspective is that directionally I have been correct. The path of progress that PLM has taken has validated the ideas that I proposed in my book. I have seen some of the ideas I proposed, such as Virtual Collaboration Rooms, being embraced and implemented by major corporations. I've seen some of the terminology and definitions that I created find its way into industry usage. (If the definition of PLM contains the words "culminating in final disposal," it's my definition — the word "culminating" sees pretty rare usage.)

With a new discipline comes some new terminology, and PLM is no exception. Old words generally come with old meanings, and new disciplines need new words. I have taken some grief over the over the use of the word "singularity" to refer to the need for one controlling or master version of information. I still like it over the often-repeated "single version of the truth." I'm still not sure what "truth" has to do with information that is collectively agreed on.

There is still some confusion with basic terminology. Some organizations still refer to this area as Product Data Management (PDM). Terminology does matter. How we talk about things is how we think about them. I find that organizations that still refer to PDM have one foot in older concepts. They still prefer drawings to models. Their use of the technology is still predominately an engineering orientation.

I proposed that PLM is made up of three elements: people, processes/practices, and technology. People are obviously the same people they were when I wrote the first book. However, there has been some new and interesting work about how people think and change, especially in the area of neuroscience, which I would like to explore further. I proposed the process/practice distinction in a few pages in my first book, but since then have given it much more thought and have expanded those ideas. Process has gotten the lion's share of the attention in today's discussions. Process is important, but it really doesn't describe the really interesting thing that people do, engage in practices, that is the real driver in creating, building, supporting, and disposing of products.

Computing and communications technology continues to advance and is truly amazing. There are those readers of the first book who would have liked me to spend more time talking about the actual technology that implements PLM. However, I am reluctant to do that, because at the pace that technology is changing, it would date any book. What I do try to accomplish is to look at underlying technological concepts and the informational constructs that drive PLM.

I maintain and become more convinced over time that information is the key driver in producing products that are both lean and innovative. My premise that information is a replacement for wasted physical resources, i.e. time, energy, and material, is a keen sense of the obvious, but has been rarely articulated. The idea of information is a critical one, but can be confusing to explore and explain.

PLM and its concepts have improved the creation, building, supporting, and disposing of products. I hope to do the topic justice by extending the thinking of my first book and providing some new and interesting concepts to accompany thinking about lean *and* innovative virtually perfect products.

I have benefitted from discussions with many of my friends, colleagues, and acquaintances in the PLM area. I have been especially fortunate to work with NASA at the Marshall Space Flight Center (MSFC) and Kennedy Space Center (KSC). My discussions with Dan Dumbacher, Pam Caruso, Mike Galluzi, Paul Gill, and Pat Hunt have caused me to refine my concepts. John Vickers, who initially brought me into NASA, is a constant source of new insights and applications and works tirelessly to network the right people and projects in order to advance the concepts of PLM.

I enjoy my reasonably frequent dinners with the Dean of PLM, Dr. Richard Riff of Ford. His insights into the direction of PLM are invaluable. Alan Fisk, also from Ford, is both a source of a wealth of how things are done at a major auto company and is now a fellow doctoral graduate from Case Western's prestigious Executive Doctorate program. I also appreciate my friends at the Purdue PLM Center of Excellence giving me a platform twice a year to try out my new concepts. Fred Thomas and Frank Saad, long time industry friends, have been supporters of my work.

I also cannot underestimate the advantage of having seven grandchildren (Nick, Bianca, Jake, Gabby, Bella, Sienna, and Sophia) from my son, Rob, and my daughter-in-law, Chris. They always are a reminder that the world is changing and needs to be not taken for granted. My lovely wife, Diane, is supportive of the time I spend on PLM. She has no interest in the topic, but she does like to accompany me to PLM conferences when they are held in nice places.

Cocoa Beach, Florida 2011

1

VIRTUALLY PERFECT

Virtually Perfect. This is a phrase that has undergone a transformation in the last decade or so. As it was originally used, it was an indication of a state of not-quite-so perfection. A perfect product only existed as an ideal in our mind. There was no way to capture it in information.[1] We could create sparse informational representations of the product as drawings on paper. When we engaged in the messy business of turning our ideal product into atoms, the best we could do was make it "virtually perfect."

We did not realize it then, but our terminology reflected that only if we could make our ideal product virtual, it would be perfect. However, our information technology, up until now, has not been up to the task. As I will argue throughout this book, we are approaching "perfect" products through virtual products. "Virtually Perfect" will transition from indicating a lack of perfection to a description of how we can make "perfect," or at least substantially better products, by using virtual products.

"Virtually Perfect" was also somewhat of an oxymoron. If something was perfect, we did not have the capability to think of it as virtual. Our best hope of rendering products virtually was atom-based. We could draw the representation of the product on atom-based paper or we could model it in atom-based clay. However, no one would mistake those renderings as a perfect representation of the actual product. These renderings and models might have been virtually perfect, but they clearly were not perfect.

We clearly had the ability to think and describe the virtual product mathematically. We had the ability to define height, width, length, and thickness dimensions to the nth decimal place. However, no matter how precise the draftsman, the two-dimensional drawings were merely rough approximations. The dimensions could only been safely relied upon if they were noted on the blueprint. Measuring the lines on drawings themselves could not be relied upon where precision mattered.

However, in the world of the 21st century, "virtually perfect" has taken on a new meaning that has transformed the way we create, build, service, and dispose of products. Virtually perfect has become the new condition of product information. Perfection is only achievable in a virtual product.

With the advent of the computer in the last half of the 20th century, we could begin to separate the information about the product from the actual product itself. We could then store and manipulate that information without any loss of precision. Up until then, we were forced to use atom-based computing, i.e., pencil and paper, to perform those manipulations and calculations.

The ability to translate the mathematical geometric information about products into visual representations started to occur in the 1960's when we started outputting crude drawings on line printers. This capability improved as soon as cathode ray tubes (CRT's) and plotters could be hooked up to digital computers. However, practical geometric representation did not come into existence until the last quarter of the 20th century with the development of true Computer-Aided Design (CAD) systems.

However, no one would have labeled the output of those early CAD systems as "virtually perfect." The early renderings were literally, as the name suggested, "computer-aided drawings." These computer-generated drawings were simple two-dimensional blueprints. The difference between the blueprints that were generated by computers and the ones generated by hand was that the computer ones could be changed and redrawn a great deal faster, with a great deal less manpower than the hand drawn ones. In addition, once the geometric representation was in the computer it could be re-used for other purposes.

With the exponential growth of computer technology, the situation today is amazingly different. Today, the computer-generated representations of physical products are "virtually perfect." The designs themselves, with the ability for precision to the nth decimal point, are the definition of mathematical perfection. Instead of the virtual representations of the physical product being a less than perfect image, the actual physical product is a less than perfect representation of the perfect virtual product. As we will see throughout this book, this has changed how we think about products and their lifecycle: creation, build, support/sustainment, and disposal.

The idea of a virtual product is not limited to the creation phase, when all that may exist are representations of a potential physical product. As we will discuss throughout the book, the virtual product also continues to exist as a product takes physical form. The virtual product can be used as an informational substitute that does not require being in possession of the actual physical product.

"Virtually Perfect" takes on a slightly different interpretation from that of the ideal product. A virtually perfect product that is linked to an actual physical product is not the ideal product, but instead it is the information about the state of the product as it actually exists. If I can get the same information from my virtual product that I could get from possessing and inspecting my physical product, then that to me is virtually perfect. In this case, the perfect part reflects not an ideal product, but the fact that it perfectly reflects the information from the physical product that it represents.

In many cases, assuming that I have designed in the appropriate sensors into the physical product, the virtually perfect product can actually be better than being in possession of the physical version. If I have to disassemble or even destroy parts of the physical product in order to get the information that I need, then having that virtual product is far more useful than being in physical possession of the physical product.

Product Lifecycle Management (PLM) is an information-driven approach to the creation, manufacture, support, and disposal of products. The informational or virtual aspect of the physical product is key to enabling this approach.

DEFINING PRODUCT LIFECYCLE MANAGEMENT (PLM)

With this idea of virtual product in mind, I would like to revisit the definition of Product Lifecycle Management. My definition of Product Lifecycle Management is as follows:

Product Lifecycle Management (PLM) is an integrated, information-driven approach comprised of people, processes/practices, and technology to all aspects of a product's life and its environment, from its design through manufacture, deployment and maintenance—culminating in the product's removal from service and final disposal.

This is identical to my first definition of Product Lifecycle Management with the addition of three words: "and its environment." Without this addition, my definition has the implication that all we are concerned about is information about the product itself. While this was not reflected in the models, examples and use cases that I described in my first book that clearly showed the product interacting with its environment, I would like to make explicit the addition of a product's environment as part of what Product Lifecycle Management encompasses.

This change to the definition further enforces the idea of a virtual product in a virtual environment as having as its counterpart the physical product in the physical environment. This adds to the idea of virtual products serving in place of physical products in a wide variety of use cases.

WHAT IS A PRODUCT?

A core question concerning PLM is what is a "product"? Is it something we make a number of such as airplanes or automobiles? Is it something we make one of, such as a nuclear power plant? Is it an end product like a rocket or can it be components that make up end products, such as rocket engines?

My definition of a product is that it is a man made object that performs a function or functions for a user. By that definition, all the items mentioned in the above paragraph are products. By my definition and use of PLM and products, products are like Russian dolls with discrete products nestled inside more inclusive products.

What constitutes a product will also depend on my perspective. If I am a jet engine manufacturer, my perspective of the product is the jet engine. I am concerned with the geometry and status of the individual components. If I am an airplane manufacturer, my concern is the entire airplane, its geometry and functionality. While I am concerned about the jet engines, my concern is more macro. I am concerned about the geometry of the engine as a whole, or its outer mold lines (OML), so I can properly fit it on the airplane and understand its aerodynamics. I am also concerned about macro elements of performance such as fuel intake and power output. However, I leave the micro aspects of the engine components and functionality to the jet engine manufacturer.

If it is a product and has a lifecycle, then by definition it falls under the purview of PLM. By this definition of product, PLM concerns itself with a wide range of things. This includes items that would be easily recognized as products: automobiles, airplanes, pacemakers, refrigerators, and earthmovers, to items that might not be obvious as products: aircraft carriers, fossil and nuclear fuel power plants, and even roads and bridges.

If it is man-made, has geometry, performs a function for its user, and has a lifecycle, then PLM, as a concept, has applicability to it. It may be that as time goes on specialization will occur as solution providers specialize on a particular product type, e.g., Airplane Lifecycle Management (ALM), or a particular product category, e.g., Transportation Lifecycle Management (TLM), or a particular asset type, Factory Lifecycle Management (FLM).[2] However, the general concepts and characteristics of PLM will be applicable.

VIRTUAL PRODUCT PREMISES

There are some underlying premises that govern the use of virtual products and therefore of the Product Lifecycle Management area. These premises are as follows:

- Physical objects have an informational equivalent
- Information is a replacement for wasted physical resources
- Bits instead of atoms[3] are used until the last possible moment and wherever possible
- Products are dual in nature — they are both physical and virtual
- Physical world models are continually refined for use in virtual simulation
- Information is required to mitigate risk

These are the premises that will drive the use of virtual products and are incorporated into the premises of Product Lifecycle Management. I will discuss each of these below.

Physical objects have an informational equivalent

All physical objects have the information about themselves embedded within the physical object itself. Obvious informational characteristics such as height, width, and length are clearly information that is embedded within a physical object. Other characteristics such as the hardness of steel, the viscosity of fluid, and the pliability of rubber are all information that is embedded in the physical object itself.

The atoms and molecules that make up the physical object determine this information. This information is relatively consistent for all physical objects that have a makeup of specific material. A rod of a specific type of metal and of a certain length and diameter will contain the same amount of atoms within a small range.

Human intelligence has the ability to find and extract information from a physical object. We can extract for example the length and diameter of the aforementioned metal rod and convey that information to other recipients without requiring the recipients to be in physical possession of that metal rod.

This information is partial and abstracted but it is complete enough to serve the purposes of specific use cases. If we need two parts to fit together, we simply need the measurement of those parts within a certain tolerance. We certainly do not need to know the number of atoms and their structure in order to perform this operation.

In the past, the information that we could extract and convey was relatively small. With respect to geometry, this information generally consisted of the length of lines and the angles at which these lines met. With the advent of computers, we could collect and convey much more information than we did in the past. At the level of the current state-of-the-art, we can have highly detailed geometric information, along with a wealth of metadata about characteristics and properties of the material that makes up the physical product.

There are a number of challenges in separating information from its physical counterpart. We first need to define an informational characteristic or property. We then need to create a common, consistent definitional system for that characteristic. Finally, we need to define a method for describing and/or measuring the characteristic within that common definitional system.

For example, we have naturally defined spatial characteristics as height, width, and length. These are the informational characteristics. We then created a definitional system for these characteristics, inches and feet. We then had to create a method for describing and measuring those characteristics. We created rulers, measuring tapes, micrometers, and lasers.

While we take our spatial measurement system and capabilities for granted, it has not been that long that this has existed. Before the mid 1800's, two of the three requirements for spatial measurements did not exist. While inches and feet existed, there was no common definition of what they were. While there was rough agreement, there was great variation in how long an inch or foot was. There was also no methodology for determining how long an inch or foot was.

It was not until the mid 1800's that the Pratt & Whitney Machine Tool Company in West Hartford Connecticut defined the standard inch and built and sold measurement tools such as the micrometer.[4] It was not until then that there could be any separation of measurement information from the physical product. If I needed to fit a part to another part, I would need to be in possession of that physical part that I wanted my part to fit to. I would then handcraft the parts so that they fit together. I could not rely on the measurement of the part because I could not know nor determine whether my inch was the same as the inch that the other part used. Virtual products, even very simple ones that consisted only of spatial dimensions, could not exist before the mid 1800's.

After the mid 1800's, virtual products could and did exist. Interchangeable parts could now be made because there was now both an agreement on and a method to determine what the characteristics of measurements of parts were. This was the first huge leap in productivity, because mass production was now possible. We could now use the informational equivalents of the physical products rather than having to be in possession of each individual physical product each time we needed to fit a part.

As we progressed in time, we continued to differentiate the categories of informational properties and to increase the granularity of information that we needed and used. Today, it is no longer enough to simply have spatial measurements of length, width, and height for all products. In some cases we need to know where points all over a products' surface are positioned in space. When we are fitting two different surfaces together, it is not enough to know the length, width, and height of the perimeters of those surfaces. We need to also know where are the interior points of those surfaces

The Ares I launch vehicle has a two-part common bulkhead design in its upper stage. Rather than simply creating two pieces to common measurements, NASA will create one of the bulkheads, measure that bulkhead, and create the second so that it fits perfectly. A micrometer will obviously not suffice for this level of granularity. NASA will use a white light scanner to create a cloud of points in space of the first bulkhead, so that NASA can create the complimentary bulkhead that matches not a theoretical design of the first bulkhead, but the actual physical bulkhead itself. This level of fit and precision would not have been possible a few short years ago.

These are the same basic principles that Pratt and Whitney used when they started creating measurements of physical parts. The parts they dealt with and the parts we deal with are defined in the same three-dimensional space. However, the granularity, volume, sophistication of information, and measurement methodology are light-years apart. However, in both cases, informational equivalents of physical products served in place of the physical products themselves.

The other issue is that the atom-based physical products are comprehensive. All the characteristics are built into the product by virtue of the type of atoms that make them up and how those atoms are arranged. Physical products either possess certain characteristics or they do not. A product of a certain material of a certain length, width, and height will have a certain weight whether we choose to observe it or not. The properties are indivisible.

That is not true of virtual products. The properties of virtual products are additive in the sense that our management of the virtual product information needs to explicitly include properties we have an interest in and those properties need to reflect the physics of our physical world in order to let us use virtual products in place of physical products in specific instances.

If all we are concerned about is spatial arrangement, then having the dimensions of virtual products are sufficient. However, if we are also concerned with the overall weight, then we need that property when we are fitting different components that may have the same geometric dimensions but very different weights.

The trend of the software technologies that are implementing virtual products is toward increasing complexity of product properties, increasing granularity of information, and increasing cohesiveness and consistency of product behaviors. Single domain uses of virtual products, such as assessing geometric fit, are moving to multi-domain uses as computer capabilities continue their exponential increase.

We are rapidly reaching the point where we do not have to have the physical object in our possession in order to have a full understanding of what the product looks like and what its other characteristics are. Instead, we can have all the information that we need about the product simply by examining its informational equivalent.

Information is a replacement for wasted physical resources

The second premise has to do with the value of the product's informational equivalent. As I introduced in my first book,[5] one of the most obvious but least articulated observations about information is that it is a replacement for wasted physical resources, such as time, energy, and material. In any given physical task, there are basically two categories of resource usage. The first category of resource usage is the minimum amount of resources that are needed to perform the physical task. The second category of resource usage is the remainder of the resources that it actually takes to perform the task.

The left side of Figure 1.1 illustrates this relationship. The lower half of the bar represents the minimum amount of physical resources needed to complete a task. The upper part of the bar represents the resources that are expended over and above that minimum amount of resources necessary. The complete bar represents the total physical resources expended to complete the task.

This arguably is an omniscient view of the task, in that it presupposes an ability to determine for any given task what would be the minimal amount of resources necessary to complete that task. For a one-time task that may not be possible, but for a task that is repeated over and over again, performing that task in different ways and evaluating the resources necessary for that variation of performing that task would allow an observer to determine a minimal or close to minimal amount of resources needed to perform that task.

How do we determine the amount of physical resource usage? Since we can trade one form of resources for another, for example material in the form of equipment can replace human labor, how do we determine the amount of resource usage? The answer is that, in a capitalistic society, we can translate the different categories of resource usage into its financial equivalent, i.e., money, which can then be summed.

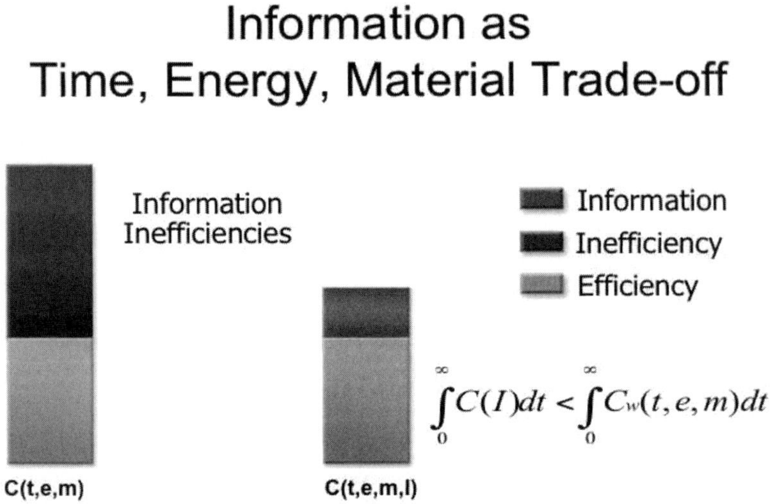

Figure 1.1

Different resources have different costs depending on the geographical area. Chinese labor costs are substantially different from American or European labor costs. This does not invalidate the premise that there is a minimum amount of physical resources needed to complete a given task. However, this minimum in terms of financial units and the specific components of physical resources that make it up are relative to the geographical region.

The way nature approaches this problem of finding the most efficient way of completing a task is to try every possible combination of a task and let the environment select which is the best combination. What nature has that we do not have are unlimited resources. Nature can afford to try all possible permutations and combinations or, in our terms, perform the task over and over again until it gets it right. In addition, nature only has a single task to concern itself with: survival

Humans have many other tasks that they undertake, in addition to survival. Humans do not also have the luxury of unlimited resources. What humans attempt to do is to use a minimum amount of resources in order to accomplish their tasks. What humans do is to use information as a replacement for wasting resources. The right side of Figure 1.1 shows that information can serve as a substitute for wasted resources. It cannot serve as a substitute for the minimum amount of physical resources needed to perform the task, but information can serve as a substitute for the wasted resources over and above that minimum amount of physical resources needed.

So what is information that serves as this replacement for wasted physical resources? Information is a sense of the state of the present and past of the physical environment and an understanding of the repertoire of the actions and effects allowable in our physical universe. With information we can know the state of things and we can plan to take actions to obtain the desired results we are after. If we do not have these two elements that I define as information, i.e., an understanding of the current situation or state and an understanding of the actions we can take that will bridge the current state with our desired state, then we will expend needless resources over and above the minimum necessary in order to obtain our desired state or goal.

A simple example may be useful in order to clarify the thought. If we are placed in a maze and asked to find our way from the beginning to the end, we can expend substantial time and energy in attempting to work our way through the maze. Unless we are supernaturally lucky, we will select ways to go that will prove to be dead ends, and we will need to double back and pick other ways to go, wasting time and energy on backtracking from dead ends.

However, if we are equipped with a map of the maze and a GPS system, which are both elements of information, we can know exactly where we are at all times within the maze and plot a path through the maze that eliminates any wrong turns and ensuing dead ends. By using this information, our map and GPS system, we could easily plot a direct route from the beginning of the maze to the end of the maze. By knowing where we are every step of the way, we could transverse the maze using the minimum amount time and the minimum amount of energy. The information that we have about the maze and our position in it has been traded for the wasted time and energy it took us to complete the maze without that information.

Examples abound of the use of information as a replacement for wasted resources within products. We transverse intellectual mazes every day where due to the lack of information we make wrong turns, encounter dead ends, and have to backtrack to a past decision point. These waste of resources are caused by not understanding the current state of things or in not understanding which actions will lead to which results.

During the create phase, not having the latest version of the product design can lead us to performing work that has to be redone once we obtain a revised version. Not having information about other components that have to fit in a specific space means that when we put together the product, not everything fits and has to be redesigned. Not having information about the high heat level of a specific component that runs alongside a fuel line means we have to redesign the routing of that fuel line.

In the build phase, lacking measurements of parts as they are manufactured can mean that these parts fail to fit together at assembly time, necessitating costly rework. Not having information about the inventory of raw materials at workstations results in idle workstations waiting for material replenishment. Workers that do not have work instructions about how the product was designed to be assembled waste resources in trial-and-error assembly attempts.

In the service phase, not having information on how parts should be disassembled leads to trial-and-error in diagnosing and repairing failed products. Lacking information on how to obtain certain product functionality, users of the product waste resources in trying different actions to obtain that functionality. Worse, they may give up completely, wasting the resources these users expended in obtaining a product that fails to perform for them as expected.

In the disposal phase, not having information about how the product was designed for recycling leads to the waste of potentially recyclable parts that will be simply thrown away without the knowledge of how and what should be recycled.

There are two final points about using information as a replacement for wasted resources. The first is that information is not free. It takes physical resources to sense the present and past state of the environment. It also takes resources to organize, maintain, and present both the state of the environment and the actions and effects that are allowable. It is clear that this resource usage has been responsible for the remarkable progress in the human condition. The advent of computing and communication technology has greatly increased our ability to collect and use information not only to replace wasted resources in activities we already knew how to perform, but also to allow us to perform tasks that in the past would have been impossible to do.

The issue is and will continue to be the costing of information to determine if we should use information as a substitution for simply wasting physical resources. Unlike physical resources, we do not have a unit of measure for information. We have hours for calculating labor usage, quantity for calculating material usage, flow for calculating energy usage, but we have no unit of measure for calculating information usage. The current solution is to consider the costs of all the information system components, hardware, software, communications, and manpower necessary to collect, organize, and present the required information. There is also some progress by solution providers in creating services that manage information on a transaction basis, but that capability is still in its infancy.

The second point is that organizations performing tasks that have not been done before have to expend resources in order to create information. This is the definition of innovation — performing tasks that have not been performed before or performing those tasks in a manner that reduces the resources required. There are some organizations, such as NASA, that their main objective is to perform tasks that have never been done before and to create information about how to monitor the physical world and understand its rules.

The issue with this second point is that this information is a new resource that can be used over and over again. It is an asset and not an expense like the wasted resources this information replaces. However, for this to be the case, this information needs to be captured, organized, and reused. Some organizations neglect that. They believe that the physical product that they develop is the asset. However, the information is their true asset.

This idea of using information as a replacement for wasted resources is an obvious yet fundamental use of virtual products in place of physical products. It has a role in both lean efforts and in innovation.

Bits instead of atoms are used until the last possible moment and wherever possible.

If information is a replacement for wasted physical resources, then we can reduce the waste of physical resources by effectively using this information. The underlying assumption is that the cost of obtaining, maintaining, and using information is less than the cost of wasting physical resources. Except in trivial situations, such as combining a few parts in an assembly operation, this has usually been the case historically. Assuming that this is the case, we should delay using physical atoms as long as we possibly can. In the case of creating, building, servicing, and disposing of physical products, we should use bits for as long as we possibly can before we have to use physical atoms. We have the ability in varying degrees to digitally create products, analyze those products, test those products, and simulate the manufacture of those products, thereby reducing or even eliminating the need to build physical prototypes. Our capabilities in these areas will only continue to improve.

For example, in the past at very early points in the design process, we had to build physical prototypes because physical drawings and blueprints could only take us so far. Two-dimensional drawings, no matter how well they were represented, were not rich enough for people to understand the three-dimensional aspects of the product. Prototypes, in essence, are very expensive pieces of information, because its method of developing information is based on physical atoms and not virtual bits. Using virtual products, we can create fully formed and fully represented three-dimensional models that we can use in place of physical prototypes. Some of the use of these physical prototypes was to simply see whether physical parts would fit together. Virtual parts can perform that function and automatically detect and highlight interferences or clashes.

But using bits is not limited to the visual realm. We can use bits to determine behavioral properties of potential products. The cost of building physical prototypes for testing and analysis purposes is a very expensive proposition for complex products, running into the hundreds of thousands or even millions of dollars. If we are able to get our physics right and do the assessment of products using virtual bits, the cost savings are enormous. One automotive company estimates that it has saved over $100 million in using computer-aided analysis and testing in place of physical testing. The cost of the virtual tools to do this was a fraction of that cost.

For example, airplane manufacturers flex the wings of their airframe to the point where they fail, since, to put it mildly, it is considered unacceptable to have a plane's wings fall off in flight. The cost of building physical prototypes to physically test this in today's environment is economically prohibitive. However, the cost to do this virtually is extremely reasonable.

In the past, airplane manufacturers might have to build a number of prototypes until they obtained wings that sustained the maximum amount of required bend. Today, they can do that testing virtually. While they still do need to do a final test or, to be more precise, a final validation of their computer-based testing, they now only do one. The cost savings of this is enormous.

While we want to delay the use of atoms for as long as possible, once we start using atoms we want to use bits wherever we can. Just because we start using atoms does not mean that we cannot find places to use bits in place of those costly atoms.

In the create phase, we can certainly postpone the use of atoms in prototypes and test articles in numerous situations. In the build phase, we clearly have to make physical products, as that is what the build phase is all about. However, we can use bits in order to simulate the manufacturing of what are soon to be physical products. In fact, what is a necessity in today's economic conditions is to get our equipment, manufacturing processes, and people performing tasks simulated in as many different ways as we can, so that we can find the most efficient way to manufacture these products.

The issue to remember is that moving between domains always involves inefficiencies.[6] The physical and virtual are different domains. While using bits is more efficient than using atoms, moving between bits and atoms introduces inefficiencies. So while we need to replace atoms with bits wherever possible. We need to minimize moving back and forth.

Using information instead of physical resources indeed is what lean is all about. To the extent that we can eliminate waste and resource usage using bits instead of having to physically experiment on the factory floor, we can surpass traditional perspectives of lean manufacturing.

Products are dual in nature — they are both physical and virtual

In addition, while we are creating the physical product during the manufacturing process, we would also like to create the virtual product. These virtual products or "as-builts" as they are often called can be used further in the product lifecycle in place of having to possess and disassemble the physical product in order to know what is in it.

This premise captures the primary concept of Product Lifecycle Management and the use of virtual products. We need to think of products both as physical and as virtual. While there is nothing inherently wrong with only thinking of products as physical, there is an inherent inefficiency in the use of physical resources when we do so. While there is a cost of information, this cost is hugely outweighed by the savings in wasted physical resources. Even if the savings in wasted resources balanced the cost of information, we should still develop the information. This is because the cost of information and the cost of physical resources are going in opposite directions, albeit at much different rates. The cost of information is becoming much less expensive, and the cost of physical resources is becoming more expensive in the future.

In the support phase, we would like to use bits instead of the physical atoms wherever we can. The main issue during this phase is that rarely is a physical product in the possession of the product manufacturer. By the very intent of products, they need to be out and about in the world performing useful tasks for their owners. In some cases, such as transportation products like cars, trucks, and planes, their purpose is to continually move about in the environment.

In addition, to the extent that we can use information to predict potential failures, we can save essential resources by predicting the failure, moving the product to the repair facility in an orderly fashion, repairing the product, and returning the product to service. Scheduled maintenance is always less costly than emergency maintenance.

If we can use the bits of the virtual product in place of having to be in physical possession of the product itself, we can reduce, and in numerous cases reduce dramatically, the use of physical resources.

In the disposal phase, if all we have in our possession is a physical product, the task of disposal and recycling becomes much more complex. Without the information about how the product was meant to be disposed or recycled, in the best case situation it will take additional time and expense to attempt to ascertain what the product is made of and how it can be recycled or disposed. In the worst-case situation, the decision is simply made to throw the entire product into a landfill because the disposer has no incentive or desire to expend the physical resources required to dispose of the product as the designer intended. Without this information from the create phase of the product lifecycle, the calculus for the product disposer can easily be that the cost of trying to understand how the product should be disposed of properly outweighs the benefit of proper disposal.

Continually refine physical world models for simulation.

The final premise that drives our use of virtual products and Product Lifecycle Management is that we will continually improve upon our understanding and our ability to simulate the physical world. The physical world is extremely complex and if the requirement were to have a full understanding of it before we could engage in meaningful simulation, then it would never happen. However, luckily that is not the case, and two things are happening that allow us to evolve both our understanding of the physical world and our ability to simulate it.

First, our understanding of the physical world increases each and every day, and we are able to continue to build upon ever-increasing knowledge of how the world works. As Isaac Newton once stated, "if I have seen further, it is by standing on the shoulders of giants."

At the same time, our computing capability continues to increase exponentially. This allows us to continually increase both the granularity and fidelity of our simulations. Moore's law is still alive and well and is predicted to continue for the foreseeable future. While Moore's Law has been with us for the last 30 plus years, what has changed is that the performance curve of computers has gone nearly asymptotic. The doubling of performance is such that we are seeing truly exponential increases in our capability.

What this means is that not only are we able to increase the granularity and fidelity of our simulations, but we are also better able to integrate a more cohesive perspective of our products. For example, the Finite Element Analysis (FEA) mesh used to be completely independent of the geometric design. Today, that mesh is integrated with a geometric design so that as we manipulate the mesh to improve structural capabilities, we also affect the geometric design.

Information is required to mitigate risk and reduce uncertainty

This is a premise that I did not fully appreciate until I started working with the aerospace industry, particularly NASA. It is one thing to incur waste in performing a task. It is quite another thing if the waste of resources results in the task not being able to be completed or the task ending in a disaster. If the task is to launch a spacecraft, then failure is that spacecraft not launching. Failure moves to outright tragedy as in the case of the Challenger and Columbia space shuttles.

Ignorance is bliss — right up to the point in time when whatever we are ignorant about jumps up and bites us. Bliss bought by ignorance may be the most expensive quality we can ever acquire. It may be that ignorance is bliss if what is going to happen would happen no matter what we knew. However, in the vast majority of cases, having information about a situation may take us out of our blissful state, but at the same time it gives us the opportunity to take action that would change the situation that is about to make our life miserable.

The assumption in the premise that information is a replacement for wasted resources when performing a task is that the task is one that can be completed. The issue is that we waste resources, but we at least complete the task. However, a worse situation is that the task is not completed and *all* the resources we deploy are wasted. It is expensive if the wasted resources are material things. It is a tragedy if the resources we waste are human lives. Information is the key to mitigating the risk and reducing the uncertainty of this situation occurring.

While many people use risk and uncertainty interchangeably, there is a difference between the two. Risk is the quantifiable probability and economic impact of events occurring. Uncertainty is the absence of these quantifications. In other words, we can quantify risk, but we cannot quantify uncertainty.[7]

It might be helpful to look at risk and uncertainty in our example of the maze. If only risk is involved, we can quantify the probability of getting through the maze. At each juncture, we would have a 50% probability of selecting the right path. We could then compute the probability or risk of getting through the maze with no information. For each juncture, where we could either eliminate or reduce our probability of picking the wrong path, we could then understand the change in risk. We could also compute probabilities over the entire maze and predict an expected value of the time it would take to complete the maze.

Uncertainty, in the context of our maze, means that we do not know where, or even if, there is an exit to the maze. We may travel through our maze only to find out that there is no way out. Computing the probability at each juncture is now irrelevant. We can no longer compute a risk, nor can we compute the expected value of the time it would take.

If we have risks involved in our tasks, then we can take actions to mitigate those risks. In product development, we can create a portfolio of projects so as to improve the probability that we will have a successful product. We may not know which one it will be, but given our understanding of the risk profile, if we have enough projects at least one or more will be successful.

If we have uncertainty, this changes. It means that we cannot calculate the probability of success. We can have as many projects as we like, but we have no expectation of success, because we cannot compute the risks.

Information is the means, and the only means, to mitigate risks and reduce or eliminate uncertainty. To the extent that I can collect information that informs me about outcomes, I can reduce my risks. For example, if I know that one in three parts fails, I can add an information collecting process to reduce my risks that faulty parts will be installed in my overall product. If I have an inspection process, which is about collecting information, then I can weed out the one part in three that is faulty. In fact, if I collect the right information, I can find out why the one part is faulty and correct the issue at the source.

The situation is a little different with uncertainty. I cannot mitigate uncertainty by probabilistic techniques. In the previous example of one part in three being defective, my mitigation strategy could be to produce four parts for every three. I would then be assured of having three good parts. Mitigating risk assumes that I have the ability to compute risk. Uncertainty is the absence of computability.

What I need with uncertainty is to be able to create information. I need to know that my task can be completed. This means that I need to undertake tasks that are designed to show that what I am trying to do can be accomplished. I also need to be able to do enough of these tasks to show what my probability of success should be. Failures are important in that they show what can go wrong.

Change, risk, and information.

When there is little or no change, there may be little requirement for information or rather for information over and above what is currently available. If we are producing a simple variation of a product that we have produced for a long period of time, then we probably do not need any addition to the information we have already incorporated into our process. In fact, the information that we are relying on is the history of past events. If our assumption is that the present and future will be like the past, we really are not in need of any additional information.

We know that our design will work, because past designs worked fine. We know how our factory will produce, because we have a history of production. We know how our suppliers will perform, because we have a long track record with them. In short, there may be some minor issues, but we can rely on the information implicit in our history to be comfortable that we will not encounter any major issues. Our risk of using substantially different resources is low.

When we add change into the situation, the risk profile increases. Let us say that we are designing a product with substantially different technology or with completely different materials or with a completely different process. We no longer can rely on our history of how things were done before. While we need to have eliminated uncertainty — what we are trying to do can be accomplished — we have not eliminated the risk that what we are attempting to accomplish can be accomplished with the predicted amount of resources.

As Figure 1.2 illustrates, this risk is proportional to the amount of change. If we are introducing some change, we will have a modest increase in risk. If we are doing something highly innovative, then we should expect a high degree of risk. It is not unreasonable to assume that this relationship between change and risk in non-linear. More changes leads to much greater risks.

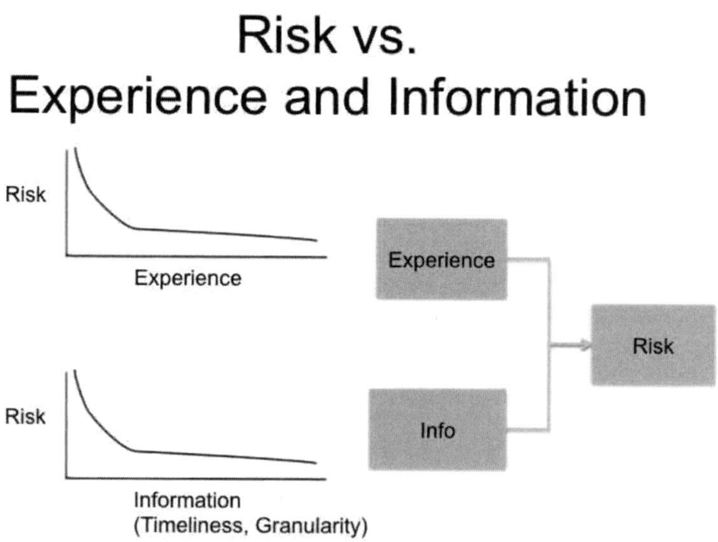

Figure 1.2

Information is a moderator of risk under the condition of change. In order to reduce the risk of consuming substantially more resources than predicted, we need information more frequently and more granularly than we otherwise would in the absence of change. Catching and remediating problems early is always less expensive than catching and correcting them later. If we do not know that there is a problem, then we cannot take action to correct it.

This means that in the design phase, we need to have high visibility into all aspects of the design and to perform more analysis and simulation of the product performance. We need to be constantly looking at information on design progress and performing product integration at earlier stages.

For manufacturing, we need to simulate the manufacturing processes in conjunction with product design in order to catch potential manufacturing processes problems as early as possible. The later we catch problems, the more expensive it is to correct them. We need constant information on the status of the manufacturing processes of suppliers. This will help reduce the risk that the suppliers will not produce on schedule or will not produce to the specifications we require.

In the support phase, we need information on how the product is performing in actual use. If we wait until warranty information starts to dribble in, we may incur substantial risks in having to make product modifications to a substantially higher number of products than we otherwise would. We need in-use information to have reliable information, unfiltered from a warranty reimbursement scheme, about what problems our products are having in actual use.

However, over and over again, I see organizations embark on new product initiatives with new product designs, materials, and suppliers. Their approach to information is the same approach that they use for established products. An aerospace company I recently visited is embarking on a new plane using composites rather than the aluminum that they have historically used. They have the same information collection plan for this new plane as they had for previous planes. They do not view their risk profile as substantially different. It will simply be a matter of time before they experience some unplanned and unpleasant surprises.

Information by itself does not address problems induced by change. However, information coupled with corrective actions does. The earlier information about problems surface, the less costly are the remedies to address them. Ignorance is really never bliss!

These six premises underlie our focus on virtual products and therefore the value of Product Lifecycle Management. We continue to employ these premises as we move deeper and deeper into creating virtual products and using the bits of virtual products in place of the atoms of physical products.

Virtual products are not a replacement for physical products, but an augmentation that allows the use of these virtual products to reduce the waste of physical resources. The cost of these virtual products, i.e., the cost of information, may in some cases be substantial. However, the cost of virtual products has been and will continue to be substantially less than the waste of physical resources. In addition information is a renewable resource, while physical resources, no matter how abundant, are finite.

LEAN AND INNOVATIVE

Between the dual objectives of lean and innovative, lean is a much easier objective to accomplish. As we saw above, we can use information in place of wasted resources. Lean by definition is a reduction or elimination of wasted resources in the accomplishment of a particular task. Whether it is the Toyota Motor Corporation producing vehicles or a hippie commune pottery shop producing bowls, lean is the idea of using information to reduce the waste of resources. (The issue with the hippie commune pottery shop is that excessive drug use is not conducive to creating and using information).

The problem with having lean as the only objective is that eventually the value that it provides comes to an end. In the ideal lean world, we would eventually obtain our goal of producing our product with a minimal amount of resources. Once we got there, we would want to continue doing that task in exactly the same way, day in and day out. To do anything else would mean that we would expend resources over and above the minimal amount of resources, which is by definition waste. The problem is that our competitors would work on creating new products that would provide more value at potentially less cost for our customers.

At that point, it would not matter that we could produce our products with the minimal amount of resources. Customers would prefer our competitors' products. It may have been that buggy whip manufacturers had leaned out their production processes, such that there were no wasted resources in producing buggy whips. However, customers ceased to have any use for them.

So it is not enough to be lean in this changing world. Product producers must also be innovative. They need to be focused not only on reducing the waste of resources in making their current products, but in creating new information and knowledge that make new and innovative products possible.

In the premises cited above, performing simulations of product performance and creating new and better models of the physical world will lead to innovation. The reason that lean and innovation are dual objectives is that lean activities can provide the resources that organizations need to perform innovative activities.

If we assume that organizations have a specific amount of resources available to them - a not unreasonable assumption - then to the extent that organizations waste resources, they will not have resources for innovation. Being lean in the tasks where information can be substituted for wasted resources is a source for the resources necessary for innovation. Because innovation is a journey into unknown territory, there certainly may be a waste of resources. Depending on the industry, many if not a majority of innovative attempts could be failures. However, even in these cases, wasted bits are much, much cheaper than wasted atoms.

Innovation and lean are financially compatible objectives. Companies that are innovative and not lean run the risk of running out of resources and/or being less profitable than their competitors. Companies that are lean and not innovative may enjoy short-term profitability, but will surely be overtaken by innovative competitors.

The key to being both innovative and lean is to have products that are both physical and virtual. This duality of product and its resulting objectives will be echoed time and time again throughout this book.

Virtually Perfect, as a phrase pertaining to products, has gone from indicating a product that is not quite up to perfection to meaning that only the informational equivalent of a product can be considered perfect. Major technological advances have enabled this transition in the last quarter of the 20th century and into this millennium in the form of computers, communications, and software. This ability to strip information from a product and fully represent it in virtual space is a new and driving phenomenon. It is what enables Product Lifecycle Management.

The premises behind virtual products and Product Lifecycle Management are as follows: physical objects have an informational equivalent; information is a replacement for wasted physical resources; bits instead of atoms are used until the last possible moment; bits replace atoms wherever possible; products are dual in nature — they're both physical and virtual; physical world models are continually refined for use in virtual simulation; and information is required to mitigate risk.

It is these virtual products that drive both lean and innovative new physical products. By substituting information for wasted physical resources, organizations can become lean. But in today's competitive environment, that is not enough. Organizations must also produce new and innovative products that create new value for their users. Product Lifecycle Management, through the use of virtual products, can drive both lean and innovative products.

Notes

1 The term "information" gets thrown around as if there is agreement as to what it is. However, on closer inspection that is not the case. Of the three terms in this area, data, information, and knowledge, data is the best defined. It is simply a stream of observations that need to be put into context. The data of 78, 82, 85 could be the temperatures of three days in June, the ages of three nursing home residents, or the IQ's of three members of a liberal chat board. We do not have information that we can use unless we organize this data and put it into context.

Information and its cousin, knowledge, are less well understood and differentiated. There are some who claim that information needs a sender and a receiver, i.e. the "inform" in "information." In particular, communications theory deals with information as the amount of "surprise" that a message contains (For the seminal work in this area, see: Shannon, C. E., & Weaver, W. (1949). *The mathematical theory of communication.* Urbana,: University of Illinois Press.)

For others, information and knowledge are pretty interchangeable. I am in that camp and will primarily use the term "information" throughout the book to mean both information and knowledge. I have a decidedly utilitarian and practical view. Information is what I can use to replace wasted resources.

For those inclined to want to delve into the understanding of information, let me recommend the collection of essays in Machlup, F., & Mansfield, U. (1983). *The Study of information: interdisciplinary messages.* New York: Wiley, which is the best book I have found on the topic. I especially recommend Machlup's essay, *Semantic quirks in studies of information* (pgs. 641-671). Professor Machlup was one of the first economists to view information as an economic resource. This was one of his last works.

A really interesting perspective on information is that our universe *only* consists of information. What we perceive as physical objects is really just information. For that perspective, see Vedral, V. (2006). *Introduction to quantum information science.* Oxford: Oxford University Press.

2 The building industry has what it calls BIM, Building Information Modeling. While BIM claims to be about generating and managing building information throughout the building lifecycle, it seems to be more about the design and construction of buildings. I would consider BIM to be a subset of PLM and to use PLM concepts.

3 When I use the term "atoms," unless I otherwise specify, I am using it in the generic term of a physical phenomenon. It may be that electrons, photons, or other particles and not actual atoms cause the physical phenomenon.

4 Browne & Sharpe has been cited as the source of this development (See: Roe, J. W., & Yale University Press. (1916). *English and American tool builders*. New Haven, London[Oxford]: Yale University Press ; Humphrey Milford; Oxford University Press.) However, a business partner of mine was the last CEO of Pratt &Whitney Machine Tool Company. I saw the original records that showed Pratt & Whitney were the originators of the capabilities that created our common measurement system and the tools that implemented them.

5 That book was Grieves, M. (2006). *Product Lifecycle Management: Driving the next generation of lean thinking*. New York: McGraw-Hill. Technically, I introduced this premise in a guest editorial for the Society of Manufacturing Engineering magazine. See Grieves, M. (2003, March). PLM - Beyond Lean Engineering. *SME Manufacturing ENGINEERING, 130,* 23.

6 This is true even within the physical domain itself, as pointed out by Arthur (Arthur, W. B. (2009). *The nature of technology: what it is and how it evolves* (1st Free Press hardcover ed.). New York: Free Press). Shipping by sea is very efficient as is shipping by rail. However, the process of transferring cargo between ships and rail adds inefficiency in both time and costs.

7 This distinction begins as far back as 1921 with the economist Frank Knight (See: Knight, F. H. (1921). *Risk, Uncertainty, and Profit*. New York: A. M. Kelley. For the impact on human society of being able to compute risks see Bernstein, P. L. (1996). *Against the gods: the remarkable story of risk*. New York: John Wiley & Sons.

2

VIRTUALLY EXPLAINABLE

Product Lifecycle Management (PLM) is "virtually explainable" in a chapter, meaning that the highlights of my version of PLM concepts can be explained in summary form. For those familiar with my first book, this chapter will serve as a refresher of the PLM framework from a slightly different perspective. For new readers, this chapter should be enough of a virtual tour of PLM and its framework so as to acquaint them with the major concepts of PLM.

DEFINING PLM

A primer of Product Lifecycle Management should logically begin with a definition of exactly what is Product Lifecycle Management or, as it is commonly referred to, PLM. The definition that I presented last chapter and use throughout this book has been in use since approximately 2002. This definition is in relatively the same form as it was when published in the management periodical, *CIO Magazine*. The article, *There is a New App in Town*,[8] was a seminal article about PLM. It was the first time an executive-oriented magazine featured Product Lifecycle Management as a topic that the executive suite should be interested in.

The definition in its present form, without this short but important revision, was developed for my first book on Product Lifecycle Management, although I had used this definition in my University of Michigan executive education classes previously. While there are some other definitions of Product Lifecycle Management that differ, and some that differ very radically, from the definition that I will present here, the leading practitioners in the field would generally agree that this definition captures what most people familiar with Product Lifecycle Management would consider when thinking about PLM.

As slightly modified in the previous chapter, the definition for PLM is as follows:

Product Lifecycle Management (PLM) is an integrated, information-driven approach comprised of people, processes/practices, and technology to all aspects of a product's life and its environment, from its design through manufacture, deployment and maintenance—culminating in the product's removal from service and final disposal. By trading product information for wasted time, energy, and material across the entire organization and into the supply chain, PLM drives the next generation of lean thinking.

The important revision of the definition for this book is the addition of "and its environment." This was an omission that had bothered me for a while. Products do not simply exist as independent entities, but are situated in their environment that is acted on and, in turn, acts on the product.

We will explore the various aspects of this definition of PLM and its implications later in this chapter. However, we first should understand just what do we mean by a product lifecycle and what are the various phases in a product lifecycle.

WHAT IS A PRODUCT LIFECYCLE?

When we talk about a product's lifecycle, we are talking about, as the name implies, the life of the product throughout its existence. The common references to this existence are: from cradle to grave, from birth to death, or my favorite, from lust to dust. The product's lifecycle encompasses the time from its creation until it is disposed of in some fashion.

When we talk about a product under the Product Lifecycle Management concept, we talk about it under two perspectives. The first is the generic product which refers to the group of individual products that share a great deal, if not all, of their characteristics in common. Generally, these products share a common identifier, such as a part number or model number, and, for purposes of dealing with the product characteristics, these products are considered to be identical.

We also refer to an individual product as an *instance* of the product. So, two products that are identical in every way and could only be distinguished by the fact that they occupy different spaces in the physical world are considered two different product instances and would necessarily have two different lives. Although identical, these products may have been created at different times; different people may use them; and they may be disposed of at different points in time and in different ways.

When we talk about Product Lifecycle Management, we refer to both of these perspectives of the product. For the very complex, expensive products, such as nuclear reactors, jet fighter planes, oil tankers or, on a smaller scale but of no less importance, medical pacemakers, we may pay special attention to each individual instance of the product. This is not unsurprising, given the large price tag of each of these particular products. However, for commodity products such as bolts, we may not be very concerned about the instances of the product at all. However, we may be concerned about an aggregate of these products, such as the specific manufacturing run or lot that produced them.

The view of product lifecycle information then is very dependent on the value and often accompanying complexity of the product and its components. In high value, complex products, even mundane parts, such as bolts and screws, take on importance that they might not otherwise normally have. This will determine whether we are simply concerned about product information of the product class as whole, or whether we are concerned with each instance of the product.

As shown in Figure 2.1, the product lifecycle is generally divided into four phases: create, build, service and dispose. In the creation phase, we take the product from an idea to a physical artifact that can actually be built. In the build or manufacturing phase, we take the specifications of the product and obtain as the output of the manufacturing process a product that functions according to our designs. In the support phase, which we will also refer to as the service or sustain phase, the product is in use. Our focus is on supporting it such that it maintains the functionality that was designed into it. The final phase, disposal, is when the product is no longer of use, and we go from a functioning, physical artifact to something that is taken out of use and discarded in some fashion.

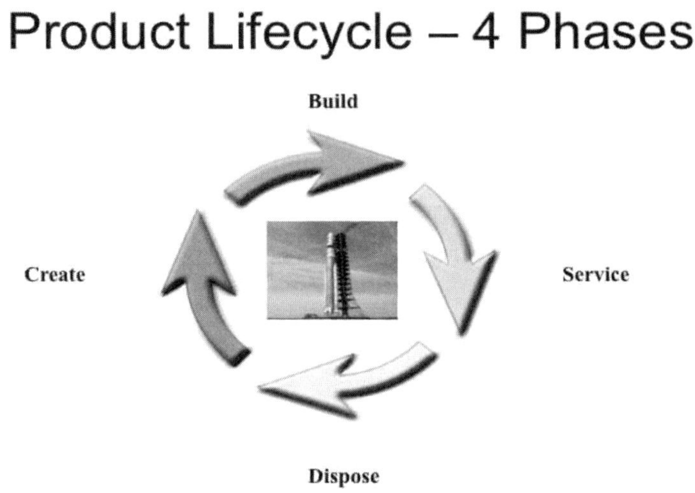

Figure 2.1

The create, build, support, and dispose phases are a useful way of thinking about a product's lifecycle. These phases may not be perfectly demarcated. For example, the line between creating and building is blurred, as multiple versions of the product are designed and then manufactured until a product that not only meets the specification but also actually works the way the designers envision it to work is created. (PLM is aimed at eliminating this iterative, costly approach.) However, for purposes of thinking about the product, the "create, build, support and dispose" model works well.

As shown in Figure 2.2, the four main phases of a product life cycle can be further subdivided. The model that I propose and is generally considered to be the model for most product manufacturers is one that starts with a perceived value and then has the following components to the product lifecycle: requirements analysis and planning; concept engineering and prototyping; product engineering; manufacturing engineering; manufacturing and production; sales and distribution; service; and disposal and recycling.

Other organizations may have slightly different terms for these various functional areas, and they may have their companies organized around these areas slightly differently. However, for purposes of our discussions, this is a pretty useful way of looking at the phases of the product lifecycle. We will next describe these functions that make up the lifecycle phases.

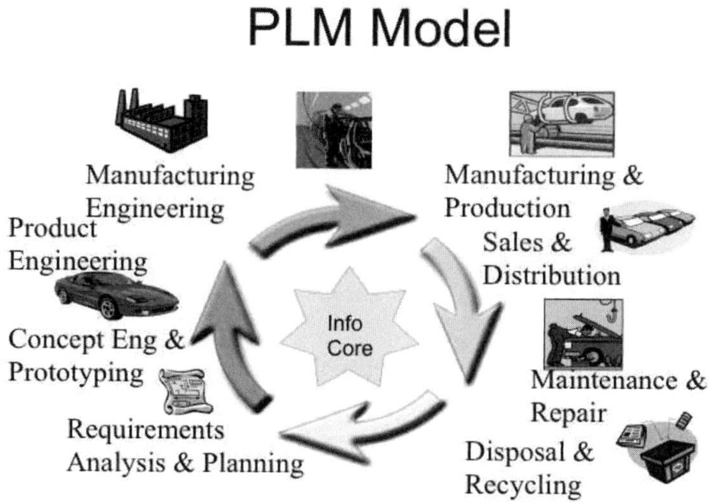

Figure 2.2

Perceived Value

All products start off with the concept of a perceived value. The assumption is made that if a product existed that embodies certain attributes, then it would be valuable to the acquirers and users of that product The perceived value can be in one or more of a number of different categories in our human society. These value categories are economic, safety, social, experiential, and belief-driven. I will discuss these categories and the implications for products later.

There are product lifecycle models that start with *ideation*, rather than *perceived value*. Ideation is defined as "the capacity for or the act of forming or entertaining ideas." I do not have a particular problem with the product lifecycle starting with people bandying about ideas. However, merely random ideas do not beget a product, at least not one that will be considered valuable by the product user. These ideas all must exist within the framework of, "will the user of the product perceive the new product to have value to him or her?" If the answer is "no," the idea is discarded. If the answer is "yes," then this perceived value must be mapped to specific requirements of the proposed new product. The sieve through which all ideas for new products must pass is one that only passes those ideas that have perceived value. I prefer to explicitly state that premise by using "Perceived Value" as the lifecycle starting point rather than the vague "ideation" label.

Requirements Analysis and Planning

In this next phase, the task is to analyze the perceived value and to determine the requirements that this product will have in order to meet this perceived value. If the perceived value is to travel quickly from point A to point B, then the task is to specify the particular realizable requirements that allow us to do just that. While teleportation might be the quickest and easiest way to travel from point A to point B and has the highest perceived value, its minor drawback is that currently it is a physical impossibility and our requirements set ought not include "zero travel time."

So we have to then look at what are the realistic requirements that allow us to obtain the highest *realizable* perceived value. It may be that those realistic requirements are that we can safely travel no more than 90 miles an hour and that we have to be able to have braking capabilities, such that we can stop in a specified distance. It would also be nice that we have a certain level of protection for the vehicle occupants.

However, we have to link these requirements to the perceived value. This is one of the more difficult aspects of the product issue in that the perceived value could entail a number of tradeoffs, say between speed and safety. We could guarantee that people would be safe in a vehicle that traveled no more than one mile an hour. However, it certainly would not meet our "quickly" requirement. On the other hand, we could develop cars that could travel at 150 miles per hour. Under current conditions, these cars would not fulfill acceptable safety requirements.

This phase of requirements analysis and planning that develops perceived value into a product concept is the most difficult, most creative, and most ill defined aspect of the product lifecycle. Interpreting the perceived value into requirements that are feasible to realize is a complex, ambiguous task. As I will discuss later in the book, the ability to virtualize will greatly enhance this phase of the product lifecycle.

Concept Engineering and Prototyping

This is the phase when the requirements are now turned into a physical realization. In concept engineering and prototyping, the requirements are mapped to specific physical mechanisms that can realize these requirements. If the requirement is a vehicle that can stop in a certain amount of time, then concept engineering needs to determine what sort of devices will allow that to occur. Potential possibilities range from frictional devices on the wheels to an anchor that would embed itself into the surface of the roadway to a chute that would pop out of the back of the vehicle. Clearly, engineers have gone with the frictional devices on wheels rather than the other options because it better fits the requirements than an anchor or a drag chute would.

Prototyping allows these concepts to be tested. Prototypes have been physical realizations of engineering concepts in order to test the assumptions as to the characteristics of the concepts. Physical prototypes are generally expensive and time consuming to realize. The move to virtual or digital prototypes greatly reduces both expense and the time to realize prototypes.

Product Engineering

In product engineering, the concepts are taken a step further and detailed specifications are developed for the product. In this stage, we move from the general to the specific. In the general concept engineering stage, we determine that frictional devices on wheels would be the best alternative as a stopping device. In product engineering, we now have to specifically define what components will need to go on to those wheels in order to be able to implement the concepts that we developed in the Concept Engineering and Prototyping stage.

The results of product engineering are detailed specifications and descriptions of the product that we think will meet the requirements that we have defined. The products we are concerned about occupy three-dimensional space. One of the main realizations of these specifications is a geometric and/

or dimensional model. Previously manifesting themselves as blueprints, in this day and age they are very sophisticated mathematical representations of where in space the atoms of our products will reside. Today, computer-based creations or CAD models are three-dimensional representations of the physical objects as they will exist once they have been manufactured.

We would also expect to get a Bill of Materials (BOM) at this stage of product development. While we need to have physical geometry, we also need a complete list of all material and the specification of the material's physical characteristics, which also provides the product structure. The BOM specifies all the items that make up the product, including things like lubricants or the grade of steel that would not show up on a geometric representation. I will deal with BOM and how it represents the product information in a later chapter.

Manufacturing Engineering

This stage starts the "build" part of our "create, build, support and dispose" cycle. The elements of building physical products are: making the first one, ramping up production, and making the rest of them. In manufacturing engineering, we take the steps to "make the first one." We need to specify exactly what material, labor, and equipment we will use and what operations in what sequence that we will perform in order to realize the specifications that come out of product engineering.

There is (or should be) generally a great deal of overlap between product engineering and manufacturing engineering. In order to determine the exact specifications of the products, we need to know the operations that we will need to perform in order to realize those specifications. For purposes of the product lifecycle model, we will look at product engineering and manufacturing engineering as distinct areas. As we will see later on, the benefit of Product Lifecycle Management is the ability to share information between these two areas such that we can avoid the circular and iterative path of specifying the product, trying to determine how to build it, only to determine the product cannot be built, and having to revise the specifications.

In manufacturing engineering, our intent is to develop the specific operations that we need to perform in order to actually move atoms around and turn theoretical specifications into a real physical product. The list of specific operations is called the Bill of Process (BOP).

Manufacturing and Production

In manufacturing and production, what we want to do now is to attempt to minimize the amount of resources necessary to create the product that we've designed. This generally entails the two phases of ramp-up and "building the rest of them." While product engineering and manufacturing engineering are still involved, at this stage the focus is on the manufacturing and production groups who are tasked with getting product out the door to customers using a minimal amount of resources.

In ramp-up, our intent is to drive down the experience curve such that we get better and better at minimizing the use of resources to create the same amount of product. Experience curves are the phenomena that as we build more products we take fewer resources to do so. At the beginning of manufacturing ramp up, we use a certain amount of time, material, labor, and equipment in producing the product. The intent during ramp up is to continue to minimize the use of those resources until we reach the minimal amount possible in order to be able to produce that same product.

We will discuss later in the book the idea of virtualization and how it impacts these experience curves. However, whether we are performing ramp up by physically manufacturing products or we are performing ramp-up virtually, the manufacturing and production phase is an attempt to create products in the most efficient way possible. Ideally, we would like to completely eliminate ramp up using physical builds, but more realistically we can drive down the experience curve only so far using virtual techniques. For the foreseeable future, there will always be gaps between what we can do virtually and what realistically happens out on the plant floor.

Sales and Distribution

In sales and distribution, we have a physical product that we now have to get into the hands of the individuals who will be using them. Sales and distribution is not only involved in physically moving the product, but in also providing information for the users and acquirers of the product. Product users need to know what the product can do and how it can do it. Product users need to have enough information to draw conclusions about the perceived value the product will produce for them. Creating sales and marketing materials, such as specifications, advertisements, marketing collateral, and video commercials are part of the way that product producers use information about the product to inform product acquirers of what the perceived value of the product is and how they will obtain that perceived value.

Service

Service is the aspect of the product's life, which for many if not most products, will be the longest period of time of the product's existence. The requirement during this phase of the product's life is to ensure that the product continues to provide to the user the perceived value embodied in the product. Service involves both the support and maintenance of the product. For complex products, this may be a difficult task in that the product may require a great deal of support and maintenance in order to maintain the functionality that was designed and built into it.

All products are subject to entropy, which is the tendency of the universe to move from an ordered to a disordered state. All things being equal, the complexity of the product generally increases the entropy rate of that product. This means that, the more complex the product, the more maintenance it needs to keep it fully operational. The service phase of the product's lifecycle has been for most manufacturers under appreciated.

Most manufacturers' perception was that once the product had left their factory door, they were no longer responsible for it. It was somebody else's responsibility, usually the user of that product, to maintain and service that product. This view is rapidly vanishing as manufacturers determine that there are opportunities for new sources of revenue by maintaining their attachment to the product after it has left the factory door. In addition, the legal and regulatory climate has a major effect on product manufacturers' view of their requirements during this phase, with a steady trend to mandating more and more manufacturer responsibility.

Disposal and Recycling

The final phase of a product's life is its disposal. In the simplest of scenarios, it is simply thrown into a landfill and buried under other items disposed of in a similar fashion. However, as we will discuss later, this approach to product disposal is changing. Manufacturers of the product are becoming increasingly concerned with how their products are disposed. Specifically, they are concerned about the ability to recycle the product material so that it can be, at a minimum, not a hazard to the environment and, ideally, provide new value in a different and recycled form.

Summary

These are the various functions of a product's lifecycle. They make up the create, build, service and dispose phases that are the major divisions of a product's lifecycle. While there may be other sub areas that are discussed and there may even be other ways of organizing the different functions that we discussed above, for the purposes of this book, this is a fairly useful and accurate portrayal of the major phases and functions that make up a product's lifecycle.

PRODUCT LIFECYCLE AND PRODUCT LIFECYCLE CURVES

The question I most often get when talking about the model of the product lifecycle that I described above is "this doesn't look like the product lifecycle I learned about in marketing class." This is indeed the case. Figure 2.3 shows a Gaussian curve[9] that divides the product lifecycle into stages, usually referred to as innovation, early adoption, maturity (sometimes divided into early and late), and laggards or decay. The product goes through stages where a small amount of "innovators" acquire the product. More "early adopters" then follow on and acquire relatively more of the product. The bulk of the product is acquired during the maturity phase, and then finally less and less units are sold during the decay or laggard phase.

This model describes the product lifecycle in the aggregate. The curve shows the volume of acquisitions of the product over time. This model does reflect that products in a general or in an aggregate sense go through periods where a small group of daring individuals gives the product a try. More people, who are less daring than innovators but nonetheless more daring than the general population, acquire the product. The general public then picks up on the product in the maturity phases until the product becomes stale. Less and less people buy it during the decay phase.

Product Lifecycle Curve

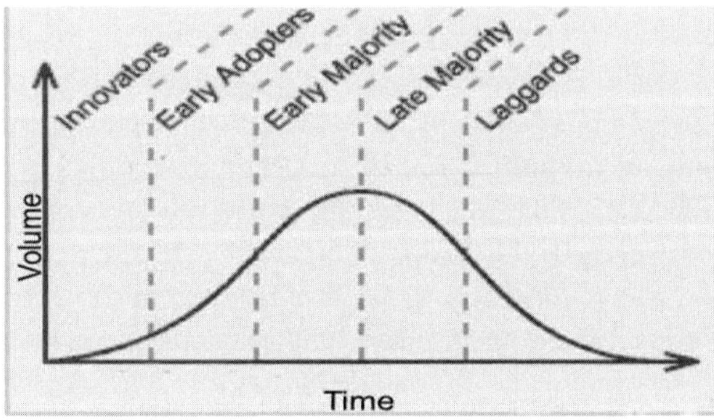

Figure 2.3

As an example, CRT televisions are in the late maturity to decay stage, while LCD televisions are probably through the early adopters and reaching the maturity stage. While products do exhibit the "innovation, early adopter, maturity, and decay" tendencies, the normal distribution curve that usually represents these stages is not representative of actual products. The automobile has had a long maturity relative to it initial phases. The pet rock's maturity was thankfully exceptionally short.

The product lifecycle model that I have presented here is a model of an individual product lifecycle and not an aggregate volume/time curve. However, a variation of this aggregate product lifecycle model will be of use later in this book when I talk about the value of PLM.

THE PLM DEFINITION: ELEMENTS AND IMPLICATIONS

There are a number of elements about my definition of Product Lifecycle Management that are fairly striking. First, the scope of PLM is broad. PLM concerns itself about a product from the cradle to the grave, from birth to death, and again my personal favorite, from lust to dust. Second, it is an approach, which means that we cannot simply go to the store and buy PLM. Third, it is about people, process/practices, and technology. And fourth, PLM is an extension of lean thinking and all that "lean" implies. These are the main elements of Product Lifecycle Management that we need to deal with.

Scope

PLM is admittedly very broad in scope. The information about the product is tracked from product conception to product disposal. Figure 2.2 is a visual model of the product lifecycle. The product lifecycle is divided among functional areas such as design, engineering, manufacturing, sales, service, and support. As Adam Smith famously described in his pin-making example, division of labor is necessary for real productivity. However, division of labor also leads to siloing of information.

An "information core," as illustrated in Figure 2.2, reorients the product information from a functional oriented approach to a product-centric approach. The purpose of this reorientation is to "de-silo" product information from functional siloing in design, engineering, manufacturing, service, and disposal. This allows for product information to be used in all aspects of the product's life, reducing wasted time, energy, and material. The separate functional areas both populate and consume information from this core, rather than hoard information in their own informational silos.

The demarcation between the phases of create, build, service, and dispose can be a little fuzzy. For example, during product launch a product may be both in the creation and building phase. However, dividing a product's life into these four phases is useful for thinking about the various stages of information.

As described above, PLM is broad in scope and, as some of its critics point out, it may be overly broad. Among the people involved in the PLM arena the standard joke is that it must have been a marketing group who created the concept of PLM. No group that had to actually implement this broad of a scope would have had the audacity to develop a concept that was so broad as to encompass the beginning to the end of the product's life.

The marketing group of PLM software companies generally relates this joke in a way that indicates that they are secretly very proud of having claimed such a large territory with respect to their product offering. However, the software application development groups that are responsible for creating products to fill all the gaps between product conception and product disposal are fairly careful in delineating just where their offerings fit within the PLM model.

The interesting issue here, though, is that even if the originators of such a broad scope were overreaching, it is irrelevant. In today's world, product companies must be responsible for their product from product creation through manufacturing, into use, and finally into disposal. While in the past, companies could wash their hands of the product once it left their factory door. In today's current environment, that simply is not possible.

Whether it is regulatory enforcement by the government about the responsibility of the product manufacturers or, as is common in the United States, lawsuits by predatory plaintiff attorneys, outside parties are notoriously effective at holding product manufacturers responsible for the use and/or misuse of their product throughout its entire life.

In some of the more memorable class action suits, manufacturers who did not even manufacture the product that caused the harm are lumped within the pool of defendants and held financially liable for damages because they manufactured a product that was in that same class of products. In the disposal phase, Europe has been ahead of the United States in defining regulations regarding the disposal of product.

The reality is that this has had little impact to date and that the European Union has not had tremendous success in holding manufacturers accountable for the disposal of their product. However, there does not seem to be much question that this trend is continuing and eventually companies will have to follow ever-stricter regulations with respect to disposal of the product.

So while some may argue that the definition of Product Lifecycle Management is too broad by far, given the current state of the art, there is little question that the overall requirements on product manufacturers are to be able to track their product from product inception through manufacturing into the usage stage and finally into disposal. While there may be some leeway at the current time, the direction of this trend is clearly one where information about the product will need to be created, maintained, and even updated throughout the entire life of the product.

Approach

PLM is an *approach*, which means that it is not an artifact in its own right. Social scientists would call this a *technology*. By social scientists' definition, technologies not only encompass physical artifacts, but also the manner in which people organize and develop processes and practices in order to impose their will on the environment. For our purposes, and so as not to confuse those who may confuse technology with an tangible artifact of technology, we will call it an *approach*. What this means is that we cannot buy Product Lifecycle Management as some software in a shrink-wrapped box. While the software component of Product Lifecycle Management is an integral and enabling part, there are other components of PLM that are equally important.

The issue is that often there is confusion between companies that are considered to be PLM software vendors and PLM itself. Confusion arises when people think that unless the PLM software vendor provides it, it is not PLM. This is incorrect. While there are a few dominant PLM software providers, the reality of it is that there are hundreds, if not thousands of companies that provide software solutions in the Product Lifecycle Management space.

When the term, Product Lifecycle Management, was first emerging, it was fairly natural to only associate Product Lifecycle Management with the products of either self-described or agreed-upon PLM vendors. However, as PLM matured and the underlying conceptual framework for PLM became clearer, there is a need to differentiate between PLM and PLM vendors. In addition, companies that had point solution offerings in particular product related areas, such as product development or manufacturing, are looking at PLM as an overall framework in which to position their products.

The issue with point solution software products is that they only encompass a small area of the PLM space and that the interface of information in those products and other information systems is done on an ad hoc and haphazard basis. If these point solution products are able to integrate into the overall PLM framework, they stand a better chance of being used not only for the particular function for which they were intended, but also for other uses that this information enables.[10]

So, for example, quality control information today is used primarily to specify whether a product should pass or fail a particular control station. That is not only useful for that inspection process, but also may be fed back into the design process such that the tolerances are determined to be too close for the product as it becomes produced over time. The longitudinal quality information reflects tool and die wear over time. Using this longitudinal quality information, design engineers could decide that loosening the tolerances allows for better manufacturability of that product over the life of the product.

The approach aspect of PLM encourages cross-functional sharing and use of product information. This is a very different paradigm than currently exists in many organizations, where information is siloed and not shared outside a specific function.

Components of PLM

Related to the definition that PLM is an approach and not a specific technological artifact is the issue of what components make up PLM. Per my definition, Product Lifecycle Management is made up of people, processes/ practices, and technologies. Of these three things, the people component is always the most important. It is only people that can decide to make a conceptual framework become accepted. People can choose to have a silo mentality about product information, covet that information so that only they have access to it, and not share that information across the product lifecycle. If they do so, then PLM will never work. So Product Lifecycle Management has to start with the basic premise that people are going to cooperate so that this new framework becomes enabled.

The issue of process/practices is an under-examined one. The focus of most business and technological discussions have been about processes and not about associated practices. While clearly Product Lifecycle Management is involved with processes, as we will see in a later chapter, defining and understanding the role of practices is a major aspect that needs to be considered. The other aspect of the process/practice discussion is that previously the information technology that existed would only allow us to effectively deal with the processes because of their well-defined information structures.

Product Lifecycle Management, with its new technological base of software applications and systems, allows us to deal with unstructured information that is relevant to the issue of practices. However, we will discuss this in a great deal more depth later in this book.

Last, although certainly not least, is the issue of technology. The amazing advances in computer technology, which includes not only processing power with its 30-year plus exponential growth, but also the associated exponential growth of storage and communications, allows us to do things that were only dreamed of a few years ago. Clearly technology advances allow us to deal with virtual products in a way that would have been inconceivable even a few short years ago.

Lean and its Extension

A continuing pressure on organizations is to do more with less. PLM extends this "lean" thinking, but does so differently from the past. The focus of PLM is to use information to substitute for wasted time, energy, and material. In the past, the information necessary to substitute for physical resources was stored in individual's heads or, more often than not, simply lost. PLM makes an asset of information.

PLM also relies on the virtualization of products in order to reduce or eliminate the waste of physical resources. By trading bits for atoms, PLM allows for a much less expensive way to test hypotheses for reducing and even eliminating wasted resources.

CHARACTERISTICS OF PLM

There are a number of characteristics that I have identified as being associated with and are an integral part of PLM. These characteristics are: singularity, correspondence, cohesion, traceability, reflectivity, and cued availability. PLM needs to exhibit these characteristics in order to implement a product-centric perspective.

Singularity is the idea that there is a singular and unique representation of information. Duplicating information is quite easy and uses almost no resources. There is also no inherent problem in duplicate information. The issue is that duplicate information rapidly becomes inconsistent information. Unless rigorously controlled, a change to only one version of the information renders it inconsistent with another version.

For product information to be useful, the users of that information need to know that they're working with the latest, most up-to-date version of that information. When faced with different versions of that information, they need to know which is the version on which they can rely. They need to know which is the master, authoritative, or controlling version. Unlike the physical world, where, even if there were such a thing as an exact duplicate when it comes to atom-based objects, physical objects can be identified by where they reside in physical space. There is no unique, geographical identifier of a virtual object.

PLM Characteristics

- Singularity
- Correspondence
- Cohesion
- Traceability
- Reflectivity
- Cued availability

Figure 2.4

PLM needs to maintain and control a logical equivalent of the geographical location of an authoritative or controlling object. This needs to be done to ensure that users of virtual products all have the same reference to the same information, so that they are not wasting time and other scarce resources working with out-of-date and obsolete product information.

Correspondence is the idea that for every physical object there is a virtual one. This means that the information that is inherent in physical objects can be stripped and made into a virtual object. This connection between the physical object and its information needs to be maintained throughout the life of the physical object. This is so that individuals who need information about that physical object need not be in physical possession of it.

In the design phase, where there is no actual physical object yet, correspondence is the idea that there can be a unique implementation of that virtual object. If that is not feasible, then the design simply qualifies as a pretty image. The idea of the duality of a physical product, i.e., a physical one and a virtual one, is foundational to the concept of PLM.

Cohesion is the idea that virtual products are coherent in their obedience to the physical laws of the universe. While the universe enforces its laws on all atom-based objects, virtual-based objects have to rely on the software systems that implement them in order to have the same cohesiveness. What cohesiveness requires within PLM is that the different views of the virtual object have consistency across views.

What this means is that the geometric view, the electrical view, and the product structure view all change when one of the views change. If we change the schematic circuitry in the electrical view, then the physical wires in the mechanical view must also change. Currently, we sometimes have challenges even within the same views. For example, we could theoretically change the length of an object without changing its weight if the software did not enforce cohesion. As software applications implementing virtual objects get more and more sophisticated, the ability of virtual objects to be cohesive will extend across more and more product views.

Traceability is a characteristic that we can implement better with virtual objects than we can with physical objects. Traceability is the idea that we can capture the changes to products over time. This is important if we are to assure ourselves that what we think has been done to our products actually has been. Traceability is important, especially for products where safety is of paramount importance.

As envisioned for PLM, traceability is the idea that we can capture and track changes to the product over time. In the design phase, knowing how the product design changes over time and knowing what testing was done to what version is extremely important. In the manufacturing and support phases, capturing and tracking what was done to the product gives us confidence that the product was manufactured and maintained to the correct specifications, irrespective of which supplier worked on it.

We can theoretically do this for virtual products. It is a matter of capturing and organizing the right data. For physical products, all we have is the product at a certain point in time. We may be able to deduce what happened to the product in the past, but we have no way of knowing if what we think happened actually occurred.

Reflectivity is the idea that as the product changes over time then we capture and reflect the state changes that have occurred to the product. As noted above, we can have traceability for virtual products, but only if we capture the state changes as they occur. The concept of reflectivity is more associated with the usage or support phase, when product manufacturers no longer have physical possession of the product. Given that many products, such as automobiles, airplanes, and ships, disperse all over the world after their manufacture, reflectivity is the idea that as these products change that no matter where they are in the world, the information about their changes are captured in virtual space.

The manufacturers of the product, with the owner's consent, can use this information to ascertain exactly the condition of the product even when they are not in physical possession of it. Manufacturers can use this information to understand exactly how the product performed in use. The information can also be used in the aggregate to understand not only how the individual product is being used, but also how the overall product class is performing in its environment. For example, the Federal Emergency Management Agency (FEMA) uses information from General Motor's OnStar operations center in order to determine which roads are open during a natural disaster.

The final characteristic, cued availability, is the idea that the mass of product information that PLM is responsible for is required to be organized and presented when it is needed. I'm now also referring to this characteristic as Embedded Knowledge Management (EKM). This product information is embedded in that it is presented on the basis of the context of the task. If I have to search an untold amount of information in order to find what I am interested in, that information may as well not exist.

While cued availability may be considered a daunting technological task, the state-of-the-art in searching for information is improving at an exponential pace. We can now Google a world's wealth of information and, more often than not, find what we're looking for. While searching for the geometric aspects of products presents a degree of difficulty that taxes our current search capabilities, even this area is rapidly improving.

This is a fairly cursory view of PLM characteristics. However, I have attempted to give a feel for these characteristics without going too much in depth, as I did in my previous book. However, these characteristics have stood up over the last few years and are considered by many in the PLM area to be the main characteristics PLM needs to deal with.

DRIVERS OF PLM

The underlying driver of PLM is that it creates value for both the manufacture of the product and the user of the product. While I will discuss the aspects of value creation for both the product user and the product producer or manufacturer in a later chapter, I would like to highlight the environmental drivers that are at work in making PLM a necessity.

These environmental drivers are of two types: external and internal. The external drivers are scale, complexity, cycle times, globalization, and the regulatory and legal climate. The internal drivers are productivity, innovation, collaboration, and quality. I will discuss each of these very briefly below.

PLM Drivers

External

- Scale
- Complexity
- Cycle times
- Globalization
- Regulatory and legal climate

Internal

- Productivity
- Innovation
- Collaboration
- Quality

Figure 2.5

External Drivers

The external driver of scale refers to the situation that organizations have gotten and continue to get much larger in terms of size. While in the 1960s a multibillion-dollar corporation was considered huge, today many corporations have revenues in the hundreds of billions of dollars. This increase in revenue means a corresponding increase in the number of employees, the number of locations, and the sheer number of products that these organizations create, build, and support.

As importantly, the amount of information that these organizations have to deal with has also exploded. I would argue that the increasing capability of computer information systems is not only correlated with the increase in size of organizations. It has enabled this increase in size. This means that these organizations could not grow to the size they have were it not for the exponential increases in computing and communications capability. While there may be an argument to be made that some of these organizations have outpaced their ability to manage their information, we are seeing no indications that organizational size will decrease.

The requirement to handle the amount of data and information required for today's products drives the need for PLM. With this increasing scale comes a need for better managing product information.

If it were simply scaling up an organization to deal with the increased volume in products, then that would be a daunting task. However, in addition to the increase in the volume of products that organizations produce, we are also seeing a huge increase in the complexity of the products produced.

From cars to contact lenses to cereals, the number of different products that organizations make has rapidly increased. Where we once had one model or version of a product, we now have five. So not only has the volume of products that we are producing gone up dramatically, but we have increased the complexity of those product suites. We need to add to this a whole new component of today's products, namely computerization. The addition of software to almost every product dramatically compounds the complexity of the situation.

It is not enough that we are substantially increasing the scale and complexity of our product lines. At the same time, we are also dramatically decreasing the cycle times that we are operating with. Even for major, complex products such as airplanes and automobiles, we have decreased the development cycle times by over half.[11]

Longer cycle times provided us with the slack in order to resolve issues between different functional areas such as manufacturing and engineering or design and engineering. We no longer have this slack time to work with, which means we need to do a much better job of sharing information. PLM, with its product-centric rather than functional-centric view of the product, is not a luxury. It is a necessity.

Compounding the increase in scale and complexity and the decrease in cycle times is that, during the last quarter of a century, we have gone from local to global. In the past, we could get everyone involved with the product in the same room to iron out issues. Ignoring the fact that the slack time no longer exists for this reconciliation process, we can no longer get all the people involved with the product into the same room without putting people in airplane seats.

There is no major organization that I deal with or even know of that does not have global operations. But it is not that they simply have global operations, because most major organizations have been global throughout the 20th century. It is that these organizations now have integrated global operations. Unlike in the past, when these global operations were independent and isolated, the global operations of today are integrated and interdependent.

These organizations need to work with the same product information across the world, simultaneously. Since product manufacturers no longer have the capability of gathering in one room spontaneously to view a physical prototype, they need to have virtual prototypes that they can access anytime, anywhere.

The last environmental driver is the regulatory and legal climate. Organizations can no longer wash their hands of a product once it leaves their factory door. Whether they like it or not, organizations are and will increasingly be required to be responsible for their product throughout the product's life and into disposal. While we have no way of knowing what governments or the legal community have set their sights on in the future, we can pretty much be assured that it will be in the direction of more responsibility for the manufacture rather than less responsibility.

Internal Drivers

The internal drivers for PLM are productivity, innovation, collaboration, and quality. The rest of this book is about these issues. Lean is productivity that is optimized. As we will see, using information or bits in place of atoms is to be as lean as an organization can be. However, being lean is not enough in today's environment. Organizations must also be innovative. As we'll see throughout the rest of this book, being lean helps in being innovative in that it frees up wasted resources that can be used for innovative purposes. However, that is not sufficient to make an organization innovative.

To be innovative, organizations must free up their people to be creative and think outside the normal parameters that constrain their products. This goes to the issue of process versus practice that we will look at in-depth later in the book.

A recurring theme throughout this book will be the need for collaboration. Again, this is not driven by process but by practice. Collaboration is not mindlessly going about the routines of the organization, but requires thoughtful interaction by not only people within the organization but by and with their customers and suppliers.

The final internal driver, quality, requires a redefinition of how we think about quality. Products only have true quality if they perform for the user of a product according to the user's expectation. For product users to perceive a product to have quality and therefore real value requires that the product meet or exceed the users expectations. Quality is not simply about meeting specifications on the factory floor. Linking quality to the product lifecycle is a key component of PLM.

These are the external and internal drivers of PLM. The external drivers are fairly self-evident. The internal drivers are key topics of this book.

BACK TO THE FUTURE

A primary reason for PLM's rapid acceptance is that it is not a new concept. In fact, it is a very old concept. Before the modern era, products were created, produced, supported, and disposed of by one or a few individuals. Cobblers, black smiths, chariot producers, and bicycle manufacturers, to name just a few product producers of old, were involved with all phases of their products.

These product producers did not need information technology because their products were simple, few, and stayed within close geographic proximity.

These individuals could and did remain connected to their products throughout the product life. The chariot manufacturer designed the chariot and manufactured it out of wood, metal, and other materials. He repaired it when it came back from battle, and he recycled the materials when its useful life was over.[12]

The problem was that this was a very inefficient use of resources. Division of labor and mass production could produce the same chariots cheaper and more efficiently. The concept of a product-centric view of product information made good sense, but it was inefficient to say nothing of the product information being ephemeral and short lived. Product information perished with the individual.

We now can have the best of both worlds. We can have division of labor and mass production efficiencies, along with a product-centric view of the information needed to create, build, support, and dispose of our products. With information technology, we can overcome the limits implied by relying on the memories of individuals as it concerns product information.

Product Lifecycle Management has been adopted so quickly because it is a back to the future strategy. The ability to virtualize product information enables us to work with products both efficiently and effectively.

This is only a brief overview of Product Lifecycle Management. PLM is a complicated concept and has a great number of entailments that need to be considered as part of the overall framework. The chapter began with a definition of Product Lifecycle Management (PLM). It then stepped back and defined the main elements of a product lifecycle: create, build, use, and dispose. It went on to further break those elements into the functional components and describe their purpose.

The chapter went on to examine the aspects and considerations of the PLM definition. It described the characteristics of PLM and discussed what may be the most important aspect of PLM: its components. People, process/ practices, and technologies are the components that make up PLM.

The chapter finished up with a description of the environmental drivers of PLM. It focused on the external drivers: scale, complexity, cycle times, globalization, and regulatory and legal climate. The internal drivers of productivity, innovation, collaboration, and quality are the topic of the rest of the book.

The chapter concluded by pointing out that PLM is really not a new concept. PLM has been adopted so quickly because it is a back-to-the-future strategy that combines division of labor with a product-centric perspective.

Notes

8 See Stackpole, B. (2003, May 15). There's a New App in Town. *CIO Magazine*, 92-101.

9 Most people who ask this question remember the product lifecycle curve as Gaussian or normally distributed, and it has been described that way. Some have also described it as an S-curve or some other shape. In fact, the product lifecycle curve can take a variety of shapes. This includes the dreaded "flat-line" where the product flops spectacularly at launch. The Gaussian curve is an idealized model that is useful for illustrating the basic concepts of the product lifecycle. See Kotler, P. (2000). *Marketing management* (Millennium ed.). Upper Saddle River, N.J.: Prentice Hall.

10 There is movement to develop a framework and standards in order to transfer product lifecycle information between software applications. It is called Product Lifecycle Support (PLCS) and is an ISO standard (10303-239). While PLCS shows promise, it is too early to tell whether its adoption by PLM users, software providers, and PLM thought leaders will enable PLCS to reach critical mass.

11 Or tried to. Airbus (A380) and Boeing (787) announced decreased cycle times, but ran into substantial and expensive delays. As I have argued elsewhere, their problems were not with PLM, but with not adhering to PLM principles as it pertained to product information.

12 For a more extensive treatment of PLM as a "back to the future" concept, see Grieves, M. (2008). Back to the Future: Product Lifecycle Management and the Virtualization of Product Information. In M. Tomovic & W. Shaoping (Eds.), *Product Realization: A Comprehensive Approach.* New York: Springer.

3

VIRTUALLY USEFUL

Virtually Useful has had the same "almost, but not quite" quality as the term Virtually Perfect. Under the PLM understanding of the term, virtual products can provide substantial value by using information in place of wasting physical resources. However, we need to move from general descriptions of value to specific, concrete uses of virtual products and their associated information.

These "Use Cases," as they are commonly called, describe the specific ways that both product producers and product acquirers will use the information that Product Lifecycle Management applications collect, organize, and present. Without use cases, it is difficult for organizations to justify and allocate the resources necessary for PLM. Use cases can also help organizations move from a conceptual understanding to a specific understanding of the value and benefits of a product-centric view of information.

My intent is to present here a number of common PLM use cases, organized by lifecycle phases. This is not meant to be an exhaustive list, and I am continually seeing both additional use cases and extensions to current use cases. I would encourage readers to engage in developing use cases for their own organizations. As I will discuss in future chapters, the creation of virtual products will allow novel and innovative uses of product information. Removing the constraint that in order to have product information we must be in physical possession of the product will open up a myriad of other opportunities. It is simply up to us to think about product information in new ways.

CREATE

Requirement Development and Verification

Product design is driven by requirements. These requirements are in turn driven by what product acquirers and users value. The issue is often that these requirements conflict, such as safety and fuel economy in vehicles. Additionally, it is sometimes difficult to ensure that these requirements continue to be fulfilled as changes in the product design constantly and normally occur during the creation phase.[13]

The use case here is to define the requirements and track the product's ability to meet these requirements as it evolves from a concept to physical entity. True requirements tracking does not mean simply tracking features, but means tracking the actual requirements themselves. Where product changes are made that will impact these requirements, notification mechanisms need to be implemented in order to alert the participants that this has occurred. As trade-offs present themselves, requirements may need to be changed, but there should be clear traceability as to what requirements have changed and why. In addition, if requirements are found to be no longer necessary, the elements that are implementing them need to be identified.

Requirements always need to be matched to corresponding verifications. This means that requirements need to be specific enough to allow for a verification that can be evaluated. Verifications can be of different types: tests, analyses, simulations, and even qualitative assessments.

As products have gotten more complex and sophisticated, requirements have proliferated and can number in the thousands. Understanding and tracking them requires integration into the product structure and design. In addition, requirements have often been an engineering exercise in tautology. If the product passed the verification procedure, then the product met the requirement, regardless of how it performed in actual use. Requirements and verifications need to extend into the build, sustain, and dispose phases and that information needs to be fed back into the create phase. Even if too late to impact that current product, this methodology provides information to refine future assumption of requirement/verification correlations.

Model Release

Model release is the function of translating requirements into a product form. In some organizations this is still referred to as "drawing release," even though what is being released are 3D CAD models and not 2D drawings. At this stage, we have conceptualized the components that our product should have. We now must translate this conceptualized model into specific, buildable components. What this requires is that we parcel out conceptualized objects and that we collect fully-defined models that can be integrated together.

What is required in this use case is that we track the status of each of these components. As the engineers responsible for these components complete their work, we need a checking mechanism to ensure that the models that are submitted contain all the information that we need. While the CAD structure itself is important, there is other information that we may require, such as general dimensioning and tolerances (GD&T), characteristic descriptions, and lightweight models that can be generated from the CAD.

The intent of this use case is that at any point in time we will know the status of each component, that each component that has been received meets our requirements for completeness, and that participants who are collaborating together are continually kept up-to-date as to the status of adjacent or integrating components. Ideally, we would like to have the ability to visually look at our model so that we could see those components that have been released and, by their absence in our visual model, those components that are still missing.

There needs to be an authoritative source or a system of record that these models are released to. There should never be any question regarding which model is the latest or "official" model.

Design Review

All organizations conduct regular design reviews in order understand how product design is progressing. In order to do this effectively, the latest information as to the status of the design, how it is meeting the requirements, the individual components' physical design, and integration of all the physical components need to be available.

Ideally, the design review can be conducted at any point in time. This means that all information should be readily available. There should not be a period of preparation required in order to bring information together from locally controlled repositories. Since products are physical in nature, the design review should include a visual representation of the product and all its parts and pieces.

Issues that arise from the design review should be identified and assigned for resolution. An approval process to sign off on the resolution needs to be determined and tracked. The participants with an interest in these issues should be kept updated as to the status of issue resolution. A history of issues and resolutions should be maintained for both the current product and for future product development.

Digital Mockup Unit (DMU)

Creating physical mockups and prototypes can consume a good deal of resources. Consequently organizations are extremely interested in anything that can reduce the number of mockups and prototypes that need to be created. The purpose of mockup and prototypes is to create information: will the design that we have created have the form and function that we desire?

Digital mockup units (DMU's) are virtual representations of products. As the name implies, the initial use of these virtual objects was as a spatial representation of the product. Initially, these virtual representations were to serve in place of mockups of the product that might be built of plywood, clay, plastic, or some other reasonably cheap and pliable material. The purpose of these physical mockups was to provide a full-scale model of the product that could be used to understand how things fit together, whether components were accessible, and, in general, let humans interact in order to assess the design.

However as digital analysis tools became more sophisticated, DMU's could be used for much more than simple spatial purposes. These DMU's can now be used to analyze such things as structural analysis, component integration, aerodynamic analysis, or crash testing. In short these DMU's can now exist in place of physical prototypes.

As I have constantly pointed out, physical prototypes are very expensive propositions. If we can use digital mockup units in place of physical prototypes, we can perform much of our design and engineering verification in a much less expensive manner.

This is not to say that there is a distinct choice between two alternatives, physical prototypes or digital mockup units. We may need to employ a combination of both. For example, we can use the digital mockup unit to produce cheap and lightweight prototypical models in a material like Styrofoam. By using the digital mockup to generate cheap, physical ones, we can produce an exact replica of what the final physical product may look like. This can produce a full-size model that we can climb in, look over, and in essence do everything that we might have done in the past with a full-scale machined model.

We can also go from physical to virtual. We can scan a model that we might do in modeling clay and produce that model in digital form. Especially for artistic endeavors, where the artist looks at his model until he or she is appropriately pleased with it, we can then capture the model at that point in time.

By using digital mockup units, we can bypass the cost of this expensive machining and similar operations in expensive materials like metal and either completely replace these with digital versions or use a combination of lightweight materials and rapid prototyping to produce cheap prototypes for specific use cases.

Engineering Change Process

Engineering changes should be controlled in a well-defined process. Change notification should be made to all participants that the change will affect. The change process should be monitored so that the status of the change is available at all times.

Requests for approvals should be triggered automatically and should be done digitally. Alerts should be automatically generated for changes that fall behind schedule. Changes should include all participants in the product lifecycle, not just engineering. Manufacturing and support should be notified of changes so that they can evaluate the impact of the changes.

Component Update

Once an engineering change that has a change to geometry associated with it is approved, that component needs to be updated in the system of record or authoritative source. This component update should be an automated process and not require substantial manual intervention.

Where a visual update using native geometry is not possible, the update should include an automatic generation of a lightweight model. All participants who have a connection with that component should be automatically updated when the new component is in place. In addition, if the new component changes the outer dimensions, an automatic check for infringement on other components should be done.

Pre-Release Collaboration

The engineering release process for most organizations is a relatively formal process. In order to be released, the part will have been required to meet certain characteristics of completeness. The released part will be considered to be a complete part that can be relied on for all forms of usage.

However, with all parts, there is a pre-release period when the part is beginning to take shape. While the information about the part during this period cannot be used for all forms of usage, certain information is available for some forms of usage. Requiring that a part be formally released before any other work such as analysis, manufacturability, or integration takes place unnecessarily delays the product development.

During the period that the product is taking shape before formal release, we would like to be able to use product design information in a more informal manner. What this requires is a collaborative space where the developers can put their work-in-progress so that others associated with elements of the product can begin to get a feel for the specific characteristics. The issue is to not only have the product available for view, but to indicate the level of maturity that the product is at so that other people relying on this product information know the limits of what they can use that product for.

For example, as the form takes shape, the engineering analysis group would be interested so that they can prepare the types of analysis that they are going to perform on this part. At one level of maturity, the analysis group can determine what analysis they are going to perform. At another maturity level, they may begin to do some preliminary analysis. However, they know enough not to go to the time and expense of doing an exhaustive analysis until the product is released.

This allows for concurrent work to be done, prior to formal release. It is important that along with presenting the product design for collaboration that maturity levels are also defined. Without that, the other activities might be done too early or too late. It is a waste of resources for an exhaustive analysis to be done at the preliminary stage of development. It is a waste of elapsed time to wait to do preliminary setup of the analysis until the final product has been released. Collaborative pre-release workspaces with maturity levels will allow for organizations to do the appropriate work at the appropriate time without the formality of an official release.[14.]

Product Integration

Components always exist in a space container. In some cases the space has been predefined. In other cases, the space container is somewhat flexible. However, at some point in the design, the space container becomes fixed and components need to fit together in a specific space with specific connections.

In addition to fitting together, other checks may need to be performed. For example, fuel lines need to be sufficiently separated from components that generate heat. Electrical components need to be separated from magnetic objects.

For product integration, a subset of the geometry is required. This subset is the outer shape, which is sometimes called the outer mold line (OML). While the parts inside the outer shape are integral to the operation of the product, for product integration only the outer shape is important.

These outer shapes should be automatically generated for each component. Currently, these would be lightweight models. The requirement is that each component be approved by product integration before being considered a completed part. If the space requirements change, all participants with responsibility for components in that space would be notified.

Product Configuration Control and Validation

The issue with most products is that there is not one product, but a multitude of products. With simple product, there is only a single product involved. However, products that are complicated or complex generally have options. Each combination of options is in essence a unique product. The number of potential products goes up rapidly as we add options. Compounding the issue is that not all options are buildable or should be built because they will not perform properly.

What this means is that we have a twofold problem. The first problem is to be able to determine which combinations of options are legitimate. The second issue is to ensure that each unique combination not only can be built but also will perform properly.

Table 3.1 gives some idea of the magnitude of the issue. The numbers are representative of a global automaker. As we can see, this is a staggering number of possible combinations. In addition, only a subset of these vehicles can actually be built. This is because some combinations simply won't work. For example, configuring a heavy-duty engine with a lightweight transmission is a recipe for failure.

Variants

Series	6	
Body Style	5	30
Powertrain		
Engine	6	180
Axle	3	540
Transmissions	2	1,080
Seating	5	5,400
Drive	2	10,800
A/C	3	32,400
Trim Color	3	97,200
Wheel/Tire	5	486,000
Region	10	4,860,000
Options 1	3	14,580,000
Options 2	3	43,740,000
Options 3	3	131,220,000
Options 4	3	393,660,000
Options 5	4	1,574,640,000
Options 6	4	6,298,560,000
Options 7	4	25,194,240,000
Options 8	4	100,776,960,000
Options 9	6	604,661,760,000
Options 10	6	3,627,970,560,000

Table 3.1

The purpose of virtual products in this situation is to act like geometric products with respect to physical fit. We can use these virtual products to determine whether or not they are legitimate products to build. It also becomes more and more expensive to find out that there is a problem with a specific configuration the farther through the product lifecycle that the product gets.

It is embarrassing to take an order from a customer and then have to tell that customer that the configuration cannot be built. It is expensive to start putting together that configuration on the factory floor and find out that it cannot be built. It can be disastrous to build a specific configuration that performs dangerously in actual use.

Going back to tell a customer that the truck with the towing package that he or she has ordered has to be revised to add heavy-duty brakes that will cost more can result in a canceled order and/or an unhappy customer. Trying to build that truck on the factory floor and finding out that the brakes are not compatible will require expensive handling of that truck. Selling that truck without the heavy-duty brakes and causing a terrible accident as a result is disastrous.

This product configuration control and validation requirement has a number of different elements. The first is a mechanism that embodies all the rules that govern legitimate configurations. This in itself can be quite complex, since some options may require other options and some options may be incompatible with other options.

The second is to be able to virtually test each of these combinations in order to insure that they will perform to their requirements. This is a step up from the current state where the assumption is made that most options do not affect performance. That may be true, but it only takes one or two exceptions to cause substantial liability for an organization.

Behavior and Performance Analysis

Behavior and performance analysis and testing information should be associated with the components of the product. Analysis and testing used for requirements should be associated with those requirements and available via links from the requirements and their associated components.

Both static analysis, such as formulas, and dynamic analysis, such as simulations, should be connected to the product and available to participants with an interest in the component. Analysis and testing that fall out of acceptable ranges need to trigger appropriate notifications.

Figure 3.1 shows a still from a simulation of a NASA rocket launch. The inset is video of the actual launch itself. The actual flight mirrored the simulation in all significant respects. In watching the combined video, it is difficult to distinguish which is the simulation and which is the actual launch.

This information needs to be available through the support phase, especially when product failure occurs. Feedback loops need to be established between the support function and engineering function in order to alert engineering when their analyses models and simulations deviate from the actual, physical performances of the product.

Figure 3.1

Procurement

Procurement is the interface between the individuals who define the product and the suppliers who provide a spectrum of items from material to commodity products to highly engineered products. On the input side, the procurement group has to have the specifics of what they are to acquire. On the output side, the procurement group needs to define specifically what the supplier is to provide.

In the past, what the supplier provided was almost entirely physical. Suppliers provided things that were atom-based. If the supplier provided items that met the specifications that the procurement department defined at a specific loading dock at a specific point in time, then the supplier met the requirements.

Today, organizations need not only the actual physical items but they need the information about the physical items, i.e. the virtual items. Organizations can then use those virtual items to make decisions about the suitability of the physical items. They can also incorporate those virtual items so as to create virtual products that they can evaluate and manipulate.

Currently in most organizations, the procurement department had not been educated on the need to acquire both the physical and the virtual product. As a result, these organizations are experiencing a mismatch between what they want and what they are getting. Even worse, their suppliers are using this lack of knowledge to improve their negotiating position. When the organization comes back to the supplier to request what arguably they should have gotten to begin with, the supplier only agrees to provide this information at an additional cost.

With the procurement group understanding and working with a virtual product as it is being developed, organizations have the opportunity to obtain what they need at the right cost. In addition, having information about the product that the supplier can deliver well in advance of the physical delivery gives the organization an opportunity and the time to address issues that the physical product may have.

Marketing Material

The use of virtual products for marketing, albeit physically based, is probably as old as physical products themselves. The chariot maker for Achilles probably whipped up a scale model of a new war chariot to show off its improvements. "See, Achilles, how the razor-sharp protrusions extend from the wheels spindles to nicely disembowel anyone getting near?"

There has been and always will be a need to get people interested in a product before investing the substantial resources in engineering and building it. There is also the need to expose people to the product without requiring that they be in the product's physical presence. That was the drawback with Achilles' chariot manufacturer. His virtual product was physically based, and so his clients had to be in physical proximity to model. Today's virtual products are not physically based. Anyone in the world with access to a computer and the Internet can view them.

Marketing material covers a wide variety of items: brochures, specification sheets, print ads, and video ads. The issue in the past was that these items were independent of the actual product. These materials were developed independently of the actual product and may or may not have represented the actual product accurately. There are numerous incidents of product launches being delayed or even cancelled because the marketing material was not ready or incorrectly represented the product.

Having access to the virtual product as it changes through the development process allows the marketing material to always represent the product, as it will actually be. In addition, the graphics illustrating marketing material can be derived from the actual geometric designs rather than being developed independently. This is currently being done for print media and is increasingly being done for video. The commercials we see on television are increasingly developed in digital studios with virtual products in a virtual environment rather than being shot with actual products in the physical environment.

In addition to the cohesiveness brought about by using the common digital product, organizations pick up valuable elapsed time by being able to have access to this product information earlier in the product lifecycle. By using virtual images, marketing material, such as print ads and video commercials, do not have to wait until there is a physical product with which to take pictures or video.

Next Generation Product

Some organizations have had the philosophy of starting the next generation product from scratch. They start with a blank sheet of paper on which to build their new product. The thought here is that this is a means to obtain innovation. The reality is that there is a substantial waste of resources because a substantial part of the new product can be reused from the previous generation product.

Starting from scratch with a new product generally means making some of the same mistakes over and over again. In addition, a lot of resources will be spent on parts of the product that customers will not value as innovative. Creating a new fuel pump that will be pretty much the same as the old fuel pump creates no real value for the customer.

Organizations are coming to the realization that their real assets are not their plant and equipment, but the intellectual property that they have created that is embodied in past products. Organizations can reuse a great deal of those assets in new products. In addition, even where components are being redesigned, information about the development, testing, and usage of the older components can provide valuable information on what to do and what not to do.

As we move to virtual products, the linkages between physical and virtual products are costly to create. Reusing previous parts and components will allow savings of resources.

Where Used

It is often important to know where a part or component is used not only within a single product, but also in all products throughout the entire organization. It may be an issue of safety, in that there is a discovery that the part does not perform as it should. It may be an issue of cost. Understanding how many of a certain part is used in all products is useful if the purchases of those parts can be aggregated to obtain better pricing. It also may be an issue of understanding design standards compliance within an organization. A component may be mandated for use, but individual design areas are ignoring that mandate.

Obsolescence is an issue during the support phase, especially if the product has a long life. If a particular part or component stops being produced, organizations need to know how many of their products are affected and take proactive steps to mitigate the loss of that part. Mitigation may take the form of buying up all available parts for inventory, finding an alternative, or even buying up the plans to manufacturer their own part. The first and critical step, however, is simply knowing what products are affected.

Organizations need the ability to search through their designs to determine where parts and components are being used. The requirement is a necessity within an individual product, but it is extremely useful to interrogate all products throughout the organization.

Packaging

The issue of packaging as it pertains to product information is often overlooked, but it is an extremely important aspect. There are two aspects of this use case. The first is the form of the packaging and the second is the informational content on the packaging. We will look at both of them.

There are three purposes for packaging. The first is to allow the product to be safely and efficiently transported. The second is to inform the product user of the package contents and approved uses. The third is to appeal to the product purchaser.

The first and second purposes are applicable to both industrial and consumer purchasers. The third is really only applicable to consumer goods. However, in all cases, packaging requires geometric design, with the first purpose, transportation safety and efficiency, taking precedence. No matter how informative and appealing the packaging, if the product is damaged or broken during shipping, then the packaging will not have done its job.

While package design for appeal has elements of art and practice in it, package design for safety and efficiency is about lean results. Product designers can use the virtual product to design packages that will transport products safely and efficiently. For mass production, such as automotive vehicles, being able to fit additional parts on a pallet or in shipping container can reduce transportations costs substantially. Part layout in containers can also lead to more efficient and less expensive storing and retrieving of parts on an assembly line.

The informational content on a package is also of extreme importance. For products that have a chemical composition, such as drugs, detergents, cleaning supplies, etc., it is extremely important, if not required by regulation, that the packaging has accurate information. Failure to do so can have substantial economic and legal consequences. Changes in product composition needs to be conveyed and enforced in packaging material.

While not a liability issue, package art is an area that organizations spend tremendous amounts of resources in establishing. Distinctive package art is an important part of brand recognition. Packaging colors and shapes both directly and subliminally influence consumers. This is also product information, and packaging color, artwork, and brand schemes need to be controlled as rigorously as the geometric shape of the product itself.

BUILD

Rapid Prototyping

Rapid Prototyping uses digital design information to create a physical representation of the product. Rapid prototyping machines are an inexpensive way to create physical prototypes. This physical representation can be used to perform physical tests, assist in developing manufacturing and assembly processes, or provide physical training artifacts.

While the goal of PLM is to use bits in place of atoms, these atoms are relatively inexpensive. The primary reason for this is that the material used in rapid prototyping is much easier to work with than the actual material that will be used for the part. Since the purpose of rapid prototyping is primarily to work with the form of the product and not its behavior, material such as plastic, which is inexpensive to shape, can be used instead of titanium, which is much, much more expensive to form.

Automotive companies have long been users of "mules" to obtain a feel for new car designs. A mule is a car frame that has hung on it exterior panels that have been formed from some lightweight material. The purpose of these mules is to give designers and engineers an inexpensive feel for what the new car will look like.

Rapid prototyping can be done with machinery used in normal production, such as milling machines, lathes, etc. This is classical "subtractive" manufacturing. It is subtractive in the sense that material is subtracted from the original block of material in order to develop the appropriate shape.

However, "additive" rapid prototyping machines are also coming into existence. Additive manufacturing adds material little by little to build up a form. These machines generate the physical forms by depositing material on a layer-by-layer sequence. The material being deposited is in soft or liquid form that hardens rapidly in place. Some of today's rapid prototype machines are actually rapid prototype printers that "print" a 3D object.

Rapid prototyping fills the gap between traditional physical prototypes and virtualized environments. Until virtualized environments in which humans can see, feel, touch, and manipulate virtual objects are indistinguishable by humans from the real world environment, there will be a role for producing cheap and quick physical objects.

Manufacturing by Printing

While rapid prototyping is a source of time and resource savings, the additive manufacturing approach would be the source of tremendous value if it could be used in the actual manufacturing process. Even when products are produced perfectly in today's manufacturing process, there still is a substantial amount of scrap material that is produced. This is because subtractive manufacturing always starts out with more material than the finished part requires and subtracts material until it get to the desired part.

In addition, in many cases the desired feature cannot be obtained because the subtractive equipment, cutters, milling machines, stamping machines, etc., cannot produce the holes, cavities, or other features due to other material being in the way. As a result, less material efficient but more manufacturable designs have to be used.

"Printing" parts would be far more efficient. Printing parts is akin to printing on paper, but does so in 3D. Printing on paper lays down a quantity of ink in a specified space on paper. Printing parts would lay down a quantity of material at a specified location, harden the material, lower the printing surface, and repeat. This would allow the build up any shape, including shapes that could not be performed by current, subtractive machinery.

Because the virtual part exists in 3-D, the information of where there should be material and where there should not is fully known. The technological issue is the ability to accurately deposit the needed material in a pliable liquid or powder form and harden it appropriately. While the ability to do this with plastics is well developed, the ability to do this with more durable material, such as titanium, is still in the early stages for anything but small parts. However, it should be only a matter of time before we can scale up this technology to print any size part, from the small parts of today to an entire wing of an airplane tomorrow.

Bill of Process Creation

Bill of Process creation is an extremely important step in the realization of a product. Without a process that results in a producible design, the design is merely a pretty picture. Creating a build process on the factory floor can be very expensive and time-consuming.

If the process can be created digitally, then substantial time and resources can be saved. In addition, understanding that an existing build process produces the desired result can also save resources from being used in recreating something that already exists.

Both having a library of known, reliable processes and having the ability to simulate new processes in building a product is critical to saving resources and reducing time to manufacture. In addition, in multiple factory situations, having each factory developed their own way of doing things is wasteful and leads to potentially unreliable manufacturing.

Factory Simulation

Factory simulation has rapidly emerged as one of the top PLM use cases. Factory simulation is essentially behavior simulation in a tightly controlled situation, the factory. The behavior that is being simulated is the actions and sequences necessary to produce a physical product from material, equipment, and human actions. If the actions and sequences cannot realize the as-designed product, then this is an indication that changes will need to be made to the design.

Factory simulation uses the digital design as both an output to be realized and as an input into the factory simulation. It is an output because the actions and sequences on and with material, equipment, and human actions need to result in a form that matches, within tolerances, the digital form. The digital design is an input because the forms that make it up need to be worked on by the digital equipment and humans. Digital material needs to be digitally bent. Digital components need to be reached and welded by digital robots. Digital human forms need to be able to reach into the digital parts to insert and tighten digital bolts in ergonomically safe ways.

The granularity of factory simulation ranges from an individual workstation to a work cell to an assembly line to a factory to a factory complex. Factory simulation has rapidly moved from simulations that could perform one of those types of simulation to integrated simulations where the view of the simulation can be selected at any level.

NASA created a factory simulation of the Michaud Assembly Facility (MAF), located just outside of New Orleans. MAF is one of the largest assembly facilities in the world, with almost two million square feet under air-conditioning. MAF is where the fuel tanks for the space shuttle were manufactured and assembled.

NASA laser-measured the entire facility and created a virtual MAF complete with production equipment. NASA uses this simulation to simulate proposed production by equipment and humans. NASA requires special-built equipment costing in the millions of dollars. By simulating this equipment, NASA can ascertain that this equipment will perform the tasks as envisioned. NASA has saved millions of dollars and significant time by discovering issues with equipment and processes that in the past would have only been discovered once production started. Figure 3.2 is a still shot extracted from a full simulation on a rocket engine assembly process.

Factory Simulation

Source: NASA

Figure 3.2

Work Instructions

Unless it is an extremely simple manufacturing process, work instructions are a necessity in conveying both how the manufacturing process needs to be done and in providing procedures for checking that the work has been properly performed. While tribal knowledge has been the de facto mechanism for this in the past, in today's environment of rapidly changing products, it is inefficient.

Work instructions can be limited to text, but can also include graphics and even video. Rich work instructions can train the manufacturing staff quicker and reduce errors more than past methods, such as 2D drawings and notes.

For new, innovative, and complex products the work instructions need to go both ways. Even with performing exhaustive simulation, when the manufacturing group starts to work with the physical product itself, there will need to be changes in processes and procedures in order to actually produce the product. This learning can be both extensive and expensive. This information needs to be captured and used in the manufacturing process, plus it should be fed back to engineering so that they understand that what they thought was their manufacturing processes did not really perform the required tasks.

I recently came across an illustrative case study of this need. An aerospace company had developed very complex manufacturing processes for building their components. The management of this group was very impressed by their improvements in both productivity and quality. Management decided to reward this group, surprising them by sprucing up their work area.

Over the weekend, the management group had the facilities people come in and paint their entire area in very cheery colors. Management wanted this manufacturing group to feel special and have a bright new facility to come in to work to everyday.

The manufacturing group came in on that Monday and productivity and quality plunged immediately. The reason is that the work instructions that this manufacturing group had developed over the course of a number of months were written on the walls of the facility. Covered up by a coat of fresh, new paint, these expensive lessons, learned procedures, processes, and practices were lost.

They obviously could be re-created, because the people who had developed them were still working. However, it took 3 to 4 months in order to get this operation back to its previous quality and productivity levels. These redeveloped work instructions were not written on the facility wall!

Capturing both the proposed work instructions and the actual work instructions is an important use case for Product Lifecycle Management. This will become more important as the more experienced workers of the baby boomer generation starts retiring. Work instructions have long been treated as tribal knowledge, but that needs to change in order to produce gains in both productivity and innovation.

Error Proofing

Having information about how the product needs to be manufactured as each process is performed can result in error proofing the product. Whether collected automatically or manually, key characteristics about the process can be required at each step. The key characteristics can then be compared to the desired characteristics in order to ensure that the product is meeting its requirements as it moves through the manufacturing cycle.

In advanced implementations, information about the virtual product can actually drive the processes on the manufacturing floor. As the product progresses to each station, information about the product configuration can drive the picking of the proper components and identification of the proper procedure with which to assemble those components.

As-Built Creation

Creating the as-built is fundamental to providing value to the product user in the support stage of the product life, which is usually the longest phase of the product lifecycle. Creating the as-built requires the creation of a virtual version of the physical product that has been manufactured and assembled.

Depending on the product, as-builts will vary in detail and complexity. For simple products that are assembled out of commodity components, the as-built might be as simple as a bill of material that lists part number and quantity. For custom engineered products, the as-built could contain the bill of material, the bill of process used to manufacture and assemble the components, measurement and inspection data for key characteristics, and any deviation or nonconformance data. The as-built information might also point back to the geometric designs of the product.

The creation of this virtual product allows the product producer to ship the physical product, while retaining the information about that product, the virtual product. By having this virtual product, the product producer is in a position to provide support and sustainment services more efficiently than third parties. In addition, the product producer can also use this availability of virtual products as a competitive advantage. The product producer can use this availability of virtual products to convince its potential buyers that its products do indeed meet their specifications and that supporting the products will be cheaper for the product user by having the as-built virtual products as a starting point for maintaining the products throughout their usage phase.

SUPPORT

Configuration Management

Most products do not maintain their form and functionality in the usage phase without support. Products break down, are damaged, and have parts that wear during usage. Unless the product is very short-lived, it would be unusual for a product to go through its entire life with the same parts and components with which it started off its life.

So even if the product maintains the same form and functionality throughout its entire life, the individual parts and components of that product will change. If we desire a complete view of the product as it goes through these changes, then we will need to update our virtual product whenever we change out a component in a physical product.

Maintaining the virtual product as the physical product changes is often referred to as configuration management (CM) or the "as-maintained." Again, this may be as simple as noting in a Bill of Materials that one part has been retired and another part installed. Additionally, if the parts have been serial numbered, then the history of serial numbers would need to be maintained. For more complex products, we again might maintain the entire history of the replacement part, including its geometric design, the process by which it was manufactured, and testing and verification data.

Figure 3.3 shows a still frame from the simulated assembly and checkout of a rocket in the Kennedy Space Center Vehicle Assembly Building. As parts are replaced, the virtual rocket is updated to reflect the new configuration.

Figure 3.3

For those products that possess computing capability, which today is most products, the product may not be the same product as it goes through its life in use. For today's products, software updates and changes, and even hardware changes, are not uncommon. This means that after a period of time, products that left the factory as identical may not be. Making the assumption that the as-built reflects the current configuration will generally be erroneous.

One automaker discovered this when the dealers uploaded new versions of the software as cars came in for service. In many of the cases, the software required a different version of the hardware than the cars possessed. Customers taking in their cars for minor, routine maintenance would get back an automobile that now performed poorly.

Maintenance, Service and Repair

The value to the product user will depend on the product maintaining its performance level throughout the life of the product. As noted above, products will rarely go through life without some maintenance, service or repair. If this is not done efficiently and effectively, the perceived value of the product will suffer.

This will require a well-developed Bill of Service (BOS) that will provide the necessary information for the product servicer to diagnose, disassemble, repair, and reassemble the product. This is much more complex than the Bill of Process (BOP) used to manufacture the product. The BOP is a one-way process that builds up the product in a sequential fashion. The BOS is a two-way process. Selected areas of the product have to be both disassembled and then reassembled.

Use of virtual product simulations is instrumental for service personnel in both initial training and in providing step-by-step refresher instructions as the actual service is being performed. In the case of repairs to complex and critical equipment, such as aircraft or nuclear reactors, an implementation of BOS could require sign-offs to indicate compliance with specific repair steps and provide an audit trail of such compliance.

While service is often an after-thought or ancillary activity in the create phase, effective BOS will be created as part of PLM in the create phase. Simulating service and repair activities should be part of the design of the product. If service or repair activities are found to be difficult, designs can be changed to improve those deficiencies. Once the product is built, that option is not available.

Part of the F-35 advanced airplane design activity was to simulate service activities of the F-35 in a simulation cave. During those simulations using actual humans, a number of problems were discovered that were corrected. Without PLM, those problems would have caused severe inconvenience to service personnel.

Counterfeit Part Prevention

In addition to maintaining a current configuration, requiring information on replacement components can act as deterrence against counterfeit parts. For products in general, let alone products where safety is of paramount concern such as aerospace, using counterfeit parts generally will degrade the performance of the product. Understanding that the parts used in support are the appropriate quality and specification as the original part is extremely important. Maintaining not only the configuration of the current product but also the pedigree and provenance of its replacement parts is a requirement for products to maintain the desired level of functionality.

Product Augmentation

Ideally, product producers would like to use product augmentation as an additional revenue source. To do so, they will need to not only have the as-built information for the products that their customer has acquired, but they will need to have the as-maintained information so that they can give the customer the appropriate version of the software that delivers the new functionality.

Examples of product augmentation certainly include Apple's iPhone. However, there are numerous products that could be tailored as a result of their environment and usage conditions. For example, automobile producers might offer performance packages for high-speed highway driving or off-road use.

For product augmentation to be successful will also require that the product producer instrument their product to collect and transmit the data that reflects how the product is performing. Collecting information about the state changes of the product will help the product producer not only understand how their product is being used, but will also help them develop new additions to the product that they can turn around and sell to the product user.

Performance Feedback

As will be discussed extensively in this book, the key determination of product quality is whether or not a product performs according to user expectations as the product is being used. Feedback of product performance from the support to the create phase will be required to understand whether or not the product actually performed to its designed requirements.

As argued in my previous book, warranty and survey data are woefully insufficient to provide this feedback. Products need to be instrumented and the data collected during the product's actual usage in order to provide objective data on performance.

How the product changes during its life, or what is referred to as "state change" information, can be sensed and collected in order to understand how the product's components respond to changes during its life. For example, the data on the pilot of an airplane advancing the throttle and the readings of various jet engine sensors such as the rate of fuel flow, turbine speeds, and engine temperature can provide valuable information on how an engine performs versus how it was designed to perform.

This performance feedback can be used as diagnostic and even prognostic information in order to maintain the product to its desired level of performance. The development group can also use this information to evaluate how well their prediction of design performance matched actual performance both initially and over time.

Product as a Service

This is potentially the most interesting and extensive use case of all. In the past, the functionality that the product had when it left the factory was the functionality it would have throughout its life. In addition, the last contact a product producer might have with the products it produced was as the product left its shipping dock. Beyond indirect contact via warranty and parts, product producers might have little or no contact with their products throughout the rest of the product's life.

By staying connected to the product, product producers have the potential to not only maintain the initial functionality that the product is shipped with, but to add functionality throughout the product's life. As the product user's requirements or simply their tastes change, the product producer can update its product to meet those changes. Instead of the product being a static product, it becomes a dynamic product that blurs the line between product and service.

In order to provide this capability, product producers will need to treat the information about their products differently than they have in the past. They will need to produce two products. They will need to produce the physical product that they have always produced. They will also need to produce a virtual product, which is the information about the product. They will also need to instrument their products so that the product producer can maintain a digital connection with that product throughout its life. This digital connection is a two-way connection. As the state of the product changes, the changes are reflected in the virtual product that the product producer maintains.

There are already current examples of this use case in existence. The Apple iPhone and OnStar by General Motors Corporation are but two standout examples. There are huge opportunities in almost every product sector to create the same capabilities. In fact, organizations whose products do not move to this model will not survive long term.

Service as a Product

If the product producer instruments their product to produce data on product performance that they can collect, they can have a competitive position in providing service for that product. If they have this information for the universe of products that they have produced as that product operates in a wide variety of circumstances, then they may be uniquely positioned to correlate product behavior with subsequent component failure. That capability could allow them to predict failures and provide their customers with preventive maintenance services that is far superior to a third party or even the customers themselves performing service when the product fails.

This is occurring today in the airline industry. Jet engine manufacturers collect data on all the airplane engines that are in the air. Given that their population of products is substantially larger than any one airline, they have better capability in diagnosing and predicting future engine failure. As a result, they can be more effective at keeping engines in operation than any third party maintenance organization or the even airline itself. Product producers who have not been in the business of maintaining their products may look at this as a new opportunity. At a minimum, the provision of this information could be a new and lucrative source of revenue, even if the product producer does not want to perform the actual maintenance and repairs.

DISPOSE

Regulatory Compliance

Product regulatory compliance continues to become more strict and proactive. The trend toward product producers being held responsible for the regulatory compliant disposal of their products is expected to continue unabated. It will not simply be enough to design a product to be disposed of in a particular fashion. It will become the responsibility of the product producer to confirm that it actually has been disposed of according to the approved method.

This means that a Bill of Disposal will need to be created for each product that defines how the product is to be retired from service, how it is to be disassembled, and how each part or component is to be recycled or disposed of. In an increasing number of cases, the information on the actual disposal process will need to be conveyed to a regulatory agency for confirmation and audit.

Project Archiving

All products come to an end of life from a production perspective. The development has been completed, and the last manufacturing run has taken place. There comes a time when the information associated with the product is "packed up" and put away.

There are two schools of thought about what should be done with this information. One school is that this information should remain available because issues that have been discovered and resolved will reemerge in other product production. Having availability of this information will reduce rediscovery and re-solving of these problems.

The other school of thought is that this information should be discarded according to a defined information sunset policy. The thought behind this is that this information can become a liability in some later product litigation. Even issues that within the context of the development and manufacturing process in which they occurred are innocuous can be extracted and made to look sinister by plaintiffs' attorney many years later. Pulled out of context and without the individuals who worked with such issues to provide clarifying explanations, this information could produce substantial financial liability for the organization. The rationale is that this information should be eliminated as soon as legally possible so as to prevent that from occurring.

Either position requires that a mechanism be put in place to archive the product information. In the first case, an additional mechanism needs to be put in place to make this information available to the organization as they develop and manufacture their new products. In the second case, an additional mechanism needs to be put into place to eliminate the information at the time set by the sunset policy.

FUTURE USE CASES

Again, this is not meant to be an exhaustive list of use cases. It is meant to describe the more meaningful and representative use cases that product organizations will have use for. It is expected that different kinds of organizations will have different requirements that will be more specific to their particular kind of product. It is also expected that these use cases will generate sub-cases that will be more specific as to the type and kind of uses.

As PLM matures and as computing and communications technologies advance, new and valuable use cases will emerge. The expectation is that the use cases listed here will still continue to exist and that they will soon become standard in all organizations if they already have not.

The success of PLM will rest with the value of the use cases that PLM provides to organizations. This chapter described some representative use cases in each of the four phases of PLM: create, build, support, and dispose. This was not meant to be an exhaustive list of uses, but a collection of the more significant use cases that organizations will select to provide value.

In the create phase, the use cases are: requirement development and verification, model release, design review, digital mock-up units (DMU's); engineering change process, component update, pre-release collaboration, product integration, product configuration control and validation, behavior and performance analysis, procurement, marketing material, next-generation product, where-used, and packaging.

In the build phase the use cases are: rapid prototyping, manufacturing by printing, Bill of Process creation, factory simulation, work instructions, error proofing, and as-built creation. The support phase use cases include: configuration management (CM), maintenance, service, and repair, counterfeit part prevention, product augmentation, performance feedback, product as a service, and service as a product. Finally in the disposal phase we have as use cases: regulatory compliance and project archiving.

Use cases will continue to emerge as new and valuable uses of product information continues to be created and exploited. The use cases presented here will become standard in most if not all product organizations.

Notes

13 For a good source on the product design process, see Ulrich, K. T., & Eppinger, S. D. (2008). Product design and development (4th ed.). Boston: McGraw-Hill Higher Education.

14 This use ties into my concept of Virtual Collaboration Rooms (VCRs) that was introduced in my first book. For an example of how VCRs might be used, see this video produced by BT: http://www.youtube.com/watch?v=n-DbWyxrlag.

4

VIRTUALLY PRICELESS

No one really *wants* or even *needs* a product. This may seem a silly statement for a book about products. However, as we will see in this chapter, this indeed is the case. People do not need or want products. What they need or want is the results that the products will give them.

The claim has been made that people hire products to do a job.[15] That is a utilitarian way of looking at things, but it is not the whole story. As I'll describe later, there are a number of categories by which people value products. The utilitarian or economic basis is one of those categories. However there are other categories under which people desire products.

While the consumer of products always understand that products are acquired to give them something, producers of products sometimes get confused about this issue. Product producers or manufacturers sometimes become so enamored with the idea of their products that they fail to understand that they are not providing value that product users would want.

When we say that people do not want a product, but only want that which the product will give them, we can look at a few utilitarian examples. People do not want a watch. They want to know the time. People do not want a car. They want to go from point A to point B in style. People do not want a drill. They want a hole.

A senior executive at Boeing asked me if I knew what the first thought that people had when they got on one of his airplanes. I suggested that it might be the size of the seats, the amount of overhead bins, or the number and placement of lavatories. He laughed and said that the first thought that people had when they get on an airplane was when they could get off of it.

While all those things about the airplane that I mentioned may have been important and certainly Boeing pays attention to those things when it designs its airplanes, it does illustrate the point that ultimately people do not want a product they want what a product does. While the examples here are utilitarian, this concept extends to social, safety, experiential, and even belief for belief's sake needs and wants. People want what the product does for them, not necessarily the product itself.

The trick of creating a product with value is balancing the benefits of the product producer with the product consumer. The product consumer would like to obtain great value while expending minimum resources. The product producer would like to obtain great value while also expending a minimum of resources — think "pet rock."

However, there is a solution to the seemingly incompatible clash of objectives. Product consumers will expend their resources for new products that provide more value than previous alternatives. For example, a washing machine frees up many hours of manual labor and does a much better job of cleaning clothes than the manual hand-washing alternative.

For product producers to be successful, they must be able to produce their product at such a price that will meet the calculation by the product consumer that the value of this product is worth the resources they will expend in acquiring and using it. As the phrase "virtually priceless" implies, we do have to expend resources to acquire products. There are things in this world that are priceless as the MasterCard ads point out, but products are not one of them. However, both product producer and product purchaser balance the price against product value. In looking at product value, we will first look at it from a point of view of the product purchaser.

PERCEIVED VALUE

I would like to make the point before I start that when I use the term "value" that I always mean "perceived value." In my product lifecycle model, I use "perceived value" of the product user as the main driver of product creation and the main evaluator as to whether a product is successfully delivered.

Products in and of themselves do not have intrinsic value. It is only the value that we humans placed on them that gives them the value that they have. For products that are belief driven, this is pretty obvious. But this is also true for products whose value is based on supposed objective criteria, such as economic analysis.

Economic analysis is not always objective in spite of the apparent concreteness of the numbers it works with. What we choose to include and to exclude in our economic analysis can take an economic analysis from highly positive to highly negative. The assumptions that we make about our selected economic variables can also have the same effect. As I will discuss later, looking at the acquisition cost of the product versus the total cost of ownership may cause a dramatic swing as to economic value.

The assumptions of cost levels in future periods versus what costs are actually incurred in those future periods generally have major differences no matter how rigorous the financial analysis. To paraphrase a saying about statistics, "if you torture the economic analysis enough, it will eventually confess." More often than not, economic analyses are tortured enough to give the values desired by their analysts who have a desired result in mind or at least a predisposition to a particular result.

The other issue about the perceived value of products is that it persists even when a more objective analysis would not support this perception.[16] The U.S. headquartered automobile companies are suffering from this issue today. I hear many comments from people outside the Detroit area that automobiles from General Motors, Ford, and Chrysler are not nearly up to the quality of foreign cars. This is in spite of quality surveys that do not support this contention. However, correct or not, it is the perception of people who now will only buy foreign-made or, more accurately, non-Detroit 3 automobiles.

This means that it is not enough to create and build products that have value by some objective standards. Companies also need to contend with subjective perception that is difficult to control. Perception, once established, is difficult to change, although product perception can go negative much more quickly than it can go positive. Firestone, a true pioneer in the tire industry, spent decades building a positive perception of its tire products. This perception was destroyed and replaced by an extremely negative perception in a few short months when Firestone tires were blamed for the rollover accidents of Ford SUV's.

For the U.S. headquartered automobile industry, the perception of poor products was an issue that they brought on in their past by making inferior products. While they have made major strides in producing quality automobiles, they are still living with perceptions that they created 40 years ago. The argument here is that companies cannot ever afford to produce products that do not live up to their users' perceptions. They may get away with it for a period of time, but it will eventually catch up with them. The time frames to erase these perception problems can, as the Detroit 3 automobile companies have shown, run to decades.

This again argues for having information about our product as envisioned by PLM. If we don't know that we are having problems with our products, then we are not going to be able to take steps to address those problems. We need to continually tie the perceived value of the product user to the product creation, building, and sustaining of that product.

PRODUCT PURCHASERS

Product acquirers purchase products from product providers. I will use "purchase" to include the spectrum of product use. Purchase, by my intent, spans the spectrum of actually taking title to the product for its entire life to simply using it for a period of time. I can purchase an automobile, lease one for two years, or rent one for a day. In all these situations, in my usage, I am purchasing the use of a product. Also, in the case of organizations, the person purchasing the product may not be the actual individual using it. However, there is still some linkage between the purchaser and user. The users of the product within an organization influence the product purchasers group to some extent.

For purposes of our discussion, I would like to divide product purchasers into two groups. The first group is personal consumers (PCs). Personal consumers acquire products for their own personal use. They are not acquiring the products to use in a business, at least that is not their primary motivation.

The second group of product purchasers or acquirers is what I will call organizational consumers (OCs). Organizational consumers acquire the product for use in an organization: business, non-profit, government, etc. Ostensibly, these products are acquired with a purely economic focus in mind. However, as will be described in this section, other factors come into play. Product producers who only assume an economic motive for OCs will be inaccurate in their assessment.

For the product purchaser, the value of the product is its benefits compared to its costs. If the product purchaser can make this calculus work, then they will perceive that the product has value and will want to acquire that product. This relationship is illustrated in Figure 4.1. Figure 4.1 is similar to the IT Value Map that I introduced in my first book. Like the IT Value Map, the Customer Product Value Map visually illustrates the components that go into analyzing a product's value from the customer perspective.

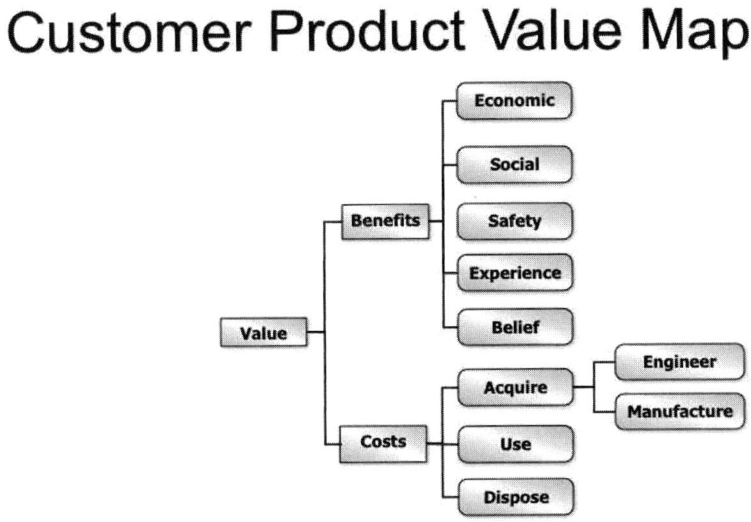

Figure 4.1

The top part of the map shows the benefit categories. What are the categories of customer benefit? I will contend the categories are: economic, safety, social, experiential, and belief driven. While the classical focus has been on economic benefit, the other categories have an equal if not greater importance in product consumers defining benefit.

Product Costs

The bottom part of the map shows the cost categories. I have divided the cost categories along the lines of the product lifecycle. While we look at the product lifecycle as being create, build, support, and dispose, the product lifecycle looks a little different from the product consumer's point of view.

For the product consumer, the product lifecycle starts usually with product acquisition. While in days long past, personal consumers may have been their own product producers, it is rare to find that these days. What differentiates a modern society from a primitive society is a division of labor that allows people to acquire the products that they need without having to produce them.

Organizational consumers may be in an organization large enough or specialized enough that it both produces and consumes its products. However, even in those cases, the production and consumption groups are distinct enough that the analysis here still applies.

So for the product consumer, the product lifecycle starts with product acquisition. The next two phases are product usage and product disposal. Product usage for the product consumer corresponds to product support for the product producer. The disposal phase is the same for both product consumer and product producer.

While we have different categories of benefits, for costs we will primarily focus on economic analysis. While there may be social costs, experiential costs, and belief costs, these are vaguer and much harder to quantify than their corresponding benefits. As a result, we will focus more on economic costs, although pointing out these other categories of costs as appropriate.

With respect to benefits, we have a pretty good understanding of economic or utilitarian benefits. Product consumers value products that give them economic benefit. Product consumers will acquire products that give them greater economic benefit than alternatives that give them less economic benefit, the cost being equal.

The study of how people make economic decisions is the subject of innumerable economic books and papers. At the end of the day, there is a reason that economics is called the "dismal science."[17] This is because there is much unknown about how people make economic decisions. In fact, a good deal of the time, when we really want to talk about the general principles under which people make economic decisions, we reach back in time and cite the most famous economist of them all, Adam Smith. In addition, we may (or may not as evidenced by the severe financial problems in 2008) understand the macro aspects of economics. Understanding the micro aspects of how individuals make individual decisions is much fuzzier.

With respect to Product Lifecycle Management, I would like to highlight some of the economic elements that come into play in making decisions about products. The first has to do with the categories of cost that people consider in making decisions about products, and the second has to do with how well they can compute those costs.

While a great deal of attention is given to the acquisition cost of the product, product consumers need to concern themselves with the costs of the product throughout its lifecycle. As illustrated in Figure 4.1, these categories of costs are acquisition, usage, and disposal. This can be referred to as the Total Cost of Ownership (TCO).

While TCO seems to be an obvious concept, it is not always taken into consideration. Even companies that use sophisticated financial techniques such as Net Present Value (NPV) or Internal Rate of Return (IRR), sometimes fail to take into account the total cost of product ownership.

As an example of this, when personal computers started to make their way into the corporate environment, companies based their justification of them almost solely on the purchase price. They ignored or substantially underestimated the cost of supporting, maintaining, and servicing these personal computers. Oftentimes, very expensive employees within the organization who simply gravitated to supporting personal computers because they were trying to be helpful or because they simply liked fooling around with them did the support of the personal computers.

However, if these expensive employees were assisting other employees with support problems, they generally were not doing the job that they were being paid a significant amount of money to do. While this was a real cost, companies neglected to account for these costs in their analysis of the cost of personal computers. So even for companies with sophisticated financial analysis tools, accurate economic analysis was lacking.

This does not invalidate the concept of TCO but does point to the issue that unless the proper framework is used, the right economic analysis cannot be made. For TCO to have meaning, the product acquirer has to have an ability to accurately assess the cost of acquisition, the cost of using the product, and the cost of disposal. We'll discuss each of these cost phases below, working our way backwards.

Disposal Costs

The cost of disposal has been under-recognized except when there was a benefit. What this means is that if the product had residual value at the end of its life to the product acquirer, i.e., it could be sold, then this was taken into consideration in the financial analysis of the product cost. However, if this was not the case, and the product was simply disposed of, there was rarely any consideration of this cost.

Both companies and individuals have historically considered the cost of disposal as zero. The product was simply gotten rid of. It was sent to a landfill, given away, or simply banished to a corner of the property where it rusted in peace. However, there is a trend to having a heightened sense of the environment, and, if disposal costs are not an issue today, they will be tomorrow.

As evidenced by the European Directives for End of Life Vehicle (ELV) and Waste Electrical and Electronic Equipment (WEEE), there are now costs in dealing with disposal from the product producer side. It is not hard to imagine that product acquirers will have similar regulations imposed upon them that will create added costs. Product Lifecycle Management, with its management of the product from cradle to grave, will not only be used by the product manufacturers to stay in touch with their products, but will eventually be co-opted by governments to allow them to mandate the proper disposal of products.

It is difficult to argue that product consumers should not be responsible for the environmental costs associated with the disposal costs associated with their products. It is also not a stretch to imagine that Product Lifecycle Management technology will create the opportunity to track products in their disposal phase.

Usage Costs

While disposal is a specific event with a fairly good ability to specify its costs, the longest period of a product life and the hardest period of the product life to accurately estimate costs associated with it is generally the usage phase. Both because the time period can be long and the ability to associate costs can be difficult, the ability to accurately assess the cost of product usage is problematic. While it may be possible to account for the costs as a product is being used, the ability to estimate the product costs over the usage phase at acquisition time can be very difficult.

While admittedly 2008 was a highly unusual economic year that hopefully will not be repeated anytime soon, changes in prices do occur. Given a product with a long useful life, it may be very difficult for product acquirers to develop an accurate model of the costs over that lifetime of usage. This is an issue that is equally valid for both personal and organizational consumers.

For personal consumers, the product lifetime that they're concerned about may be shorter. However, their capability and resources to be able to compute those costs is less than the organizational user. For the organizational user, their resources and capabilities to compute these costs can be significantly greater. However, the timeframe that they have to consider can be significantly longer. The net result is that the ability to compute these costs can be difficult for both categories of product users.

The tendency for both these categories of users is to simply extrapolate from the present. Given that tendency, product producers may have a difficult time in convincing product consumers of the value of their product if this value is based on substantially different assumptions about the cost structure. If the product producers are assuming much higher or much lower costs than the present costs, their estimate of how the product consumer should value the product will probably differ markedly from the value that product consumers actually ascribe to their product.

There are a number of reasons that we will examine as to why this may be the case. The main issues are: uncertainty about future costs, inability to compute future costs, and rationalization of future costs. We'll look at each of these.

The 2008 radical fluctuation of gas prices is highly illustrative of uncertainty about future costs. Buyers of trucks and SUVs before the 2008 run up in gas prices probably severely underestimated their cost of product usage. Likewise, buyers of fuel-efficient cars who bought these cars at $4.00+ a gallon might have made very different decisions because they really didn't want small vehicles if they knew that gas prices would drop very shortly to below $2.00 a gallon. In simply a few months' period, estimates of the cost of the usage phase for automobile products would have been wildly inaccurate.

This is the issue bedeviling automotive producers today. The value that both consumers and organizations have placed on high-mileage vehicles has fluctuated as rapidly as gas prices. Unfortunately, no automotive producer can change its product offerings in such a rapid fashion.

In addition to uncertainty, there is an inability to compute future costs because we do have no idea what they may be. As an example, utilities have no idea what the Environmental Protection Agency (EPA) may do with respect to regulation of coal-fired plants. It is not that there may be a fluctuation in the price of some known expense. The EPA could very well create a whole new class of expense, such as carbon sequestration, that does not exist today.

Finally, there simply may be a rationalization of future costs. Organizations may have a cost model that they wish to come true. They simply create their assumptions to make that cost model operative. Congress does this all the time with the Congressional Budget Office (CBO). The CBO is required to score the financial impact of bills by using the assumptions that Congress provides them with, no matter how ridiculous the assumptions. Some organizations are equally delusional.

Acquisition Costs

Product acquisition costs are the costs that are known with the most certainty. Obviously these costs are the most immediate, and the transaction where the product consumer pays a certain amount of money and acquires the product is the most certain.

For simple products, this may be the case. However for complex products, the acquisition costs need to incorporate the cost of being able to actually use the product. For example, while acquiring an actual airplane is fairly straightforward, the cost of training people in the use of an airplane may also be quite significant. In addition, for products like industrial equipment, there may be a substantial cost of installing products.

It is often that these ancillary costs are either underestimated or overlooked by product acquirers, only to find out that their true cost of acquisition is much higher than they had predicted. Virtual products can assist in identifying and helping quantify these particular costs. Training and installation can be simulated so as to fully understand the costs of these categories.

Product Benefits

As mentioned earlier, the categories of product value or benefits are economic or utilitarian, safety, social, experiential, and belief driven. Each of the categories is discussed below.

Economic Value

The economic benefit of a product is the cost in resource expenditure of performing the task with the product compared to performing the same task without the product. Both organizational consumers and personal consumers perform this analysis. Organizational consumers may perform this analysis with more rigor, because their tasks can be more readily quantified. For example, it is readily quantifiable how long it will take a steam shovel to dig a hole rather than using men with shovels. The price of the men with shovels is a readily quantifiable amount.

While more subjective, personal consumers engage in the same sort of analysis. In buying a power lawn mower versus a hand mower, a personal consumer will place some sort of value on the time and energy that he or she may expend in using the hand mower versus the power mower.

While economic analysis has long been used as the primary analysis that product consumers use in acquiring products, as will be discussed below it may be completely overwhelmed by other value considerations.

Safety Value

Safety, which also can be considered security, is an ontological or basic human need. People are born with an innate desire to be safe. Intrinsic in an evaluation of a product acquisition is an evaluation of that product's safety. The value that consumers place on safety in most cases trumps any economic value. However, the concept of safety spans a fairly wide spectrum. For product consumers, safety can mean anything from incurring no discomfort whatsoever to having a reasonable chance at survival.

On a conceptual basis, product acquirers may claim that economics plays no part in their decisions when it comes to safety. The reality is that there is some trade-off between safety and economics. For example, people make trade-offs in automobile safety all the time. If there were no trade-off between economic value and safety value, then people would be prepared to spend any amount of money to ensure the safety of themselves and their family. However, that is not the case and people do buy cheaper vehicles that are less safe.[18]

So how do people value the safety of products? The answer is that it seems to be a hurdle decision. What this means is that people are prepared to accept a certain amount of risk in their lives. What is acceptable risk? When it comes to human lives, it would be hard to argue that producing products that harmed or killed people at any level was "acceptable" so how do we reconcile this?

At a launch of the space shuttle that I attended, the Director of NASA at the time, Mike Griffin, addressed this issue. I was invited to view the launch from the director's balcony at the Kennedy Space Center. This balcony is as close as one can get to the space shuttle at launch, except if one is in the shuttle itself. Prior to launch, the Director of NASA gave a little talk describing the launch and NASA's view of safety.

Director Griffin said that there was no acceptable risk regarding the safety of the astronauts. However, he said that NASA and the astronauts took an *accepted* risk. While no loss of life is acceptable to NASA, they understand that there is risk involved in such a dangerous endeavor. NASA and their astronauts accept that risk.

Humans view their products in much the same way. They understand that there is accepted risk in many of the products that they acquire and use. Safety therefore is a hurdle issue as to the value that product consumers attribute to their products. Personal consumers are probably less acceptable of risk than organizational consumers. However, the differential of acceptable risk between the two categories should not be considered to be very large.

Basically, if the products safety risk profile is below a certain level, then product consumers will consider it valuable. If the products safety risk profile is above a certain level, then product consumers will consider it to have no value and will not acquire it. This trumps economic considerations. If a product consumer was offered a power drill that was exceptionally cheap but 1 in 1,000 of these drills electrocuted their user, neither a personal consumer nor an organizational consumer would ever consider purchasing it.

The societal trend in favor of product safety continues to increase. Fifty years ago children rode around on bicycles with no protective gear and piled in the back seats of cars with no seat belts. Today, it's considered child abuse to let your child ride his or her bicycle without a helmet, and, forget about seat belts, children are ensconced in car seats that could probably take them safely through atmospheric reentry.[19] Even if individual product consumers do not place a value on safety, this value is built-in by the government and its regulations, sometimes to an absurd degree.[20]

Both the hurdle rate and the safety of the product are in part set by societal perception. While safety metrics for products are available, they are statistics. People interpret those statistics in light of how likely they believe they personally will be affected. Many people buy small cars and use chain saws in spite of statistics that show that these products can increase their risk of injury and even death.

There may be some national differences in product consumers' view of safety. However, that seems to be harmonizing as the world becomes more global. Even China, which historically has had an extremely poor record of producing safe products, is becoming much more vigilant. Neither the Chinese consumers nor the Chinese government tolerated a recent milk-tainting incident. In fact, the Chinese government acted in a way that no Western government would. They tried and executed executives responsible for the dangerous milk in under a few months.

Below a certain hurdle rate, safety value trumps economic value. Above that hurdle rate, product acquirers make trade-offs between safety value and other values.

Social Value

Social value is an extremely powerful criterion for evaluating products. It regularly trumps economic value and probably trumps safety value more often than we would care to acknowledge. There is an age-old question that parents have asked their children when told that it was a requirement to have something because their friends had one. "If your friends jumped off a cliff, would you jump off a cliff also?" This would be answered in the affirmative if the children were truly honest. Sadly, a significant number of them would indeed jump off a cliff under the right peer pressure conditions.

Even as adults, the need for social value is a basic human need. The latest studies in neuroscience give indications that the need for social value is hardwired from birth and may be as basic as our need for food, clothing, and shelter.[21] We use products as an indication of our social value. Humans need and use social capital as much as economic capital.[22]

While the economists of the past would have liked to portray us all as rational, economic beings, examples abound that shatter this myth. As much as we would like to think that we are rational economic animals, the social aspect of our makeup is as important, if not more important, than our economic perspective.

A Timex watch and a Rolex watch tell the same time, at hugely different costs. Yet people will buy a $20,000 Rolex watch rather than $100 Timex watch. A Ford Fusion and a Lincoln will carry us from point A to point B in the same amount of time, but the Lincoln costs much more than the Ford.

However we buy the Lincoln, as much for status as for the additional features.

While you might think that this behavior is only applicable to personal consumers and not to organizational consumers, examples also abound to the contrary. In offices, the simple, utilitarian, green metal desks and tables have given way in numerous organizations to sleek office cubicles with ergonomically designed furniture. While the claim may be made that these products help people work better, a good deal of the reason is to promote the organization's social value. The thinking goes that if this company has all this nice furniture, over and above what they need for utilitarian purposes, then this must be an organization whose social standing is high.

Clearly, a great number of organizations understand that their products need to be created with social value in mind. Companies in the luxury goods market, such as jewelry, clothing, and high-end automobiles, create and position their products as having high social value. In the computer industry, Apple designs their products not only to have high utility, but also to promote social value. Apple's designs say, "People who use Mac's are cooler and more with it than people who use PC's."

From a product producers' standpoint, the difficulty is in understanding how much of a premium that they can command for a product that has social value over the same product that only has economic value. Product producers can get a fairly decent idea of the economic value of their product by comparing it to the economic value it generates for the product acquirer. A machine tool can produce X amount of widgets that would require Y amount of labor hours if done manually. That is a relatively straightforward calculation. It is not very straightforward to calculate what social value a luxury watch creates for its product acquirer.

Social value is obviously socially constructed. It has a value that people agree it has. So how do virtual products play into this formulation?

The problem with creating products that have social value is that it requires that the product acquirer attach a value over and above the economic value that the product may have. The product producers need to convince the social community that its product is worth the price that the product producer wants to sell it at. If the product producer cannot do that, then the product producer has a very expensive flop on its hands.

Some product producers have developed and positioned their luxury products over a substantial period of time, decades and decades. The brands that they have established are associated with social status and are easily recognizable all over the world. Examples of these brands are Mercedes, Cadillac, Gucci, and Rolex.

While companies that produce high social value products spend much time and money in advertising, product placement, and endorsement by high status individuals, these companies also have something else in common. These companies use materials of high-value and manufacture these products with attention to superior quality. Creating social value that is not the result of a short-lived fad requires products that perform well for the people acquiring them.

Virtual products can assist in two areas. The first is that virtual products are the key to high quality. By simulating the manufacturing of these products, product producers can work out quality issues before the physical production ever takes place. By capturing the as-built information, product producers can ensure that products are being produced to exacting specifications that high-end products require.

Virtual products can also assist in the social positioning of the products. As described above, one of the methods of social positioning is advertising. The difference between old and new methods is that virtual products make advertising much more realistic. Using the digital product in print and video advertising adds a realistic aspect to the presentation. Much of today's advertising for products such as automobiles uses digital representations from the create phase in producing both print and video advertisements.

The social aspect of our life is extremely important. A product producer who can tap into this social need will be able to charge much more for a product than the product producer who only meets economic needs. While we might think that this applies only to personal consumers, it can easily be demonstrated that it applies to organizational consumers. Organizations project social value as much as individuals do.

Experiential Value

The experiential aspect of products is a relatively modern phenomenon. Prior to the 20th century, products had economic, social, and a veneer of safety value. Experiential value of products was mostly unknown. The vast majority of people gave little thought to needing their products to provide them with exciting experiences. Products for the most part were utilitarian tools.

That began to change in the 20th century. People began to select products for the experiences it gave them. It occurred at the high end of society with automobiles, such as the Duesenberg and Cord. For the wealthy, it was not simply enough to take advantage of the ability to get from Point A to Point B much more quickly than before. Some of them also wanted the excitement and thrill of the ride between those points.

The desire for experiential products also occurred at all levels of society with the advent of the radio and phonograph. People sought products whose main value was to give an experience to people. With the exception of musical instruments where the experience is pretty much dependent on the user's ability, products that gave experiences as their main function were a new phenomena.

Even the high end products that indicated social value began to differentiate themselves on the basis of experience. A Mercedes and BMW are comparable in terms of their economic and social benefit. They both transport people and convey a sense of social superiority. However, the experiential aspect of the two cars is different.

The experience that the Mercedes driver looks for is a feeling of solid luxury and security. The BMW driver on the other hand wishes to experience the thrill and performance of a responsive and well handling automobile. The two drivers want experiences from their high-end automobiles. However, they want different experiences.

The experiences are not instead of the other values. They are in addition. The drivers also want social value and safety value. This adds a dimension of complexity because now the product needs to not only be safe and convey a sense of social value. It also needs the added dimension of an experience.

This sense of experience is not limited to personal items that we may acquire and use. This sense of experience also applies to products that, on first blush, looked to be utilitarian commodities. Earlier I mentioned the Boeing 787 and that people's first thought upon entering a commercial aircraft is when they could disembark from it.

Boeing, however, is very cognizant of the need for positive experiences, as well as safe, economic transportation. The experience on a Boeing 787 promises to be much more pleasant than current aircraft. This is because both the air pressure and humidity will be significantly increased, making it more comfortable for its passengers.

A major factor for Boeing in developing the 787 was clearly economics.

Boeing needed to create a plane that was more fuel-efficient and thus more economical than the other planes in the market. They could have done this without considering passenger experience. The result might have been a lightweight, stripped-down airplane that packed passengers in like sardines.

Instead, they added a dimension of value, the experience, that they incorporated as a design criteria in order to create an airplane that was not only safe and economical, but that would provide the passenger with a better flight experience. This obviously required more innovation, such as the use of composite materials, than a product without the experience criteria would require. Boeing's calculation was that airlines would recognize and want this experience dimension for their passengers.

Adding this experience dimension often means that the product that leaves the factory door is not the final product. The idea of a duality of products, one physical mirrored by one virtual, is important if product producers are to continue to provide the experiences that the product acquirers desire.

Apple's iPhone is a great example of this. The iPhone as simply a phone does not provide any more experience than any other phone. However, couple it with iTunes and the experience dimension changes dramatically. Now, I don't just have a standalone device whose information I would lose if it malfunctions. Instead, iTunes fully mirrors my iPhone, so if my iPhone were to fail, I can fully restore it to its operational state by reconnecting it to iTunes.

In addition to Apple staying connected to my iPhone by being able to upgrade the phone's operating system to add enhancements and fix bugs, it has enabled an entire bazaar of new applications that I can select and download for entirely new experiences. Apple has a "Genius" function to look at the music that I have and make recommendations for new music that might appeal to me for purchase.

The iPhone that came out of the box is very different than the iPhone that changes with me as I look for new experiences. There are clearly two products at play here, a physical iPhone and the virtual iPhone. Apple stays connected with its virtual iPhone long after it has shipped from its factory. This is a virtual product mirroring a physical product at its best.

Even product producers making major ticket item products are catching on. The automotive companies are incorporating technology in order to stay connected with their products and provide their users with better experiences.

General Motors' OnStar manages to combine experience and safety value. In the event of a crash, it knows that the automobiles air bags have deployed and OnStar will send emergency help. Ford Motor Company, with their Microsoft Sync product, will monitor road conditions, send alerts to their drivers and update travel directions to help the driver avoid traffic delays.

The ability to add this experience dimension for product producers requires that they know what product the user has ("as-built" and "as-maintained") and how that product has changed throughout its life ("reflectivity"). This is information that Product Lifecycle Management needs to organize and maintain in order for product producers to truly exploit this experience dimension of perceived value.

Belief-Driven

We also acquire products for belief-driven reasons. The value of these kinds of products drive us to acquire them simply because we believe that they have value. While tautological in nature, this is no less a reason for product consumers to expend resources on these kind of products than any other reason. While religious artifacts are probably the purest example of this category, there are other products that fall into this category. To a greater or lesser extent, the new category of "green" products is belief driven. The issue with product producers chasing this category of products is that, not unlike the Emperor's new clothes, if something happens to undermine the belief, the value of the product dissipates.

The other main issue with belief-driven products is that product producers often do not understand or simply pay lip service to the things that are necessary in remaining consistent with the underlying belief. In the "Emperor's New Clothes," the two swindlers went through the motions of pretending to create the wonderful new clothes. Sometimes product producers do not even do that.

One area where a number of product producers are going through the motions is in the green product area. Many organizations are engaged in a Design for the Environment (DfE) initiative that goes to great lengths in order to design products that are recyclable and environmentally friendly. However, a good number of these organizations have not really embraced PLM. As a result, the information that will be necessary to recycle these products will not be available when the product finishes its service in years or decades from now.

These companies are touting their environmental credentials and appealing to the belief system of the product acquirers. However, without the necessary information, these products will wind up in the same landfill as the not-so-friendly environmental products. These products producers can only tap into this environmental belief system as long as their customers fail to understand what is really happening.

Product producers whose product value derives from beliefs need to ensure that they remain consistent with those beliefs. Products whose only value is in this category are risky propositions. Beliefs change over time and product acquirers often figure out that the effort that product producers make on these products really does not add value.

PRODUCT PRODUCERS

The category of value that product producers focus on is primarily economic value. Product producers first and foremost need their products to produce profits. Without profits, product producers cannot survive long-term. Organizations often times have secondary reasons that they promote as a reason for producing their products, such as the benefit for humanity or the good of the environment, but in the end, if their products do not produce profits, then they will not survive.

The ability of the product to produce a profit depends on the revenue that the product generates to be more than the cost of producing the product. The IT Value Map, as shown in Figure 4.2, illustrates the value creation of products over the product life. The costs of the product are the costs that the producer incurs in the various stages of the product's life: create, build, sustain, and dispose. Revenue is generated almost exclusively during the build and sustain phases of the product life.

Revenue in the build phase is simply a function of the number of units sold times the price per unit. While pricing can greatly depend on external economic conditions and organizational goals, looking at products in isolation, pricing can be thought to be dependent on two things: the functionality of the product and the quality of the product.

All things being equal, which is the economist's weasel wording that nothing ever is equal, the more functionality a product has the better price that it can command. This assumes that the functionality translates into a value for the product acquirer. This product functionality must produce something of economic, social, safety, experiential, and/or belief driven value to the product acquirer. If it does not, then it is extraneous functionality.

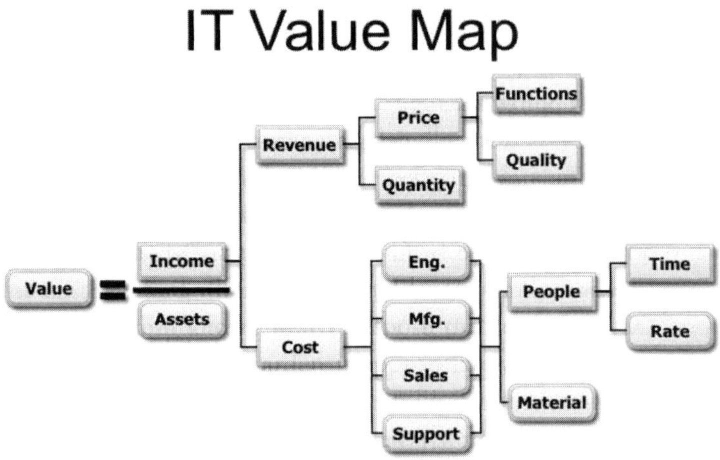

Figure 4.2

The common mistake that product producers make is to confuse product features with product functionality. Product developers become so enamored with their ability to produce technological marvels that they lose sight of whether these features will produce valued functionality for the product acquirers. "Feature creep" is an insidious phenomenon, because it adds to the cost of a product without creating corresponding value.

With respect to price, the higher the quality of the product the higher the price it can command. Unlike functionality, quality is a bracketed characteristic. What this means is that below a certain level of quality, the price can go to zero without a product acquirer being interested. If I build a car that only operates one out of every 50 times, I could not price that car low enough to attract buyers, except those that want to buy the car for scrap.

Likewise, if I create too much quality, there is a price above which product acquirers will not value the product. If my hypothetical car above is of such a quality that I am prepared to offer a warranty of 100 years, I will find that the vast majority of product acquirers will not be prepared to pay the premium that I need to create such a quality automobile. Above a certain normal and customary level of quality, product acquirers will pay little if any premium.

For product producers, the build phase has historically been the primary source of revenue. Once the product was sold and left the factory door, the product producers' source of revenue stopped. This is not entirely true in that some product producers did have a robust aftermarket for parts. However, many product producers were content in letting other organizations sustain their product and were satisfied to simply provide parts. In fact, some organizations felt that the headache of producing parts for products that were no longer in production was not worth the potential profit. This resulted in laws that required product producers to continue to make parts available for specific periods of time.

This perspective on products is changing under PLM. More and more organizations are viewing the opportunity to remain involved with the product after it has left the factory door is a substantial source of profits. These are organizations that recognize that people do not want products. People want the functionality that products deliver. If organizations can continue to help people obtain this functionality, then they can profit from it.

This does require that organizations stay connected to their products. Rolls-Royce stays connected to its airplane engines. General Motors stays connected to its automobiles. Apple stays connected to its iPhones. In all these cases, these organizations now have the opportunity to provide innovative services to their customers and, in turn, profit handsomely for doing so.

Product Profit Curves

Revenue and costs do not all come in the same time period for product producers. Instead, costs occur first as a product producer develops its products for market. Revenue only occurs later as the product is built and sold to the product acquirer. In the traditional product model, cost can continue to occur after the product has been sold and the revenue received. These costs are the costs of warranting the product to a certain level of performance for a certain period of time or a certain period of performance. Product producers are in essence guaranteeing the quality of their product, i.e., it will perform at a certain level of performance.

Present and New Product Curves

Figure 4.3, shows two product lifecycle profit curves. Curve one, the Present Product Curve (PPC), is the one described above. Profit is negative during the product development phase. It turns positive as the product begins to be manufactured and sold. It then may turn negative as the product producer incurs costs for warranting their product after the product has been sold and production discontinued.

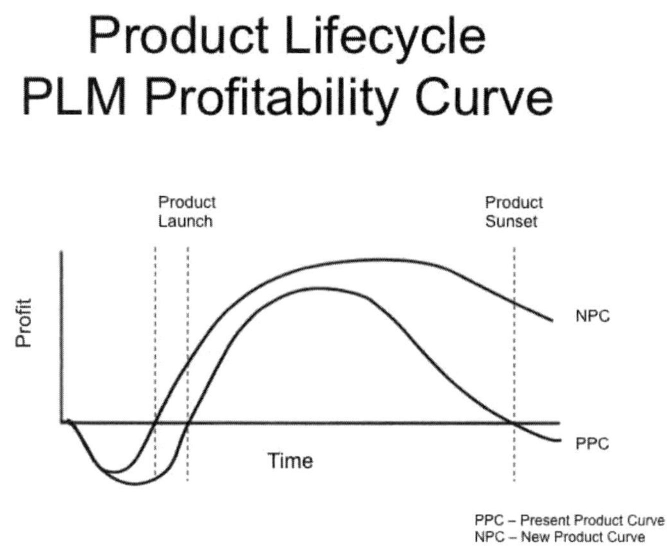

Figure 4.3

The second curve, the New Product Curve (NPC), reflects the impact of applying PLM concepts to the product lifecycle. At the beginning, profit is still negative. Because we are making more efficient use of information, we expect that the cost of development will be less and, even more importantly, the time frame for incurring those costs will be reduced. It is difficult to put a value on reducing time-to-market. There clearly is the obvious value of spending a set amount of resources for a lesser period of time. That is easily measurable.

What is not so easily measurable is that being first to market with a product may mean the difference between having a successful product or an unsuccessful one. Market leaders with the right product first are overwhelmingly more successful than late-to-market entries with me-too products.

With PLM, we would expect that we would expend fewer costs in the product development phase. We may need to condition the organization that, under PLM, costs may be incurred faster than the traditional product development method. This is because we can do more of the development concurrently than we can with the older methods. We also can engage in more analysis and virtual testing in the beginning of the development phase when we are creating virtual products rather than physical prototypes.

However, this is not a bad thing, except maybe to the accountants who are not familiar with this sort of early cost accruals. Finding and fixing design issues early in the development process is much, much less expensive than finding and fixing these same issues later. The "rules of 10" is an industry guess that addressing problems later in the development phase is a factor of 10 more expensive in costs.

Overall, by the time we reach product launch, we would expect, as Figure 4.3 shows, that the overall cost of product development under PLM is less costly than the traditional method. In addition, as illustrated here, product launch occurs earlier in time producing benefits that may make the difference between the success of the product and mediocre performance or even failure.

Moving into the next section of the profit curve, we also see the advantages of applying PLM concepts over the traditional methods. Under the traditional methods and even following the tenets of lean manufacturing, we would expect to incur higher costs compared to PLM as we continue down the experience curve. Even though we are applying kaizen on the factory floor, we are building products less efficiently than the final optimal method. Products made earlier in the build cycle are more costly than products produced later in the build cycle.

Under PLM, we would be seeking to explore this experience curve virtually. Long before we built a physical factory, we would have built a virtual factory and experimented with the most efficient way to build a virtual product. Because this would be done virtually, we could afford to not only investigate the usual methods to reduce costs, but we could experiment with less traditional methods that would allow us to create new and innovative processes. In addition, in factories where machinery is being built for our specific purposes, we could simulate this equipment in order to determine whether we have the desired functionality defined. Once that machinery is physically built, we are stuck with it. Changes to plant equipment, once it has been physically built, is an inordinately expensive proposition.

In addition, given that a great deal of the equipment on the factory floor now has intelligence, we can create and test the programs that this equipment will execute in operation. In simulation, we can work out the program bugs that in the past consumed physical time on the factory floor. With today's tools, let alone what will be available tomorrow, we can create and test a fully operational factory before the first shovelful of dirt is moved at the factory site.

As we continue on in the product lifecycle, the traditional profit curve begins to bend down and may even turn negative as production ceases and revenue stops coming in. Yet warranty costs continue to be incurred. The PLM curve does not show the same phenomenon. This is because, by staying connected to the product, the product producer can continue to receive revenue by producing additional services for the product acquirer.

In some cases, this is simply recapturing services that some third party might have previously performed. As I have already mentioned, in the past, product producers viewed sustaining the product as not something that they wanted to do. In fact, they often viewed it as a burden that was required by law for them to produce parts for a specific period of time.

However, product producers who have embraced PLM and the concept of making two products, a physical product and a virtual product, realize that even though the physical product has left their factory door, they still possess the virtual product. They can use that virtual product as a competitive advantage in seeking revenue during the period that the physical product is in use. Under PLM, product producers have the as-built information about the product. They can use that information as a base to create and track the as-maintained information about the product.

In addition, product producers have a population of products over which they can collect information about product failures. Even if third-party service organizations could do the same quality of repairs on failing products, product producers have the opportunity to develop prognostics. Product producers can offer services that collect data about the product while it is in use, analyze that data against data that predicts potential future failures, and schedule service before an actual failure occurs.

This is not science fiction. Companies such as Rolls-Royce are doing this today. It gives them a tremendous advantage over other service organizations, including airlines themselves that could not provide this capability. This is also a win-win situation for the product producer and the products acquirer. The product producer now has an additional source of revenue, and the product acquired has better product usage and less product crisis failures.

So while the traditional product profit line turns down and even negative, the PLM product profit line stays steady into the future. Organizations are under tremendous stress for profits in today's global economy. Using virtual products as a new source of reoccurring revenue is a potentially huge opportunity.

PPC vs. NPC Impact

It is difficult to quantify the cumulative impact of PLM on product development. Companies are understandably reluctant to share this information. It also is difficult to compare the costs of a new product being developed today with one that was developed previously. That said, talk to enough people, and one gets a feel for the magnitude of difference.

I currently would put that difference between 25% and 35% in cost savings through the manufacturing phase. I would also expect that this number would improve once new sources of revenue are created during the sustainment phase. The most common issue is not that companies do not think that they will receive benefit from adopting PLM. The most common issue is that the projections of improvement are so large that managers are reluctant to propose them to senior leadership because senior leadership would find them unbelievable.

Value versus Price versus Cost

The issue for the product purchaser is to balance the value of the product against its price. I may think a Gulfstream jet has great economic benefit in reducing my travel time, would nicely convey my social status, and flying in it is a great experience. However, if I can't afford it, the benefits are irrelevant. We all have to balance our product wants against our economic resources. We all do it, but how we do it is idiosyncratic.

For the product producer, the task is to set the price of their product such that the product purchaser will make the determination that its value is worth the price. Three common methods that product producers employ are cost plus, cost of alternatives, and product proxy.

Cost plus is the easiest. Product producers add up the cost of producing their product, tack on their desired profit, and use that as their price. This method works if the product purchaser will view that value of the product as equal to or greater than this price. For products that have significant value to the product purchaser over and above economic value, this method may be acceptable. Mercedes used this method for a long time. Mercedes engineers would build the car that they wanted, add up the costs, set the price, and purchasers paid it because they valued the safety, social and experiential characteristics.

The problem with this method is that if function creep occurs or the product is over-designed, the cost of the product may increase beyond its perceived value. Even Mercedes found this out as people began to balk at the prices Mercedes was charging. Mercedes then had to design for specific price points.

Product producers sometimes approach the cost plus from both sides of the cost. Some product producers will charge substantially more than their cost and see how many people will buy at that price. They then continue to lower the price to a point that will get them the most purchasers. Other product producers will price below their cost in order to induce people to buy. They then hope that once the product takes hold that they will be able to raise their prices. What they are attempting to do is buy market share. Buying market share is one of the most expensive purchases a product producer can make.

For products that can be compared to alternative methods of doing the job the product purchaser wants done, pricing a product against this alternate method is an option. This method works for more utilitarian products where the primary value of the product is economic. An earthmover can do the work of men with shovels and so can be priced to compete with the cost of paying laborers to perform the same amount of work.

The third method is to price the product in the same range as a similar product. The price of this similar product acts as a proxy for the value that the product purchaser has shown a willingness to pay. Even highly innovative products often must be priced in this fashion. Innovative cellular phones that had capabilities beyond current models could not be priced much beyond those current models.

Getting the value to price to cost relationship is more art than science, although product producers do perform a great deal of analysis using methods similar to the ones described above. Perceived value of product purchasers is in the end analysis just that — perceived. Product producers can use virtual products to some extent to acquaint potential product purchasers with the physical product in order to help set the price of that product.

Given the accelerated pace of product creation, introduction, sales maturity, and fall-off, product producers need to make innovative products that create new and unique value for their potential customers. They also need to make them as lean as possible to give them the maximum flexibility in setting price. Product producers cannot survive long term if their products do not produce a profit. They stand no chance of doing that unless they produce true value for the acquirers and users of those products.

Virtual products can clearly benefit product producers in the create, build, sustain, and dispose phases of a product's life. The remaining chapters will contain numerous examples of this.

This chapter explores the idea of the value of products. No one really wants a product. They want what a product can do for them. The challenge with products is to balance the value it creates for their product acquirer with the value it produces for the product producer.

Value is always perceived value in that we socially construct the idea of value. Value is subjective and not an objective concept. This is something that product producers often overlook.

Product purchasers can be divided into two groups personal consumers and organizational consumers. The values that product purchasers used to evaluate products are economic, safety, social, experiential, and belief driven. Personal consumers deal with all of these values. Organizational consumers may be more focused on economic values, but these other values also play a role. Product producers need to concern themselves with all of these dimensions of value, and not simply focus on economic value.

Product producers are primarily concerned with economic value. If they do not have that, then they will not survive. Product producers need to concern themselves with product profit curves. PLM shrinks the cost curve and extends the profitability curve. As importantly, it shrinks time-to-market, which often determines the success or failure of a product. Product producers can provide more value to their product by producing two products, a physical product and a virtual product.

Both product producers and acquirers have to concern themselves with the monetary aspect of the product. Product acquirers have to determine what price they will pay for the value they perceive. Product producers must set that price to induce buying that covers their cost and provides them with the profit necessary to survive and thrive.

Notes

15 For example, see Christensen, C. M. (1997). *The innovator's dilemma: when new technologies cause great firms to fail.* Boston, Mass.: Harvard Business School Press.

16 Perceived quality does not fully reflect objective quality for as much as six years, although high-reputation brands enjoy a quicker reflection of good quality and a slightly slower reflection of poorer quality. See Mitra, D., & Golder, P. N. (2006). How Does Objective Quality Affect Perceived Quality? Short-Term Effects, Long-Term Effects, and Asymmetries. *Marketing Science, 25*(3), 230-291.

17 Economic historians will no doubt find fault with my use of the term in this way. The term is said to have originated with Thomas Carlyle in the 1800's in reaction to either Malthus' dire predictions on population growth and starvation or in Carlyle's defense of slavery over the concepts of supply and demand of labor — there is support for both explanations. (Galbraith, J. K. (1977). *The age of uncertainty.* Boston: Houghton Mifflin.) I would contend that, even though most people do not know of that origin, the name resonates well because the ability of economists to agree on economic drivers, let alone accurately predict economic outcomes, is pretty 'dismal'.

18 How less safe? The Insurance Institute for Highway Safety (IIHS) reported that the death rate for minis in a crash is twice as high as that of larger cars. See Kazman, S. (2009, April 17). Small Cars Are Dangerous Cars. *Wall Street Journal.*

19 Government regulation may simply be the government's perception of "protecting the public" and may have little factual basis. Data suggests that children might be just as safe wearing seatbelts as being ensconced in car seats. See Levitt, S. D., & Dubner, S. J. (2009). *Superfreakonomics: global cooling, patriotic prostitutes, and why suicide bombers should buy life insurance* (1st ed.). [New York]: William Morrow.

20 The recent regulations on lead in children's toys are a case in point. Retailers are removing bicycles from their shelves because bikes have lead that exceeds the statutory requirements. Children would have to lick their bikes for an extended period of time to suffer any adverse effects.

21 See Lieberman, M., & Eisenberger, N. (2008). The pains and pleasure of social life: a social cognitive neuroscience approach. *Neuroleadership Journal, 1*(1), 38-43.

22 For an explanation of social capital, its formation, use, and power, see: Lin, N. (2002). *Social capital: a theory of social structure and action.* Cambridge ; New York: Cambridge University Press.

5

VIRTUALLY INSEPARABLE

We take for granted that we know what the term "virtual" is, but do we really? We use the word "virtual" in a number of different ways that have inconsistent and sometimes contradictory meanings. As discussed earlier, the term "virtually perfect" has undergone the transformation from an idiom to a descriptive condition. "Virtual" seems to denote some unreal or imaginary quality, such as the virtual world of Second Life. However, in other usage, "virtual" implies a concreteness that might not otherwise exist. A "virtual dictator" is generally a real dictator in everything but the name.

The origin of "virtual" confuses more than it enlightens. "Virtual" evolves from the Latin "virtus," meaning "strength" or "virtue." While the ability to create virtual representations of products has proven virtuous, it is difficult to imagine the Romans predicting our current usage of the word when they coined it.

However the word 'virtual' has evolved from strength or virtue, we now have enough experience with how we have come to use it. However, it is not just a passive term. We have also come to "virtualize" things. We should also define how it is that we do that.

What is a "virtual product"?[23]

Here is the definition that I would propose for a *virtual product*:

A virtual product is a use-specific informational or bit-based representation and its associated rule-based environment of a physical or atom-based product and its natural behavior.

This definition gets to the idea that a virtual product is a representation of a physical product. By a physical product, we mean something that is atom-based. In order to be tangible in the physical world, a product needs to be made up of atoms. A virtual product by contrast is bit-based. We would like to obtain the same information from the virtual product that we would get from possessing, inspecting, and testing the physical product itself.

Additionally, it is not enough to simply have the information about the physical product. We need a bit-based environment for that information that can perform operations on that information. At its simplest, the bit-based environment needs to display information to us using rules that reflect how the product would appear to us if we were in its physical presence. At its most complicated, any operation we can perform on the physical product, we can perform on its corresponding virtual product.

The operations that we can perform on the virtual products need to mimic the natural behavior of its corresponding physical products. Two lines that are parallel cannot intersect. Two solid products cannot occupy the same space. The rules that the virtual environment has must be consistent with the natural laws of the physical world.[24]

Currently, there are two bit-based environments that we have access to. One environment we have had for a very long time, and one environment is relatively recent. The environment that we have had for a very long time is the human brain. The relatively recent environment is the computer. While they both are bit-based, neuron-based for the brain and silicon-based for the computer, they differ with respect to different dimensions as discussed later.

There is no intrinsic need to have information about a physical product. There is always a use-specific need that we are trying to meet. If we are designing a component with multiple parts, then, from a geometric perspective, we need to make those parts all fit together. If we are interested in aerodynamic capabilities, then we need to understand the wind resistance of the product design. If we are interested in maintaining the product to a certain standard of performance when it is in use, then we need to have information about the status or condition of that product.

The issue for the foreseeable future of virtual products is that the cohesiveness that is naturally enforced in atom-based products may not be enforced depending on the specific use of the virtual product and its environment. For example, in a specific-use environment that is used for spatial representation, it may be possible to lengthen a virtual bracket that supports a virtual cylinder.

However, if the lengthening of the corresponding physical bracket were done, it would not support the weight of the physical cylinder. Only if the rules involving weight were built into the virtual environment could we rely on the virtual products behaving in the same fashion as its physical counterpart. This structural analysis might or might not be included in this use-specific environment.

It may be possible some day to create an atom-by-atom representation of a physical product that would allow us to use the informational representation for any purpose since we could duplicate in information anything that might be done to the actual physical product. However that day is a long, long way off.[25]

I would propose this definition of *virtualization*:

Creating an informational or bit-based representation of a physical or atom-based product.

There are two cases that I would like to look at. The first case is where the physical product already exists. The second case is where the physical product is yet to exist i.e.. where we are creating a new physical product.

The first case is obviously a simpler case. We have a physical product that already exists. We can see it, feel it, and touch it. We can take measurements of it. We can look inside, although if we do that by cutting cross-sections of the product, we risk destroying that product.

The task in this first case is to abstract the information that we need in order to create a virtual product that mirrors the physical product. Depending on our use case, we might abstract a little or a lot of the information from the physical product.

The early computer accounting systems were an example of abstracting only a little of the information from the physical product. For some of the early inventory systems that I programmed, the common information that I collected was a brief description of the product and its weight, height, width, and length. Along with the quantity of the number of products that existed, this was all the virtual product information that I needed for the use that I desired: namely controlling inventory.

Today, while inventory control systems do not require much more information about the virtual product than they did in the past, they do require and have available much more information that we need for other uses.

We are now able to abstract much more detailed information about the physical product. Using CAD systems, we can create detailed spatial and geometric information of each and every component that makes up our physical product. We can associate characteristics such as weight, color, and material composition with a geometric design. We can use this information to perform tasks such as assessing the structural or aerodynamic capability of the physical product.

For this first case, we have the actual physical product as a reference. The task is to have our virtual product mimic this physical product for the specific use cases that we have in mind. When in doubt as to the accuracy of this virtual representation, we can always refer to the actual physical product.

In the second case, where the purpose of the virtual product is to create a physical product, the issue is a little trickier. We do not have a physical product to serve as a reference for our virtual one. In fact, the purpose of this exercise is to create a virtual product that has all the characteristics and performance that we desire in a physical product. Only when we fully create that virtual product do we expend the physical resources that are required to manufacture a physical product.

This requires that the virtual environment in which we are creating a virtual product have the same characteristics and rules as the physical environment. Again, the robustness of this virtual environment will depend on the use case. Depending on the use case, there will be various levels of abstraction. The general rule of these virtual environments is that while they may not enforce all of the physical rules, they should be explicit in identifying the rules that they do enforce.

As computing and communication technology continue on their exponential path, we would expect to see these virtual environments become richer and more robust. For example, it used to be that CAD systems and Finite Element Analysis (FEA) systems were completely independent. We would have to create a mesh of points that abstracted the shape of the product. We would then manipulate the mesh until we got a desired shape with the desired structural characteristics. We would then have to go back to the CAD system and modify the design until it matched the geometry of the desired mesh. Today, CAD systems and the FEA systems are integrated. As we modify the mesh in the FEA system, the geometric design automatically changes.

Information Mirroring Model[26]

As introduced in my first book, the idea of physical and virtual products goes a little farther than one product being able to exist from the other. What I proposed by way of my Information Mirroring Model is that physical and virtual products exist together in a linked manner. This means that there is a duality of physical and virtual products. By keeping them linked throughout the life of the physical product, there is opportunity to save on physical resources such as time, energy, and material. This was and continues to be my conceptual premise for Product Lifecycle Management.

As shown in Figure 5.1, the Information Mirror Model consists of a real space with physical products and a virtual space with virtual products. There are three main components of the Information Mirroring Model. These components are: a) real space, b) virtual space, and c) the information and data linkages between these two spaces.

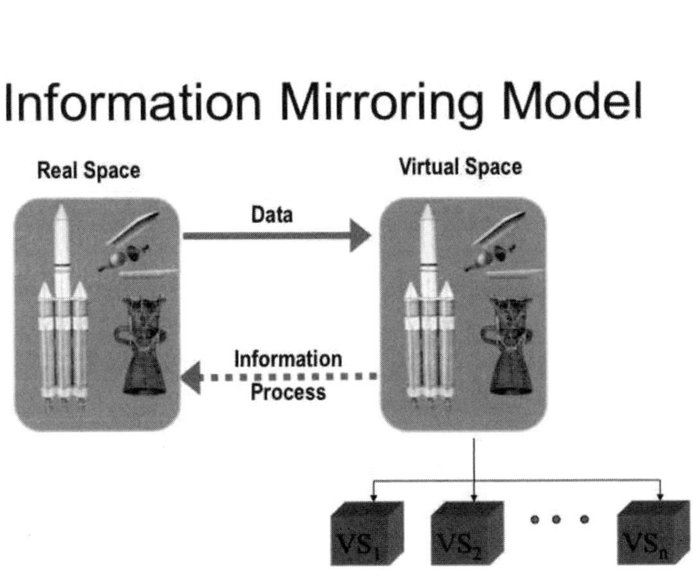

Figure 5.1

As I explained in my first book, we are extremely comfortable with working in real space. We humans have spent thousands and thousands of years in discovering and understanding the rules that govern the behavior of atoms in real space. That is not to say that there is not a great deal more to learn. However, for the materials that we deal with, we generally have a fairly good understanding of how they will behave. When we do not, we craft experiments and tests whose purpose is to enlarge our understanding.

Virtual space, however, is both old and new. It is old in that, as humans, we have possessed a bit-based virtual space for as long as mankind has had self-awareness — our brains. However, this capability, while amazing in itself, has substantial drawbacks.

The first drawback is that the fidelity and permanence of our human memory leaves a great deal to be desired. Our ability to create and maintain detailed information in our memories over a long period of time is not very good. Even for simple objects, asking us to accurately visualize its shape is a task that most of would be hard-pressed to do with any precision. Ask most of us to visualize, let alone spatially manipulate, complex shapes, and the results would be hopeless.

The second major drawback is that this virtual space cannot be shared. Only in science fiction can we telepathically look into someone else's mind and see what they see. The reality is that we have to use some atom-based media, such as pen and paper, in order to convey the representations that we see in our own minds. While language is truly a wonder, even speech requires the atoms of the air to convey what is inarguably a very sparse representation of what we would see in our minds.

The virtual space that is new is obviously the virtual space that we can create in computers. Unlike our human memory, this virtual space can have almost perfect fidelity and unlimited permanence.[27] In addition, it overcomes the problem of a lack of shared space. With a degree of control of computation capability that we do not possess over our own minds, we can manipulate virtual representations to whatever degree we choose to exercise.

While our personal hardware in the form of our minds can do amazing things, for the purposes for which we would like to use our virtual products, the computer virtual space is vastly superior. As the Information Mirroring Model represents, what we require of virtual space is that it mirrors the products of real space in sufficient detail to allow us to use information of the virtual product in place of the real product.

What we would also like to do is to have the virtual product capture and reflect the changes that the real product goes through in real space. Additionally, we would like to have the information about the real product that we are collecting and organizing in virtual space to be available to us back in real space.

That is the purpose of the linkages between real and virtual space. We want to collect the data on the current state and the changes of the real product in real space, transmit the data into our virtual space, and organize the data into useful information. Conversely, we want to be able to access the information that we have created in virtual space and be able to use that information in real space

There no longer is simply one physical product that exists in real space. There are now two products — the physical product and the virtual product. These physical and virtual products are linked. Data from the state of the physical product updates the virtual product. Information from the virtual product is available for our use in real space without having to have physical proximity and access to the real product.

Value of Virtual Products

There are two cases identified earlier that we need to examine. In our first case, where we already have a physical product, we collect data about that physical product and create our virtual product. In the second case, where the physical product has yet to exist, we create a virtual product and use the information that we learn as we experiment with the different permutations and combinations of shapes, forms, and behaviors in order to create a physical product in real space.

So what is the value of virtual products? As I discussed earlier, information is a replacement for wasted physical resources, i.e. time, energy, and material. From a physical resource perspective, using information takes substantially less physical resources. Virtual products are, in essence, information. We can use this information as a substitute for wasting scarce physical resources.

What we would like to do is use bits instead of atoms wherever possible. As we will see throughout this book, there are a myriad of opportunities to use bits instead of atoms. As an example, if the Navy would like to know whether a certain radar component is in all the ships in its fleet, it has two ways of doing that. Without having any virtual ships, the Navy can go to the substantial expense of tracking down each ship wherever it is in the world, traveling to that ship, and opening and inspecting the radar system on that ship.

Or, if the Navy has virtual ships, it can connect to the virtual environment independent of wherever in the world the individual who is inquiring is located and, with a click of a mouse, request information on each and every radar system in each and every ship no matter where these ships are in the world.

It is pretty easy to see which method is more efficient in terms of saving scarce physical resources.

In addition to using bits instead of atoms wherever possible, we also want to use bits for as long as possible before we have to use atoms. Anytime we have to manipulate atoms it is an expensive proposition in comparison to using corresponding bits.

This means that when we are designing a product we want to do as much as we possibly can with a virtual product before we have to make a physical product. What we would like to do is create a design, ensure that the design meets all the spatial requirements, test out that design in as many different ways as we can, and only when we get a design that does what we think it needs to do, do we actually build it using physical atoms.

Every physical prototype that we build is an expensive proposition, even for trivial products. To the extent that we can eliminate physical prototypes by creating, building, and testing virtual prototypes, there are substantial savings of real physical resources to be had.

This use of virtual products to reduce or eliminate wasted resources is clearly a definition of "lean." What we hope to accomplish with virtual products is to reduce or eliminate the waste of resources needed to produce their physical counterparts. Bits have proven cheaper to use than atoms. The use of virtual products is all about using bits.

That covers the lean aspect of product development, but what does that do for innovation. There is a twofold answer to this. The first is that by using virtual products to be lean we can free up resources that we can use for innovative activities. The second is that, because bits are cheaper than atoms, we can do more exploration, more experimenting, and more testing with virtual products than we could do with physical products.

This not only pertains to the creation of the product itself, but it also pertains to the process and methods of manufacturing and assembling the product. The virtual products that we create are not only the products themselves, but these virtual products can also be the means of making those products. We can and do create and use virtual tools, virtual robots, virtual assembly lines, and even virtual humans. Using these virtual capabilities, we can create and test innovative manufacturing and assembly operations that will in turn produce lean operations.

This means that we cannot only innovate with the products themselves, but we can innovate with the means of production. This is the value of virtual products.

Evaluating Virtual Products

If we are going to create virtual products, then we will need to evaluate how well these virtual products mirror their physical counterparts. In my previous book, I proposed a series of tests to evaluate how well virtual products mirrored their physical counterparts. I call these tests the Grieves' Tests of Virtuality.

The premise of the tests was fairly straightforward. In the test, a human observer is positioned in a room that has two windows. One window looks into a room where the physical product is present. The other window is a computer screen.

There are three tests that the observer can perform. These three tests are: a Sensory Visual Test, a Performance Test, and a Reflectivity Test.

In my first PLM book, the second two tests were the same. However, the first test was called the Visual Test. It was pointed out to me that we have other senses than simply our eyes. This indeed is true. However, as I have pointed out in my previous book, our visual sense is our highest bandwidth sense.

The other senses are important, and I do not want to give them short shrift. In fact, with respect to the sense of hearing, the throaty roar of a Chevrolet Corvette and the rumbling of a Harley-Davidson motorcycle are clearly distinctive. In fact, with respect to the Corvette, engineers actually tune the exhaust system in order to give it the right tone and pitch. So a Sensory Audio Test certainly is not only feasible but is actually being done.

In addition, the work in haptics technology continues to evolve. We have the ability to put on special gloves and actually feel virtual surfaces, with the gloves providing the necessary feedback to convince us that we have touched a solid object. We can grasp a virtual steering wheel. We can turn a virtual wrench and feel the resistance of the bolt.

I am not sure that we will ever have available and/or need a Sensory Smell Test. However, with respect to technology, I have learned never to say "never." In addition, one of the more attractive things about buying a new car is the "new car smell." Maybe at some time in the future, we will need the ability of a sense of virtual smell.

However, to be consistent with my previous book and because of the importance of the visual sense, I'm going to only focus on a sensory visual test. I will leave it up to the reader to fashion tests for the other senses. It will be along the lines of the sensory visual test. My acknowledgment of the other senses will be in changing the name from the Visual Test to the Sensory Visual Test.

For the Sensory Visual Test, the observer can ask that any spatial manipulation can be performed on both the physical and virtual product. These products can be rotated, lifted, and even disassembled. If the observer cannot tell which is the physical product and which is the virtual product, then the Sensory Visual Test is said to be passed.

For the Performance Test, the observer can ask to have any action performed on the physical and virtual product. He or she can ask to have power applied to it; to have stresses placed on it; to place it in a wind tunnel; or any other action that could be applied to the product. Again, if the observer cannot tell the difference between the behavior of the physical product and the behavior of the virtual product, then the virtual product is said to have passed the Performance Test.

The last test is the Reflectivity Test. This test requires a little imagination, because the observer is going to know that the physical product is out and about in the physical world. Again, we have the same observer. This observer looks into the same two rooms, one of which holds physical product and the other of which holds a virtual product.

The observer can ask to see the status of any aspect of the product. For example, he or she could ask for the odometer reading of an automobile or the fuel gauge reading in a helicopter. Or, he or she could ask to see the model and serial number of the fuel pump on an airplane. If this observer can get the same information from the virtual product as he or she could get from inspecting the physical product, the virtual product is said to pass the Reflectivity Test.

Virtuality Test Progress

So as we begin the second decade of the 21st century, how are we doing with our Tests of Virtuality?

Visual Tests

If we look at the Sensory Visual Test, the answer is that we have made a great deal of progress since the year 2000. While at the beginning of this decade, the visual representation of products was getting pretty good, it was fairly easy to tell the virtual product from the physical product. As the decade moved along, the visual representations kept getting better and better.

Today, in many situations, virtual products pass the Sensory Visual Test. Many companies now have life-size power walls[28] upon which they project their digital designs. By rotating them on the screen, these virtual products can be looked at from any angle, and, in the case of automobiles, doors and hoods can be opened and closed. The view from the interior of the car is as if we were sitting in it.

However, it goes farther than static projections. Some of the print and video ads that we see featuring the latest automobiles are produced virtually. This has probably caused a great deal of dissatisfaction on the part of some marketing executives. In the past, they got to travel to exotic locations with gorgeous models (referring to both the cars and the women). Today, the same photo shoots are done on digital computers.

Since the improvements will continue, for all practical purposes we can say that we are passing the Sensory Visual Test. No doubt we will continue to expand our requirements in this area. For example, we can expand the Sensory Visual Test to be the Sensory 3-D Visual Test.

The requirement for the 3-D version is to no longer confine the observer to looking through the windows of a physical and virtual room. In this test, we can require that the observer be allowed to walk around the product. In keeping with this being a visual test, we can confine the observer to simply visually inspecting the products, still allowing him or her to perform any spatial operations.

Alternatively, we could allow a more extensive version of the test and let the observer hear, touch, feel, and/or smell the product. We need to understand that adding each sense complicates the tests. This 3-D test will require a leap from flat-panel displays to holographic technology. While this may seem infeasible today, I, for one, am not ruling this out.

Performance Tests

The Performance Test is moving along more slowly. The requirements for this test are much more expansive. We not only have to sense the virtual product as if it were physical, but also this virtual product must behave exactly like the physical product. The requirement of this test is that we can have any operation performed on this product that we could have performed on the corresponding physical product.

This means that our virtual environment would need to have all the physical laws of the universe built into it — a daunting task. But what we can hope for in the near future is to build into our virtual environment selected laws of the universe.

This is where we are today. The issue is that we can abstract certain features of products today and subject them to specific kind of tests. These tests are generally referred to as "solvers," and there are different solvers for different kind of problems.

We have solvers for finite element analysis, stress testing, heat analysis, material deformation, aerodynamic airflow, and other tests. The issue is that we generally have to prepare the product for the test by abstracting the relevant information that we are interested in studying. This abstracted information is then used in the solver. This information is changed until the solver produces the results that we are looking for. The resulting information then needs to be incorporated back into the virtual product.

Because this information has been abstracted and subject to manipulation in the solver, integrating it back into the virtual product may require interpretation and trial and error. As I had mentioned earlier, in the example of finite element analysis, the trend is to integrate these solvers with a virtual object so as to eliminate abstraction and reinterpretation of the solver results back into the virtual product.

I would expect this trend to continue. Although unlike the Sensory Visual Test, there may not be a specific point in time where we can say that we have "passed" the Performance Test. It may be that we simply integrate more and more solvers with their virtual products.

One of the main issues of the Performance Tests is how do we evaluate performance? What we have done with physical products is to create instruments that measure the characteristics that we are interested in. We then correlate those instrument readings with performance characteristics so as to make decisions whether we are getting the required performance. Some of the instruments that we have created are temperature gauges, force meters, flow meters, and impact gauges.

While we do use our visual senses to evaluate performance, they are generally not broad or precise enough and need to be augmented to really assess performance. For example, we insert smoke into a wind tunnel test in order to "see" aerodynamic performance. We use high-speed photography in order to capture the results of a crash tests, because our natural vision is not fast enough to neither see the details of the crash as it occurs nor to accurately capture the sequence of events.

The virtual environment cannot only emulate the creation of our instruments, but it can translate those results so that our senses can be brought to bear in evaluating virtual product performance. So for example we can see the heat level of a virtual product by using a color-coded gradient to indicate the temperature of each part of that product. We can see the aerodynamic properties of the vehicle in motion by making visible the virtual particles of air.

As an example of what we can do today, I sat in front of a huge screen at NASA where a simulation of the yet to be built Ares I spacecraft was launching. As a realistic spacecraft climbed up from its pad at Kennedy Space Center, I could see the outline of the Florida coast recede into the distance, and I could look out and see the curvature of the Eastern Seaboard come into view. This was very realistic and quite impressive. Although maybe not quite good enough to convince me that this was a view of an actual event, it was pretty close.

However, this was not all that I could see. On separate screens, I could also see a wireframe of the same spacecraft. One of the important aspects of a rocket's behavior is the bending that occurs to its structure as it climbs out of the earth's gravity well. While that behavior could be represented as numbers from some instrument that I would then have to interpret, I could actually see this behavior visually on the computer screens.

The wireframes of the rocket were color-coded so that its deviation from the center could actually be seen. The wireframes changed from black to blue and back again as the stresses to the rocket were recorded. The fact that the wireframes never changed to the color red was an indication, without looking at instruments, that the rocket remained within acceptable limits. This was an example of actually seeing performance.

Reflectivity Tests

With respect to the Reflectivity Test, we are clearly in its infancy. The idea of a company maintaining a link with its product after it has left the factory door is very much a 21st century concept. The links in the past were only maintained by taking possession of the physical product on a periodic basis, such as bringing it into a repair hub or bringing it back to the factory for an overhaul.

Today, it is difficult to find a product that does not have a microprocessor integrated into it. There is more computing value in today's cars than there is steel value. But it is not just large ticket items such as automobiles and airplanes. Almost any product that you can think of has a microprocessor in it. This includes washers, dryers, refrigerators, thermostats, pacemakers, and even running shoes.

With these microprocessors and their ability to communicate, companies can continue to stay in touch with their product long after the product has left their factory door. This will allow for these products to communicate back the current state of their condition at all times.

While this concept is still in its infancy, this does not mean that there are not some worthy examples of companies staying connected with their products. Two companies that are notable in this regard are General Motors and Rolls-Royce.

General Motors captures a substantial amount of information about the status of its vehicles. It then transmits this information through its OnStar vehicle tracking system. Not only can General Motors tell the status of the oil in its customer's vehicle and the amount of gas in its fuel tank, but it knows where that vehicle is at all times and if the vehicle's air bags have deployed. This means in the case of an accident, General Motors knows instantly that a problem has occurred and can immediately direct emergency services to that customer and his or her vehicle.

Rolls-Royce has sensors in every one of its airplane engines. Information about the status of those sensors is collected and transmitted to Rolls-Royce's monitoring center in Derby, England. The status of the sensors is collected at predefined times in each cycle of the engine's performance, where a cycle is defined as a takeoff and landing.

This information is analyzed and compared against the thousands and thousands of other profiles Rolls-Royce has for the performance of its engines. Rolls-Royce can determine whether or not the profile for a cycle is normal or abnormal. If it is abnormal, Rolls-Royce can determine a course of action for the airline to follow. It can ask to have the engine looked at the next landing, or, as is more usual, Rolls-Royce will instruct the airline to have the engine looked at the next time the plane is back through the maintenance hub.

These are both good examples of companies whose products are starting to meet the Reflectivity Test. In the past, these companies would have had to physically possess their product in order to assess its condition and take remedial action. Now, they can look at the virtual product and make much of the same assessment.

General Motors and Rolls-Royce are on the vanguard of the movement to maintain a linkage with their product after it has left the factory door and while it is in service. Even these companies have a long way to go in order to pass the Reflectively Test. Other companies have not even begun to address this issue. However, the trend is clearly in this direction.

Virtual Product Representation Evolution

As the virtuality of products has rapidly accelerated, the methods of dealing with this product information are also changing. We are increasing the amount of product information we deal with, as well as increasing the amount of complexity in that product information. Figure 5.2 shows the current and proposed evolution of products and the information needed to represent them.

Product Models

If we were going to talk about models, it would be good if we had a common understanding of what we are talking about. The issue is that the term "model" can refer to as diverse things as a complicated mathematical formula and someone who sashays down a runway in Paris wearing the latest fashions. While we are probably not going to confuse our model with an ectomorphic individual wearing unusual clothes, there is much room for misunderstanding when we can refer to a "model" as such different things as a logic schematic of how a product behaves and a spatial model of the geometric design of the product itself.

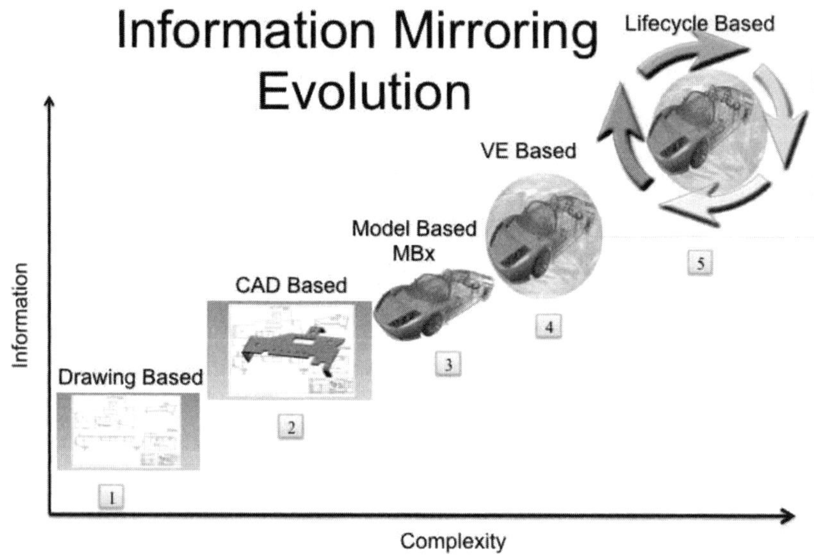

Figure 5.2

For its purposes, the Department of Defense defines a model as "physical, mathematical, or otherwise logical representation of a system, entity, phenomenon, or process." While narrowing down the definition of model, it still is fairly broad and leaves an opportunity for confusion among individuals who may be talking about different kinds of models. Even under this definition, one individual could be talking about the spatial model of the product itself and another could be talking about a systems engineering model that defines the behavior of the product in a schematic form.

While both may be correct in their references, there is a huge difference in what they are talking about. When talking about product models, I would like to propose that we are talking about two different kinds of models, spatial models and behavioral models. Spatial models are geometric representations of the physical product itself, i.e., what the product form is. Behavior models are logical or mathematical representations of the product's behavior, i.e., what the product does. These two kinds of models can exist separately, or they can be integrated in simulations that would use both the physical shape of the product and also show its behavior in the environment.

I will attempt to identify the use of product models as either spatial or behavioral whenever the context of model usage is not clear. However, I expect some confusion in the usage of the term "model" to persist as organizations employ it to describe their use of product information.

Phases of Evolution

I am proposing that there are five phases of the virtual product representation evolution. The five phases are: Drawing-based, CAD based, Model-based x (MBx), Model-based Environment (MBE), and PLM-based. As I describe below, the common perspective is that we are in the third phase, model-based design, engineering or systems (MBx). However, I will argue that we are at least partially involved in the fourth and fifth phases. I will describe each of the phases below.

Drawing-based phase

Drawing-based designs have been the standard from the point in time that man began to create and build products. As Figure 5.2 shows, there was very little virtuality involved in drawing-based design. The amount of information in drawing-based design was low, as was the complexity of that information. Drawing-based design, as the name implies, was based on drawings made on material, with the latest material being paper. As time progressed, the drawings became more and more precise, at least as it pertained to the annotations on the drawings.

The term "blueprint," which is synonymous with drawings, came into being in the mid-1800's. The term "blueprint" conveys more precision than simply the term "drawings." However, blueprints were merely a method developed by the British astronomer and photographer Sir John Herschel to reproduce drawings. The blueprint method of coating paper with chemicals so that the drawing could be reproduced has nothing to do with precision. However the term "blueprints" became synonymous with the plans necessary to create products with a high degree of precision.

Both the drawings and their ensuing blueprints are two-dimensional representations of products. This means that there needs to be different views of the product in two-dimensional form in order to specify the entire height, width, and depth of the product. The only virtuality that comes into play here is a virtual representation that these drawings invoke in humans that see these drawings and attempt to create three-dimensional objects from them in their minds' eye.

The core problem with drawing-based designs is that there is always room for interpretation between views. Even when the design contains angles only along the normal three-dimensional axis, there could always be interpretations between views, such as the top view to the front view, or the front view to the side view. When the angles were not oriented along three-dimensional axes, there could be major differences in interpretation.

To realize a product using drawing-based model techniques, the physical drawings were transformed into physical objects or prototypes. Designers and engineers attempted to assemble these individual prototype parts into the desired complete product in real space.

Prototypes were and are information in a physical form. They also are an expensive form of information because they involve moving atoms around instead of bits. By having to fit the physical prototype parts together, product developers obtained information about what worked and what did not work. The physical prototype in essence stored that information as product developers made whatever changes to the prototype parts that were necessary in order to get the product that they envisioned in their initial drawing-based design but was not being realized.

When the product developers got the product in the shape and form that they wanted, they took the various physical components apart, measured them to see what changes that they had made, and went back and updated their two-dimensional drawings.

The two-dimensional blueprints were the controlling source of design information. As such, they had very little virtuality. As a result, there generally were many iterations between the blueprints and the physical prototypes in order to get a physical product that reflected the real intentions of the designer.

The extensive use of atoms in physical drawings and prototypes meant that this phase was hardly lean. A blank sheet of drawing paper can lead to innovation, but the reality of having to iterate between drawings and physical prototypes made innovation an expensive proposition.

CAD-based phase

The second phase in the information mirroring evolution came about with the advent of computer systems that moved paper-based blueprints into the digital realm. This was called Computer Aided Design or CAD for short. While attempts at CAD computer programs began as early as the 1960s, true CAD systems did not come about until the mid-1980s. At that time a number of very specialized and very expensive dedicated hardware and software systems came on the market.

As the name implied, CAD was meant to assist in the creation of drawings and was not meant to be a replacement for them. The idea was to not have to rely on the drawing skills of specialized draftsmen to accurately represent a desired design. With CAD systems, even the most artistically challenged could produce precise and accurate drawings. As with drawing based blueprints, the drawing was the authoritative source. The difference was that a computer generated the drawings rather than the drawings being rendered by a draftsman with a pencil and T-square.

In addition, the drawings were still two-dimensional and not three-dimensional. Therefore, they required the same high-level skill of the user of those drawings to envision three-dimensional objects. This meant that while there was some increase in productivity because using the computer was faster and more reliable than relying on human draftsmen, it did nothing to reduce the number of prototypes that needed to be made along the way in order to help people translate two dimensions into three dimensions.

Moving to these CAD-based drawings also contributed to a loss of control of design drawings. Because the CAD-based drawings were digital, they could easily be copied and moved around. Copies of the same design proliferated and were easily modified leading to multiple and uncontrolled versions of the same design. While CAD-based drawings improved some efficiencies, they caused other inefficiencies.

The CAD-based phase was a transitional phase between drawings and models. As such, it probably had minimal impact, if any, on making organizations lean. The draftsman was simply traded for a CAD-operator. "Shoulder surfing," the designer leaning over the shoulder of the CAD operator, was the established but inefficient method of working on designs. The innovation of this phase was in the process of transitioning to a new way of handling designs.

Model-based (MBx) phase

The phase that the leading edge organizations claim to be transitioning to today is that of models. This is called a number of different things including Model-Based Design, Model-Based Engineering, or even Model-Based Systems. For purposes of covering all these, I will refer to this phase as "MBx."

The term "model-based" refers to the fact that this phase is involved with three-dimensional models as opposed to the two-dimensional drawings of the past. The move from 2-D to 3-D in terms of capability is not to be underestimated. The move from two-dimensional drawings to three-dimensional models was not simply an incremental improvement. It literally was a quantum improvement in a whole new dimension. It was not simply a matter of transforming two-dimensional drawings into three-dimensional objects, but it was also integrating these various objects into a complete model.

The information that a three-dimensional model conveys is incomparable to that of two dimensions. With two-dimensional drawings, the work of developing a cohesive three-dimensional view required a substantial special cognitive skill that few humans possessed. More commonly, as described above, three-dimensional physical prototypes had to be created at substantial expense in order for the information to be displayed and understood.

Model-based design changes this way of doing things. The three-dimensional components are collected into a three-dimensional model. If the proper fit and tolerances are not obtained, the components can be modified virtually until the desired results are obtained. This then becomes the new design, and there is no requirement to propagate these changes, with its inherent possibility of errors, back into any other drawing or design component.

With these three-dimensional integrated models, there is no need to use one's imagination as to how the components will fit together, nor is there a need to expensively move atoms around in order to create physical prototypes. Model-based design can dramatically reduce if not eliminate physical prototypes.

With the move to MBx, we made a tremendous leap from separate sheets of paper to a three dimensional, virtual representation of the product. In addition, unlike drawings, we could aggregate and build up the models from separate components. In essence, we changed from a flat model of disconnected views of a product to a cohesive, integrated model. From a visual perspective, we substantially reduced and even eliminated the need to build physical prototypes, because we now had our prototype virtually.

However, like all new major transitions in technology, there always are issues. For example, with two-dimensional drawings it is relatively easy to make notations. We just pick up a pencil and mark our notations on the drawings. In earlier versions of model-based systems, the focus was on accurately portraying three-dimensional models. The other information that drawings contained was often secondary in nature and either omitted or tacked on in an ad hoc fashion.

The other issue was that the ability to build up cohesive, integrated models came to tax the computing technology on which they were created. Some of the products that are created such as planes, ships, automobiles, and rockets have thousands to hundreds of thousands to over a million parts. Refreshing a model that contains these many parts required so much computing capability that these products often had to be chunked up into assemblies and subassemblies. Otherwise, it might require a week or more of computing time to refresh a model.

While most people working in the PLM area consider that we are in the MBx phase, the reality is that we are rapidly progressing through that phase and are into the next two phases. Unlike their counterparts in two-dimensional drawings, models simply do not exist in an empty vacuum. Instead, there is a wealth of information that is or should be attached to these models.

The MBx phase began to get us both lean and innovation. Reducing the need to build physical prototypes reduced physical resources, including the all-important time-to-market. We could also afford to be more innovative, since the cost of trying new designs could be done virtually with cheap bits.

Model-based Environment (MBE) Phase

In this phase, the geometric models do not simply exist floating in empty space. These models must integrate with the world in which they operate. It is not simply enough that a model is geometrically complete and consistent. It must also meet performance requirements that are the purposes of the product.

If an airplane was fully created as a integrated model and looked sleek and terrific, but was aerodynamically unsound, it would be of little use other than as a neat picture to hang on the wall or even as a great plastic model to put on a shelf. It is not enough to have a perfect looking geometric model. That model must also implement the performance requirements that make it useful.

What this phase indicates is that we need the capability of performing Computer-Aided Testing (CAT) and Computer-Aided Engineering (CAE) on that model in order to determine if the model could meet its requirements goals. These are things such as being structural sound, being aerodynamic, and having certain sound level characteristics.

For example when the Joint Strike Fighter, the F-35, was designed, one of the main design issues was whether or not it could perform as a short takeoff and landing (STOL) vehicle. The potential problem was whether or not the hot exhaust from the rear engine would leak over into the front lift fan. If it did, the hot exhaust would dramatically reduce the efficiency of the front lift fan, rendering it unstable or unusable.

This model was simulated with the simulation making visible the various exhaust gases and color-coding them according to their temperature. The simulation showed that the hot engine gases would not affect the front lift fan. This could be visually seen from the simulation. The simulation definitively showed that the model would meet its performance requirements. More importantly, when the airplane was built, its actual performance mirrored almost perfectly the simulation.

One of the most important elements to engineer in the development of a new airplane is the wing. The flow analysis of air over the surface of the wings and fuselage is a key element in understanding the capabilities of the new airframe. The Boeing 787 is the first design where the entire airframe could be analyzed in one piece. Prior to this plane, Boeing could do component analysis but could not analyze the entire airframe at once.

This phase also starts to extend us into the product lifecycle. In the previous phases, the activities were pretty much based in the create phase. Manufacturing did come into play, but only as a passive user of the designs. It is still not uncommon for organizations in the MBx phase to produce two-dimensional drawings that are then thrown over the wall into manufacturing.

However, in the MBE phase where we are reacting with the environment, we now start to integrate the build or manufacturing phase. The model is not simply a geometric design floating in its own universe. The model is now reacting with the environment. While CAE and CAT is part of the model's environment, the manufacturing processes and the factory in which those processes occur are also part of the model's environment.

Having a product model does no good if we cannot produce it efficiently. So we need to also be able to simulate the Bill of Process, which defines the resources that we need, the operations that we need to perform on and with those resources, and the sequence in which we need to perform those operations. To do this, we need a model, i.e. the virtual product, and we need a virtual environment, which is the virtual factory and all the elements in that factory: machines, labor, and material.

This is not the full product lifecycle that we concern ourselves within this next phase, but by specifying environment along with the model, we expand from a model-only perspective. Again, even though the common wisdom is that we are in the MBx phase, there are a number of organizations, especially those at the leading edge of PLM, who are into this MBE phase.

Organizations in this phase or striving to be in this phase also use the acronym MBE to refer to Model-based Enterprise. While a bit confusing, it is consistent. Organizations that standardize on spatial 3D models for use across their organization will use these models in behavioral simulations. In the create phase, they will perform analysis and testing. They will simulate the manufacturability of the products in the build phase. They will simulate both the support and maintenance activities to produce a product that is more efficiently sustained.

In this MBE phase, we are extending both lean and innovation. While in the MBx phase, we reduce or eliminate prototypes that we need for form and fit, we still need to build expensive prototypes for testing. Virtually engineering (CAE) and testing (CAT) products means that we can reduce, and, in some case, dramatically reduce these costs. We can also be more innovative since we can now afford to not only perform the "usual suspects" test, but we can now try a wide variety of testing and analysis. We can start to extend the use of our product models into the rest of the lifecycle.

PLM Phase

The last phase, where we have made progress in some aspects, is the Product Lifecycle Management (PLM) phase. In this phase, we are not only interested in the virtual model and the virtual model in the environment, but we are also interested in capturing the information about the product throughout the product lifecycle.

This means that we not only have the model and the model's simulated performance, but we are also tracking the information about the physical products that have been derived from this model throughout its life. One of things that we are very interested in obtaining is how well the performance of the actual product matches the predictions of how the product would perform as it was developed and manufactured.

For example, for heavy truck manufacturers we would like to track how long the product went between repairs, what kind of mileage performance that the engines actually got, or how well the axles stood up to the weight of the cargo.

The other aspect of this PLM phase that is different from previous phases is that we are now concerned with instances of the product. In the previous phases, the virtual product was representative of all the products that could be created. In this phase, we are now creating individual instances of that virtual product and our intent is to track those instances throughout their life.

It may be, that as we further refine our ability to capture the information about the product as it is being used and mirror that information, we may separate this phase into further phases. However at this time, since we are early on in understanding and using product information from the service and disposal stage, we will not separate the model out further.

This chapter explored the issue of just what "virtual" means. In an era where we truly have the ability for a virtual environment, the meaning of "virtually perfect" has morphed from an indication of inferiority to a description of what actually can be. The chapter attempted to remove the ambiguity surrounding the term "virtual," defined that term, and went on to define "virtualize." The chapter went on to clarify how virtual products have come to be an integral part of our modern environment.

The chapter also described the Information Mirroring Model (IMM) as a framework for conceptualizing PLM and explored the implications of the duality of physical and virtual products. The ability to use virtual products in place of their physical counterparts drives the value of the IMM.

In order to understand our progress in the use of this virtual environment, we revisited the Virtuality Tests. Specifically, we discussed the Sensory Visual Test, Performance Test, and Reflectivity Test. We assessed how well we are doing against those tests and provided some examples of how they are actually being used today.

Finally, the chapter provided the evolution framework of virtual products. The phases described were Drawing-based, CAD-based, Model-based design, engineering, or systems (MBx), Model-based Environment (MBE), and PLM-based. While the common wisdom is that we are moving into the model-based phase, a closer examination shows that some organizations have moved past models and are engaging with the MBE and PLM phases.

Notes

23 In keeping with the fact that this is a book on Product Lifecycle Management, I will use the term "product" or "part," rather than the more generic term, "object." In the way that I am using "product," I can mean an individual part, such as a piston, an assembly, such as the fuel pump, or even entire entity, such as s an automobile or an airplane. I will try to use "part" if I am talking about an item in the context of a more encompassing product. However, I will probably not always be consistent. One person's "product" is often the "part" of some other person's product. Hopefully, the context will make it clear as to what I am referencing.

24 We could relax the requirement that the virtual environment must be consistent with the natural laws of the physical world. This would account for the virtual objects of imaginary, virtual worlds, like World of Warcraft, Second Life, etc. Magic swords and flying carpets are interesting for imaginative games, but, since these objects cannot really exist in our physical world, this would not be relevant to people who were tasked with creating real products.

25 It is estimated that a BMW automobile has 10^{28} atoms in its makeup. We do not even have a word for that number of bytes. The highest number, a yottabyte, is only 10^{24} (approximately) and we would need more than one byte to represent the information of each atom.

26 This concept was originally introduced under a slightly different name in an earlier paper. See Grieves, M. (2005). Product Lifecycle Management: the new paradigm for enterprises. *Int. J. Product Development, 2*(Nos. 1/2), 71-84. John Vickers of NASA has a simpler and more evocative name: Digital Twin.

27 This is in theory. A very real problem yet to be adequately addressed is how can information about a product that may have a life of fifty to a hundred years or more be successfully maintained for that period? Equally important, how can that information be interpreted, presented, and manipulated long after the programs that initially did that are gone? These are yet to be answered questions.

28 Power wall is the name given to a bank of viewing devices that is built into the wall of the room or a small auditorium. A bank of computers drives the viewing devices, generally plasma or LCD screens. This bank of computers divvies up and displays in an integrated fashion a digital object, such as an automobile or airplane. These digital representations have evolved to be full size so that they are indistinguishable from looking at an image of a physical object itself. Such is their value that these power walls were still being installed by General Motors in the summer of 2008, even though the company was in dire financial straits.

6

VIRTUALLY REAL

Up until now, we have been segregating the physical from the virtual. We have talked about physical parts in the physical world and virtual parts in the virtual world. That was not only a useful way to look at things. It reflected what we could do from a technological standpoint.

However, we can now start to mix the physical with the virtual. This allows us to be more extensive in trading bits for atoms and reducing the waste of resources, time, energy, and material. As a result, we need to develop a better taxonomy of just what can operate in both real and virtual environments.

While previously we have discussed "products" and "parts" as the inhabitants of both real and virtual space, I would propose that there are three inhabitants that we need to look at. The first inhabitants are what we will call Passive Inhabitants. When we think of our products of the past, we are probably thinking of passive inhabitants. We have talked about these products as having behaviors, but not really about having robotic or intelligent behavior.

A second group of inhabitants do have quasi-intelligent behavior of a sort in that they can make decisions based on sensing eternal stimuli and take actions based on those decisions. This second group of inhabitants can be referred to as robots. This group is often discussed as having "machine intelligence," although I would argue that is an oxymoron.[29] Robots have computing capability that allow them to sense, decide, and respond to environmental stimuli.

The term "robot" often evokes a machine in human form, an android. Androids figure prominently in movies, such as the Terminator series or "I, Robot." Androids are a form of robots. However, these form of robots are currently the least prevalent and certainly the least capable in real life. While they may be potent and versatile in movies, the current android is pretty primitive. The current androids can barely do what the average two year old can: walk and grasp objects.

The second most common understanding of a robot is that of the industrial robot usually found on assembly lines. These robots, while only vaguely humanoid, have torsos and arms that move, grasp, and perform vaguely human-like activities. They lift, weld, paint, and turn screws and nuts — work that was previously performed in a similar fashion by humans.

However, this class of robots is far, far more extensive than androids or industrial robots. By my definition of robots and the definition of many others, the span of robotic equipment is very broad. By the more general definition of robots, a robot senses stimuli, decides according to rules, and responds with some action. This sense, decide, and respond covers product forms that vary widely. This covers something as mundane as the cruise control in automobiles, which sense the speed of the car and take actions to speed up or slow down, to the automatic pilots of a modern airplane, which can take-off, fly across country, and land safely. It clearly also covers factory robots, which can sense positions of parts and take actions such as welding, assembly, and painting

The third group of inhabitants is not made up of products at all, but consists of humans. While heretofore, we have given humans only the role of observers in our real and virtual spaces, the reality is that they can also be participants. Humans do not simply stand outside a window and observe our parts. They're also in the room with them and interacting with them. In fact, the success of a product depends on how well our product interacts with humans and performs a job that humans have "hired" it to do.

Figure 6.1 is a template for a series of three matrices that lays out the interaction of real and virtual space against our three potential inhabitants of those spaces. We will now look at each of the quadrants in each of the matrices and explore what these interactions mean. Some of these quadrants already have established names, and we will use those names in our discussion.

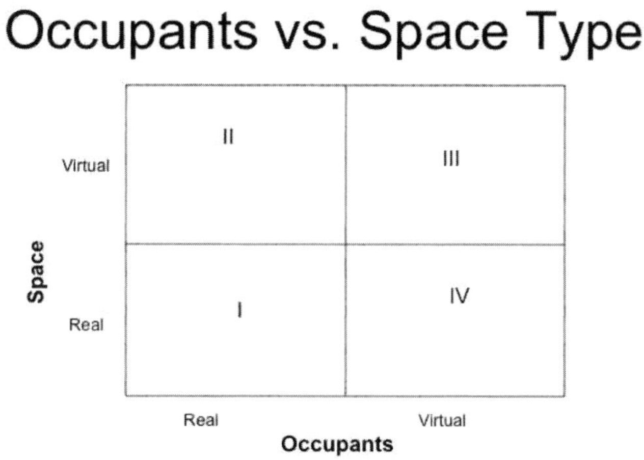

Figure 6.1

PASSIVE PRODUCT INHABITANTS

In the second matrix, Figure 6.2, our real and virtual space inhabitants are passive products. The category of passive products in real space, Quadrant I, is what we are most familiar with them. This is the natural condition of products. As discussed above, until very recently, humans only dealt with real objects in real space.

At first glance, the category of real objects in a virtual environment, Quadrant II, seems to have no real interest. Put a passive product in virtual space and nothing happens. Passive products only respond to physical forces. Since there are no physical forces in virtual space, there can be no reaction of passive products in virtual space. Environmental simulation has no meaning for passive products.

However, if we are going to mirror physical products in virtual space, then those physical products need to, at a minimum, identify themselves. In the past, this identification took the form of bar codes. The issue with bar codes is that the bar codes must be readily visible for line-of-sight scanning to take place. For a product that contains many parts, the bulk of them that may be hidden from view, bar codes can only provide information about a small subset of the parts and components of a product. In addition, the capture of that information requires a device that that can "see" that bar code.

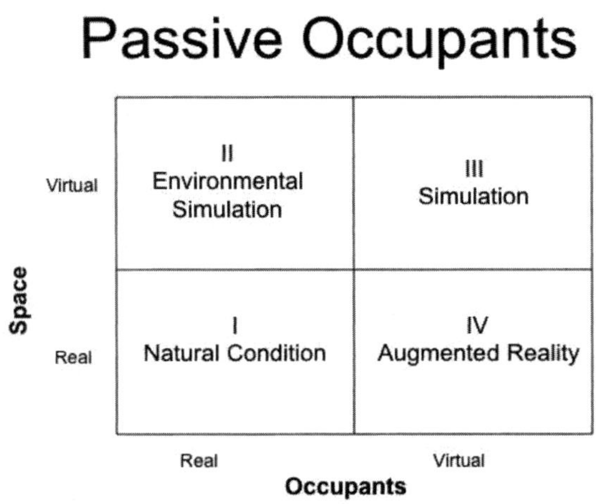

Figure 6.2

A much better solution is RFID (Radio Frequency Identification) tags. These are tiny electronic chips that contain a small amount of information. Each chip or tag has a unique address so that anything that has one of these tags can be distinctively identified. The readers simply must be in geographical proximity with the tagged item in order to identify that the item exists and to read any information embedded in the RFID tag.

Simply to inform virtual space that the item exists is useful. An early use was identifying all the components and parts at a nuclear construction site. Not surprisingly, these sprawling sites invariably have parts and equipment that are misplaced. This causes delays and even the repurchasing of items that exist but cannot be found. Once a day, an individual drove around the construction site in a golf cart with an RFID reader. This updated the virtual space, which showed the location of each item and piece of equipment. Anyone wanting to know the location of anything could simply interrogate the virtual space, saving wasted resources looking for the object on acres and acres of the physical site.

The issue with equipping every object with an RFID tag is the cost of the tags and the cost of installing them. As with all computing technology, both costs are rapidly coming down. It is highly likely that these RFID tags could be embedded in every item within a few short years. This means that every distinct part or component would have the capability of being identified in virtual space. We would no longer expend the wasted resources of disassembling anything in order to know what was inside of it.

The category of virtual objects in virtual space, Quadrant III, is one we have discussed extensively in a previous chapter. While we have had the ability to virtualize objects in our own minds for as long as the human race has had self-awareness, we really had no ability to have independent virtual spaces until the last half of the 20th century with the invention of the digital computer.

Quadrant IV is our next area of investigation. As it happens, the category of virtual objects in real space is an interesting one. It is called Augmented Reality (AR).[30]

In Augmented Reality, we project virtual objects into the real world to produce real benefits. For example, we can project the inner structures of an object onto the external structure of that object, in essence giving us the ability to "see inside." If we want to see where the pipes and wiring are in a building today, what usually happens is that we get out the blueprints for that building, look at those blueprints, and then look at the wall mentally matching up the blueprints with the wall and trying to ascertain where those pipes and wiring might actually be inside that wall.

That assumes that we even have plans or blueprints. With commercial properties that I have dealt with, that assumption was iffy. Even if blueprints existed, it took time and resources to track them down. For residential properties, the assumption is ridiculous. I recently rearranged a room in my house. The cable TV outlet is on the opposite wall from where it needs to be. I would like to know where the cable comes into the room so that I could reroute it from that point. I have no clue where that is.

With Augmented Reality, we could look at the wall and, by merging the virtual room with our physical wall, we could "see" where those wires and pipes actually were. What this requires is some enabling technologies. We need some projection device to overlay the virtual object on the real space. We also need some sort of positioning system in real space so that the projection system can accurately integrate its virtual object with real space.

While both of these technologies are in their infancy, just this sort of integration has been done and has been shown to be feasible. There are examples, too numerous to be mentioned, where this would be extremely useful. Certainly, the building example of trying to match blueprints with a blank wall occurs millions of times each day. However, we could also apply the same circumstances to an airplane mechanic looking at a jet fuselage and tracing its internal wiring. We also do not need to limit ourselves to simply projecting a structure. We could also project other information, such as a step-by-step description of how to disassemble this jet engine.

Medicine could be made safer and more effective by using this capability. A surgeon operating on a patient could use the information from a CAT scan to more accurately identify the area that he or she was operating on. While laparoscopic surgery employs cameras, AR projections could allow a surgeon to know exactly where he or she was in relation to where they should be.

Augment Reality is also not limited to static projections. We can project arrows on a car windshield that would show us exactly which turns to make in order to get to a destination. Street addresses could be projected on any car window to help us find our way. Heads-up Displays (HUDs), which are a simplistic form of AR, have been around since the 1950's when the technology was incorporated into fighter planes. It is now on one of my Corvettes. What differs is that rather than presenting instrument information, we can now present any type of information.

This technology is in use today on mobile phones. There are apps that take the camera view of a street and overlay information onto the picture. If I am looking for a restaurant, I only have to hold up my phone, and it will overlay the street view with the restaurant names, the type of food, and how highly it is rated.

Augment Reality relies on the delivery of information from virtual space to real space as indicated by the arrow in the Information Mirroring Model. It also requires an accurate positioning of the physical object in real space and that positioning information captured in virtual space. Augmented Reality requires much more sophisticated technology than a simple inquiry through a computer terminal would require.

Wearable displays are certainly possible. While today's technologies dictate independent devices that allow people to both look at real space and a view of the corresponding virtual space, it is highly likely that this technology could in the not-to-distant future take the form of wraparound glasses that allow the viewer to see both the real world and its virtual projections.

ROBOTIC INHABITANTS

In Figure 6.3, the next category of participant who can populate the real and virtual environments is the robotic-controlled product. This participant is a very interesting one for a number of reasons.

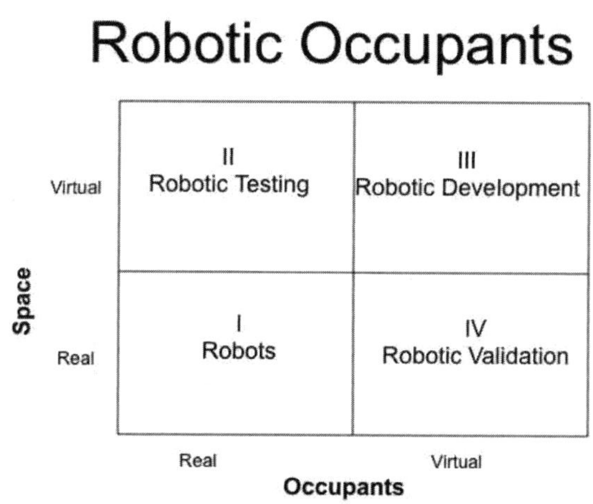

Figure 6.3

First, robots are a fairly recent phenomenon. Prior to the development of the microprocessor, products had little or no intelligence. Intelligence of products up to that point in time incorporated what has been described as "frozen knowledge."[31] This refers to the fact that the behavior of these products was prescribed by the gears, levers, valves, and all the other mechanical elements that were built into the system at the product creation.

Absent costly mechanical conversions, the capabilities of the machine throughout its life were defined when it was manufactured. These capabilities or the knowledge of what this product could do were "frozen in" when the machine was created.

The arrival of electrical components dramatically enhanced the flexibility of machines, but the capabilities were still defined at product creation. The circuitry of these electronics was implemented in discrete componentry. While circuit boards could be replaced, we were still talking about making changes in a physical fashion. We had to be in physical possession of the product in order to make changes.

There was an ability to sense, decide, and respond, but it was extremely limited and highly inflexible. Such capability had to be incorporated into physical circuitry. Physical circuitry had no flexibility. Once the circuit was wired that was what it did. Computing, such as it was, was highly limited to what could be wired up.

The arrival of the microprocessor radically changed the nature of products. In fact, today it is difficult to find products that do not incorporate microprocessors. While large ticket items, such as airplanes and automobiles, have a multitude of microprocessors working in them, products such as microwaves, washers, dryers, refrigerators, medical devices, and even running shoes contain microprocessors in them monitoring and/or governing the behaviors of those products.

In addition to microprocessors, products were also given sensors to allow them to sense the environment in which they were operating. This combination of sensing and computing allows products to sense, decide, and respond to their environment. Rather than the "frozen" knowledge of pre-computing products, we now have the era of "liquid" knowledge, whereby these products can fluidly sense, decide, respond, and even adapt to their environment.

This was a great benefit when the only space that these products had available to operate in was real space. However, these products are also naturally suited to operating in virtual space. Why? Because these products have no way of knowing whether their sensors are getting their data from real space or are being artificially fed their data from virtual space.

So how do these products behave in real and virtual space? If we look at Quadrant I, this is a quadrant where the robotic product operates in real space. This is the normal habitat in which these products grew up in, so, as indicated, it is their normal existence. Up until recently, these robotic products were created, tested, and validated in real space.

The normal sequence for development of robotic products was to program it, take it into an actual environment, and see how its performance differed from what it was suppose to do. It was then taken back to the development environment and the cycle was repeated until the robotic product performed as required. This was a time consuming process and required expensive testing using real resources. If the task was welding, it required actual welds on real parts that had to be scrapped when the robot did not perform correctly.

If we move up to Quadrant II, this is a quadrant in which the physical robotic product operates in a virtual environment. What this means is that we have the physical product, but what it is sensing and responding to is a virtual environment in which we control the data this product receives. What we can use this situation for is to test the product in a highly controlled environment.

As an example of this, NASA would like to test the avionics of a new spacecraft. As a major understatement, it is extremely expensive to test the actual avionics in real space, ("space" in both senses of the word!) because it means trundling a rocket out to the pad and shooting it off into space. The Ares I-X test launch in the fall of 2009 ran about $500 million. So how does NASA use the virtual environment to test the actual avionics?

What NASA does is to mount the actual avionics in a ground facility, whereby the avionics are fastened and hooked up much in the manner that they would be if they were installed in actual spacecraft. However, instead of getting their input from external sensors on the spacecraft, these avionics systems get them from a virtual environment. This virtual environment is a library of actual sensor readings from many spaceflights. The technicians testing these avionics systems can feed these actual sensor readings from actual space flights into the avionics systems and see how they respond.

In addition, the technicians can create their own data sets of sensor readings to explore the outer boundaries of the avionics systems' performance.

In doing so, NASA can test the avionics systems on not only what has occurred in the past, but what can occur. In fact, NASA can even test what "cannot" occur. It is the things that cannot occur but do that are usually the source of catastrophic problems.

While doing this kind of testing is possible using real products in real space, it is not feasible. In this particular case of NASA, but also in the case of most product manufacturers, the cost of this kind of testing in both monetary terms and elapsed time terms is prohibitive. What generally happens is that even in a Design of Tests only the usual suspects get tested. However, it is the unusual suspects that cause the major problems, especially in complex systems.

Over in Quadrant III, we have a robotically controlled virtual product operating in a virtual environment. The situation is highly useful for product development. This is the case where there is really no physical manifestation of the product itself. The components of the product, including its robotic control, are being simulated in a virtual environment.

It is here where we create a robot with the behaviors we desire. The programs that we write and test will someday be embodied in tailored silicon, but today they exist as simulated instructions in a virtual environment. This means we have the opportunity to write and test our code without going to the cost of affecting anything that is atom-based.

It's not simply the computer code we can create and simulate, but we can also simulate the hardware associated with it. For example, if we are working with an industrial robot, we can not only test the computer code that would drive its robotic arm, but we can simulate the entire robot to ascertain it is doing the job as we envision it.

With the appropriate factory simulation, we can see in a visual fashion exactly how a welding robot can make the appropriate welds on an automobile frame. We can check to see if the robot clashes with other robots or if there is anything interfering with the robot making the correct welds. But by utilizing the simulation, we can even do more than that.

We can not only try to implement the sequence of welds that we need to make, but either through an optimization program or even good old-fashioned human trial and error, we can attempt to optimize and minimize the number of robots necessary to make the required welds. Trial and error is awfully expensive to do on the factory floor, but it is very inexpensive to do in a virtual environment. One automotive company reduced the number of robots required from over a hundred to the low teens, with payback on their investment in the simulation technology measured in weeks!

Finally, down in Quadrant IV, we have the virtual product working in a real environment. While a machine doing virtual work doesn't produce real products, we can look at this quadrant in a different fashion. We can perform validation that our robotically controlled products are doing what they are supposed to do by feeding them data from the physical or real environment.

By capturing past data on real activities, we can use this data to feed into our virtual machine in order to validate its behavior. The more extensive our data on what has actually occurred in a real environment, the more robust our validation. While we have certainly had extensive real data in the past, the time and cost to validate new designs with all this data using physical equipment would, in most circumstances, be cost and time prohibitive.

We can also place the robotic controlled product in a real environment. We can let it sense, make decisions, and execute commands based on those decisions. However, we can disable its control of physical equipment and simulate the control of virtual equipment. This allows us to see what its response would be to stimuli without having it have an impact in real space.

Examples of this would be placing a robot on an assembly line and having it sense and make decisions on recognizing parts and orienting a virtual arm to pick up those parts. We could test a new autopilot on an airplane by having it sense, make decisions, and display the necessary required responses. A human pilot could execute those responses if he or she agreed with them and not execute those responses if they felt that those commands were inappropriate. Capturing those inappropriate decisions and responses enables a learning loop for the system developers to improve their robotic product. As technology progresses, these systems may "learn" on their own until their decision and responses match those of an experienced human.

Again, we not only trade-off bits for atoms in order to reduce resource usage, but we also enable a level of testing and validation of products that was effectively impossible to do in the past. While the lines between the real and virtual blur with respect to robotic products, it is clear that there is tremendous value in mixing real and virtual products in real and virtual environments.

Autonomous Robots

As I have mentioned before, no computer has yet to pass the Turing test of intelligence and is unlikely to do so in the foreseeable future. However, that does not preclude computers from making complex and robust decisions based on stimuli that they receive as inputs. It does require that we program these computers with ever more complex software to take advantage of the increasing speed and capability of these computers.

Computers for a long period of time have made and executed decisions on physical products. Cruise control, airplane autopilots, and the last minute in a Space Shuttle launch are increasingly complex examples. However, up until now, a human has overseen these decisions.

The obvious next step is to allow these computers to have autonomy. While this is a major step, this would multiply the impact of humans by freeing them up from routine tasks and lowering costs because over time computers are less expensive than humans. The military is especially interested in this because in addition to lowering costs, computers are much more reliable in performing routine tasks. They do not get bored, distracted, or uninterested.

The issue is how do we perform verification and validation (V&V) on the software that will drive these autonomous products. Understanding how these products will behave in all situations is an imperative. This is especially the case if these products have weapon systems that they control!

Virtual products will be required for this effort. The proposal would be that V&V would be a multi-stage effort. After development, the software would be required to undergo exhaustive testing in Quadrant III (Virtual Product in Virtual Space) that would run through all possible combinations and permutations of stimuli. The product, in physical form, would then be tested in Quadrant II (Real Product in Virtual Space), using a library of actual stimuli selected for its diversity and comprehensiveness. Finally, the product would be tested in Quadrant IV (Real Product in Real Space), with its ability to execute subject to human override or in a controlled physical space, so that any unexpected action would be either not allowed or harmless.

The other requirement for these autonomous robots would be to instrument them from the beginning so that they collected stimuli information that could be used to improve the suite of testing routines. Again, it is not the usual suspects that cause the most problems. It is the unusual suspects. A robust sensoring and collection of stimuli and reaction from the outset of the creation of this category of products is critical.

HUMAN INHABITANTS

The last inhabitants of our real and virtual environments that we will examine are the human inhabitants (Figure 6.4). While strictly speaking, there is no such thing as a "virtual" human. There are virtual human figures that can occupy our virtual environment. There is the also the ability, as we will see later, for humans to act in real space as if they are virtual.

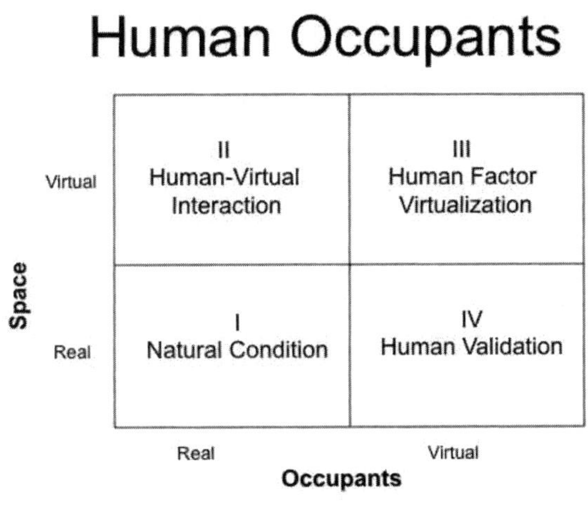

Figure 6.4

If we look at Quadrant I, again, this has been the normal situation for as long as there have been humans. Indeed, separating human intelligence from our connection to real space is effectively impossible. Even if the physicists are correct and that there really are nine dimensions plus time, our entire existential existence - the way we think, the way we talk, the way we act - is based on our ontological understanding of a real space that consists of three dimensions plus time.

Up in Quadrant II, we have human intelligence in a virtual environment. This can be extremely useful, because we can create parts and products that only have a virtual existence, yet test human interaction with them. With the right kind of equipment, humans can interact with virtual products and can and will respond as if they have a tangible existence. Again, because vision is such a major input as a human sense, simply presenting a visual representation of a virtual product can enable humans to interact with it as if that product was real.

One of the important elements of aircraft design is making sure that the support team provisioning and repairing the airplane can do so in a safe and effective fashion. For the new Joint Strike Fighter (JSF), the testing and training of this was done using real humans in a virtual environment. In this particular case, the virtual environment was a Cave that can support four humans. These humans were equipped with goggles that projected a realistic 3-D image of the airplane. The humans then performed normal tasks such as opening access doors, checking gauges, replenishing munitions, and doing other chores that ground maintenance crews would normally do on an airplane.

While it was highly amusing to an outside observer to watch people in a dark, empty room ducking around nonexistent protrusions, opening nonexistent doors, and cooperating in tandem to attach nonexistent munitions to nonexistent wings, the participants, even though they were fully aware of the airplanes nonexistence, rapidly became accustomed to acting as if the environment was real. This wasn't just a game, because they learned valuable things about the proposed airplane.

They also, through going about these tasks, were able to provide feedback to the airplane designers about the ease or difficulty of performing these tasks. Clearly, once the airplane had been built, it would be way too late to make any changes that could improve the operations. However, at this stage, before any atoms had been moved, it was a lot less expensive and a lot less time-consuming to improve the efficiency of the airplane as it pertained to its ground operations. Without this capability, too often sustainability and efficiency in the support stage of the product is often overlooked or even ignored. By using human participants in virtual space, we can, at minimal cost, examine the support phase and improve it before the design is cast in concrete.

Over in Quadrant III, we have a virtual human in a virtual environment. While I stated earlier, there are no such things as virtual humans, simulating virtual human form is an important aspect of products and their creation. Humans manufacture products and humans use products. So having the capability of simulating their activities in the manufacturing of the product and the usage of the product is extremely advantageous.

In manufacturing the product, humans are the most versatile "machines" on the factory floor. However, they can be very fragile, and requiring them to perform tasks that stress the human body is inefficient and costly, both in monetary terms and in human suffering. Therefore, being able to simulate human activity in a virtual factory in order to ascertain the ergonomics of the manufacturing and assembly tasks is extremely important. In addition, using our virtual human forms, we can test these tasks not only for the "average man," but also for a wide variety of both male and female human forms. This allows us to design factories that are safe, efficient, and productive.

From a products use perspective, we can also use these virtual humans in our virtual products to ascertain that they are designed correctly. In automobile design, virtual humans are used to ensure that the controls and equipment of the interior of a car can be safely and efficiently used by a wide range of human body types. In addition, we can use the same human forms to determine fields of vision to understand what humans can and cannot see from their seat in the automobile.

Again, finding out after the automobile is manufactured that there is a field of vision problem or blind spots is extremely expensive to remediate. By trading bits for atoms, we can inexpensively address this problem at the very front of the design cycle. This is only one of many examples of simulating human form in product design that is both efficient and effective.

For products that need to be maintained where safety is an issue, virtual humans serve an important role. Nuclear reactors periodically require divers to go into water to replace instrumentation rods. Simulating this activity allows the work to be planned so that it minimizes the potential exposure to radiation of the divers.

In Quadrant IV, we have a virtual human in real space. We can instrument human forms and gather information about the impact of forces on those human forms in situations where we would not subject humans to these experiments. One use of this is "crash dummies."

One of the funniest video clips I have seen was an early crash test of a General Motor's vehicle. In that test, a car was driven toward a wall. At the last moment, the driver opened the door, bailed out of the car, and rolled away. Clearly, the driver had no interest in seeing how the vehicle crash would have impacted its occupants!

Crash testing has come a long way. While the testing will be done virtually, there will for the foreseeable future have to be a physical validation of the tests. Using real humans is obviously out of the question. Using virtual humans is the only solution.

Virtual humans are also starting to be used in medical training. Again, if we can simulate human medical behavior, it is clearly better for medical students to make mistakes on a virtual human rather than on a real human. We can run the simulation until the medical student gets the treatment right. We are trading off bits for atoms, but in this case the trade-off is literally priceless, preserving human life.

These three matrices only scratch the surface of dealing with the opportunities of real and virtual combinations. The examples presented above are impressive, but we are only at the early infancy of what we can do. The idea of using the virtual environment that dramatically improves efficiency and effectiveness of our products is only in its early stage. Every day we are getting a better grasp of what is virtual and how we virtualize things that only previously existed as atoms.

VIRTUAL PRODUCTS, REAL PRODUCTS, AND HUMAN INTERACTION

Up until now, the assumption has been that humans interact with physical products in real space. Humans use virtual products in virtual space to minimize the amount of resources they need for those interactions. They simulate product behavior of virtual products so that they can test their designs before they build physical ones, reducing or eliminating the need to create physical prototypes. They simulate manufacturing processes to eliminate wasted resources. They interrogate virtual products so that they do not have track down and disassemble physical products to know what components are in them.

The Information Mirroring Model is illustrative of that paradigm. However, we are rapidly seeing a new kind of human interaction with both the physical product and the virtual product. Rather than simply using the information about products to interact directly with the products, humans are operating and controlling physical products through their virtual products.

As shown in Figure 6.5, this expanded model, the Virtual Control Model, has humans interacting with the virtual product. The virtual product interacts with the physical product, receiving information about its state and its environment on a constant basis and responding in turn by sending instructions and commands that it receives from a human operator to be executed by the physical product.

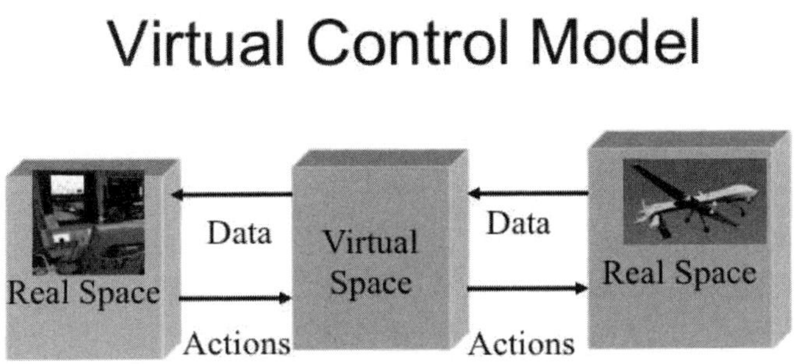

Figure 6.5

In the Information Mirroring Model, communications between physical and virtual products was loosely coupled. With some exceptions, updates linking the physical and virtual model could be done periodically. But those exceptions, such as an immediate alert if the airbags deployed on an automobile, were rare events.

In the Virtual Control Model, communications are two-way, constant and real-time. Humans interact with the physical product as if they were actually with it. The physical product performs as if a human was physically present and operating it. However, the virtual product sits in the middle.

This new model has been made possible by the rapid advancement of computing and communications technology. The model requires immediate, high volume data transmission between physical product, virtual product, and humans. It requires highly sophisticated sensing equipment. It requires computing control and feedback of equipment that was previously mechanically controlled locally.

The term used to describe this capability is telepresence. Telepresence is defined as a human operating equipment over a distance as if he or she were physically present.[32] In these situations, humans use the sensors and communications of distant equipment to give them the cues and information that they need to operate the equipment as if they were physically present in that equipment. For the equipment, it is as if there was a human present in that equipment.

An example of this is Unmanned Aerial Vehicles (UAV), often referred to as drones.[33] In the past, aircraft could only be operated if there was a physical pilot present in the cockpit. Today, the airplane drone operators, who legitimately should be called pilots, sit in front of an instrument panel with video screens in a room far away from the actual aircraft. However, they operate that aircraft as if they were actually sitting in the cockpit. Like the pilot that is physically present in his aircraft, these drone operators can take off, fly thousands of miles, identify and attack a target, and return their aircraft safely to the ground, all from the comfort of an easy chair.

A primary driver of this capability has been for situations where it is dangerous for humans to be physically present, such as flying low speed aircraft in war zones, or where humans simply cannot go, e.g., Mars. The issue in the past was that technologically we could not provide enough communications capability to deliver the required sensory stimuli, especially video, that humans needed to make decisions, nor transmit control commands fast enough. That is changing.

I expect to see this trend continue. For example, the Coast Guard is working on a vehicle, Vertical Unmanned Aerial Vehicle (VUAV), which will provide homeland security, search and rescue, and marine interdiction functions. Remotely operated battle tanks would seem to be a natural. Tank operators today do not have a direct connection with their environment. They see and operate through cameras.

While unthinkable today, tomorrow's commercial airplanes may be flown by pilots on the ground. If the pilots have all the visual cues and stimuli that they would have sitting in the cockpit, why could they not fly remotely? I personally would feel much more comfortable with Captain Sully at the controls, but the next generation of airline passengers might be just as comfortable with remote pilots.

As our ability to create sensors and successfully transmit these sensors across large distances to humans and, in return, transmit the human responses to the sensory stimuli presented to them, the Virtual Control Model will continue to improve. Even today, doctors are operating on patients far removed from their physical presence. Again, this is a way of trading off bits for atoms to perform activities effectively and efficiently that were impossible to do in the past.

As we will see over and over again throughout this book, it is the "virtual" that allows products to extend their reach to be "perfect." Trading bits for atoms is not simply about reducing resources needed to create, build, support, and dispose of products, although that clearly is a benefit. Trading bits for atoms also allows more possibilities and opportunities to be explored in creating and building products that are more robust with better functionality.

The chapter explored combining and integrating virtual and real worlds. It explored the use of virtual and real environments by three categories of virtual and real inhabitants: passive products, robotic products, and humans. The three matrices created here highlighted the roles of mixed mode reality, augmented reality (AR) and human virtualization.

The chapter proposed extending beyond the loosely coupled Information Mirroring Model to a more tightly coupled Virtual Control Model. The Virtual Control Model uses the virtual product to interface a physical product and a human operator.

This capability called telepresence is rapidly coming into existence. UAV's are the first wave, but we would expect to see many more creative uses. In all these instances, the theme of trading inexpensive bits for expensive atoms showed up again and again. Having both the real and the virtual product provides the promise of both efficiency and effectiveness.

Notes

29 True machine intelligence would require the machine to pass the Turing Test. This is something that has yet to be done. While it is common to talk about a product with computing capability as "intelligent," I will try to avoid doing so wherever possible. For Turing's original description of his test of computer intelligence, see Turing, A. (1950). Computing Machinery and Intelligence. *Mind, LIX*(236), 433-460. For a view that there will be no need for computers to pass this test because humans and computers will merge, see Kurzweil, R. (2005). *The singularity is near: when humans transcend biology*. New York: Viking. If so, I trust any man-computer reading my book in the future will find my work quaint.

30 For a more extensive description, see Feiner, S. K. (2002). Augmented Reality: A New Way of Seeing. *Scientific American, 286*(4), 8.

31 The term "frozen knowledge" was used by the Nobel Economist, Kenneth Boulding, in Boulding, K. E. (1996). The economics of knowledge and the knowledge of economics. In D. M. Lamberton (Ed.), *The economics of communication and information* (pp. 411-423). Cheltenham, UK; Brookfield, Vt., US: E. Elgar Pub.

I extended the metaphor to intelligent products by referring to them as being "liquid" in Grieves, M., & Tanniru, M. (2008). PLM, Process, Practice, and Provenance: Knowledge Provenance in Support of Business Practices in Product Lifecycle Management. *Int. J. Product Lifecycle Management, 3*(1), 37-53.

32 The confusion here is that the term "telepresence" has been used to describe the new visual communication technology used for interactive meetings provided by Cisco, HP, and others. Technically this is "visual telepresence." Telepresence, without a modifier, refers to the sense that a human is fully present at a geographically remote location.

33 The terminology is unfortunate in that these vehicles are not "unmanned." They are manned. However, the "man" is just not physically present in the vehicle. He or she is clearly manning the vehicle. UAVs and robot vehicles are often talked about as if they are in the same category, but they are very different. I would argue that only robotic vehicles are unmanned and that UAV's are really TAV's (Telepresence Aerial Vehicles), but the confusion in terminology has already been ingrained.

7

VIRTUALLY IN MOTION

The major value of virtual products will come through the ability to simulate the major phases of their physical counterparts' life. In the create phase, the role of simulation is to forecast the behavior of the product in its operating environment. This is the product's function. In the build phase, the role of simulation is to produce the steps that will result in the manufacturing of a physical product. This is the product's form. In the support and sustain phase, the role of simulation is to plan and train on the actions needed to disassemble and successfully reassemble the product.

If the goal is to substitute wasted physical resources with information, then being able to simulate the form and function of virtual products in order to determine if they can be manufactured and will perform as expected has been and will continue to be a major source of conserving physical resources.

While being able to create and manipulate three-dimensional objects is useful in order to ensure that different components will have geometric fit with each other, the most important aspect of products is not their form but their function. While creating and using virtual geometrical models has delivered huge benefit in terms of creating components that did not interfere with each other and fit perfectly together the first time, the major benefit from virtual products promises to be from simulating their behavior in their intended environment and the processes necessary to bring these products into physical existence.

Simulation is not something new. Humans use simulation each and every day in order to visualize the potential outcomes of actions. In our everyday activities, we engage in simulation almost constantly. When we are driving, we mentally simulate the motion of an oncoming car in order to decide whether we have enough time to turn in front of it or not. When we are playing golf, we simulate the flight of our golf ball based on our position of the ball in our stance, the direction toward which we are pointed, and our understanding of our golf swing. Unfortunately, for many of us, our understanding of our golf swing differs from our actual golf swing.

In creating products, we have used this mental simulation in order to produce products that gave us a desired behavior. The first caveman that developed a spear would have simulated in his own mind that taking this pointed stick and hurling it at a certain animal would produce the results that he desired, namely dinner.

As people developed more complex products, the success of those products depended on their ability to simulate how those products were going to perform. The issue with human simulation is that we are relatively limited in the amount of detail that we can manage successfully. While we may be able to get the gross behaviors directionally correct, we lack the ability to do simulations in sufficient detail.

We could easily simulate mentally that a vehicle that consisted of a tubular cage made of aluminum foil would do poorly in protecting its occupants in a head-on crash with a two-ton steel vehicle. However, we are unable to process the sufficient amount of information that would enable us to understand the much more complex situation of whether an automobile of conventional design and materials could also protect its occupants.

In the past, computer simulation has had a similar problem. Computers did not have sufficient capability in order to process the amount of information needed to do sophisticated simulations of complex products. Until very recently, complex simulations existed only in the realm of supercomputers. Even then, they were relatively limited in their abilities. However, as Moore's law has led to exponential increases in computing capability, we are rapidly reaching the point where computer simulations of complex products with complex behaviors are executable on everyday computers.

As a result we are seeing simulations play a role in at least three of the four phases of the product lifecycle. The phases that we are seeing simulations play a role in are: the create, build, and support phases. While there has been little activity in the dispose phase, simulation has a role to play there, and I expect that we will see simulation in this phase in the not-too-distant future.

DEFINING SIMULATION AND CLASSES OF SIMULATION

What is simulation? For our purposes, simulation is the application of forces to our virtual product and the prediction of the behavior of that product and its environment as a result of the application of those forces over time. As Figure 7.1 illustrates, the state of a virtual object and the forces affecting it are evaluated over a certain time period. These forces change the virtual object state in some fashion during that time period. The output of the simulation is this new state of the virtual object, which then becomes the input to the next time period with its new application of forces.

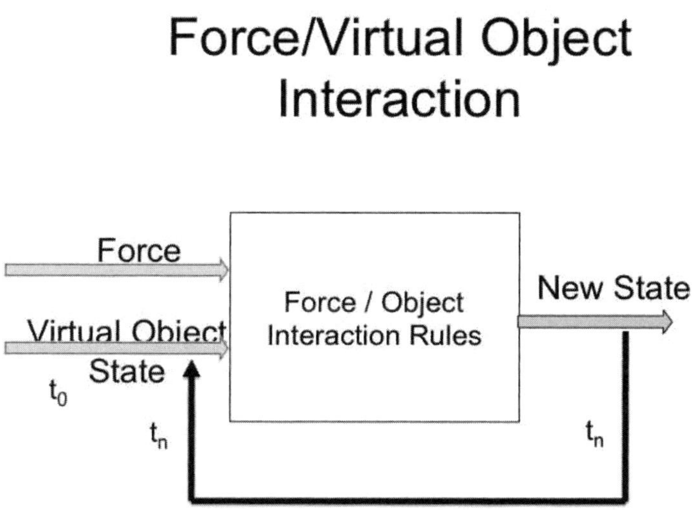

Figure 7.1

While these look like static analyses, strung together they become dynamic motion of the virtual object over time. The concept is much like the picture books that we did as children, where we drew a sequence of pictures that showed objects in slightly different positions on subsequent pages in our book. We then flipped through the book that showed our images in motion. Even as children, we had an intuitive sense of forces acting over time on virtual objects!

Simulation does in essence the same thing. For each time division that we intend to deal with, we apply forces on our virtual product and compute the impact that those forces have in that time. The output of that frame becomes the input to our next frame. We continue that process until we run it for the time period that we have an interest in.

Engineering analysis is a limited form of applying formulae determining the impact of forces on an object. It is a very simple form of simulation, but it is simulation nonetheless. The impact of applying a formula is that at time zero (t_0), no force is applied. At time one (t_1), the force is fully applied. For a great deal of engineering analysis, where the interest is simply in analyzing the impact of a fully applied force on an object, the timing of the application of that force is relatively unimportant. If the interest is to understand whether an axle can support the weight of the chassis, then the issue as to whether the axle breaks in seconds, minutes, or even hours is irrelevant. The sequence of how the axle may buckle over too great a weight is also irrelevant. A great deal of engineering analysis both past and present is merely concerned with the full impact of force irrespective of the time that this force is applied.

If we are interested in the airflow over an airplane wing, the force that we are interested in is the flow as it meets the surface of our wing. For each tick of the clock, we compute what happens at the intersection of the air and our wing and adjust both the air and our wing accordingly. We do that over many time periods and over many points of the wing. We then translate that into images so that we can visually see the impact of this force of air on our virtual wing.

There are basically three classes of simulation of virtual products. The first class is a simulation of virtual products with its environment. In these simulations, virtual products only interact with natural, physical forces. The second class is a simulation of the virtual product with electronic circuitry and/or a computer program or a controller to adjust the state of the virtual product, i.e., reduce fuel flow, increase voltage, toggle a relay, so as to bring it in line with some desired state (See Figure 7.2).

These first two classes will be treated the same, because they are deterministic. The same set of circumstances will produce the same results each and every time. Since the controller has its set of rules baked in, the same forces and virtual object state will result in the same adjustments each and every time.

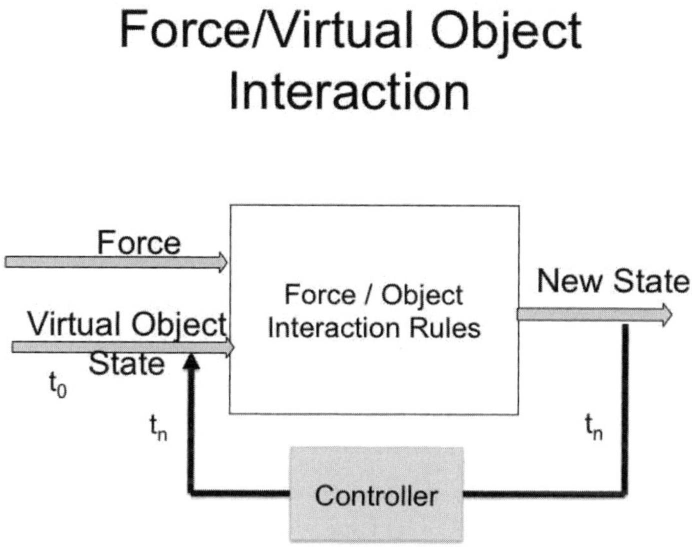

Figure 7.2

The third class is a simulation of virtual products interacting with human intelligence. This simulation is a three-way interaction: the virtual product, natural, physical forces, and human intelligence. As I stated before, computers can simulate the first two, but cannot simulate the third. Human intelligence has to come from actual humans and not from computers attempting to simulate human thought.

I would like to make the distinction between human structure and human intelligence. Human structure or the physical human form can be simulated with virtual products as part of the environment. Simulating the human form in conjunction with the virtual product is well within the capability of the first type of simulation. Simulating human intelligence and decisions requires the second type of simulation with actual humans participating.

PHYSICAL FORCE SIMULATION

There are a number of different kinds of physical force simulations. The advantage of these simulations is obviously seeing how virtual products will respond to their physical environment. In theory, each of these simulations could be performed as physical tests with physical products. The obvious constraint is cost. Physical tests can cost thousands of dollars for simple products and into the millions of dollars for complex products such as airplanes and spacecraft.

Assuming that our knowledge and ability to model all of the physical forces involved is robust and complete enough, virtual simulation can be done at a fraction of the cost of physical testing. In addition, a substantial part of the costs of physical testing is in the instrumentation necessary to collect the desired data. In simulation, since we are computing all the different states of the virtual product and its environment, we have no need of separate instrumentation. We can simply interrogate the simulation for the desired data at any point in time.

The other tremendous advantage we have with simulation that we do not have with physical testing is the ability to control time. In physical testing, if things happen in either brief periods of time or in long periods of time, we are at the mercy of the clock. The issue with short periods of time is that critical things may happen in such short time periods that we need to develop extremely expensive equipment in order to capture critical data.

Automobile crash tests occur within a few seconds. At one tick of the clock, we have a perfectly normal automobile. A few ticks later, we have a mangled piece of metal and plastic. In those few ticks of the clock, critical things happened in a specific sequence. We need a detailed understanding of what happened in those few ticks of the clock in order to understand how and why the automobile performed in protecting or not protecting its occupants.

On the other end of the spectrum, we can have long periods of time occur before the appearance of the events that we wish to study. If our interest is in the life of a turbine fan blade, then with physical testing, we might have to wait years before the phenomena of metal fatigue comes into play. If we are interested in evaluating different materials for products that we wish to release in a few years, waiting a decade or more for physical test results will not work.

With simulation, we can control the time of virtual space to our advantage. For our crash test, we can slow our virtual clock down and analyze our crash millisecond by millisecond. We can freeze time at any point during the crash tests to take a closer look at the state of the virtual product. For our turbine fan blade, we can speed up our virtual clock, whirring past the years like HG Wells' Time Traveler. Assuming that we get our physics right, we can examine the effect of virtual decades of operations on a turbine fan blade in a short period of physical time.

The other advantage that simulation gives us is the ability with minimal cost to perform a wide variety of virtual tests. With physical testing, we need to carefully determine which tests we need to perform. Since this testing is invariably expensive for complex products, we need to select the conditions of our tests such that we examine the usual suspects for failure and/or the performance boundaries of the product, although there is usually a substantial amount of overlap between these two categories.

While this is not a bad strategy, the failures from complex product performance often times come from the unusual suspects and not the usual suspects.[34] Using simulation, we can afford to not only test for the usual suspects of failure, but we can also afford to test for those regions of operations that may be the source of unusual failures.

While we have techniques that we have developed for physical testing because they are cost-efficient, we can now use more probabilistic techniques that would be uneconomical and prohibitive for physical testing. For example we can and should use Monte Carlo simulation to probe for potential product failures, especially in regions where we have complex interaction of variables. It is in these regions that nonlinear effects may cause products to fail and fail quite spectacularly.

It was known that there was a deformation of O-rings in the space shuttle Challenger's booster rockets. This deformity allowed hot gases to escape. While speculative, simulating these O-rings under a wide variety of conditions, including low temperatures might have predicted the Challenger disaster. While the technology was not available for this type of simulation in the 20th century, there is a real possibility and potential for simulation to prevent a Challenger type disaster in our future spacecraft.

Human Interaction Simulation

Adding humans into simulation changes the nature of simulation. The model simulation with simply the state of the virtual object and the applied physical forces is both deterministic and repeatable. It is deterministic because we can calculate the impact of applying the forces to the virtual object. In the same way, it is repeatable, because the impact of the same physical force on the same virtual object should yield the same result over and over again.

Adding human intelligence, or more specifically human decision-making, results in simulations being nondeterministic. Since we have no way of knowing what the human response may be to a particular situation, we have no way of knowing ahead of time the results of the simulation. It is only repeatable in the sense that the same human decision combined with the forces and virtual object will yield the same outcome. However, humans often behave differently in the same situations.

As Figure 7.3 shows, the simulation model gets a little more complicated. Human decisions are added as input to the model. Human analysis of the new state of the virtual object is now subject to human analysis before it is fed back into the system. Humans constantly attempt to make sense out of their environment as a precursor to making decisions. Even when faced with what seems to be identical situations, humans may make different decisions based on subtle nuances.

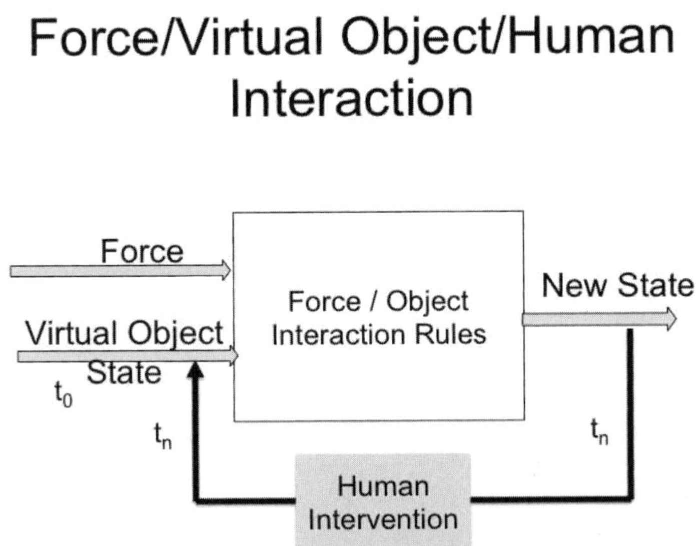

Figure 7.3

As shown in Figure 7.4, human interaction in simulation can span a spectrum from involvement to immersion.

On the involvement end, humans are simply involved with the simulation by making decisions. The simulation model is merely looking for a human decision in order to proceed. The interaction with the simulation from the humans' perspective is abstract. It may be as simple as responding to a question from the simulation model.

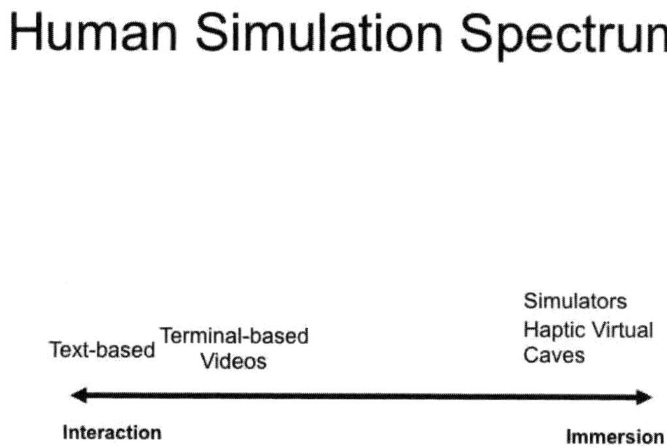

Figure 7.4

An example of this is the Beer Game that most MBA students encounter. This is a supply chain simulation model that requires the students to place an order for the delivery of beer for a number of different weeks. The students are given some information such as beer consumption levels and the lead-time of beer production in order to make their decisions. The simulation can give hugely varied results on the basis of the student's input, even though the model is relatively simple.

As simulation models become more sophisticated, human involvement increases. The general proxy for this is a higher engagement of human senses in the model. At the next higher level of involvement, the simulation model may present visual images as its way of conveying information to human participants. A simulation model that is assessing different handling characteristics of an automobile could present the road to the human participant and various responses as to the position of the car on the road as a change in steering decisions by the human participant and the handling characteristics of the automobile.

Since we are engaging our highest bandwidth sense, vision, we would expect a much greater degree of involvement than if we were simply typing in answers to text. We should expect that the greater the image fidelity to real life, the greater our immersion. While playing Space Invaders on a Nintendo was engrossing, playing Call of Duty on a high definition television connected to an Xbox or PS3 is at a whole different level. The Department of Defense (DoD) has taken that even farther with life-size projections of battle simulations on high speed computers.

The flight simulators that the airline pilots use engage even more senses. In these types of simulations, not only are visual cues presented to the pilot, but also hydraulic devices simulate the position of the plane and therefore the orientation of the pilot as a pilot makes his or her decision. These additional sensory cues enhance the reality of the simulation. The physical responses, such as breathing and heart rate, of pilots in simulated stressful situations mirror the responses of pilots in actual situations.

As computing power rapidly increases, immersion into the simulation becomes extremely feasible. Today, it is possible to put people in simulations that incorporate visual devices in the form of goggles and biofeedback devices that provide similar indications as if the people were handling physical equipment. These allow simulations that put people into situations with their virtual product that are as realistic as if they were dealing with that physical product. Mistakes made in these situations save valuable resources compared to making mistakes using the physical products themselves.

However, careful attention must be paid to the fidelity of the simulations. If the simulations are not accurate in their reflection of how products would behave physically, we can cause problems, especially if the simulation is used for training. People will react in actual situations as they have been trained to do in simulations. If the product does not react in the real world the way it reacted in simulation, people will perform improperly. This has been a problem with airplane simulators, where pilots have made fatal mistakes based on their training in simulators. It is estimated half of the fatalities in the first decade of the 21st century of U.S. airline accidents were linked to faulty simulator training.[35]

Simulation Versus Testing

The outcome that we desire from testing is reliability and completeness. By reliability, we mean that the test results will reflect what will occur with the product in actual use. By completeness, we mean that testing will cover all the possible conditions that the product will encounter in the environment. While reliability is achievable, completeness is an ideal. We can never hope to test for all possible conditions, but we can try for all probable ones. Where human safety is involved, we need to go beyond probable and even test for improbable conditions. This is something that is cost prohibitive for physical testing, but quite feasible for virtual testing.

As our virtual products and our virtual environments continue to gain in richness and robustness, the question becomes when and how should we replace physical testing with simulation. The costs of physical testing and simulation are moving in different directions. The cost of physical resources continues to grow over time, even if it is simply at the rate of inflation. Virtual costs will continue to decrease over time as Moore's law and its corollaries continue to remain in effect. PLM's main premise, that we should replace atoms with bits, will become more and more attractive.

It is important to note as part of this discussion that physical testing has not been and will not be a guarantee of desired product performance. While in the past, physical testing was the best tool we had in order to predict product performance, it has been by no means an unqualified success. If it had been, we would not see the level of product recalls that we do. We would also not see some of the spectacular product failures, such as the DC-10 airplane engine mount failure.

Because product testing requires physical resources, and, often substantial physical resources at that, physical testing is limited. While the engineering discipline has devoted substantial time and effort to devising methodology and techniques in order to make testing as efficient and effective as possible, physical testing is a limited subset of all possible combinations of environmental effects that the product would encounter in actual use.

While physical testing lacks completeness, it does have the attribute of reliability. Given the methodologies that we have developed, we can be confident that the test results will reflect the attributes that we are interested in. When we perform the wing flex test on an airplane test object, we have great confidence that the planes we will build can have a certain degree of wing flex without the wings breaking.

The issue in deciding whether we can substitute simulation for physical testing is whether or not the simulation will give us the same results that the physical testing gave us. What we need to convince ourselves is that our informational bits will perform in the same way that the physical atoms do. In order to convince ourselves that this is the case, we need a methodology that does this. One instance of the simulation giving us a result similar to the physical test result is not enough.

Figure 7.5 is one such methodology. The first step is selecting a number of physical tests that have been previously performed. The sample size should be representative of the complexity of the physical tests: the simpler the test - the smaller the sample size, the more complex the test - the larger the sample size.

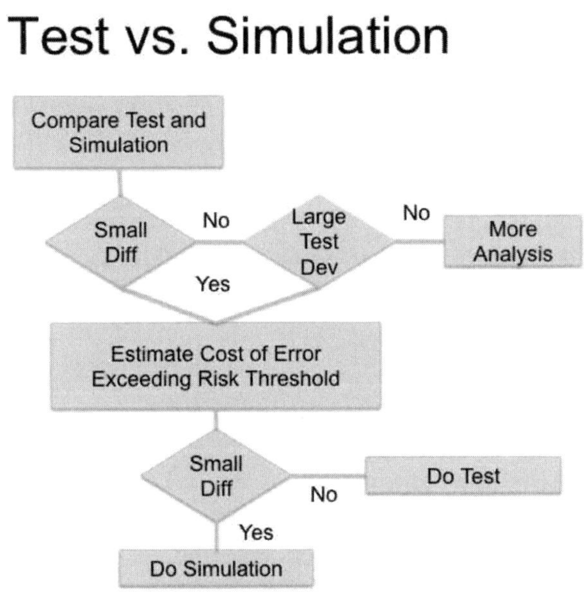

Figure 7.5

The tests should then be performed in simulation. If the difference between the physical test and the simulation a small, meaning that the mean is close to zero and the deviation is small, then the simulation is a candidate to replace the physical test.

Even if the deviation of the simulation to the physical tests is large, it may be that deviations of the physical tests themselves are also large. If there is a large deviation between the physical test and the simulation, but intra-test simulation deviations are small, then clearly more analysis needs to be done in order to understand and model the physics involved.

The last step is to estimate the cost of making an error above a certain monetary threshold in doing tests and simulations. That cost should be reduced by the cost of performing the respective physical or simulation tests. If those costs are comparable, then we should consider replacing the physical test with the simulation test. Since cost of the simulation will be less than the physical test, sometimes by a magnitude or more, the initial cost will be much less. It is only if there is an error, i.e., the simulation test does not catch a problem, that there will be additional costs. However, these additional costs could also be incurred if the physical test also fails to catch the problem.

If the simulation produces the equivalent reliability as a physical test, what we gain is in the area of completeness. We can now afford to do many more simulations than we could afford to do physical tests. For example, in crash tests where we might have done a front impact and a side impact, we can now perform simulations of impact angles in between those right angles. It may be that an oblique impact causes a structural collapse that a front or a side impact would not uncover. The costs of these additional simulations would be a fraction of the costs of performing the physical crash tests.

Simulations have the potential to yield a huge reduction in physical testing costs. For complex products such as airplanes or automobiles, the cost savings can easily be in the hundreds of millions of dollars. While it is clear that simulation will add to the completeness of testing, the need is to be convinced that simulation has the same reliability as physical testing. This requires a methodology similar to the one that I have outlined here.

SIMULATION THROUGH THE PRODUCT LIFECYCLE

Simulation is useful throughout the entire product lifecycle. While some of the more robust uses may be in the create phase, all phases can benefit from using the virtual product to predict how the physical product will behave. Even when there is a physical product in the support phase, the benefits in cost and safety of having humans interact with a virtual product will validate the trade off of bits for atoms.

Create

The create phase is rife with opportunities to use simulation. At the beginning of its life, all products are virtual. The trick is to turn the virtual products, i.e., the ideas of the designers and engineers, into products that have the actual functionality and behavior that they envision. Simulation helps them do that without having to translate their virtual ideas into expensive physical prototypes.

Crash Safety

This has been and continues to be the poster child for simulation. This is a premier example of trading expensive atoms for cheap bits. In addition, crash tests, especially of automobiles, requires a complex interaction of forces and materials.

Because of the substantial costs of a physical crash tests that can run into the hundreds of thousands of dollars or more, crash simulation have long been worked on. However, the computing requirements could only be fulfilled by very expensive supercomputers. However, the major automobile manufacturers paid the price for simulations on these expensive computing systems, because simulations, even in a primitive form, saved these manufacturers significant amounts over physical testing.

The other reason that manufacturers invested in crash test simulations is that they were aware that computing performance was increasing at an exponential rate. Because of the complexity of simulating crashes, most of these manufacturers felt that it was an investment well worth making in order to develop and prove out the mathematics that would model the forces in a crash. The issue that they realized was that it was not enough that computing capability was increasing exponentially. They would need to gain experience in developing the necessary techniques to take advantage of this computing capability.

Those investments have proven out. While automotive companies still run major crash simulations on supercomputers, some simulations can be run on much, much less expensive PC clusters today. Given the advances of computing, they will in all probability run on the smart phones of tomorrow.

The other issue of physical crash testing costs, in addition to the obvious cost of destroying a $20,000 to a $100,000 automobile for each test, is that there is a substantial cost of the instrumentation in attempting to capture the data that a crash test creates. High-speed photography can capture a millisecond-by-millisecond picture of the crash as it unfolds. However, it can only record the surface of what the cameras are pointed at. The results of the impact on internal components in most cases needs to be deduced from comparing the deformed crash component to its pristine original.

In simulation, we can look at the impact of forces on components in any degree of detail and for any degree of time division. We can also look at the impact on each individual component regardless of whether it is visible from the outside or is very deeply buried inside the car. We can get this data without expensive instrumentation and without trying to deduce what occurred by the end result, assuming that the vehicle can even be dissembled in its mangled condition.

The key to crash test simulations is how well it reflects an actual physical crash test. The state-of-the-art today is that it is accurate enough to make good decisions regarding component structure. It promises to get better over time. However, until we have virtual crash tests that are indistinguishable from physical ones, we will continue to perform physical crash tests, although there will be less and less of them.

Even when the virtual test is indistinguishable from the physical test, we will still perform a physical crash test to validate our virtual findings. Even if physical crash testing was not required by law, which it in fact is in the developed world, the physical world can always unpleasantly surprise us. In fact, the premise of testing virtually but validating the virtual tests with a final physical test will be the standard for most types of simulations.

Aerodynamics

NASA announced the end of an era recently when they released a notice that they were shutting down and demolishing the wind tunnel at Langley Field. The wind tunnel dates back to 1931. It boasted involvement with such aerospace luminaries as the Wright brothers, Charles Lindberg, Howard Hughes, and other noted aviation figures who used the wind tunnel to validate their designs. It was responsible for testing early biplanes to Boeing's X-48C, a futuristic, delta-wing airplane.

Not coincidentally, the Boeing 787 was the first major airframe to have its entire wing structure simulated on computer. These two events are related. Computer simulation of aerodynamics is moving from massive wind tunnels to the virtual environment of computer systems. While the Langley wind tunnel was being constrained by the increasing size of the new airframes that it could test, computer capability was removing the constraints on the size of the airframes that it could simulate.

While the Langley wind tunnel could adequately test the airplanes of the past, the new airframes were of such a size that they needed to be broken up into pieces in order to test them physically at Langley. Computer simulation was rapidly moving in the other direction. It was moving from an ability to only simulate pieces of an airframe to the ability to simulate the entire airframe. It only became a matter of time to make the determination to trade off atoms for bits - the atom-based Langley wind tunnel for the bit-based computer simulation.

Aerodynamic simulation is a matter of evaluating the force of the virtual object as it moves through air. The wind tunnel was based on a phenomenon that was known as far back as Leonardo da Vinci. That phenomena as stated in da Vinci's Codex Atlanticus and his notebooks was "as it is to move the object against the motionless air, so it is to move the air against the motionless object." Wind tunnels were built to exploit that physical phenomenon.

The issue with physical wind tunnels is that air is not visible. In order to understand the effect of air against the object, engineers needed to not only generate air with high-speed fans, but they needed to generate a source of smoke so that they can observe the air flow. While this sufficed for many aspects of aerodynamic analysis, it did limit wind tunnel testing to unidirectional forces. In addition, where the cross-section of the object to be tested was large, the use of multiple sources of smoke to cover that cross-section meant that some smoke trails could easily be obscured.

Computer simulation does not suffer from the same constraints. Since we control the environment, we can change some physical phenomena rules to suit our needs. We can make air visible, so that we can easily see how it flows over certain areas. We can not only make it visible, but we can color-code air flows so that each cross-section of interest has its own color. We can ascertain from the color not only the airflow past the object, but the turbulence that may cause cross-sectional deviation.

With simulation, we also do not need to rely on our eyesight, not even the augmented eyesight of photographic capture. We can have our simulation follow individual virtual molecules of air in order to see if they passed by our virtual object in a desired manner or they deviated unacceptably.

We can also engage in more complex aerodynamic analysis than may be afforded to us by unidirectional airflow. There is no reason why we cannot have multiple sources of airflow to simulate crosswinds or microbursts. It is some of these phenomena that have proven deadly to aircraft in the past.

Aerodynamic simulation is useful for a wide variety of vehicles. It is clearly essential for aircraft and spacecraft. But it is also highly important for automobiles and trucks. One way to obtain better fuel economy is to lessen the resistance of the vehicle to the air passing over it. A great deal of aerodynamic research is involved in making cars and trucks more aerodynamically efficient and thus more fuel-efficient.

This is also a safety issue for vehicles such as boats, ATVs, and personal watercraft - in addition to automobiles. If these vehicles are not engineered properly from an aerodynamic perspective, the force of the flowing air can cause these vehicles to lift and even turn over. Ralph Nader made his career on the aerodynamic flaws of the Corvair.[36]

The additional attractiveness of aerodynamic simulation is that it has proven more accurate than wind tunnel testing. Wind tunnel testing requires an enclosed area, whereas the actual vehicle will be in open space. While the impact of the enclosed wind tunnel space may be minor, it does exist. That effect is not present in simulations.

Of all the types of simulations, aerodynamic simulation may be the first to go completely digital. The information gain from aerodynamic simulation is as good if not better than physical wind tunnel testing. The cost to build, maintain, and test in a wind tunnel is many magnitudes greater than virtual simulation. If we add in the cost of having to build a physical prototype early in the design cycle, the economics and efficiency of simulation dwarfs that of the wind tunnel. It is easy to see how trading these atoms for bits is highly beneficial.

Durability

Durability is a highly prized attribute for today's products, especially ones that are expected to be in service for years or even decades. The issue in the past was that products were engineered to produce the required functionality, but it was unclear for how long they would produce that functionality. The only way to ascertain durability was to obtain that information empirically. This meant that testing laboratories intended to put the product through a lifetime of uses. Refrigerator doors were opened and slammed shut hydraulically. A heavy weight was repeatedly dropped on a sofa cushion. A car was continually driven around and around a test track.

While this testing certainly helped, the assessment of durability was not very accurate, as evidenced by the fact that the products of yesteryear were fairly unreliable compared to today's products. Where there was an attempt to really obtain durability, the answer was to over-engineer the product. This meant that the product user was overpaying for the functionality that he or she really needed.

Some of this philosophy has carried over to today. I particularly enjoy the ad by Mercedes where they show an automobile with its doors open and four hefty men sitting in the open windows of those doors. The message was because it was a Mercedes, its doors were expected to support weight on the door hinges that would never happen in normal use.

While the intent of the ad was to emphasize durability, what I saw was over-engineered costs. However, that was to be expected in the past, when we had little in the way of tools to assess durability. Today, we can dynamically calculate the stresses that occur to automobile bodies as they encounter forces similar to those that they would encounter on the road. We can look at wheel displacement as the vehicle travels over virtual bumpy roads and calculate the stresses that the vehicle incurs.

We do have enough empirical data from physical tests to correlate the stresses that we calculate against the stresses that a physical vehicle incurs under harsh conditions. We can then predict the durability of the parts on that car based on the failure that we obtained from physical vehicles. We no longer need to run a vehicle 100,000 miles around the test track. We can run that same virtual vehicle around our virtual test track and any number of variations of that test track, in order to understand the durability of our designs.

Heat Management

Heat is an energy force that is a requirement to deal with but is difficult because of its lack of visibility. Even over time, unless the product heats up enough to be in the visible range or we view it in infrared, a product looks the same regardless of the amount of heat it is retaining. The inability to manage heat can range from the product user being uncomfortable, as in a passenger compartment that retains too much heat, to being dangerous, as in a fuel line that is routed too close to a part that heats up.

We can simulate the effect of heat over time. We can also map heat levels onto color so that we can visually see the impact of heat over time. We often map heat to color because the color gradients are distinct enough that we can differentiate even small heat changes visually. Heat can originate from a number of different sources such as friction or combustion. We can simulate these different sources in order to determine heat problems in product use.

Noise and Vibration

Noise and vibration are more difficult to simulate because of the various conditions that create these phenomena. One of the main ways to reduce noise and vibration is to enforce design guidelines during the engineering phase. For example, there are some plastics that should not be put next to each other. The design guidelines can be enforced in the design authoring tools.

However there are other simulations that can determine if excitation structures are well enough isolated from vibration sources. They can also simulate whether the structures are self-dampening, which will reduce or eliminate noise and vibration. Noise and vibration are not simply an annoyance factor, but, especially vibration, can lead to durability issues.

Ergonomics

Ergonomic simulation is a simulation that does span the spectrum from involvement to immersion. At the involvement end of the spectrum is the simulation of the human physical form. With these types of simulation, we use information about the physical form to determine the suitability of the design.

Examples of this are determining if human drivers of various sizes can reach the pedals of an automobile. We can simulate various human size forms to determine the range of seat positions that we will need in order to successfully handle that size range. In addition, we can also then specify the upper and lower limit of human sizes that we can comfortably accommodate. What we attempt to do, since human sizes conform to a normal distribution curve, is to accommodate everyone that falls into a normal range.

Another example of this is field of vision. For a range of sizes we can project fields of vision that show us where our designs will have blind spots. We can also determine how far in front of a vehicle and how far behind the vehicle we can begin to see the road. These simulations are fairly routine and can be incorporated into design rules that alert us when we are attempting to design something uncomfortable or unsafe.

On the other end of the spectrum, we use immersion in order to involve human intelligence with these design decisions. While we can use simulation participation to project a field of vision in order to determine if the instruments on a dashboard are visible, this does not tell us whether the information on these instruments is easily recognizable and understandable. We need human intelligence, i.e., putting humans in situations where they can see those instruments, to give us feedback.

This immersion can be single sense or multi-sense. In single sense, we may equip our participant with virtual goggles that display our instrument panel. In multi-sense, our participant might be equipped not only with virtual goggles, but with gloves employing haptic feedback mechanisms that give our virtual driver tactile feedback on the virtual controls in a virtual cockpit.

It is a bit eerie to watch one of these simulations, where the virtual driver sits in the driver seat surrounded by nothing but air. However, his motions are that of a physical driver. He grabs a virtual steering wheel, glances around at virtual instruments, tilts his head to look into virtual rearview mirror, and shifts the virtual gearshift. However as a virtual driver, I can attest that, although I knew that the automobile interior was not real, it did feel exceptionally realistic.

Ergonomics simulation has been successfully used by many organizations to not only get the form factors right, but also to understand "look and feel" issues. While these are not the most expensive prototypes that organizations have to deal with, being able to simulate a range of potential vehicle interiors allows the exploration of many more possibilities. Organizations can afford to innovate with combinations that they may not otherwise try if they have to build physical prototypes. In addition, the simulation in bits will be quicker and less expensive than creating prototypes in atoms.

Build

Some of the best simulations that currently exist are in the build or manufacturing phase. The reason is that the manufacturing phase is the most controlled of the product lifecycle. In the build phase, we control what material we use, what machines we use, the order of operations, and the overall environment. In fact, in the build phase, the more things we can control the better that we can be assured that our Bill of Process will produce exactly the same results each and every time. Ideally, we would like no variability at all in the production of one product instance from another. We can build up our simulations from individual stations to a line of the stations to an entire factory.

Workstations and Cells

We can simulate how individual workstations and cells can perform the activities of moving material into it, performing the operations on those materials, and moving material out of it. We can determine if various elements of the tool conflict or clash and whether these tool elements have enough degrees of freedom to carry out the tasks that we need.

In addition to the control aspects of the build process, even small increases in efficiencies can have large effects. Inefficiencies in the design process can often be tolerated because the design is only done once and may be a small part of the resources employed in order to produce a product. The manufacturing process, on the other hand, is done over and over again, so that even small inefficiencies can have major cost effects.

Companies have counted on the experience curve where as production volumes increase the cost of production decreases. All types of production have empirically shown about a 20% experience curve. A 20% experience curve is that for every doubling of production, costs decrease by 20%. The Toyota Production System (TPS) prides itself on driving down this experience curve through continuous improvement. However if this continuous improvement is done on the factory floor, it means that Toyota is producing a large number of products in a less than optimal and efficient manner. If this experience curve can be driven down in simulation to the most efficient manner of production, then, when physical production starts, waste is kept to a minimum. Again, it is far cheaper to expend bits than it is to expend atoms.

Human Ergonomics

Humans are the most versatile, but one of the most fragile pieces of "equipment" that factories have. Humans can perform an infinite variety of tasks and can adapt their methods to the situation at hand. However, compared to the other industrial equipment in the factory, humans are much more fragile and susceptible to injuries and fatigue. For most of the history of industrial production, organizations gave these issues little attention. When a worker was injured, they simply replaced him with a new worker.

However, this mindset changed throughout the 20th century. Governments in the developed countries created substantial regulations that dictated to organizations that working conditions could not impair or endanger the health of their workers.

While the analysis of ergonomics in working conditions has been around for decades, simulation takes this analysis and work planning to a whole new level. The static ergonomic analysis of the past was limited primarily to gross body movements and for an average body type. This made the workplace safer, but workplace injuries continued to occur because not all body movements are gross body movements and certainly everyone does not have an average body type. In addition, until the operations actually were done on the factory floor, a complete understanding of the required body motion was unavailable.

Simulation changes this. We can simulate human actions both large and small. We can also simulate these operations for a variety of body types, so that we can understand whether the motions that we are proposing are acceptable to all body types or are only suitable for a certain range of body types.

We may think that a certain motion looks feasible for workers to perform. However, we may find in simulating that motion that this operation requires the wrist to be bent beyond a safe and comfortable level. We may also find that once we begin simulating this activity for the volume of production that we desire, that this particular motion will result in fatigue for the worker. These may be subtle issues that would not arise until we had begun factory production. At that point, we would incur costly injuries to the workers and costly changes to factory operations as we attempted to mitigate the issue.

In a relatively short period of time, we have moved from very rough forms of human simulation that simply show the feasibility of humans being involved in manufacturing operations to a very rich, robust human factor analysis that allows us to have a high level of confidence that the operations we are asking humans to perform are safe, reliable, and efficient. We can do this for not only an average body type, but for a range of body types that reflect the actual population of our factories.

While it may not be a requirement today, it is not unthinkable that tomorrow's requirement is that we must simulate factory operations with human factor forms in order to demonstrate that all operations requiring humans are safe. It also may be that, in the future, if we have not simulated these operations and if a worker becomes injured, it will become a de facto proof of negligence. Using these simulations, we can prevent harm from coming to our workers, create a much safer workplace, and, as a bonus, increase productivity.

Factory Simulations

The simulation of work cell operations and human factor simulation can now come together in full factory simulations. This means that we can put together the entire factory and perform analysis and planning from both the highest level of factory throughput to the lowest level of individual and discrete operations. What this gives us is the ability to plan and optimize our factories in the way that lean manufacturing never anticipated.

The key to a factory's success is to produce products using the minimal amount of resources. Simulation allows us to do this with cheap bits of simulation rather than expensive atoms of experiments on the factory floor. As I have said many times before, even the Toyota Production System with its kaizen methods requires us to produce products inefficiently as we attempt to minimize the use of resources. It may be that we cannot get to perfect fidelity between the real and virtual worlds for simulation, but if we can drive down a significant length on the experience curve using simulation rather than trial-and-error on the factory floor, the savings for most industrial organizations is tremendous.

The examples of these kinds of savings are numerous. NASA has saved millions of dollars in simulating their manufacturing activities. In one instance, they determined that a weld from a custom piece of equipment was inadequate to perform what they needed to do. This piece of equipment costs in the neighborhood of $10 million. If they had placed this equipment on the factory floor and discovered the problem there, it would have cost them hundreds of thousands of dollars to correct that deficiency.

By using simulation, NASA uncovered the problem long before the equipment was built. As a result, the equipment plans were modified at minimal cost so that the physical equipment would perform properly when it reached the factory floor. The cost of discovering this problem and modifying the equipment once it had been built was substantially more expensive than the cost of doing simulations.

Sustain

The goal of the sustain phase is to maintain the product in the condition that it first entered service. In addition, the product can be tailored and enhanced as it is required to perform new and different tasks. There are a number of different opportunities for simulation to provide value during this phase.

Service Training

The in-service phase of the product can dwarf the other phases of the product's life in terms of duration. Product lifetimes cannot only be years, but they can be decades and even a century or longer. The issue here is that long-lived products are serviced by humans, whose work life does not match up to products' lives of decades or more.

People change jobs, move up the career ladder, change careers, and retire. Even if the product manufacturer takes into consideration the sustainability of a product and diligently trains support personnel to be fully prepared to support the product when it begins its existence, sooner or later the people who were trained on this product will no longer be available. Without these people, a product may still have useful life left, but may have to be disposed of because no one knows how to service or repair it.

Simulated training and service modules can prepare new personnel to step in and take over the support function from other personnel who are leaving that role. The simulations can guide inexperienced personnel in identifying malfunctions with the product and can provide guidance on the most efficient way to put that product back into service. This is extremely useful for products that are either highly complex or expensive, where making an error in the repair process is most undesirable.

There are also some products where making errors in the repair process would lead to highly dangerous outcomes. In those cases, we would want the new support personnel to make his or her errors on the simulated product and not on the actual product itself. Nuclear reactors would be a good example of this type of product.

Service Planning

There are numerous examples of industrial equipment and products that need to be taken out of service periodically in order be refurbished. These include assembly lines, battleships, and nuclear and fossil fuel power plants. The cost of having these products out of service is steep. If the time for refurbishment can be decreased, the savings of doing this are substantial.

Taking nuclear power plants as example, each day the nuclear facility is out of service for refurbishment can cost utilities a million dollars or more. In addition, the nuclear aspect of these power facilities makes safety a primary driver of these refurbishment activities. Ignoring the fact that regulations are extremely stringent, one simply does not go into a nuclear facility and begin dismantling things without extensive planning.

The work on these facilities can be planned so that they are done in a safe, efficient manner by using simulation. Ensuring that equipment can be moved properly and that obstacles and obstructions are sufficiently clear is of paramount importance. These simulations can provide the required information in order to understand how equipment needs to be positioned and moved in the most efficient manner.

In one nuclear power plant, the plan was to move a certain piece of equipment out of the structure that contained it. It was discovered in simulation that there was a protruding beam that blocked the straight removal of this piece of equipment. The refurbishing team developed a piece of rigging that allowed the equipment to be moved so as to avoid this protrusion. Had the simulation not been done, they would have only found out about the problem as they attempted to move this piece of equipment. At that point in time not only would it have been more costly and time-consuming to address the problem, but because the equipment was already hanging on a crane, it would have led to a potential for very unsafe conditions.

The advantage in terms of cost of using simulations to plan versus trial and error during the activity is something that can be determined. What cannot be determined is the increase of safety in these kinds of activities. While it is pretty clear that safety needs to be of paramount importance in nuclear facilities, keeping workers safe in any kind of industrial equipment movement is of major importance. The cost of these simulations in relationship to the cost of human life is insignificant.

This is not meant to be an exhaustive list of potential uses of simulation. As the technology advances, there will be many more uses.

This chapter focused on the aspect of simulation. Simulation is starting to impact all areas of the product lifecycle, and it is important to understand the different roles that simulation can play.

In the create phase, we have physical force simulation which can help us understand whether or not our product will give us the behaviors that we desire. However we also need to engage humans in the simulations, because human interaction with products is nondeterministic and cannot be simulated by computer systems that do not have the intelligence that humans have.

The goal of simulation in this phase is to fully replace physical testing. This will not happen immediately. However, we should see steady gains in this area. It is also predicted that even if physical testing is replaced by simulation, there will always be a requirement for physical validation of the product.

In the create phase, the categories of simulation that were explored here are: crash safety, aerodynamics, durability, heat management, noise and vibration, and ergonomics. In the build phase, we will be simulating workstation and cells, human form interaction, and finally an entire factory simulation. In the sustainment phase, we expect to see both service training and service planning as major uses of simulation.

Notes

34 For examples of these, see Perrow, C. (1984). *Normal accidents: living with high-risk technologies.* New York: Basic Books.

35 See Levin, A. (2010, August 31). Simulator flaws tied to airline crashes; Flight training cited in half of fatalities. *USA Today.*

36 See Nader, R. (1965). *Unsafe at any speed; the designed-in dangers of the American automobile.* New York: Grossman.

8

VIRTUALLY ACCOMPLISHED

As Einstein is reported to have said, "the definition of insanity is doing the same thing over and over again and expecting different results." Given that, if we take processes to their logical conclusion, we will never have any innovation. We can get incremental improvement, but we cannot get true innovation. Processes by their very definition are about doing the same thing over and over again.

That is not a bad thing. The way to eliminate wasted resources is to take a task that we do over and over again and identify the way to do that task that minimizes the use of resources. While in previous chapters, I have focused on virtual products and its uses, they do not accomplish anything by themselves. We must incorporate them into what we do in organizations for virtual products, simulations, and other capabilities to have any impact.

As I described previously, if we take any task, we can divide its resource usage into two categories. The first category contains the resources that are absolutely needed to perform the task, and the second category contains the resources that add no value to the task. If we then eliminate the second category, we have a textbook definition of "lean."

However, doing the same task over and over again is not all that we do in organizations, and, a good deal of the time, it is not the most important thing that we do. Often what we do is to try to accomplish things that we have not accomplished in the past. If business were simply about executing well-defined processes, there would be no innovation or new product creation.

While we might get incremental improvements, there would be no new and innovative products.

One of the other things that we do in organizations besides processes is something I have labeled as "practices."[37] By definition, processes take one or more inputs, perform specified operations or routines on those inputs, and produce outputs. Processes are defined so that different people performing the same processes will produce equivalent results. While they may not be exact results, from the organization's standpoint, they will be effectively equivalent.

Practices are very different. With practices, we are looking for desired results. What we attempt to do is to look at all the inputs that we have available for selection and all the available operations or routines that we can perform on those inputs. We then attempt to select those inputs and operations that will give us our desired results. Often times, the results that we are trying to obtain are contradictory or even mutually exclusive.

For example, we want vehicles that are both safe and fuel-efficient. Adding weight to a vehicle can make that vehicle much safer, but fuel efficiency declines because of the additional weight. A process approach would be to create a formula that would balance safety and fuel efficiencies. A practice approach would be to find or create a new material that was both lightweight and strong.

I am sometimes accused of being anti-process. This is not the case. As I will discuss later, I am very much in favor of trying to create and formalize processes. In fact, without processes, tasks are almost impossible to bring to conclusions. There is an old and not inaccurate saying that, "an engineering task is only completed when the time runs out."[38] What is implicit here is that when faced with a task that is result driven, that has innumerable input and routine combinations, and that has competing results that require trade-offs, engineers would never complete the task if they were not under some sort of deadline. Since there would always be room to improve the results, the engineering task would never be "finished."

However, while I believe in the value of processes, I also believe that other things are going on in the organization. These things are practices and even art. While I will discuss art at the end of the chapter, I would like to spend the bulk of this space discussing the process/practice distinction.

There are a couple of reasons why process has and continues to get the bulk of attention. First, processes are a lot neater and well defined than practices. Second, there is a tendency for the technical disciplines to want to believe that what they do is well defined, orderly, and deterministic. Design, engineering, and information systems are all structured disciplines.

These technical professionals would like to believe that what they do is very "Spock" like. Like Mr. Spock, the unemotional Vulcan of Star Trek fame, technical professionals would like to believe that they are oh-so logical as they go about their tasks. The idea that they only do processes fits in very nicely with this perspective. In fact, if we ask these people how they go about their job, they will provide us with very neat, orderly, and well-defined flowcharts.

But as any ethnographer will tell us, we should not accept what people tell us about what they do, we need to observe them ourselves to see what they do.[39] If we look at what designers, engineers, and even support personnel do in performing their work, it rarely resembles the neat orderly flowcharts that they would show us. In fact, if we look at the process maps of any group within an organization, we would find major gaps between what the process maps say that they do and what we would observe them to be actually doing.

PROCESS AND PRACTICE EXAMPLE

One of the clearest ways to examine the difference between process and practice is to look at two examples. In Figure 8.1, we have an example of two engineering processes. The top flowchart shows the process for defining a vehicle's weight. The bottom flowchart shows a process for approving a vehicle's design.

The top flowchart is a true process. Inputs are well defined and the routines to perform on those inputs are highly specified. Irrespective of the people that perform the process, the results that would be obtained would be equivalent. In fact, we could translate this flowchart into an algorithm or program that would provide a step-by-step definition of how to perform this process.

The bottom part of the flowchart, while a process, contains elements of practice. The box labeled as "define specifications to meet requirements," while in a neat little box, masks a very messy practice. Assuming that there are competing and even contradictory requirements that need to be accomplished, there may be a myriad of solutions that meet or at least are acceptable so that the specifications can pass the approval decision. In fact, the criteria used to define whether or not the specifications meets the requirements may be altered depending on whether a design solution could be found.

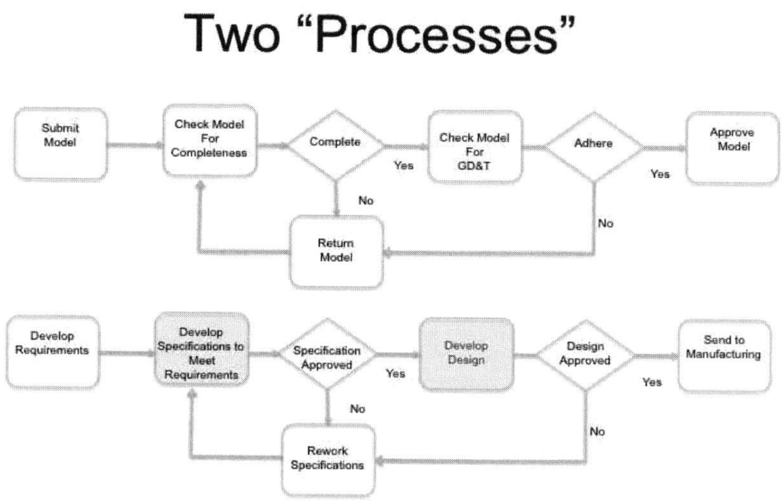

Figure 8.1

If there are competing or contradictory requirements, trade-offs will have to be defined and some of the requirements might have to be relaxed in order to produce any solution at all. This is not something that lends itself to a process. There is no algorithm or code that could be produced in order to provide the solution. In point of fact, anyone who has sat in on one of these sessions would see heated arguments and intense negotiations taking place by the participants. This is hardly a well-defined and orderly process. It is disorderly and messy.

However, as a result of being messy, these practices can and do produce innovation. In attempting to produce a result, and, in many cases a result that has never been produced before, people will attempt to combine inputs and the operations on those inputs in new and unique ways.

Innovation is not unique to humans. Nature also produces innovation through what we call mutation or genetic programming. In nature's case, it tries to produce all possible combinations and permutations and then allows the environment to select out those designs that are best suited for survival. This works for nature because it has unlimited time and resources. Humans, without that luxury, need to do things differently. And we do.

What we do is to envision the results that we want and then use information that we have acquired about cause and effect in order to get those results. In doing this, we trade off information that we have in order to avoid wasting resources on attempted solutions that do not meet the required results. Nature has unlimited resources and no information. Humans have information and limited resources.

So while nature uses genetic programming in order to obtain innovation, we need to obtain innovation through practices. Process will not get us innovation. This is my only issue with process. Unfortunately, process people fail to see this. In fact, there is almost a religious belief that process *can* get us innovation.

One of the more interesting discussions that I have had about this was with a NASA Six Sigma expert. At a meeting that we were in, she claimed that there was a Six Sigma process that produced innovation. My response to this was to ask her to code up this process so that it could be disseminated throughout the rest of NASA in order to create innovation. Her response was to inform me that I clearly didn't understand what she was talking about and then stomp out of the room.

While her reaction might have been an extreme one, people who only believe in processes have very difficult issues in addressing innovation. People armed only with a hammer believe everything is a nail. While I think that incremental improvements may be obtained through a process, true innovation requires practices.

PRACTICE/PROCESS SPECTRUM

Figure 8.2 shows the visual difference between process and practice. If we look at a spectrum, from ill defined to well defined, we can see the difference between process and practice. On the right side, the inputs and the routines on those inputs are well defined. The output is simply the result of running those routines against those inputs. At its most rigid and/or bureaucratic outcome, the output is accepted irrespective of whether it makes sense or not. With processes, we get the outputs that we get by running well-defined routines and operations on well-defined inputs. While that may not be the result that we really desire, it is what we get from processes.

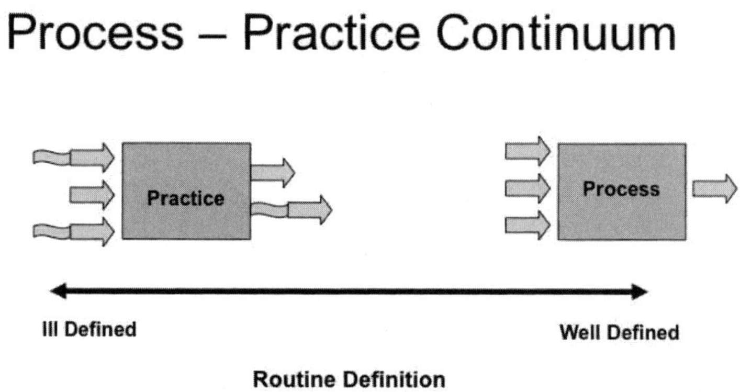

Figure 8.2

One of the better examples of this that I have observed was going through security at the airport. A man had passed through the X-ray machine a 10-ounce bottle that had a couple of ounces of liquid in it. The TSA officer informed him that he could not take this bottle through security with him. When the man objected that the amount of liquid was less than the 3 ounces that were allowed, the security officer, not without a sense of irony and amusement, informed the traveler, "Sir, I'm an official of the United States Government and not allowed to exercise common sense." The TSA official's process was that only bottles that were less than 3 ounces in size could be passed through security. Even though the intent was to limit liquids to 3 ounces, the TSA's process implemented a limitation of 3 ounces in the physical size of bottles.

On the left side of Figure 8.2, we have practices. As was mentioned previously, practices are result driven. We define the outputs that we want and then we select the inputs and the operations or routines on those inputs in order to produce the desired outputs. As indicated by the wavy lines of outputs, the outputs may not be as crisply defined as the outputs of processes. In fact, we may redefine the outputs as we deal with competing requirements and trade-offs.

With practices, we start with the result that we desire and back solve to select the inputs and routines that give us those results. We can find out a number of things in doing this, especially if the results that we are looking for are competitive or contradictory. At worst, we may find out that what we're trying to do cannot be done, at least not with the inputs and routines that we currently have at our disposal. Unlike a process, where we will always get a result, a practice might or might not be successful, where success is defined as finding a set of inputs and operations on those inputs that will produce the results we desire.

When we are unable to succeed in our quest for a desired result, we can either give up, or we can adjust the results that we are looking to obtain. Once we adjust that results, we can then reselect our inputs and routines or operations in order to obtain these new, adjusted results. Except in the most trivial cases, practices are generally iterative in nature. If that were not the case, we could probably make a process out of a practice. By selecting our output and then trying all combinations of our inputs and routines in a systematic fashion, we would then produce our desired output. This is just what nature does.

As I will cover more in depth later, there are substantially different information requirements between processes and practices. With processes, we only want to give the minimal amount of information that will allow the process to be performed. Everything else is irrelevant. For our TSA official, the amount of liquid in the bottle was irrelevant. The only information that he wanted was the size of the physical bottle.

For practices, we need to provide as much information as possible. Since we do not know ahead of time what inputs and what routines or operations are relevant to obtain the desired result, we need to make available to the practitioners a vast pool of information from which they can select what they need. If we limit the pool information, we most likely will limit the alternatives that can be considered.

DISTINCTION WITHOUT A DIFFERENCE?

While the idea of practices that is different from processes resonates well with most people, I occasionally get the objection that processes and practices are distinctions without any real differences. The objectors will say, "When I talk about processes, I'm really talking about practices, too." There is no question that we can be pretty fuzzy in our use of the terms processes and practices. For example, we almost exclusively refer to processes when we talk about what we do in our organizations. However, we then throw in the term of "best practices" that seems to refer to anything an organization does.

Huh? How is it that all this discussion is about processes and now we have this thing, best practices? Ignoring the fact that I take a very jaundiced view of "best practices," the primary answer is that we clearly haven't thought through the differences between process and practice. As a result, the phrase, "best practices," began being used and was unquestioningly picked up as a common phrase. Interestingly, I find that this phrase does bother some people, but they are unsure as to why.

The core issue is that there is a substantial difference between a process and a practice. In spite of some lexical sloppiness, we inherently know the difference between a process and a practice. In reality, we act on that difference all the time as we go about working in our organizations.

In the next section, I will outline the difference between process and practice. There are clear, characteristic differences between process and practice. This is not simply a difference in terminology. There is a difference in the way we do things.

PROCESS AND PRACTICE — DIFFERENT CHARACTERISTICS

In Table 8.1, I have listed what I believe to be most of the characteristic differences that make processes distinct from practices.

Lean versus Innovative

Processes are intended to give us lean results in our organizations, while practices are intended to get us innovation. Processes, by definition, are structured activities that are intended to give us equivalently repeatable results. What we would like to happen with a process is to obtain the same results each and every time that we perform the process. We do not want processes to be idiosyncratic. That is we do not want processes to be dependent on the individuals who run them. We want the same results each and every time, no matter who performs the processes.

Process vs. Practice

Process	Practice
Lean	Innovative
Predictable	Unpredictable
Input, routine driven	Goal seeking
Precise	Fuzzy
Codeable/calculable	Negotiable/arguable
Efficiency	Effectiveness
Frictionless	Frictional
Optimize	Satisfice
Autopilot	Sensemaking
Training-based	Education-based

Table 8.1

Processes by their very nature are definable. We define the inputs that we want for the process, and we define the operations or procedures that we will perform on those inputs. Because we have defined them, we have an understanding of the outputs that we will obtain from the operations that we are performing on these inputs. Our intent is to take variation out of the result. With processes, we would like to be able to be assured that we will get specific results if we have specific inputs. If we add up all the weights of all the components of our vehicle, then we will get the total weight of the vehicle. For this to be a process, each and every time we select the same components we will get the same weight.

How do we get to "lean" from this? The answer is that it does take some work. We cannot simply equate a process with being a lean process. To get to a lean process, we need to analyze all competing processes and pick the one that consumes the least amount of resources. Organizations can have and unfortunately often do have inefficient processes. While processes will give us defined the results, we need to go the extra step to produce not only defined results, but results that are also lean.

With practice, we are looking for innovation. The focus of practice is to attempt to find the inputs and operations that will give us the result that we are looking for. With practice, we are not telling the participants what specific inputs to select or what specific operations to perform, we are asking them to obtain a result.

Again, we need to take an additional step to get to innovation. While we can define a result that we know how to get, that really isn't the intent of practice. If we could do that, we ought to make it a process. After all, we have a result. We know what inputs and operations to perform in order to get that result, so it makes no sense to ask people to re-create this.

Innovation is another way of asking for results that we had not obtained before. With innovation in the product area, we are looking to create a product that performs certain functions better than other products or performs functions that we have not been able to perform before.[40] Before the computer chip, we had the ability to perform calculations, but the cost of those calculations was extremely expensive compared to performing those calculations on a computer chip. With the creation of cellular phones, we could do something that could not be done in the past, which was to talk to people within the phone system without being tethered to a copper wire.

In most organizations, however, we are not simply looking to be lean or innovative. We are looking to be *both* lean and innovative. For some tasks the objective is to be lean, as in repeatable manufacturing. For other tasks, the objective is to be innovative, as in new product development. What this requires is that we select either a process or practice, depending on what we want to accomplish. Processes alone will not suffice. If we're looking to reduce resources, i.e., be lean, then we need to engage in a process. If we're looking to be innovative, then we need to engage in a practice.

Predictable versus Unpredictable

Processes are predictable, while practices are unpredictable. With a process, we are interested in repeatability. We would like to know that each and every time we have certain inputs, that we will get certain outputs. Even in the case of our not-so-humorous TSA example, there will be a very predictable output. Each time a container of greater than 3 ounces passes a screening station, it will be rejected. This is very repeatable and predictable. It is one thing to be repeatable and predictable. The trick is to have the repeatable and predictable output be the one that we really want. That is an issue that we will deal with later on.

With practices, we have unpredictability by its very nature. In one possible outcome, we may not ever be able to obtain the result that we desire. In our example above, where we want a vehicle that is perfectly safe but has superior gas mileage, we may never be able to get to that result. The results that we desire may be unobtainable, or, in the case of opposing results, it may be impossible to obtain one result without precluding the competing result.

The other issue of unpredictability is that, even when the results are obtainable, we may not be able to predict how we are going to get those results. There may be multiple ways of selecting the inputs and operations that will produce the results we desire. Because the permutations and combinations of inputs and operations may be so large, there is no practical way of being able to predict which combination will be selected. This predictability is less of a problem than being able to predict whether or not the results can actually be obtained. But it does lead to the problem of evaluating how efficiently resources are being used in order produce those results.

Not being able to predict whether results can be obtained or not is the problem that most all companies face introducing new products. If they do not produce the results that they set out to obtain, they fail in creating a new product. However, if they do not try to produce results that had never been obtained before, they will produce nothing that is innovative. The issue that organizations face is how to assess the potential success of their ability to actually produce something innovative.

While processes may help organizations in making sure that they do not spend too many resources in pursuing something that cannot be obtained, the actual activities creating innovation are practices. While we can define a product development process aimed at creating new and innovative products, within that process the actual innovation is a practice.

Input, routine driven versus goal seeking

As I described earlier, processes are about taking specific inputs and performing defined operations or routines on those inputs. For true processes, we have little or no say in which inputs that we take and which routines that we perform on those inputs. These have been defined by whoever defined the process. The outputs that we get are the outputs that we get. With processes, we will always get an output, even if it is not very useful.

In practices, we start out with a goal and attempt to determine which inputs and which routines or operations that when combined will produce our goal. With true practices, we have a lot of leeway in our selections. We may even have to create new operations and find new inputs in order to produce our desired outputs. With practices, we may never get the outputs that we seek.

Processes are forward solving. Practices are backward solving.

Precise versus Fuzzy

Processes are very precise. They have to be if we are to perform operations or routines on a selected group of inputs. Certainly we would need to be precise in our selection of both the inputs and the operations to be performed on those inputs. There can be some fuzziness in the inputs and operations if we're prepared to tolerate some variability in results. This may be why some people think that process and practice are interchangeable. However, even in these cases, we are still forward solving from inputs, not back-solving from a result.

Practices, on the other hand, are very fuzzy. In some cases, we do not even know why we make the selections of inputs and operations that we do. We know we need a certain result, and somewhere in our mental processing facilities, we make the necessary connections and weightings in order to decide which inputs and which operations we need to perform in order to get the results we desire.

Codeable/Calculable versus Arguable/Negotiable

In point of fact, humans are more comfortable with practices than with processes. Contrary to the model of the mind as a computer, our minds operate significantly different than computers do. We are not sequential computational machines. We operate by associating data within our brains and by weighting those associations in a particular fashion. In many situations, our brains do it automatically, without us even being aware we are doing it or being able to articulate why or how we did it.[41]

Processes are codeable and calculable. If we are dealing with a true process, we must be able to define the inputs that we are going to deal with, and we must be able to define the routines or operations that we are going to perform on those selected inputs. We can create an algorithm that defines the selected inputs and the operations that we will perform on those inputs.

That being the case, we can also define the calculations that the operations are to perform on inputs. By calculations, I do not necessarily mean arithmetic ones. Calculations can and do include logical types of calculations of the type, "if this is the case, then do that." In fact, pure processes require us to be able to code these logical calculations. As computer systems have become embedded in almost every facet of an organization, we have replaced humans with computers in many, many processes. Computers are ideal for processes, because they will in a slave-like fashion perform exactly the same operations on exactly the same selected inputs each and every time. Humans lack that sort of consistency.

Practices, on the other hand, are not codeable and calculable. While there may be codeable and calculable aspects to practice, as noted above, fuzziness prevents the precision necessary to perform calculations. Instead, practice exhibits the characteristics of argumentation and negotiation.

With a practice, there may be a very large universe of potential inputs and operations. There may be many different combinations and permutations that create the same result. Which inputs to select and which routines to run may be a matter of personal preference. Sometimes, we select one way of doing things over another way simply because we are comfortable with that way or because we have been trained that way. Because we may feel strongly that only our way produces the best desired results, we may tend to engage in heated arguments, not because our way is the only correct way, but because we have so much invested in that way of doing things.

Arguments, stripped of their emotional overtones, are an attempt to provide rationale and evidence that our approach to obtaining a desired result is superior to an alternative one. If we were completely rational beings, which we are not, this might always be a successful method. However, often times, the decision on which argument is better is often decided on whose rhetoric is better or, worse, who yells loudest. This is a pitfall of practices and is not to be underestimated.

In addition, practice involves negotiation. Sometimes a negotiation is around a trade-off of competitive or opposing results. This is useful when the goal of the negotiation is to produce the best result. It is not useful when the result of the negotiation is to preserve one of the party's vested interests at the expense of a superior result. Again, practices have a tendency to deteriorate from result-oriented negotiation into a vested interest negotiation.

An example of this process/practice distinction is a conversation I had with a human resource manager. They told me that they had a process for setting salaries. They had salary ranges set up for different positions. The employee would then come in, and the HR department would discuss the employee's performance. HR would then settle upon a salary increase.

I explained to them that while part of this was a process, there was a major element of practice involved. Two identical employees could go through this process and come out with two different salaries. What actually was occurring with the employee was negotiation. While the employee was only negotiating within a certain range, he or she still was negotiating.

If arguing or negotiating is taking place, we are engaged in a practice not a process. This practice may exist within the confines of a process, but it is a practice nonetheless.

Efficiency versus Effectiveness

We come to a core issue regarding the distinction between process and practice. Processes are about efficiency. Practices are about effectiveness. Processes are about lean. Practices are about innovation. With processes, we want to strip out any unnecessary action in performing the process. We have already seen that we do not want to consider any data or information that is not actually needed to complete a process. We have selected the inputs and the operations, and we want to perform a process using the minimal amount of resources as possible.

Again, however, evaluating the efficiency of a practice is difficult. Two different people could have very different conclusions about how efficient a practice was. In fact, a practice that does not produce the desired results might also be very efficient. Determining that the results were unobtainable might have been very efficient, that is, it uses the minimal amount of resources to make that determination. Someone else might have used substantially more resources to reach the same conclusion.

Practices are different. With a practice, we want to produce a result or a set of results. Going into a practice, we really don't know what combination of inputs and operations that we will need in order to produce our results. If the results that we are seeking are similar to results that we have obtained in the past, we already may have a good idea of the inputs and operations that will give us our desired results. However, if our results have never been obtained before, i.e., they are highly innovative, it may be detrimental to have preconceived ideas about the inputs and operations that will be required.

With practices, constraining resources and methods may be highly detrimental. It does little good in a product development effort to create a new product quickly and using minimal resources if that new product does not produce results that we require. If the time runs out too quickly on our product development efforts vis-à-vis the adage quoted above, we may have nothing to show for our efforts. If we have minimized resource usage but do not acquire our results, we have not minimized resources but wasted them.

The issue that we have to deal with is that we can evaluate effectiveness of a process, but it is difficult to determine efficiency of a practice. With processes, we have predetermined which inputs we are going to select and how we are going to select them. We have also determined what operations we are going to perform on those inputs. We therefore can calculate the time and resources we need to expend in performing a process. If we cannot, then we do not have a process.

With continuous improvement or kaizen, we are in essence creating successive processes, where each process uses fewer resources than the previous process. The issue here is that at the beginning we do not know which combination of inputs and operations minimizes our use of resources. As we try different combinations, we calculate the usage of resources by each of these processes, and we select the process that uses the least amount of resources as the process we want to perform. While there may be some variability in the usage of resources, they're within acceptable range.

Since we know the results of our output that these processes will give us, we understand their effectiveness. If they did not give us the desired result, we would not be performing these processes.

With practice, we do not know whether we can obtain the result or not. Therefore, we may expend a great deal of resources without any results. Also, since we may be able to obtain the results in many different ways, it is difficult to create an a priori evaluation of the effectiveness of one practice over another. Evaluating the effectiveness of practice is very often a matter of experience and judgment rather than being able to use objective criteria.

I recently fired an attorney who was working on a legal matter for me. While this attorney had produced results, I felt that the amount of time that he worked on the case and, as a result, his fees were excessive. However, there were no objective criteria for me to prove to him that he was wasting resources. My criteria for evaluation was that I have spent many, many years dealing with attorneys and have spent millions of dollars on attorney fees, so I have a great deal of experience in knowing how long something should take. He was taking much longer than my experience told me he should.

However, practices are going to be inherently inefficient. Creating new information or knowledge takes resources. If information is a trade-off for wasted resources, conversely creating that information usually requires wasting resources as we explore new areas of potential knowledge. The key is to continually test and experiment with our combination of inputs and routines to determine if we are headed in the right direction. Where there is real waste of resources in practice is to pursue an elaborate theory of how selected inputs and routines will produce our desired output without developing tests and experiments of parts of that theory along the way.

Frictionless versus Friction

We want processes to be frictionless. What this means is that we would like a process to be like a well-oiled machine. When we perform a process, we want the process to go as smoothly as possible. We don't want to fumble around looking for the appropriate inputs. We don't want errors executing the operations. Ideally, we would like a process to use a minimal amount of resources each and every time no matter which people are involved in performing that process.

We do not want people asking questions about what they should do or worse questioning why they are doing it. We simply want the process to work fast and efficiently. To use our example from above, computing the weight of a vehicle, we do not want people wasting time by not knowing either what all the components they need to add up or where to find the weights of these components. We don't want two different people performing this process and coming up with two different results. Instead, when we need to execute the process, we want the list of components with their weights readily available, and we want to perform the addition flawlessly. This is the hallmark of a process.

Practices are different. We want questions as to why we are doing things a certain way. In fact, we want to generate arguments or at least critical discussions about what is the best way to obtain a result. If we do not have that, we can easily fall into complacency whereby we produce nothing new or innovative.

Also using our example from above, if we have no discussion about how best to meet our requirements in a design review, we most likely will wind up with pretty much the same product that we produced last time. If that is what we are trying to do, then we should have been engaged in a process not a practice. If, however, we are trying to produce something new and innovative, then by definition we need to do something differently.

This is why it's important to have non-homogeneous groups when we are trying to be innovative. By homogeneous, I'm referring to people that think and act alike. If I want to produce new and innovative things, we need people that have differing views and differing perspectives.

I would like to make the distinction between friction and drag. By friction, I am referring to ideas that, even in opposition to each other, move the discussion forward and result in the synthesis of new ideas.[42] This is very different than people who are naysayers and attempt to find fault with any new idea. We can always prove that we cannot do something. That is pretty easy, and that is drag. The trick is to prove that we can do something new. The friction that I am encouraging in practice is about the synthesis of new ideas and not about negativity or drag.

Optimize versus Satisfice

Because processes can be codeable and calculable, we can attempt to optimize them. We can look at the operations for selecting inputs and we can look at the operations that we perform on those inputs. We can analyze and evaluate each step in the operation and determine whether it has any role in producing the result.

Clearly, the two steps in attempting to optimize the process are: A) eliminate all steps the do not enter into producing the result; B) evaluate alternative operations that may use less resources. The first step is really value stream mapping. Depending on the complexity of the operations and the potential number of alternative operations, the second step may or may not be feasible.

Practices are different because they are results driven, and there may be a universe of possible inputs and the ways to combine them in order to produce the desired result. When that is the case, it very well may be an impossible task to optimize a practice. Instead, what we should be looking to do is to satisfice.[43] By satisfice what we mean to do is to get to a stage where we deem the result to be "good enough." This does not mean settling for mediocrity. But it does mean that we are evaluating the return on our efforts and determining that the future expenditure of resources will not produce an adequate return in the improvement of the desired result.

Autopilot versus Sensemaking

People engaged in processes are effectively on autopilot in more than a metaphoric way. As I defined processes, they are about people running well-defined routines on selected inputs. If they are engaged in normal, everyday processes, this is much like running on autopilot. People are comfortable with processes because, as I will discuss in the next chapter, they are energy efficient. We use less energy performing a routine process than we do in facing a new, challenging problem.

This is not to demean people who engage in processes. Processes make for lean organizations if the processes are well crafted. Since the process-practice distinction is a continuum, processes can run from the truly mindless to those that require some thought in dealing with exceptions. However, autopilots work best when not faced with a lot of exceptions.

People engaged in practices are sensemaking.[44] Practices are about finding the right inputs and routines to obtain the desired outputs. In essence, people work to make sense of the myriad of inputs and routines that they can select from in order to obtain those desired outputs. They are actively engaged in ferreting out those things that will allow them to reach their goal.

While processes pre-define the inputs that need to be selected, practices need to discover the inputs that will give the desired results. Often, those inputs have weak signals.[45] If they did not, it would be obvious that they were important. But being weak, they are not obvious. People engage in sensemaking in seeking them out to explain what is happening and how that will help them reach their goal.

Sensemaking is more difficult and more resource consuming than running on autopilot. However, if we are looking to solve problems and not simply looking at getting through a process, then we need to continually make sense of the inputs we deal with. Changing the inputs and evaluating how the results change is a mechanism we constantly employ. Autopilot is fine for routine tasks. We need sensemaking for problem solving.

The difference between autopilot and sensemaking can be best made by an example. Say we were led into a darkened room containing obstacles in it and told to make it to the door on the other side. Autopilot is the idea that we had been trained to take five steps, forward, two steps to the left, four more steps forward, etc., etc. in order to avoid the obstacles. Sensemaking is the idea that we turn up the light so the pattern of of obstacles emerges from the dark so that we can see the path that we need to take to the other side.

Training-based versus Education-based

We train people to perform processes, but we educate them to engage in practices. Since processes are well defined and codeable, we are interested in the people involved in process doing the same thing over and over in a repeatable fashion. We have already defined which inputs are to be selected. We have also defined which operations that we are to perform on these inputs. We are not looking for a personal interpretation of how to do this. We want the process to be performed in the same way no matter who performs it.

Given that is our criteria, we need to train people. It is not important that they understand why they do things. It is important that they perform the process in the same way each and every time. They do not need to know why they do it, but they do need to know what to do. For processes, we need to train people in what they do for as long as it takes to make them proficient.

Practices are different. For practice, we need to obtain a specific result. We have not defined the inputs, and we have not defined the operations to use. For true innovation, we need people to be free to think about different, and sometimes radically different, ways of doing things. For that, we need education.

We need people to understand and question what they need to do, because we cannot predefine the actions they need to take to get the desired results. But they do need to understand why we are attempting to obtain a result. It is only if they understand the "why" that they can create the "what" to do. With education, we teach people how to critically think about issues. Unlike processes, where we really want people to unquestioningly follow what we have determined that they need to do, with practice, we need people to question the "whys" in hopes of uncovering erroneous assumptions that can be disputed and changed.

As Figure 8.2 shows, process and practice are on a spectrum. Certainly, there are processes the need to be followed in exact detail. Likewise, there are practices where the results have never been accomplished before, and any and all inputs and operations can and should be considered. In the middle of the spectrum, there are processes where there is some discretion in either selecting the inputs or executing the operations. As an example, the purchasing process may define that the lowest bidder is selected. However, purchasing may have some leeway in the selection if they do not think that the low bidder is really capable of performing. The judgment that they use is not defined by a formula but is guided by past experiences.

Likewise there are practices that only consider a small number of inputs and a small subset of operations. When we begin to develop a variation of a product, we do not start with a blank sheet of paper. Instead, we start with the last variation of the product and make modifications to that. Rarely is something that involves people either pure process or pure practice.

PROCESSES DERIVE FROM PRACTICES

To put it in a different way, processes were once practices. It may have occurred through performing ad-hoc practices and recognizing that one way of doing things was superior in terms of resource usage. Or it may have been through a planning process that looked at the desired output and determined that a particular set of inputs operated on in a certain way produced the desired output. Either of these methods are practices.

However, once the desired method is analyzed, formalized, defined, and implemented in a repeatable way, what was once a practice becomes a process.

It is now a process, because it is no longer goal-seeking. The goal or output is now defined as what comes about by following the process. It is a good process if the output produced is always the one that is desired.

PROCESSES AND PRACTICES WITHIN THE PRODUCT LIFECYCLE

The mixture of processes and practices will vary within the product lifecycle and even within the various phases of the product lifecycle. For example, by my definition of the build process, we build the first one, ramp up production, and build the rest of them. Building the first one or to use the more traditional term, manufacturing engineering, can involve a great deal of practice, especially if we are creating innovative new processes for new products. We start off with the desired result, the new product, and should be open to widest range of possibilities to accomplish that. While Boeing has built planes for decades, the 787 Dreamliner required very different processes, as it was the first commercial airliner built from composite materials.

Depending how innovative our new production methods are, ramp-up may require a varying ratio of process to practice. If we simply need incremental improvement, we may be able to use processes to work through ramp-up issues. However, if we have problems with highly innovative processes, we may need to engage in complicated problem solving requiring practices.

Once we are in full production or building the rest of them, we want and need repeatable processes with little or no deviation. If we have developed lean processes, then by definition, any deviation will mean that we are wasting resources.

Figure 8.3 plots various functions of the product lifecycle against the relative need of process and practice for that function. This is meant as a relative indication of how the various functions fall on this process / practice matrix. Depending on the industry, these functions may position differently on the process and practice matrix.

However, I would like to make one particular observation. Most, if not all, major product organizations have groups that focus on process development, improvement, and training. Few, if any, have groups that are focused on practice development, improvement, and education.

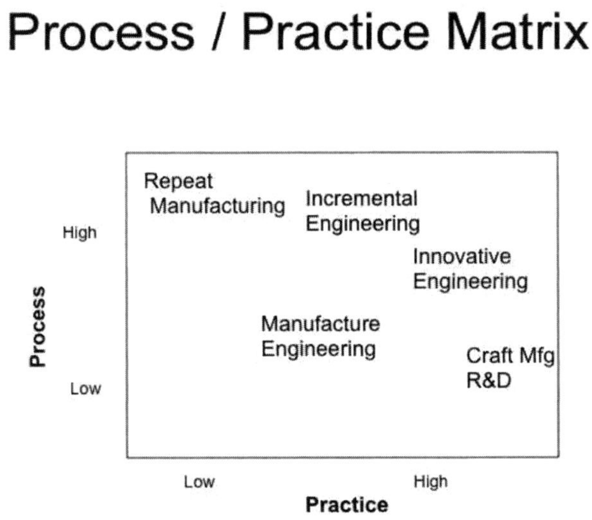

Figure 8.3

MISMATCHED SITUATIONS AND ACTIVITIES

There are some very common situations where processes should be used instead of practices and vice versa. The two that I will discuss are rote practices and bureaucratic processes.

Rote Practices

Rote practices are those activities where it looks like people are engaged in finding the right routines and inputs to obtain the desired result. However, for a number of reasons, the people that are engaged in this activity are just going through the motions.

A common example of this is a meeting that is convened in order to solve a particular problem. However, it is common knowledge by all participants that no matter what ideas are proposed and what discussions occur, the outcome of the meeting will be whatever the boss or decision maker has already decided will be the outcome. This occurs time and time again in numerous organizations. It may not occur all the time, but it occurs enough of the time that it is a common pathology.

The situation is not always a bad thing, and many times it becomes embedded in the organization, because it works. The boss or decision-maker may be in the best position to decide how the organization should best proceed. However, regardless of whether this is an effective strategy or not, the organization is wasting its resources in pretending to engage in a practice. Instead, the organization would be far better off in recognizing that this indeed is a process. The process in this case is that the boss decides and conveys his decision to the rest of the participants.

The one valid use of rote practices is to reaffirm the social system for existing members and indoctrinate new participants. People have a need to understand the social system in which they operate and to understand their role and position in that social system. Even though rote practices may not produce a useful result in an efficient manner, rote practices may be necessary for the maintenance of the social system necessary for the smooth functioning of the organization.[46]

Bureaucratic Processes

The converse of the situation is the bureaucratic process. A bureaucratic process occurs where the inputs are defined and a specific routine is performed. However, it is only by random chance that the desired output is obtained. In fact, in numerous cases the output defies common sense and appears to be absurd. The common cause of this is that the definers of this process have no real understanding of the environment in which this process is supposed to operate or simply do not care.

I recently encountered a process for a university where I am a professor. Last year, my first year teaching for the university, I had to submit an I-9 form and a letter that was signed by a third party who had inspected my passport that proved my U.S. citizenship. That certainly made sense. However, this year the university payroll department is requiring that I submit a new I-9 form and letter. If I was a U.S. citizen last year, it stands to reason that I am a U.S. citizen this year. This process is silly and a waste of resources.

PROCESS AND PRACTICE — DIFFERENT INFORMATION REQUIREMENTS

Where the process / practice distinction has the most impact is on the role of information. A process orientation results in the perspective that participants should only be provided just enough information to do their job in the name of efficiency or leanness. Unfortunately, if what the participants are engaged in is really practice, this perspective leads to starving the participants of the raw material that is needed to really drive innovation. With practices, participants do not know what information they need until after they have successfully produced the output that they are searching for.

Minimal Data versus Maximum Information

With process, we have defined which inputs we are going to consider because we have also defined which operations we are going to perform. If that operation is not going to use an input, then there is no need for the participant to have access to that data or information. In a process, we only want to consider the minimal amount of information that allows us to perform the process and obtain a result.

It was irrelevant to the TSA official how much liquid was actually in the bottle. All the data he needed was the capacity of the physical bottle. The fact that that physical bottle held the allowable amount of liquid was irrelevant to his decision. Also irrelevant to his decision was the fact as to whether or not this passenger really needed that liquid or that this liquid was the most harmless substance in the world. The process that he was following specified that he was to select the physical capacity a container and compare that capacity to 3 ounces. If 3 ounces or less, he was to pass the container. If greater than 3 ounces, he was to reject the container. Other data or information was irrelevant.

Practices are considerably different. With practices, we would like to have the universe of knowledge at our disposal. We are attempting to get a desired result. What we need to do is to explore this universe of possibilities in order to produce that result. Because we are back-solving from a result, we do not know ahead of time which inputs or operations that we need to combine in order to produce the desired result.

This of course is the extreme position. We don't always need an entire universe of knowledge at our disposal. Most of the time, we have a pretty good idea of the potential inputs we need and operations that we can perform to produce the desired result. However, to produce real innovation, we need to make sure that we do not get locked into only considering a subset of available inputs and operations. We can get locked into a situation where what should be a practice degenerates into a process, because we have gotten so comfortable with only using a limited subset of inputs and operations.

It is somewhat amusing to see proponents of "everything is a process" to call for out-of-the-box thinking in order to solve a problem. Thinking of activities as a process when we should be thinking of these activities as a practice is a major reason for getting into the box in the first place. Out-of-the-box thinking should be second nature to us if we are thinking in terms of practices. However, our single-minded focus on process limits our ability to do so.

ART IN ORGANIZATIONS

The discussion about processes and practices would not be complete without at least touching upon the role of art in organizations. If the perspective is that organizations are all about process, then organizations hate to think that art plays a role in what they do. However, with respect to a large number of products, it is a major part of their appeal.

People like products with aesthetic appeal. Automobiles, clothes, shoes, mobile phones, televisions, and a wealth of other products are designed to appeal aesthetically to the product acquirer. The problem with art is that there is no process to obtain an aesthetic product. Likewise, it is difficult to define a desired result that a practice can attack. In the case of art, the result that is obtained is socially constructed, i.e., people decide after the fact whether they like it or not.

Because the result of art is so ill defined, any input is a potential input and any routine is a potential routine. We are attempting to create a form that will please people, but we have no idea if we will succeed until we do. What we basically have to do is let people with artistic temperaments loose and hope that what they will turn out will appeal to our customers. This is as far away from well-defined inputs and well-defined routines as we can get. While we do not like to talk about art in our organization, the form of a product can mean the difference between customer acceptance and customer rejection. Think BMW and Edsel.

This chapter explored what people in organizations really do. It proposed that contrary to the common wisdom that people only engage in processes, people also engage in practices. While processes are input and routine driven, practices are results driven. Both processes and practices are needed for an organization to be successful.

The characteristics of processes versus practices include: lean versus innovative, predictable versus unpredictable, input, routine driven versus goal seeking, precise versus fuzzy, codeable/calculable versus negotiable/arguable, efficient versus effective, frictionless versus friction, optimize versus satisfice, autopilot versus sense-making, and training-based versus education based.

This chapter then defined the characteristics of processes versus practices. The idea of processes and practices has implications for Product Lifecycle Management, although it can apply to many organizational endeavors. The type, organization, and quantity of information needed for process differs markedly from the information needed for practice. The chapter finished with a brief discussion of the role of art in organizations.

Notes

37 My concept of "practice" has its origins in the sociological research on practice. Practice in that respect is about constituting and reconstituting purposeful social relationships and transmitting inter-generational knowledge. (See Bourdieu, P. (1977). *Outline of a Theory of Practice* (R. Nice, Trans.). Cambridge: University Press and Bourdieu, P. (1990). *The logic of practice.* Stanford, Calif.: Stanford University Press.) While there are definitely some elements of that in the practices businesses engage in, I am more focused on the outcome orientation of practice, i.e., producing a specific result. As I discuss later, rote practices have this element of social continuity.

38 There is a more pointed and tougher saying favored by my friend Stephen Sharf, the former Vice-Chairman and Vice-President of Engineering at Chrysler, "There comes a time in every project where you need to kill the engineer."

39 There have been ethnographic studies of engineering design that explores how engineers really work. See Bucciarelli, L. L. (1994). *Designing engineers.* Cambridge, Mass.: MIT Press.

40 What we are looking for has been called disruptive technologies. See Christensen, C. M. (1997). *The innovator's dilemma: when new technologies cause great firms to fail.* Boston, Mass.: Harvard Business School Press.

41 We are only beginning to understand through neuroscience how the specialized parts of our brain work both separately and together. One thing is very certain. Our brain processes data and information distinctly differently than a computer does. See Ramachandran, V. S. (2011). *The tell-tale brain: a neuroscientist's quest for what makes us human* (1st ed.). New York: W. W. Norton.

42 Leonard-Burton refers to this as "creative abrasion" in her book about managing a firm's knowledge assets. See Leonard-Barton, D. (1995). *Wellsprings of knowledge: building and sustaining the sources of innovation.* Boston, Mass.: Harvard Business School Press.

43 The term "satisfice" was coined by the Nobel economist and early computer scientist, Herbert Simon. See Simon, H. A. (1996). *The Sciences of the Artificial* (3rd ed.). Cambridge, Mass: MIT Press.

44 Sensemaking is the word that describes how humans make sense out of the information that comes at them in a continuous flow. For one of the best books on the topic, see Weick, K. E. (1995). *Sensemaking in Organizations.* Thousand Oaks: Sage Publications, Inc.

45 Weak signal inputs are inputs that that do not have a prominence or an obvious role in creating an output. However, they do have a major role, and they are important. In what are called High Reliability Organizations (HRO's), such as hospitals, nuclear reactor sites, or NASA, paying attention to weak signals may head off major problems. The increase in pressure readings on the Deepwater Horizon in April, 2010 prior to the well blowout was a weak signal that should have been focused on. For more on HRO's, see Weick, K. E., & Sutcliffe, K. M. (2001). *Managing the unexpected: assuring high performance in an age of complexity* (1st ed.). San Francisco: Jossey-Bass.

46 For more on social systems and their maintenance, see Berger, P. L., & Luckman, T. (1967). *The Social Construction of Reality: A Treatise in the Sociology of Knowledge.* Garden City: Doubleday & Company.

9

VIRTUALLY HUMAN

Operating in virtual space will require understanding and adapting to a new way of thinking and doing. As we begin to exploit virtual spaces, we are much like the protagonist in Robert Heinlein's science-fiction book classic of the 60s, "Stranger in a Strange Land." The protagonist, Valentine Michael Smith, was a human who was raised by Martians. When he came to earth as an adult, even though he was human, he was perplexed and confounded by a culture, which was completely unfamiliar to him.

Much like Smith, there are many of us that will find the customs and culture of virtual space unfamiliar and confusing. Some of this is generational, but not all. Certainly, much of the younger generation has grown up in virtual space. They understand the cultures and customs of this new space. They are more comfortable texting than talking. They would not know how to coordinate their activities if Facebook did not exist.

But the understanding of virtual space is not a generational dichotomous proposition. It is not simply that the younger generation is completely comfortable with it, and the older generation has no idea of what it is all about. While there may be older individuals who have no idea what the Internet is or still do not have an e-mail address, these individuals are relatively rare in developed countries. They are nonexistent when it comes to the business community, although there may be a few dinosaurs in executive suites that still have secretaries instead of administrators and have these secretaries print out their e-mails and send out responses on their behalf.

As a rule, the older generation has comfortably adopted electronic communication. They email and text as easily as they wrote memos years ago. Most executives I know are on Linkedin. There are even a number of older executives who have Facebook pages and Twitter.

As the first decade of the 21st century came to a close, one of the most talked about topics was "social computing." There are a number of PLM companies that are now touting their support of this. Some of this is hype. Some of this is simply repackaging technologies to share product information. Regardless, there is recognition that collaboration in the form of "social computing" or even plain old e-mail is critical to creating, building, sustaining, and disposing of products.

In my first book, I identified the internal strategic drivers of Product Lifecycle Management as innovation, productivity, quality, and collaboration. If we look at these four characteristics, and ask which one is different, the answer is collaboration.

Innovation, productivity, and quality are all characteristics that we are trying to obtain through Product Lifecycle Management. Collaboration is different in that it is not a characteristic we look to obtain. While innovation, productivity, and quality are all things that we are trying to obtain when we develop products, we are not seeking to obtain collaboration. However, collaboration is a legitimate driver because collaboration is the means by which we can acquire the other three characteristics. Collaboration is a second order internal strategic driver of Product Lifecycle Management, but without it, we do not get the other three characteristics.

There are two main reasons why collaboration is important. The first is that collaboration is an efficient use of resources in accomplishing our objectives. Collaboration, if done properly, increases the amount of brainpower brought to bear on an issue.

Collaboration can increase productivity, because there are more people looking at accomplishing a goal and identifying inefficient use of resources. It can increase innovation, because there are more people with different ideas and different approaches to solving problems and creating value with products. Individuals tend to get locked in to a frame of looking at things. A group of individuals, especially if they possess diverse views, will create a clash of ideas whose resolution will create new and different ways of producing a goal.

In the same way, a single individual may not recognize flaws that lead to problems with quality. A group of individuals will have different ways of looking at the same information and will tend to flesh out the problems that need to be resolved in order to really produce a quality product.

The second reason is that collaboration makes us better performers as individuals. Collaboration is not simply that the group is more than the sum of its parts, but without collaboration, the parts, i.e., the individuals, are diminished. People are social animals, and they tend not to be as capable alone as they are in a collaborative group.

In his 1943 paper,[47] Abraham Maslow proposed a hierarchy of needs that drive human behavior. He proposed that the order of needs that humans sought were: physiological needs, safety needs, social needs, self-esteem needs, and finally self-actualization. However, the latest research in neuroscience seems to indicate that social needs are so strong that they supersede even physiological needs. Man is a social animal. When deprived of the social interaction that collaboration provides, he or she is not nearly as capable as he or she can be in a group.

The process mentality that dominates the thinking in most organizations is that people are cogs in the machine independently going about their work and providing the necessary inputs and performing the necessary tasks that the machine requires. The reality is that the increases in productivity, innovation in product and processes, and quality improvements are the result of the collaborative effort of individuals.

The issue is that, as we have moved into the virtual world, we have moved from collaborative efforts to individual ones. As I will illustrate in the next section, we have moved from open areas where collaboration could take place naturally and where interactions were among individuals. We have moved people into walled cubicles that isolated individuals and moved interactions to human-computer ones.

With the advances in technology that allow us to link individual computers into a shared system, we can reintroduce the collaboration that people need to make them more capable. As shown from the rapid adoption of new technology communication mediums, such as instant messaging, texting, and twittering, people will gravitate to and actively seek out the need to collaborate. The task will be to align these new technological communication methods with the goals and purposes of our organizations. The new water cooler is a virtual one.

VIRTUAL PRODUCT ENGINEERING PRACTICES

One of the more visual examples of the increase in globalization occurred in a presentation given by Terry Kline, Vice President of General Motors, during one of my AUTO^e conferences. There were two slides that showed the change in engineering groups between the 1960s and 2000s. The first slide showed a room the size of a football field, filled with row after row of drafting boards. At many of the boards were engineers in white shirts and skinny ties hunched over their drawings. However, throughout the room, there were clusters of these engineers in what appeared to be discussions about particular drawings. This slide was representative of the engineering group circa 1960s.

The next slide represented the engineering group at the beginning of the 21st century. This was not a slide of a room and people. Instead, it was a map of the world with stars representing the many engineering centers located throughout the various continents. The slide was meant to show the transition from a centralized engineering headquarters to decentralized global centers.

The visual juxtaposition of the massive drafting room with a global map illustrated quite nicely that the companies had gone global and were now distributing their work around the world. I have since used similar visual representations to indicate the globalization of organizations.

While I understood the macro implications of these two slides, I missed the micro implication that was implicit in these two different representations. While engineering groups had gone global in a big way, enabled by technology, there were losing some of the collaborative capabilities that they had in the past. This was also courtesy of the same enabling technology.

The drafting rooms of the 1960s fostered collaboration in ways that were lost in the 2000s. As shown in the picture, the work in the 1960s was available for anyone to look at. Managers and co-workers could walk around the room and look at the work as it progressed from board to board. If one engineer was working on a design and had a question about an interface point that another engineer was working on, all he had to do was walk over to the other board and look at it.

As we moved to the CAD-based electronic systems that enabled us to work globally, we lost this openness and ensuing collaboration. We took the engineers out of the large open rooms and installed them in cubicles. We took the drawings that were open for all to see, and we moved them to personal computer screens in the individual cubicles.

As we did this, we changed the paradigm of how engineers work. Instead of the openness of the past, we made engineering work individual and solitary. The new paradigm became work on the design, clean up the design to get ready for review, and review the design. While the design review was collaborative, the other two steps were not.

In addition, the second step of getting the design ready for review is arguably non-value add. Getting the design ready to review does not really add any value. It may prevent engineers from some embarrassment because he or she has the opportunity to clean up their design. However, that means that they are not as careful as they should be in their designs. When their work was constantly available for all to review, engineers would have paid more attention, knowing that there was not a period for them to clean up their design.

In addition to being structurally inefficient, this new paradigm of engineering also fosters a more serial process, which means that it more likely than not takes more time than it should. The design - clean up - review sequence is a serial sequence rather than the design and collaborate parallel sequence of the past.

This is an example of unintended consequence of technology adoption. It is doubtful that engineering management made a conscious decision to change the environment in which engineers worked. I do not personally know of any executive who said, "Hey, let's get rid of these big drafting rooms and put our engineers in individual cubicles with their own systems. And while we're at it, let's eliminate the spontaneous collaboration that's occurring."

Instead, this new paradigm simply evolved over time. As CAD systems became more powerful and more accessible to any engineer, companies gradually moved their designers and engineers out of the large rooms and into the cubicles. The processes were adjusted to account for the adoption of technology. However, the practices were left to evolve on their own. This unfortunately had the effect of two steps forward and one step back.

I would propose that we rethink this new practice and bring technology to bear on taking us back to the previous collaboration model. I had previously proposed the idea of Virtual Collaboration Rooms to re-create the physical project rooms or war rooms of old. I would like to take this a step further and propose how we should organize engineering centers.

My suggestion is that we re-create the larger collaboration rooms along the lines of the 1960s drafting room. If we don't take the engineers out of their cubicles, then we should at least reduce the height of their cubicles so that they can see over them. I would then propose that we mount display panels around the room and project what each engineer is working on in their cubicle.

This would mean that anyone working on a project could simply look up on the wall and see what everybody else was doing. Rather than the design - cleanup - review cycle that is currently the practice, design and review would take place continuously and simultaneously. Everyone would have the same idea of the state of the project. Problems could be corrected earlier rather than later in a formal review process.

The advantage that we have today is that, unlike the drafting rooms of the 1960s, we are not constrained by physical location. There is no reason that the designs displayed on these projection screens needs to be simply the work that is being done locally. The designs of engineers working on the same project, regardless of where they are in the world, could be displayed. The collaboration could be truly global.

There are some technological issues that need to be addressed to realize such a concept, such as how to consolidate work from multiple workstations, what the latency of the displays might be, how much information we need to move on a global basis, and what the impact is on bandwidth and communication capability. These are all solvable issues. However, the major issue is now cultural.

Designers and engineers have gotten used to and, in fact, may have grown up in, this new environment where they kept their work to themselves, except for the review process. Many of these designers and engineers will be most uncomfortable in having their work available for review at all times. However, if we are to maximize the utility of virtual products, we need to implement continuous, spontaneous, and transparent collaboration.

HARDWARE RULES

Regardless of whether we are one of the new generation that is comfortable with the new computing and communication technology or whether we are one of the old generation that longs for pencil and paper, we are going to have to change in order to effectively use virtual products in virtual space. For the technologically savvy generation, the issue will be to adapt to the workplace. For those that are not technologically savvy, the change requirement will also be to adapt to the new tools of the workplace.

Moving to a world of virtual products will require change. Managing this change will separate the successful organizations from those that are not. While there has been much discussion and research on change management, the most compelling comes from the new area of neuroscience, called NeuroLeadership.

It is not uncommon in organizations to adopt a model of human thinking-as-a-computer. We talk of getting input from people, getting their output, and even developing programs for them. Especially in the technical fields, the model of the human as a computer has a great deal of appeal. People in technical disciplines tend to view themselves as having Spock-like thinking and behaving in ways that is completely logical. This in part explains why we are so enamored with processes.

The reality is that the human brain has very little comparison to a digital computer. We have very different hardware and a very different way of processing than a digital computer. We have to take this very different hardware into account if we are to successfully implement change management in organizations.

This recognition of the impact that our mental hardware has on how we behave both individually and in organizations has spawned a new discipline called NeuroLeadership. The attractiveness of NeuroLeadership is that it is very consistent with the experiences of anyone who has managed people in an organization. Most seasoned executives will come to the same conclusions about human behavior that the findings in NeuroLeadership point to, but it is now nice to know that there is a scientific basis for that understanding.

One of the seminal articles on the topic by David Rock and Jeffrey Schwartz[48] outline the major issues of change management. These issues are "the status quo is energy-efficient, change is pain, behaviorism doesn't work, people change themselves, and focus is key." Taken together, these premises form the basis for understanding how people adapt to change.

Status quo is energy-efficient

What neuroscience tells us is that people use different parts of their brain depending on whether a task is routine or whether it is novel. A routine task is very energy-efficient, while a novel task requires much more energy.

A common example of this is to sit through a couple days of an education class in lieu of the normal work routine. The tendency is for people to feel much more drained and tired than they do from their normal workday. Their spouses are usually incredulous when they complain about being tired. "How can you be exhausted when all you did was sit around all day," the spouse will usually say. It is usually tough for the class attendee to defend this.

The reality is that we use a lot more energy when we are sitting through an educational class that requires us to do some hard thinking. We use a lot less energy when we are sitting at our desks performing routine tasks that are second nature to us. Since people tend to gravitate to using less energy rather than more energy, it makes sense that people will want to do what is familiar rather than undertaking a new way of doing things. People will unconsciously gravitate to the status quo in the interest of conserving energy.

Working with virtual products in virtual space is clearly not the status quo. This means that as people begin transitioning to work with virtual products that we will be asking them to expend more energy than they have in the past. Even for those people who have grown up using technology for social purposes, the transition to a workplace where there is a requirement for efficiency and innovation will be a change to their status quo.

In addition, it is one thing to use these technologies for small, social interactions. It is quite another to use these technologies for longer-term, cohesive projects such as creating, building, and sustaining a new product. It may not matter that my texting with my friends is inconsistent and even contradictory. When I am creating a product with my colleagues, inconsistency is unacceptable.

As we move into the realm of virtual products, we should expect that we would be asking our workforce to expend more energy than they have before. Some individuals will be capable of this, while other individuals may not. We need to be alert in assessing and adjusting workloads. It also may change our evaluation of the performance of individuals. The high performer of yesterday may have been a high performer because he or she had mastered the old routines that were very energy-efficient for them. Thrust into this new model, they simply might not have the required energy for doing the equivalent work in the virtual environment.

Change is pain

We have often heard that change is painful. From the research in neuroscience, we find out that this is true - literally. It turns out that the pain centers in our brain that become active when we experience physical pain, such as spraining a wrist, also become active when we encounter major change situations. The level may not be as intense as the feeling of slamming our fingers in the door, but directionally the pain that we feel when we are subjected to change is similar.

In the same way that we tend to avoid slamming our fingers in the door, we tend to want to avoid change. It is not only energy efficient to maintain the status quo, but it is also comfortable.

In addition, humans have a strong error control circuitry. What this means is that humans quickly detect a difference between what they expect to happen and what does happen. This detection circuitry is in the primitive part of the human brain and evokes strong emotions.

This was an extremely useful mechanism in man's early existence. Our prehistoric ancestor's ability to immediately recognize that the reeds alongside his path were rippling when they were not expected to do so because there was no breeze would have alerted him that he was about to become dinner for a saber tooth tiger unless he immediately reacted. Even though we are not in much danger of becoming a saber tooth tiger's dinner, our error detection circuitry is embedded deep into our brains.[49]

This reaction to change can be deep and visceral. We can experience strong emotional reaction to change that overrides a more logical approach. Without conditioning, people can easily experience a reaction that causes a flight, fight, or freeze reaction. This has been called an "amygdala hijack"[50] and refers to the very primitive reptilian part of our brain, the amygdala, taking control from our higher reasoning centers.

Working in a virtual environment will be especially difficult because it is a totally new environment, devoid of the cues of the everyday world that makes us comfortable. People who need tangible cues such as pieces of paper, physical prototypes, and material mockups will find themselves very uncomfortable, and even painfully uncomfortable, in dealing with virtual objects in a virtual environment.

When putting people into this new environment, we need to carefully assess their reaction to it. Some individuals will be comfortable, and we can accelerate their usage of virtual objects in virtual environments. Other people will literally experience this as a painful event. If we simply dismiss their reaction as silliness, we run the risk of these individuals engaging in detrimental behavior as they seek to avoid a painful situation.

For these individuals, we will need to go slower, so that the amount of change that they have to undergo is less. We also need to be on the lookout for coping behaviors, such as printing voluminous reports or having to reproduce blueprints for any change in the design.

In some ways, changing to a virtual environment is similar to getting into physical shape. For someone who is out of shape, engaging in too much exercise brings on a substantial amount of pain, rather than benefit. That pain leads people to stop exercising, rather than continuing. The more effective solution is to engage in light exercise that slowly builds up. While there will be some discomfort, it will not be so debilitating so as to cause the abandonment of exercise.

We should use the same philosophy for people who are "out of shape" with respect to dealing with the virtual environment. We should have these people start slowly, get used to those changes, and continue to increase their involvement until they become comfortable in the virtual environment.

Behaviorism doesn't work

Behaviorism is the idea that if we present humans with the right stimulus then we will get the response we are looking for. Behaviorism emerged in the 1930s from the work of the psychologist, B.F. Skinner. It is best typified by the example of Pavlov's dog, where by associating a dinner bell with the delivery of food, simply ringing the dinner bell caused the dog to salivate.

The issue is that extending the behavior of animals to thinking humans does not work so well. Both academic research and, more importantly, workplace experience suggests that the simple stimulus-response model is insufficient to get people to change behavior. People are not simply reactive actors, waiting to be manipulated by stimuli. Instead they can be proactive in "gaming" the system to bring about outcomes that they desire.

Reward and punishment systems are routinely used by organizations in an attempt to get people to do what the organization wants them to do. The idea is that reward systems will get people to do what the organization wants them to do, and punishment system will stop people from doing what the organization does not want them to do. Even in this basic premise, organizations often get it wrong by trying to reward people for not engaging in undesired behavior and punishing them if they do not produce a behavior that the organization wants.

However, even when used in the appropriate manner, reward and punishment systems at best get short-term results. Rarely, if ever, is there a permanent change in behavior.

The reason that it is temporary is that people are awfully clever in turning these systems to their advantage. A good example of this is sales compensation systems. As I found out from having a couple of hundred salespeople working for me in one of my companies, salespeople are inordinately clever in working a compensation system to their advantage. More often than not, the sales reward and punishment system, while directionally successful, was always mediated by the unintended ways (at least unintended to me) that salespeople work the system.

Getting people to change the way that they think and interact with products will require long-term change and not the short-term effect that reward and punishment systems bring. While we may get people to try these new methods by using a carrot and preventing them from using older methods by using a stick, we will need much more than that to change long-term behavior.

In an aerospace company that I worked with, they were moving to a 3-D model-based environment from 2-D drawings. They had a well thought out work release system, and they had a compensation system that rewarded people for moving in this direction. Some of the individuals involved did just enough work according to a new procedure in order to receive their bonuses. However, they then delayed fully adopting the new system, because they were much more comfortable with paper 2-D drawings.

They delayed until such a point in time that the more time-consuming, but more information generating PLM method, could not be done without delaying the project. They then reverted to their 2-D release system in order to meet the deadline to release parts. My message to the top management was that, unless they modified this group's overall behavior, this would be what happened each and every time. Behaviorism was not going to change these long-term and system-working behaviors.

People change themselves

If behaviorism doesn't work, that is, if crafting a system of reward and punishments do not change people's behaviors, then what does? The answer is that people change themselves. The evidence from neuroscience is that people literally rewire themselves in order to change the way that they think.

While we think that we can change the people that we are responsible for, the best that we can do is to create conditions in which they change themselves. Our ancestors were onto something with the old adage, "you can lead a horse to water, but you can't make him drink." We can lead people into situations where they can change their behavior themselves, but, in the end, we cannot change their behavior.

This often gets confused in the way we look at organizational training and education. We often think that if we give people training in tools and processes that this will translate into the way they think about how they perform their jobs. We are also often disappointed. Training is useful for improving proficiency, but it requires education in order to give people the necessary resources so they can make the decisions required to effect change.

When we want people to move to a virtual environment, we will need to educate them on the reasons and benefits. Simply changing the process and telling them to follow it will not suffice. For a concept like Product Lifecycle Management, we need to educate people in what that means not only for them but for everyone else working with the product. If they are simply looking at their own area, it may seem to them that we are asking them to do more work than they have done before. That may be the case, because in looking at the entire product lifecycle, it may be more efficient to create the data that is needed downstream in an earlier phase. In the past, that information was created some time later at much greater expense.

While people may not be wildly enthusiastic on taking on more effort, if they are educated on the larger picture and understand the ramifications of this additional work, they will be more accepting of it. If we simply tell them that we have changed the process, then, without giving them the appropriate education, they will be less accepting and may be very creative in working to meet the letter of the process rather than the spirit.

Focus is key

So how do we get people to be in a position where they will change themselves? The answer is that we put them in situations where they can devote the necessary attention and focus in order to do so. When that happens, they will literally rewire their brains, and, as an additional bonus, feel good about it.

This is not an unusual phenomenon. In fact, I would bet against anyone not having experienced it. The "it" is the moment of insight, when everything seems to click, and we gain a new understanding of how things work. When this moment of insight comes, we also experience a wave of euphoria or satisfaction that accompanies this understanding.

From a neuroscience perspective, what happens at the point of insight is that there is a sudden burst of gamma rays that occurs. What this wave oscillation does is to create new links and connections across many parts of the brain. What we are doing is literally rewiring our brain with a new understanding.

This does not happen haphazardly. The key to this happening is our ability to intensely focus on a situation. We are not empty vessels in which this information is poured into us. Instead, we need to be put in situations where we focus long enough and hard enough to produce this change effect. Organizations that simply put people into training sessions where they are passive participants will not get people to effect a change in themselves.

When we are talking about fundamentally changing the way people deal with products, moving from a physical-based environment to a virtual-based environment, we will need to create the educational environments to foster the proper focus for people to make these changes. Ideally, we should immerse people into these new environments, giving them meaningful problems to solve, in order to create the attention and focus that they will need.

The final step that we should keep in mind is that we need to take the ability to revert to the status quo off the table. We should not do it prematurely, but much like the general who burned his boats once he got his troops to the other side of the river so they could not retreat, there is a point in time when we need to move people off the comfort and energy efficiency of the status quo. In my example of drawing release above, the people knew that they could go back to a manual drawing release system if they delayed long enough. That is precisely what they did. Organizations must anticipate that and prevent that from happening.

However the timing of taking the status quo off the table is important. If it is done too quickly, and people have not changed themselves, then there is an opportunity for causing much pain and turmoil within the organization. If it is done too late, organizations will lose precious time and resources in moving to a more effective and innovative way of creating, building, sustaining, and disposing of products. While there is no one time that is right for all organizations, an assessment plan of how well people are making the changes is key to determining the appropriate time.

VIRTUAL SPACE AND KNOWLEDGE RETENTION

It may be that the most important uses of virtual space will be in the capturing, organizing, and making available the knowledge assets of the organization. The contention has been made that the bulk of organizational knowledge is contained not within structured or even unstructured information that the organization owns, but in the heads of its people. Given the amount of data we are capturing on a daily basis, this may no longer be true in terms of volume. However, the critically useful information that organization possesses is undoubtedly within people's brains.

While organizations may have well-developed knowledge management systems and standards that define the knowledge of that organization, the way most organizations deal with critical issues is still through subject matter experts (SMEs). Where there is a concern about a certain issue in design, such as operational parameters that are getting close to their limits, or there is simply a thorny problem that the people involved have not faced before, the common response is to bring in an SME, lay out the issue, and get his or her recommendation as to what to do. In the majority of cases, the organization then defers to the SME as to the course of action.

However, three things are occurring that are hindering this approach. First economic pressure to reduce costs has reduced the number of SMEs that are available. Many organizations can no longer afford the luxury of having technical experts for small and sometimes highly arcane areas to be simply waiting around to be called. Generally these people became subject matter experts because they were allotted the time to investigate and understand their area thoroughly. Many organizations have been forced to eliminate individuals who do not have day-to-day usefulness to current projects.

The second issue is that as companies have gone global, SMEs may not be in the right geography in order to lend assistance. This issue is twofold. First, these individuals may exist, but others within the organization who are not co-located with them are not aware of who they are or what they know. Second, SMEs may not have enough access to the information that they need about the problem. The subject matter expert may need to be physically present with some material or prototype in order to understand what exactly is happening. This has historically been handled by having the subject matter expert travel to the location. However many organizations effectively cut out all travel during 2009, which inhibited these experts from going to where the problem was.

The global access issue can be handled by technology. The ability to use computing and communications technology in order to, in essence, telepresence into other geographical locations will become more and more effective.

The third and most serious issue is that there will be a huge knowledge gap that will start to occur as the baby boomers begin leaving the workforce. In the past, this was not an issue, because organizations had a steady stream of people training in their SME ranks so that as one person retired, another who had trained under that person took his or her place. However, in the 1980s organizations went through substantial periods of downsizing, when they eliminated a substantial portion of their less experienced workforce.

It is this workforce that would have gone on to become future subject matter experts, but because they were eliminated, there is now a gap between the individuals who are retiring now and the new hires that were added during the expansion years of the 1990s. Unless something is done, and done quickly, as the baby boomer generation retires, substantial institutional knowledge about how things work, how to solve particular problems, and why things are designed as they are will be lost.

Virtual space is a potential solution for this problem. One of the premises behind PLM stated earlier was that the understanding of the physical world would be better and better captured in the virtual world.

As we capture the knowledge of subject matter experts and build them into product-oriented knowledge bases, we will not be in the position of having lost that information. However it is not enough to simply capture that information, we also have to implement cued availability. What this means is that as the less experienced workers go about their job, rather than having to search for this information, it should be presented to them.

We're starting to see tools that associate the knowledge of the subject matter experts with the work that is being done on new products. By categorizing or even ontologically recognizing product types, we can draw upon knowledge bases to produce the required aspects for that product.

For example, if an engineer is working on a crankshaft, the system will automatically create requirements for stiffness and durability from its knowledge of previous crankshafts. In addition it will require specific tests and verifications that these requirements have been met.

It is also proposed that people will learn best by doing.[51] The issue in the physical world is that doing things can be very expensive. Crashing vehicles into walls or tearing the wings off of airplanes is not a feasible approach for having engineers learn about the limits of design. However, virtual space can provide them a high fidelity and realistic environment in which they can learn the tools and tricks of their trade. By using simulation, engineers can quickly determine whether or not they have understood and addressed their design issues completely.

At the education level, this is showing signs of being highly productive. Purdue University, for example, has started to require their students in certain design courses to actually simulate the actions of their designs. Students find out very quickly that while their design may look particularly elegant, it simply does not work. In the past they might have convinced themselves that they really understood the design, only to find out once they were required to do it after they graduated, that their understanding was woefully inadequate. Using industry simulation tools, the students get an excellent grasp of not only what the design would look like, but also how it would work in actual conditions.

While capturing and organizing information in virtual space is a productive idea, it is especially important given the demographics of the workforce as they exist. Virtual space will both capture information from soon-to-be retired-experts, along with giving less experienced employees a means to quickly and inexpensively gain the experience and expertise that they will need.

ORGANIZATIONAL CHANGES

There is no such thing as an independent organizational entity, even though we tend to talk and even treat organizations as such. However, organizations do not think and act independently of the people that make them up. Organizations are simply the sum total of the people who make up those organizations. However, organizations structure how people behave and even think. The same individual in two different organizations may act and even think differently depending on the organization within which he or she resides.

Different organizations have different processes, practices, policies, and even culture. These different approaches to behavior color the way people act and think within their respective organizations. While we may think that we are moving from a physical to a virtual world, unless this is supported by organizational constructs, the changes to people within these organizations will be superficial at best.

Roles

The impact of roles within the organization is often underestimated. I once had an organization in which there was a dysfunctional group. This group had a number of members, none of which were named as the team leader. There was constant grumbling within the group and constant pushback on the tasks that they were assigned. This was a group that was always unhappy. There was nothing that I could do that would please this group of people.

There was one individual within the group whom I will call Tom. Tom, I thought, was the most reasonable of the individuals within the group, and I found that he had some good ideas whenever he was coaxed into at least coming up with something.

I made Tom the team leader. The next day he fired his best friend in the group, Alan. When I asked him why he fired Alan, Tom said, "Alan is the biggest whiner you have ever seen. Nothing ever makes him happy. He poisons the group." When I raised my eyebrow and said to him, "But wasn't Alan your best friend? So why did you fire him?" Tom replied, "Yesterday, I wasn't the team leader. Today, I am."

Tom's behavior clearly changed when he became "Team Leader." When he was one of the group, Tom felt no obligation to do anything about Alan's behavior. Once he became the team leader, his role required that he be responsible for the cohesiveness of the group, and he took prompt action in order to affect that.

Official Roles

If we are to get new behaviors out of individuals, then we need to create and implement new roles for our people. Most of today's roles are intra-functional, which means that the people within those roles are concerned only with their own function. If we are to move to cross-functional activities within organizations, then we will need to craft roles that are also cross-functional in nature. We will need to craft roles that implement cross-functional groups, so that we can have people thinking outside of their functional area.

In the past, this may not have been possible, because organizations were arranged around physical parts. However, with the advent of virtual parts, anybody anywhere can have access to the virtual product. We can now implement cross-functional approaches to dealing with that virtual product. Marketing no longer has to wait until there is a physical prototype in order to be thinking about marketing material. Manufacturing can start to design manufacturing and assembly processes that will result in manufacturing the physical product as soon as design reaches the stage of a virtual product that allows it to be simulated.

However, as the above paragraph illustrates, our thinking about roles needs to create some new vocabulary in role description. Marketing, manufacturing, and support functions need to participate in product creation and not simply be the recipients of their output. Instead of being simply a marketing role, marketing will need to have roles such as Marketing-Product Creation. Manufacturing needs to be Product Creation and Manufacturability.

We need to give careful thought as to how we craft these official roles, how we name them, and how we define them. This will affect how people behave. If we have titles and roles the same as we had in the past, we can expect to get behavior similar to what we had in the past. If we expect new behavior and changed behavior, then we have to define and describe our roles for people differently.

Unofficial Roles

As much as executives like to think that they are in control of their organizations, organizations are also social entities. As such, people adopt social roles within the organization that are not under the control of management.

Common roles include thought leader, worker bee, contrarian, and the indispensable person. I would like to pick two of these roles that are applicable to virtual products and Product Lifecycle Management and discuss them.

It is extremely important that we get the thought leader on board with respect to virtual products. Sometimes the thought leader is the manager of the group, but often he or she is a member of the group whom the people look up to and respect his or her opinion. In any kind of change situation, it is critical that we get the thought leader to support the change.

If we intend to move to a virtual product environment, we need to pay special attention to educating and training the thought leader. While it does not solve all of our problems, having the thought leader in sync with what our intentions are with respect to virtual products and how we expect the organization to adopt them is important in getting the rest of the people also in sync.

If we lose the thought leader, we may be able to prevail in the long-term. The rest of the group usually does not blindly follow the thought leader, even though he or she generally has a great deal of influence. However, it will be much more difficult. If the thought leader is opposed to virtual products or cannot make the change to think about products differently, then my recommendation, harsh though it may be, is to eliminate the thought leader. Otherwise, progress will be hard to come by in adopting virtual products by the rest of the organization.

The other role that we sometimes find in the organization is the "indispensable person." This is the individual who people depend on whenever there is a crisis to step in and solve the problem. When an organization has an "indispensable person," there are generally many situations that require their assistance.

I've acquired over a hundred companies in my career. Whenever I have acquired one of these companies, I would ask if that organization had an indispensable person. In a substantial number of these organizations, the answer would be in the affirmative. People would say, "Yes, Sally is our indispensable person. We do not know what we would do without her."

I would then promptly call Sally into the office. I would sit Sally down and inform her that I was letting her go. As one might imagine, this usually stunned the organization. (Sally was not generally thrilled, either!) My rationale for this was that the indispensable person generally made himself or herself indispensable. They kept information to themselves so that they would be indispensable. There were numerous times for them to be called on to be indispensable, because in essence they fostered that.

In the vast majority of the cases, once I got rid of the indispensable person, and people realize that they were going to have to solve problems on their own, the organization began to run smoother. There was no longer a gatekeeper for information. People now had access to information and could use that information to do their jobs much better. Chances are that if an organization has a heroic firefighter who is always being called upon then that same person is also a pyromaniac causing their fires.

The issue here is that virtual products are about information, and indispensable people will want to control that. But under the philosophy of Product Lifecycle Management, this information needs to be widely shared in order to allow people to trade off information for wasted resources. The availability of this information will eliminate the dysfunctional need to have an indispensable person. Sharing this information freely allows all the individuals to be better at their jobs collectively.

Organizational Culture

Paradoxically, company cultures will become both more fluid and more rigid. This will only work if companies make the distinction between practice and process. Virtual products will enable anyone, anywhere, both within the organization and within the supply net, to collaborate on producing products that are both innovative and lean. Since participants can have access to the virtual product regardless of their geography, organizations can be very fluid in creating and disbanding virtual teams. The requirement to have people that are local to each other collaborate because they need to share the same physical product no longer exists.

Organizations will be more rigid in implementing processes across the entire organization. The Chinese have an old saying that, "Heaven is high and the Emperor is far away." This described that the farther that one was geographically separated from the capital, the more freedom to do things one had. This saying could adequately describe organizations. The farther away from headquarters a group was, the more independent they were.

In this age of virtual connections, geographical distance has minimal impact. Global organizations are dictating that processes they deem efficient be done no matter the location. Factories in different locations are implementing the same processes. If one factory improves on the process, that process is immediately exported to the other factories. Organizations, with virtual capabilities, can now have instantaneous visibility into all their locations.

This cultural change will have a dual effect. People involved with processes will find their ability to do things differently highly constrained. People with practices will find themselves pushed to extend who they work with and what resources they consider. They will also find that they can no longer get comfortable with a specific group of people or specific way of doing things. Practice groups will be formed and dissolved according to the tasks at hand.

Cultural change, like all other change, can be painful. It can also be slow, because organizations have a built-in inertia to resist change. The move to virtual products will force many individuals out of the comfortable way that they have done things in the past. The end result will be an improvement in both efficiency and effectivity, but it will not be without pain and resistance.

People will be "strangers in a strange land." But not for long.

This chapter explores the human element of Product Lifecycle Management in its use of virtual space. The internal strategic driver, collaboration, is necessary in order to obtain the other internal strategic drivers: productivity, innovation, and quality. People are inherently social animals and moving into virtual space does not eliminate that need.

Even though we may have taken a step backwards by taking people out of large collaborative areas and putting them in front of solitary computers, we have not lessened the need for collaboration. We need to rethink that strategy. We need to think about creating Virtual Collaboration Rooms (VCR's) that will allow people to engage in spontaneous collaboration, regardless of whether their collaborators are next to them or across the globe.

The movement to virtual space also does not mean that people should be viewed as possessing computer-like capabilities. Humans have very different computing hardware than computers have and recent neuroscience research has shed some new light on how people think and act. In looking at the change that people must undertake in order to move into a virtual environment, we need to be cognizant of these premises: the status quo is energy efficient, change is pain, behaviorism doesn't work, people change themselves, and focus is the key to having people make these changes.

This chapter also discusses the use of virtual space and that the need to retain the knowledge of workers will become increasingly important. There is expected to be a knowledge gap as the baby boomers retire. Using virtual space to capture this knowledge will allow us to better address these issues.

Organizations need to address the fact that it is organizational structure that will drive behaviors as we move to virtual space. We need to give thought to the roles that we assign to people, because these roles have a structuring effect on their behavior. We need to consider not only official roles, but also unofficial roles within the organization.

Finally we need to understand that organizational culture will become both more fluid and more rigid. The practice aspect of organizations will become more fluid, while the process areas will become more rigid. This cultural change will most likely be painful, and organizations need to be prepared to address that.

Notes

47 See Maslow, A. A. (1943). A Theory of Human Motivation. *Physchological Review, 50*(4), 370-396.

48 See: Rock, D., & Schwartz, J. (2008). The Neuroscience of Leadership. *Strategy + Business*(43), 1-10.

49 For a very readable explanation of this, see Gladwell, M. (2005). *Blink: the power of thinking without thinking* (1st ed.). New York: Little, Brown and Co.

50 The book that the term is credited to is: Goleman, D., Boyatzis, R. E., & McKee, A. (2002). *Primal leadership: realizing the power of emotional intelligence.* Boston, Mass.: Harvard Business School Press.

51 See Pfeffer, J., & Sutton, R. I. (2000). *The knowing-doing gap: how smart organizations turn knowledge into action.* Boston: Harvard Business School Press.

10

VIRTUALLY INFORMED

Product Lifecycle Management is by its definition about product information. In order to be useful and even to be "information," this product information needs to be organized and categorized. One of the ways that we have categorized product information is by its stage in the lifecycle. We can think of this product information in terms of the phase where we create this information and use it for that phase and future phases. Therefore we can categorize it according to the product lifecycle phases of create, build, support, and dispose.

The other way to categorize product information is by whether it is related to the product's function or the product's form. While the age-old premise of "form follows function" implies that the two are related, product form and product function do have different informational structures. Because product form and product function do have different informational structures, the age-old premise is also an age-old problem. Creating a product form that produces the desired product function is a difficult task.

So I will describe what I believe to be the important informational structures for products. It is not intended to be an exhaustive list, but it is intended to describe the major informational structures that Product Lifecycle Management needs to deal with. Categorization is rarely as neat and as well defined as the people who develop these categories would like.

As a result, there may be some disagreement as to my categorization. However, it will hopefully provide a starting point and an understanding of what informational structures Product Lifecycle Management needs to deal with. If any organization is ignoring one of the structures, then it may help them understand why they may be having problems in creating, building, supporting, or disposing of their product.

Product Information Structures

Phase	Structure	Type
Create	Requirements	Function
	Product structure	Form
	Schematics	Function
	Mechatronics Code	Function
	Product creation workflow	Both
	Engineering Data (CAE/CAT)	Function
Build	Bill of Process	Form
	As-builts	Form
Support	As-Maintained	Form
	Operational State Changes (OSC)	Function
	Bill of Support	Form
	Product Operational Instructions (POI)	Function
Dispose	Bill of Disposal	Form

Table 10.1

It is important to note that when I am talking about informational structures that I am talking about this information primarily residing in computerized form. Up until recently, computerized informational structures were relatively simple, with the information consisting of symbols in a structured form.

Today, information can be highly non-structured and still be easily searchable. However content is no longer limited to symbols such as text or numbers. Content can be images, videos, or, as in the case of geometric designs, proprietary structures. The informational structures that I will talk about in this chapter are organized information, but not necessarily structured information. The content can easily be symbols, images, videos, simulations, or other content packages that contain relevant information.

These informational structures that I will discuss structure the organization of the information type, but not necessarily the content details. Therefore my focus will not be on the content and its specific structure. Content will vary and vary considerably depending on the application software that creates this content. My focus will be on the categories of product information that PLM needs to deal with and a general description of the characteristics in those structures.

When I say, "PLM needs to deal with," I need to emphasize the premise that PLM is an approach and not a specific software application. There may be many different kinds of software applications, some of them not originating from traditional PLM software providers, that produce or consume these product-oriented information structures. Those individuals, both from the business side and the information systems side, who have the responsibility for overseeing PLM within their organization will need to insure that they consider all of these informational structures. They need to have the appropriate say into their formation and use in order to effectively implement PLM. Ignoring one or more of these will result in wasted resources in such areas as information re-creation or duplicate, inconsistent information resulting in time delays and costly rework.

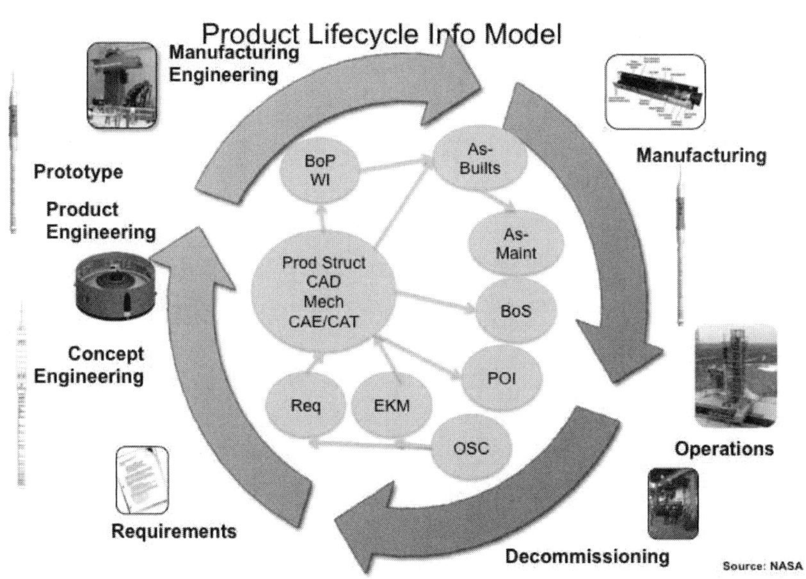

Figure 10.1

Table 10.1 contains a list of the product information structures that I will deal with in this chapter, along with how I categorize it as to it being about product structure, behavior, or both. Figure 10.1 graphically illustrates where these information structures come into play during the product lifecycle. I will move through the product lifecycle of create, build, support, and dispose and discuss the main information structures of each of these phases.

CREATE PHASE

Requirements

Defining and managing requirements is critical in creating a product that is useful to its user. It is also one of the most difficult and hard to manage aspects of product creation. The task of mapping requirements to product design is a difficult task at best. Being able to say that this design parameter allows us to meet this specific requirement can range from a simple formula to black art.

When we have the not uncommon occurrence of competing and even contradictory requirements, the problem gets even worse. When we have a requirement of vehicle safety and vehicle fuel economy, we are going to have to trade off one for the other. As discussed in a previous chapter, the question of how we do this is not a process. It is a practice with arguments and negotiation.

The issue generally becomes that the further we get into the development process the further removed from the source of requirements we become. As we start to change things, we may lose sight of the requirements that we are attempting to meet. In many cases, the product development activities take a life of its own, and we start to make changes in the product because of costs, technical reasons or even expediency without understanding how these changes impact our ability to meet our desired requirements.

This will always occur. However, what we need is for our PLM system to maintain the links between our requirements and our designs. Given the complex designs that we deal with in automobile, aerospace, and medical equipment, to name just a few industries, it is difficult if not impossible for humans to maintain all these linkages without the help of PLM applications. We simply do not have the attention to detail and the ability to process the amount of detailed information required to do this.

The problem is that many requirements may not be described in a formula. They in fact may be fuzzy, such as "we need to build a vehicle that is safe." How we link "safe" to a statement that "the vehicle will have a crumple zone that absorbs the impact of X miles an hour" is a matter of judgment and not formula.

Product Lifecycle Management is in a relatively early stage of organizing and maintaining requirements linked to design specifications. However, it is one of the more important areas and is a key informational structure.

Product structure

In the create phase, product structure is arguably the most important information construct. Much like the human skeleton is the organizing structure of the human body, product structure organizes the various components that make up a product. While product structure is an abstract concept, it is no less important to organizing a product than the human skeleton is to organizing the human body.

Because product structures are arbitrary, they may be subject to change. Different people looking at the same product could reasonably come up with different product structures. However, the key is to settle on one, even if it is arbitrary. If the groups working on different areas of the product are allowed to create their own product structures or, worse yet, have no product structure, then confusion will result. The components will only come together with an inordinate waste of resources in resolving version and interface problems.

There are two main product structures in the create phase. These two structures are Bill of Materials and CAD product structure. While they are similar, different groups within the organization usually control them. However, these two information structures need to be tightly coupled in order to provide a cohesive view of the product.

The key aspect of both these structures is that they are hierarchical in nature. They in essence have a main node, which is the product itself, with branches off into sub nodes, which are assemblies, subassemblies, and individual components. Again, the divisions of this hierarchy may be arbitrary, but they definitely need to be consistent.

The CAD structure is a hierarchy of geometric designs. The CAD structure consists of assemblies, subassemblies, components, and parts. Historically, it has been a common practice to use the part number to define product structure. For example, part AAA and part AAB may be part of assembly AA. As CAD came into being, it was natural to name the CAD files with this part number.

Relying on part numbers to define structure is generally a good recipe for problems. The reason is that if someone fails to conform to the naming convention, CAD files can be orphaned or can replace unrelated CAD files that have the same name. CAD files need to be expressly defined and maintained within the PLM system. Again, it may be that there are different ways that the structure could be organized. However the key is to pick one, communicate that structure to all participants, and consistently enforce it.

The Bill of Materials is also a product structure. While geometric structures are important to defining a product, they are not the only things that a product consists of. Products also have elements that are non-geometric in nature. Product elements such as coatings, paints, powders, and lubricants are key aspects of a product, but have not typically shown up on a CAD drawing as a feature, although that is changing as CAD systems progress from being drawing-oriented to being model-oriented.

The Bill of Materials is a complete list of all the parts and components that make up a product. The Bill of Materials is also a hierarchical structure in that an assembly is broken down into sub assemblies; subassemblies are broken down into components; and components are broken down into their respective parts. Each of these items has a part number that identifies it.

CAD structures and Bill of Material structures do not have a one-to-one correspondence, although, as shown, in Figure 10.2 aspects of their structure should be in correspondence. Neither of these structures fully defines the product. It takes both of these structures.

One of the ways that this is accomplished is that when a product is released, the Bill of Materials and the CAD drawings are packaged together as a single release element. The Bill of Materials describes all the parts that need to be consumed in order to create the product, and the CAD drawings describes all the features of all the geometric parts.

This was a method that occurred when the Bill of Materials and geometric designs were paper-based. It was and still is a very labor-intensive process to create the Bill of Materials, obtain all the drawings for the parts of the Bill of Materials, copy the entire package, and distribute it to all the engineering and manufacturing personnel who need it.

The problem with this method is that it is time and resource consuming. At the time this development package is "published," the package publisher needs to stop the development process and collect all the CAD drawings called for in the Bill of Materials. This also assumes that the publisher can determine which is the latest versions and ensure that they do match up with the Bill of Materials. Many times the first pass at this is not successful, because it does not contain the latest CAD drawings, but some previous version. This necessitates the publishing process to be done all over.

This is not lean because it slows the development process and requires not an insignificant amount of resources in order to accomplish this task. It also diminishes innovation, because work is stopped on new versions of the product while the publishing process is taking place.

In addition, it is inconsistent with the current division of responsibilities within today's organizations. Usually different groups manage the CAD representations and the Bill of Materials. Manually coordinating these groups can often become a logistical nightmare.

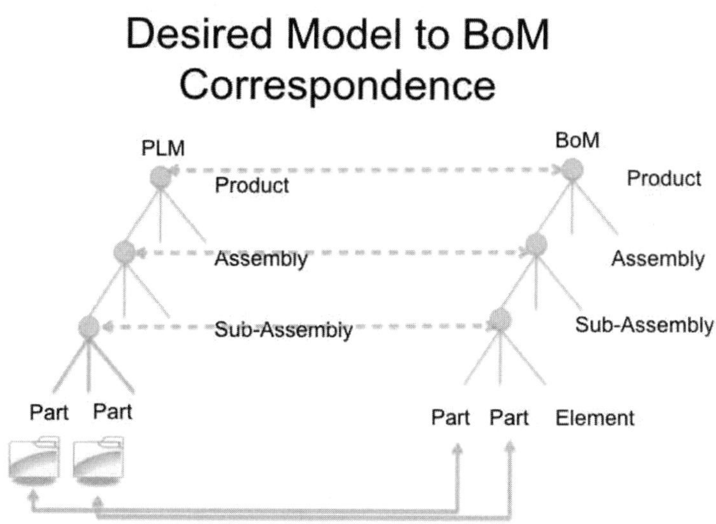

Figure 10.2

PLM's answer is to use its control of product data to link the CAD structure and the Bill of Material structure. As Figure 10.2 shows, the links between these two structures are maintained within the PLM system and, at any point in time, authorized individuals within the organization can acquire the latest Bill of Material structure, along with the correct associated geometry.

Versions

If the coordination between Bill of Materials and CAD drawings were a one-time event, then we would be talking about a relatively trivial issue. The problem is that during the create phase there will be many different versions of both the geometry and the BOM. The issue becomes how and what to version as the changes are made.

While the revision of individual component may be handled by including a revision number or letter as a designator appended to the part number, as is commonly done, or in the metadata that accompanies the CAD file, it becomes more complicated when the product structure changes. The rule that is generally followed is that, if adding or deleting a part or component changes the level of the product structure, then the next higher level is revisioned also. If only a part or component at a certain level is revisioned, then the next higher level is not revisioned.

On the Bill of Materials side, the general rule is that any time a revision is made to a level, the next higher level is also revised. Because the Bill of Materials are much more abstract than product structure, they are easier to revise. This is both good and bad news. The bad news part of this is that because the Bill of Materials is so easy to revise, it is much easier for different Bill of Materials to proliferate throughout the organization.

As it stands today, the different phases of the lifecycle can and usually do have their own Bill of Materials. Engineering can have an Engineering Bill of Materials (EBOM). Manufacturing can have a Manufacturing Bill of Materials (MBOM). Support can have a Support or Provisioning Bill of Materials (SBOM or PBOM). While they all describe the same product, each of these Bills of Materials may differ, and differ considerably, from each other.

With respect to product structure, we need to keep in mind the characteristics of Product Lifecycle Management that pertain here. Probably the most important characteristic, cohesion, is the biggest challenge. The different views of the product structure must be cohesive and consistent with each other. If cohesion fails, we easily have a Bill of Materials that call for parts that have no geometric design or we can have geometric designs that do not show up on the Bill of Materials.

Traceability is also important. From being nice to have to being legally required, traceability of the changes in either structure or geometry is a necessity if we want to understand how and why the product evolved. This is especially important if we find that we have issues with the product not meeting its performance requirements and understanding what changes that we made to the product in order to address these issues. This is critically important in the product liability area, where a plaintiff's attorney ideal dream is to discover that we found that we had a problem with the product but made no changes. We need to trace that development path in order to have proof positive that we addressed product issues as they arose.

Information singularity is always important during the create phase. One of the major sources of wasted resources is working on obsolete versions of the product design. By controlling for singularity of information, we can ensure that everyone working on the design is working on the latest version of that design. One of the byproducts of not having product structure is that we cannot enforce singularity. How can we know what is the latest version of a component, when we have no product structure context in which to place it?

Cued availability also comes into play here in that as people work on aspects of the design, the PLM system needs to be presenting them with the latest version of both product structure and its individual components. People need to be alerted to a change of CAD product structure or the Bill of Materials. While the PLM system may not be smart enough for the foreseeable future to understand the implications of the changes, simply alerting the participants that a change has occurred can be sufficient to prevent the waste of effort in working on obsolete designs.

Variants

What really complicates product structure is when the product allows for variants, as products often do. A variant of the product structure is an allowable configuration where there are multiple options for the product. For example, a vehicle may have manual door locks or power door locks. It may have an optional V-6 or V-8 engine. It also may allow for a standard or premium sound system.

Each vehicle configured in a certain way is a variant. The product structure would be such that there would not only be a specific part or component at a certain level of the structure but there may be multiple parts or components, requiring one of them to be selected for each instance of the product. Added to this multiple option selection is the issue that only certain combinations of options are legitimate. For example, if I wanted the V-8 engine in my truck, it may require that I also have a heavy-duty transmission. The configuration with a V-8 engine and standard transmission is not a legitimate selection.

The implication of variants is twofold. First, the number of possible combinations goes up dramatically. Table 3.1 in Chapter 3 showed the huge number of potential Bill of Materials against the number of options. The second implication is that there now needs to be a validation mechanism for a Bill of Material. The validation mechanism needs to be able to identify an allowed Bill of Material from one that is not. Given that there may be fairly complicated rules in order to assess the number of options and whether they are compatible, this validation mechanism may be quite complex. When we couple this with the requirement to create a valid BOM with its associated geometry, we are not talking about a trivial undertaking.

However, the failure to provide for variant validation can lead to products that cannot be built, products that do not perform as intended, and even products that are inherently dangerous. Variant validation has to be part of any PLM activity where product options are allowed.

Mechatronics

The advent of electronics in products during the last century added a new dimension of complexity to product structures. This was followed in the last quarter of the 20th century with the arrival of programmable electronics that added an entirely new dimension. Cohesion within a single dimension is a non-trivial task. Cohesion across three different dimensions, each with their own configuration control techniques has added great complexity that must be addressed simultaneously.

Mechatronics consists of the mechanical structure that has already been discussed. It also consists of electronic schematics and computer code structures. These three structures need to be explicitly linked and controlled simultaneously.

Schematics

Schematics are also an abstracted product structure. In theory, if we have CAD structures, then we shouldn't really need schematics. After all, we should be able to see the components and the wires that connect them. However, even when we had large, discrete circuitry, we had a need for schematics. As we move to smaller and highly integrated chip technology, the need for schematics has increased.

The reason that we need schematics rather then being able to rely on CAD structures is that we are limited in mental processing. Unlike computers, we are not very good at being able to sift through large amounts of information and derive what we need. Also, unlike computers, we are much better in dealing with abstract information that we can use to draw conclusions about relationships.

With schematics, we abstract information about components and their interfaces. This was important in order to be able to understand the components and interfaces when we dealt with discrete electrical components, such as transistors and resistors. With integrated components, schematics also allow us to unpack and understand the integrated circuits in terms of these components, their connections, and logic.

With mechanical engineering, understanding interfaces is relatively straightforward. Two pieces connect or interface at their physical geometric boundary. With electrical or hydraulic engineering, the connections are more logical than spatial. While a physical connection still needs to be made for electrical or hydraulic components by wires or pipes, the geometric attributes of those wires and pipes are relatively irrelevant. The information that needs to be conveyed in order to understand the structure is what electrical or hydraulic components are connected. What length of wire or what length of pipe is irrelevant for understanding the interface between components.

That is not to say that wiring or piping from a geometric perspective is irrelevant. The size and length of wires and pipes needs to be accounted for within the CAD structure. Again, cohesion is extremely important between the schematic and CAD representations. Airbus found this out the hard way when they went to wire the first A380, their new jumbo jet, in Toulouse, France. While no doubt the schematics that governed the circuitry were correct, the wiring did not fit within the conduit designed for it.[52] So schematics are an important information abstraction that allows us to understand the logical connection between electrical and hydraulic components. Ideally, we would like to integrate these within the CAD structures and be able to abstract them as we need them. While there is work to be done in this area, today's schematics are independent structures that need to be developed and kept cohesive with their corresponding CAD structures.

Computer Code

Mechatronics code is the software code that the microprocessors in products execute in order to provide product functionality. It is an element of product behavior that did not exist in products until the last quarter of the 20th century. Prior to that, all electrical controls were implemented in physical circuitry. As Moore's law continues to dictate the steep increase in capability of microprocessors, more and more product behavior is implemented via mechatronics.

There are two forms of mechatronics code. The form that microprocessors understand and operate on is pure binary, consisting of strings of zeros and ones. This is called object code. The symbolic code that programmers work with is called source code. Source code is a structured language that consists of statements and commands that allow programmers to define the operations that they want the microprocessor to perform. A computer compiler converts the structured language into the binary code that microprocessors recognize.

The issue with computer code is that each and every bit needs to be precise. Having a bit that should be a zero when it is one or vice versa can lead to a product malfunctioning. With atom-based structures, individual atoms do not have significance. We can be off a number of atoms here and there, and the product will still function properly. With bits, each bit does have significance, and even a single bit can be the difference between a product functioning and malfunctioning.

The other issue with this code is that there is no ability to adjust it between the create and the build phase. If geometric structures do not fit together in the desired fashion during product fabrication, manufacturing can make adjustments. With code, what is developed during the create phase is downloaded exactly in that form to the microprocessors in the product during the manufacturing phase. There is no ability to adjust the code so that it "fits."

Configuration management of this mechatronics code is critical to the successful operation of the product. The code that is developed, tested, and approved for a specific revision of the product needs to be tightly managed so that it is used for that version and only that version of the product. Configuration management of this code has been rapidly evolving and a topic of high interest.

There are numerous stories of companies downloading the wrong code into their product that causes substantial problems. Downloading the wrong computer code happens not only in the create phase, but extends to future phases, especially support. One automotive company had a policy of updating the code in their automobiles when they were brought in for service. They thought if they updated it with the latest release of code that they would enhance the product.

However, there were changes in circuitry between the time when the initial mechatronics code was developed and the latest code development. Downloading this latest code onto older versions of the automobile caused subtle but substantial problems. Owners who brought in their vehicle for minor repairs found themselves dealing with an automobile that was much worse off than when they brought in, with no idea as to why.

So cohesion is the most important characteristic that mechatronics code needs to adhere to. There needs to be cohesion between the source code, the object code, the mechanical implementation, and the electrical representation. Getting any of these elements out of cohesion will lead to severe product behavior issues.

In addition, traceability is also an important characteristic. Configuration management of this code needs to be able to be traced back through its different versions. Computer code is notorious for never being perfect in the first few releases. Even where cohesion is being maintained, the code that is attached to the vehicle may have bugs in it. Revisions and updates to correct those problems need to be implemented in the existing product base. Tracing which products need which releases is a key element in PLM.

Engineering Analysis and Testing

It is a stretch in terminology to refer to the information generated from engineering analysis and testing as a structure. For now and the foreseeable future, the more accurate way of referring to this information is as a collection. Today, engineering and analysis data and testing exists in as many different information formats as there are analysis and testing methods.

A good deal of this information is contained in spreadsheets and word processing documents whose format can and most often does vary from person to person, group to group, department to department, and organization to organization. While in some cases this information is formatted, in numerous other cases this information is unstructured and is often times in the form of a report. In the past, this information has been collectively referred to as Engineering Data Management (EDM)

While these issues may reduce the searchability of this information, at a minimum, we should be collecting this information and tying it to its respective product. The issue that often occurs today is that testing and analysis information that may be very expensive to collect and analyze is used at its point of generation and then filed away in some idiosyncratic system by the individual responsible for it. This information is only later available to the organization if that individual is still around and whoever is interested in reviewing that information at a later time remembers who worked on it.

What happens more often than not is that this analysis and testing information is available only at the first point of interest. If this information is needed in the future, the cost of analysis and testing is incurred again. The inability to capture this analysis and testing information and associate it with its respective product is a substantial waste of resources for organizations.

While the first step is to collect and associate this analysis and testing information under PLM, this step will need to be expanded. The issue with a great deal of this information is that it exists without any context. Often times, the analysis and testing information is not really information at all. It is merely data points organized in some fashion.

By information context, I am referring to the conditions surrounding this information. These are such elements as who performed the analysis, what instruments collected the data, what were the limits of the conditions under which testing occurred, where was this information collected, etc.

For example, if we were measuring the length of something, it would certainly make a difference if our instrument of measure was a laser versus a ruler. If we had a measurement of 12.133, we could rely on the accuracy of that measurement if the measuring instrument was a laser. However, if the measuring instrument was a ruler, we would probably find the measurement accuracy unsupportable and decide that we would need to re-measure this ourselves.

The concept of providing context with this kind of analysis and testing information is referred to as data provenance. While in the past, we have been satisfied to simply be able to collect and store this type of information, we are getting more sophisticated in our approach and abilities in dealing with analysis and testing information. We are rapidly developing methodologies to attach metadata or data about the data to information where the context of that information is as important as the information itself. A geometric design can usually stand on its own, but testing and analysis information requires the context and provenance of that information.

Product Creation Workflow

Before the new millennium, product creation workflow would have not been considered a product information structure. At its best, the product creation workflow was contained within a corporate procedure manual and evidenced by paper sign offs. At its worst, product creation workflow consisted of tribal knowledge by the participants about how a product design received approval to move to manufacturing.

One of the first applications that PLM software providers undertook was to formalize and implement into a product information structure the steps necessary to take the idea of a product to a fully formed product design. This was a natural outcome of the PLM software providers' product data management activities, whereby they created a repository in order to organize and control product designs and engineering data. The next logical stop was to implement a product creation workflow that used that repository.

There is a similarity between the product creation workflow that creates a design and the build process that takes the design to a physical product, which I will discuss later in this chapter. While the building of a product can and needs to be made a process, the creation of a product contains many elements that are practices. While there is an overall process that must exist in order for a product to come to fruition, there are significant activities within that process, such as deciding what constitutes a good design, that are clearly practices.

In addition, the manufacturing of a product is a sequential, orderly process. The creation of a product is not a step-by-step sequential process, but is an iterative and sometime messy one. In the manufacturing phase, products take shape in an orderly fashion. In product creation, product designs tend to coalesce and emerge over time.

The intent of the product creation workflow is to move the product along the creation path without driving out creativity. The product creation workflow attempts to balance innovation with lean activities. We want to create innovative products without the unnecessary waste of resources.

The product creation workflow attempts to set out the various stages of development process and approval gates that moves the product creation from one stage to the next. Since the PLM system also controls the product data management aspect, it has as a main goal the forcing of information singularity. One of the major wastes of development resources is working on the wrong and/or obsolete version of the product design. By linking the product creation process with product data management, PLM implements data singularity through design checkout and check-in or some similar mechanism.

The product creation workflow also manages the different swim lanes of product creation. The activities of the mechanical designers, electrical designers, and the mechatronics code developers need to be coordinated and cohesive across the disciplines.

As part of the product creation workflow, traceability is built-in. We can see how the designs changed over time and who approved them and when. If there is an issue with some component, we can go back through the trail of design changes and approvals and see what happened when. While we need to do much a better job of capturing the "why," it clearly is possible to do so.

One of the characteristics that product creation workflow is focused on is cued availability. As we move into the global, digital world in product development, we have lost the visibility that the physical drafting rooms of previous generations had. When all product design took place in one large facility, it was fairly easy to know when a coworker changed a design that required us to take some action with our design. With design centers spread across the world, that visibility has been lost. Part of the product creation workflow is not only to move the product design through the required steps, but it also serves as notification system to all participants as designs need to be reworked because of uncovered issues.

The purpose of product creation is to take requirements and turn them into a product design that implements those requirements. Unlike other phases of the product lifecycle, this is about the creation of a virtual product. If this product phase is done correctly, then there is no physical product until the very end of this phase. There is nothing physical to put our hands on. The product creation workflow moves the product creation along until we get a product that meets our desired requirements or at least meets the requirements that we can obtain successfully, without compromising below a certain acceptance point our vision of product performance.

BUILD PHASE

Bill of Process[53]

The Bill of Materials is what the product is made up of. The Bill of Process is the means by which the items of the Bill of Materials are created. The Bill of Process defines the resources needed and the operations to be performed in order to produce the parts and components of the Bill of Materials.

The resources that the Bill of Process deals with are material, labor, and equipment. The Bill of Process then defines for each step the operation to be performed with these resources. These operational steps are then sequenced appropriately in order to produce a part or component with the desired characteristics.

For example, to produce a metal reinforcing strut, the Bill of Process might look like Table 10.3. The Bill of Process describes the material to be selected, the equipment that is needed, the operations that the equipment needs to perform, and the labor needed for the operation.

The detail of the Bill of Process can vary with the complexity of the equipment and the familiarity of the operators with the operation to be performed. For equipment whose function is highly defined, such as a stamping machine, the Bill of Process might simply state the size of a sheet of metal to be inserted into the machine. The stamping machine merely cycles through, so there is little need for any detailed instructions.

Bill of Process Example

Seq	Operation	Equipment
1	Stamp out shape	Stamper #3
2	Grind down edges	Grinder #1
3	Insert holes	Drill Press #4
4	Inspection	Faro Arm

Table 10.3

A milling machine, on the other hand, has a multitude of settings and geometric axes. The instructions for the Bill of Process for that equipment might need to have very detailed setup requirements and a very detailed process for creating a desired shape.

Bill of Processes themselves can vary in granularity. ERP systems generally have a higher-level view of operations and routings because ERP systems are more concerned with the macro scheduling of products. Manufacturing Execution Systems (MES) have a much finer and detailed view, because these systems are involved with minute by minute scheduling on the factory floor.

Work instructions are closely related to the Bill of Process, if not actually a subset. These are generally detailed instructions for the humans that perform manufacturing and assembly operations. While the Bill of Process may call for drilling a hole of a certain diameter, the work instructions would give the human operator the methods by which he or she might determine how big of a drill bit to use, the angle on which to drill a hole, and instructions on how to deal with the tailings.

While we have done a successful job of implementing Bill of Processes in a computerized form, work instructions tend to be a lot less structured. In many cases, work instructions rely on tacit or tribal information from operators who have performed these functions many, many times. In addition, work instructions have been left to the operators on the floor to define and implement. While highly valuable, these work instructions remain localized and unknown outside of the work area.

Work instructions should be part of the information structure that is needed in the Bill of Process. If the Bill of Process itself is insufficient to produce a part or component of the same quality each and every time, then work instructions are absolutely a part of the Bill of Process.

However, work instructions should not be limited to descriptions that augment the Bill of Process. These products are three-dimensional products, and as such, should be accompanied by three-dimensional representations. A picture is worth a thousand words. While in that adage, the term "picture" was not defined more precisely, I think we can safely say that a three-dimensional representation is worth more words than a two-dimensional blueprint.

Even though we have been using three-dimensional representations in the create phase, in many organizations, those representations were dumbed down to two-dimensional blueprints for the manufacturing floor. However, we are now starting to see lightweight representations of the three-dimensional CAD models making their way to manufacturing floor. Embedding these lightweight models in the work instructions and even providing build simulations that are associated with the Bill of Process will result in manufacturing more efficiently and in turning designs into accurate, physical products.

The primary PLM characteristics that the Bill of Process concerns itself with are singularity and traceability. With respect to singularity, it is important that there be one build process for each item being built. The Bill of Process is in essence an information repository that defines the minimal amount of resources necessary to produce a specific part or component.

As information is gathered about reducing resources in manufacturing a part or component either through simulation or experience on the factory floor, the Bill of Process should be modified to reflect this new information. Again, this is an example of information substituting for wasting resources.

If multiple Bill of Processes are allowed for the same part or component, then unless they are equivalent, an extremely rare occurrence, all but one of them will result in products being produced inefficiently. In today's global environment with manufacturing being done all over the world, the Bill of Process can serve as a knowledge transfer mechanism so that each plant does not have to go through its own learning curve in order to produce products efficiently.

With respect to traceability, being able to trace the evolution of a Bill of Process can provide insight into areas of improvement for future processes. In addition, traceability insures that companies are fully armed in the continuing battle with product liability claims. Being able to show how the company was diligent in improving its manufacturing processes can serve as a bulwark against unsubstantiated claims.

AS-BUILTS

The Bill of Process is the input to the manufacturing process. It contains the ingredients and recipe necessary to produce the desired result. This desired result is the as-designed product. What actually comes out of the manufacturing process is the as-built product. The goal is to have the as-built product be identical to the as-designed product as possible. If we do not have knowledge of the as-built, then we will not have the ability to compare and resolve differences between the as-designed and as-built nor will we have the ability to use the as-built information further down the product lifecycle in the support and disposal phases.

In the manufacturing or build stage, we are moving from a prototypical or generic product to an individual instance of that product. Up until the build stage, the product has only been a virtual product. In fact, if we reach our goal of only having virtual products in the design phase, we will not have even built any physical prototypes. Again, the reason that this is our goal is that it is far cheaper in resources and less time-consuming to move bits rather than atoms.

The issue with as-builts in the manufacturing stage is the sheer amount of information that we potentially need to deal with. For automobiles, we have in the neighborhood of 6,000 parts per vehicle, and we produce somewhere between 9 million vehicles in a very bad year and 17 million vehicles in a very good year. Looking at the bad year and the number of parts, if we only keep a twenty-character part number and quantity, we are looking at a trillion bytes of data. In the past, this would have been a problem. Today, we can handle that. In the future, this will be a trivial amount of storage.

However, the trend in as-builts is to collect more and more information on less and less expensive products. It does make sense for very expensive products such as the Joint Strike Fighter, the F-35, to keep very detailed as-built information. For the F-35, each plane has its own as-built that contains each and every part with its serial number. If one wanted to know what specific circuit board was in what particular airplane, the as-built information on that plane could provide that.

But the trend in as-builts is going far beyond simple part and serial number. Data on specific operations as the manufacturing process is performed is collected and saved for each instance of the product. As each manufacturing operation is performed, what is defined as critical measurements are obtained and saved. These critical measurements can be as simple as the torque readings for a bolt to the complexity of a full point scan cloud of the surface area of the component.

This as-built information, i.e., information on each instance of the product, is in essence the creation of a virtual product that reflects the actual physical product. As I will discuss in the next section, as-built information provides the virtual product needed in the support phase.

By comparing this as-built virtual product with the as-designed virtual product, we can ensure that each instance of the product conforms to the desired specifications. However, taken in the aggregate, the as-built virtual products can also be fed back into the create phase in order to validate and improve the product design.

The issue that often occurs is that the first number of products built conform to design specifications, but over time start to drift. As tools wear and dies erode, the as-builts will reflect the drift out of tolerances. In addition, tolerance stacking, where all the tolerances start to drift to their outermost levels, can cause products to have assembly problems, if not premature performance and reliability problems when in use.

As computing capability keeps exponentially increasing, I expect to see the number of as–builts and the complexity of the information that the as-builts contain to increase. Today, expensive products such as fighter planes have as-built information. Tomorrow, we may see even mundane products, such as appliances, having as-built information.

SUPPORT PHASE

As-maintained

The as-maintained product structure is intended to keep the virtual product synchronized with the changes in the physical product. Most organizations would need a Bill of Materials-like product structure to reflect the product changes. In some cases, where the product was highly customized, as in engineered-to-order products, there also might be a requirement to have CAD structures in addition to a Bill of Materials.

The as-maintained product structure concerns itself with product form and not product function. The assumption here is that the product function stays the same irrespective of the change in parts or components. The function of the as-maintained product structure is to create a virtual product that reflects the components and parts of the physical product.

As a product ages, knowing what components have been replaced and when allows the support function to be done in a less costly, more effective fashion. To rephrase one of the underlying premises of Product Lifecycle Management - not having information will result in wasting physical resources.

A good example of this is how military depots have handled refurbishment of their battlefield vehicles. Because the military has had no as-maintained product information about their vehicles, the first thing the depot does when the vehicle arrives there is to completely disassemble it.

The parts are inspected and, if in an acceptable state, are placed back into their respective parts bins. The vehicle is effectively rebuilt from scratch during this refurbishment process, no matter what the physical condition of the vehicle was at arrival. The vehicle could have had a complete engine replacement the day before. It does not matter. That vehicle with the new engine will be completely disassembled and rebuilt from the ground up.

This lack of information and waste of resources would not work in the for-profit world. In fact, it really does not work now in the world of the military, where waste and inefficiency have a long-standing tradition. The military recognizes that resources are limited, and it is looking to Product Lifecycle Management for maintaining information that can replace the waste of resources.

The as-maintained informational structure supports the Product Lifecycle Management characteristic of reflectivity. The intent of the as-maintained product structure is to have the virtual product reflect the current product form of its physical counterpart. The characteristic of correspondence means that each physical product has a virtual counterpart. Having singularity of information insures that there are not multiple versions that reflect different parties working on the product at different times. A single source of this information that reflects the current form of the product and is kept up-to-date with all these changes is important in order to prevent people wasting their time with inaccurate representations.

Bill of Service

The Bill of Service is the informational structure that is intended to keep products at the level of performance that the user requires. The reality is that as soon as a product moves into the support phase of its life it starts to deteriorate. The environment starts to work on the product. Parts begin to wear and break. Users push products to the limits of their operational parameters and beyond.

The task during the support phase is to maintain the product at a level of performance at or above the level that the user values for that product. Products that cannot be kept at that level are not perceived to be quality products, regardless of how well they were designed, engineered, manufactured, and assembled at the factory.

To maintain the product at the appropriate level of performance requires that the product can be successfully serviced during the support phase. By comparison, the Bill of Process is relatively simple. The Bill of Process requires finding a one-way route from materials to completed product. The Bill of Service, on the other hand, is much more complicated. It requires that a problem of performance be identified, a cause of that problem be determined, the appropriate component be located within the product and uncovered if necessary, a new component be installed, and the product be reassembled.

This theoretically requires that there be a separate Bill of Service for each potential component subject to failure. The reality is that components in the same area that require common disassembly and reassembly procedures can share Bill of Services.

The issue with Bill of Services is that too often it has been the redheaded stepchildren of product manufactures. With apologies to redheaded stepchildren, product manufacturers often pay very little attention to the issue of supporting their product. Often, there is little or no sharing of information from the previous product lifecycle phases to the support phase.

It is very common for manufacturers to ship the completed product to a group who is then expected to develop and prepare the required Bill of Services. Diagnostic operations, assembly and disassembly processes, and geometric drawings are prepared from scratch with little or no access to information from the create and build phases.

Often times, these groups are so unfamiliar with the products that their Bill of Processes bear little resemblance to the most appropriate ways to diagnose and repair these products. In the best of cases, there is a substantial waste of resources required to re-create information that is available from the create and the build phase of the product lifecycle.

The geometric designs from the create phase and the Bill of Process including work instructions from the build phase should serve as sources of information and starting points for creating Bills of Service. Re-creating this information is both costly and subject to error. It is a huge source of dissatisfaction for product users, who would value the product if it could perform in the same fashion as it did when it left the factory.

Operational State Changes (OSC)

Operational State Changes (OSC) refer to the information about the changes in the condition or status of the product when it is in the usage phase of its life. It is an informational structure about the behavior, not the form, of a product. Operational State Changes are the changes in selected conditions of the product between two time periods. The lights of a car were off, and now they are on. The RPM's of a turbine were X at time t_1 and are now Y at time t_2.

In some cases the change in operational state is a constantly occurring thing that we monitor on a regular basis, such as the RPMs of a turbine blade on a jet engine. In other cases, the operational state change is a trigger that means an event has occurred either routinely — a seat belt has been fastened — or unexpectedly — airbags have been deployed. Even for operational states we monitor on a regular basis, such as the turbine blade above, exceeding a threshold can change routine monitoring into a triggering event.

The OSC informational structure contains two elements of information with an optional third. The two elements of information are the time an operational state change occurred and the changes in the state of the product. The third optional element of information is the former state of the product. It is optional because for a product that continually reports its state of operation, the old state may already have been captured. For products that intermittently reports states only when some condition has triggered a reporting requirement, we may need a product to report both its before and after state.

The Operational State Change information could be either simple or complex. It could be a simple binary condition, such as an automobile airbags having been deployed. It could be a complex set of information, such as reporting the various states of numerous instruments and sensors in an airplane.

While the as-maintained informational structure describes the change in product form over the time of the product life in the support phase, the OSC describes the changes in the product behavior during the same period of time. Together, both of these informational structures give a complete view of the product form and product function throughout its life.

The OSC is a relatively new form of informational structure for products. In the past, the collection of information about the product, if done at all, was done on a manual basis. The automobile dealership manually recorded a vehicle's mileage only when it was brought in for service. There was very little thought given to instrumenting the product so that product state information could be gathered throughout its life.

With the wide proliferation and adoption of microprocessors in almost every product, the ability to continuously, unobtrusively, and reliably collect information about the product state changes throughout its life has become widespread. Examples abound about this collection of information. Copier advertisements on television extol the virtues of a copier machine calling for repair services when needed. Automobiles notify emergency services when its airbags are deployed. The latest fighter planes transmit information about failing components to their base as they go about their mission.

OSC is the mechanism that implements the characteristic of reflectivity in PLM. As I have described earlier, reflectivity is the idea that the virtual product mirrors the physical product as the product goes through its life. OSC is the mechanism by which the virtual product reflects the current state of the physical product. This virtual product can act as a surrogate for being in physical possession of the actual product itself. Locating and acquiring the physical product is a waste of physical resources for which information can serve as a substitute.

OSC also implements traceability. By looking at the history of state changes of the product, product manufacturers can gain valuable understanding as to whether their product met the performance requirements that the product manufacturers hoped to obtain from their product. Aggregating OSC information over a population of instances of the product gives the product manufacturer much more robust information about the product's performance. The alternative used up until now was to sample some of the products and to infer the parameters of performance based on that sample. Clearly, drawing conclusions from the entire population of the product rather than a sample of the product will lead to better product performance understanding.

Implementing traceability through OSC can be critical in defending against product liability claims. After an accident, it is pretty clear without OSC whether the airbags deployed are not — we can see the wrecked vehicle. What is lost without OSC once the accident occurs is the speed of the car prior to the crash and whether the occupants' seatbelt were in use.

Airplane manufacturers have recognized the importance of OSC for an extended period of time. However, they have not carried it far enough in mirroring that information in a virtual product. Their means of implementing OSC were in "black boxes" that captured the operational state change information.

The crash of an Air France flight 447 on June 1, 2009 soon after it left Brazil reflected this shortcoming. The airplane, an Airbus A330, went down in water so deep that recovery of these black boxes could not be accomplished until 2011. While the plane was transmitting some information as it flew, there is no reason that, at our current level of technology, all the information that was being sent to the black boxes could have not been transmitted to a computer that held the virtual A330. Crash investigators could have used that valuable information to more quickly and more accurately assess the reason that this plane went down. This is not simply an issue of wasted physical resources. It is an issue of potentially wasting lives, on which no price can be placed.

OSC also helps implement cued availability. If Operational State Change information can be analyzed and anomalies spotted and surfaced, then we can react to problems before they occur. That is what Rolls-Royce does with its state change information. Information that they receive from each engine in flight is compared against other state change information that they have aggregated over thousands and even millions of flights. That flight information has been correlated against resulting problems.

Thus Rolls-Royce can make predictions that a pattern of OSC information will result in a problem at a later time. Armed with this information, airlines can undertake preventive maintenance that eliminates that problem from occurring. This is much safer and much less expensive than letting a problem occur with an engine at 35,000 feet and then addressing it.

Interestingly enough, there are network effects from collecting operational state changes. This is true even about the absence of such information. For example, FEMA, the government disaster agency, is interfaced into General Motors OnStar operation centers. Why? Because in the event of a natural disaster, such as a hurricane, FEMA can immediately ascertain which roads are passable and which are not.

Because there are so many General Motors vehicles on the road, they have a network effect. The absence of OSC information from a particular stretch of highway, such as an interstate highway, means that the road is impassable. FEMA could collect this information by expending resources in sending people to check or in collecting the always-unreliable eyewitness accounts. However, tapping into the OnStar system, gives FEMA a real-time perspective of the highway system.

OSC information is in its infancy. Work needs to be done in how to best structure and convey this kind of information. However, the computing and communications capability in even the most mundane products means that OSC information will become increasingly available. We will need to explore and understand how to best organize and use this valuable type of product information, both at the individual and aggregate level.

Product Operational Instructions (POI)

The Product Operational Instructions are most commonly referred to as the "product manual." In the past, this has not been thought of as an informational structure. For most of recorded history, products were simple objects with intuitively obvious operating instructions. For a hammer, it was "grasp wooden handle and vigorously move up and down with opposite end positioned above intended object." For a screwdriver, it was "put metal end into screw slot, grasp opposite end, and turn right-tighty or lefty-loosey." For a spear, it was "grasp object in the middle, orient pointy end at target, and hurl."

In essence, for early products, what you saw was what you got. As complex products came into being, we developed the product manual. For a surprisingly large number of products, the product manual that describes the product operation bore only a passing resemblance to the actual product operation. Even if the product manual did contain the appropriate operational information, finding it took as much effort as the search for the Holy Grail. That is if the product manual survived beyond the first few days of the product's acquisition. Most users of products were unable to locate their product manual shortly after removing the product manual from the box it came in.

The issue with today's modern products is that what you see has no bearing on what you get. At least with the mechanically complex products of the past, the mechanically inclined could deduce the operation of the equipment from looking at its parts. With today's microprocessor enabled products, that is clearly not possible.

In fact, that is how the product manuals of the past were often written. The product was thrown over the wall to the product manual group. They then attempted to deduce the operations of the product and create an instruction set that documented their discoveries. It is unsurprising that most product manuals leave much to be desired.

This method will clearly not work with today's products. My definition of product quality is that it performs the functions to the satisfaction of the product user. If the product user cannot ascertain how to obtain that functionality, then his or her perception will be that the product is not a quality product. It can have a terrific design. It can be manufactured to the strictest of tolerances. If the product user cannot make it work for him or her, it will not be considered a quality product.

This means that Product Operation Instructions needs to be integrated in the product create phase. The product functionality that is tied to product requirements and implemented during design and engineering needs to be linked to the product operations instructions. This means that the standalone manual needs to be a thing of the past.

In fact, the product manual is but one format of the Product Operational Instructions. The informational structure should include tutorials, videos, simulations, and dynamic searches that allow the product user to become familiar with his or her product and provide the right information at the right point in time to obtain specific product functionality.

The PLM characteristic that Product Operational Instructions need to exhibit is cued availability. As the user is attempting to perform a function, the product operational instructions should be embedded in the product itself. Ideally, the product operational instructions can be cued by either the context of what the user is doing or by keywords.

My wife recently bought a new Lincoln MKZ with Microsoft Sync. It has the ability to display a weather map of incoming weather. She knew she had seen it, but was unable to locate it from the menus. While I have over 40 years of familiarity with computers, it took me a minute or so of poking around before I could find the weather map.

The other PLM characteristic that Product Operational Instructions need to implement is reflectivity. In the past, the product that left the factory door contained all the product functions it would have throughout its life. Today's products can be updated and changed through the downloading of new computer code. The Product Operating Instructions need to be kept synchronized with this change in product function. While one might argue that these functional changes have been minimal, the advance of computing capability will mean that there can and will be substantial changes to product functionality in the future.

Product Operating Instructions with its disconnect from product creation and its ad hoc approach will need to be brought in line with PLM concepts. Product Operational Instructions have not been thought of as product informational structures but will need to be considered that in the future.

DISPOSE PHASE

Bill of Disposal

The Bill of Disposal is an information structure that deals with a product's form. It probably exists in few organizations today, but it needs to. In essence, the Bill of Disposal is the inverse of the Bill of Process. Where the Bill of Process defines the resources, operations, and sequences in order to produce the desired as-designed product, the Bill of Disposal defines the resources, operations, and sequences in order to effectively and efficiently dispose of the product.

In looking at the product lifecycle, I have added the desired value of "impact" in defining the value of a product. While environmental impact will depend on the cost imposed by society, there is clearly a trend toward reducing a product's environmental impact. The desire and ability to simply abandon products to a landfill at the end of their useful life will continue to decline, if only for the fact that the cost of the physical resources locked up in a product will become more and more valuable.

The time to create the Bill of Disposal is at the time the product is designed. Organizations are currently spending significant amount of resources in "green" or designed for the environment (DfE) products. They are designing products that are meant to be disposed of in an environmentally friendly fashion, recycling as much of the product as possible.

However, as I have stated before, this effort is wasted unless we create a Bill of Disposal that provides detailed instructions on how the product is to be disassembled and disposed of. Designing products to be disposed of with minimal impact on the environment is useless unless the instructions are in place for that disposal.

That is not to say that some of this disposal does not take place today. Where there is an economic opportunity, entrepreneurs will spring up to create this capability. The scrap metal business is a case in point. However, their activity will fluctuate as the market for their metals do. A few years ago, scrap metal prices were extremely high. Metal-based products, including some that were in service but accessible to thieves such as outside air conditioners, were being efficiently recycled. When the price of metal dropped, recycling was not so effective.

One of the ways to drive down the cost of disposal is to trade information for wasted resources. If the information about how to disassemble, recycle, and dispose of the product with the minimal amount of resources is available, then this drops the cost point of effective product disposal.

However, the future trend is toward regulatory mandating of effective product disposal. The cost of this will ultimately be borne by the product acquirer. So reducing this cost through proper information will save resources.

While the build process relies on the Bill of Materials in order to create the product, this Bill of Materials may not be sufficient for disposal. We may need a Bill of Substance (BoS) in order to understand what the material in the product is made of in order to understand how it may be safely recycled or otherwise disposed of properly and safely. There are issues that exist, such as companies not wishing to disclose the makeup of their proprietary materials. However, being able to disassemble and identify the parts and components that make up a product is a necessary start to minimizing the impact that that product has on the environment at its end of life.

Unlike some of the other informational structures, the Bill of Disposal will be required to be linked to the product until the product is removed from service. This could be a very long period of time, spanning decades or even a century or more. This information may outlast the organization that created it. The Bill of Disposal will need to be linked to the product by possibly embedding it into the product or by being held by some long-term organization, such as the government.

Up until now, there has been little consideration given to this specific issue of the Bill of Disposal. Forward-looking organizations should begin to consider it today before a solution that may be unpalatable is forced upon them.

This chapter describes the information structures that PLM needs to deal with. These structures deal with the form of the product or the function of the product. While there may be other informational structures that have product information, this chapter describes the more important ones.

In the create phase, the information structures needed are requirements, product structure, mechatronics, engineering analysis and testing, and product creation workflow. Product structure includes both CAD and Bill of Materials (BOM). These two structures are closely aligned and need to be tightly coupled. In addition, the various versions of the Bill of Materials, the Engineering BOM (EBOM), the Manufacturing BOM (MBOM), and the Support BOM (SBOM), need to be also kept in synchronization. Mechatronics has a need to tightly couple its structures: mechanical, electrical, and software code components.

In the build phase, the product structures we need to concern ourselves with are Bill of Process and as-builts. The Bill of Process describes the manufacturing steps that will result in a product. The as-builts identify the makeup of each instance of the product that is manufactured.

The support phase involves itself with the as-maintained product structures, the Bill of Service, and the Operational State Changes (OSC) that track the state of the product as it goes through its life. The support phase also includes Product Operational Instructions (POI), which have historically been only loosely attached to product information.

The disposal phase has a Bill of Disposal, which is the information necessary to dispose of the product consistent with its design intent. Bill of Disposals exists for few if any products today, but are necessary if we are ever to implement effective product disposal. This may also require that we go one level deeper to a Bill of Substance.

This chapter discusses how these informational structures implement the main characteristics of Product Lifecycle Management. These characteristics are singularity, cohesion, correspondence, reflectivity, and cued availability. Each of these informational structures deals with one or more of these PLM characteristics.

Notes

52 Strictly speaking, this was not a cohesion problem between schematics and CAD. Rather it was a cohesion problem within CAD itself, as different groups of Airbus used different CAD software to represent their respective geometric designs. For my analysis of this problem, please see my website at www.plmvirtualyperfect.com.

53 I am using the conventional nomenclature of "Bill of Process" and will extend that usage to the support and disposal phases. While the Bill of Materials is a list of materials, the Bill of Process is a flow of activities. It should be accurately called a process, as in "Process of Manufacturing." A "bill," which is a statement or list of particulars, is not the best describer to be joined with "process." However, we are probably stuck with it.

11

VIRTUALLY FLAWLESS

Flawless would certainly be an attribute that quality would evoke, as in a flawless paint job or a flawless casting operation. However, upon closer examination, the characteristic of flawlessness might not be the most important attribute of quality. A flawless paint job on a car that did not start would not be much use to someone who needed transportation. A flawless cast of a component that did not mate properly with other components would be of little use to a manufacturer wanting to ship a completed product. Flawless certainly has some relationship to quality, but, as we shall see, product quality is a great deal more complicated.

Quality is one of the most important characteristics of products today. Companies spend a great deal of time and effort in an attempt to build quality products. No discussion by a CEO of a product company is complete without a mention of quality. As I have discussed previously, quality is one of the main drivers of price. A product that is higher in quality commands a better price than a product that is lower in quality. Below a certain threshold of quality, the price of the product drops to approximately zero.

However the issue of quality is a complicated one. While there is much talk about quality, there is also much confusion about what quality actually is. If we look to the definition of quality in the dictionary we find that there are at least eight different definitions of quality that have very separate meanings from each other.

PRODUCT LIFECYCLE QUALITY (PLQ)[54]

The different definitions of product quality can be reconciled if we view product quality as a lifecycle of characteristics, where the preceding characteristic maps to and implements the following one. In that fashion, quality is derivative of and dependent on how well the following phase implements the previous phase.

As shown in Figure 11.1, the Product Lifecycle Quality (PLQ) model starts with the overarching characteristic of perceived value. Perceived value is supported by requirements, which in turn results in a design. Designs are turned into specifications. Product instances that are built to these specifications are the embodiment and outcome of the chain, from perceived value to requirements to design to specifications.

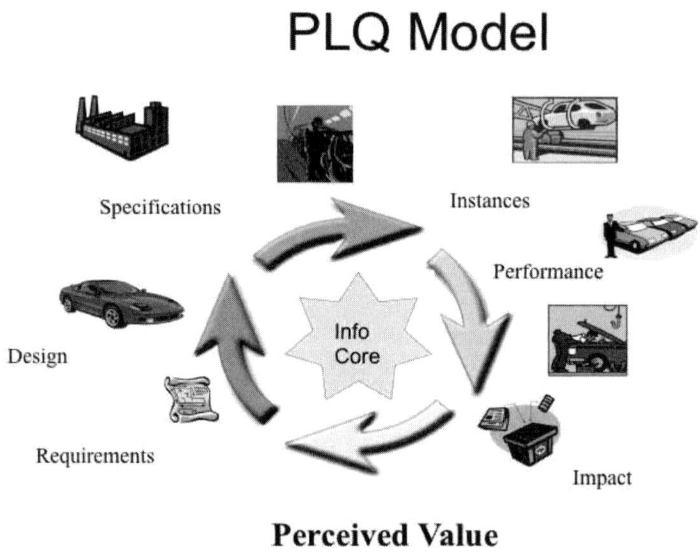

Figure 11.1

The true test of product quality comes at the performance stage when the product is to perform the tasks for which it was intended. Irrespective of anything else, if the product performs the tasks that have perceived value to the product user, it is a quality product. If it does not, then no matter how well it is designed, no matter how accurately it meets the specifications in manufacturing, it is not a quality product.

Up until recently the usage of the product until it was retired from service was the extent of the concern with the product. This may still be the concern of most individuals with respect to quality. However, the trend of modern society is to be concerned with the impact of the product on the environment when it ends its useful life, as all products must do. The product's impact on the environment will also be a perceived value. This "perceived value" of quality may be internalized by individuals or it may be mandated by society through laws and regulations. However, current trends suggest that disposal needs to be considered in any discussion concerning quality.

Perceived Value

As the model illustrates, Product Lifecycle Quality starts and ends with perceived value. As continually emphasized, perceived value is what we evaluate a product against and is the essence of what quality really is. If we perceive a product as meeting our expectation in obtaining something we value, then the product is a quality product to us. The closer the product delivers what we value, the more quality we think it has.

As previously asserted, while economic value receives a great deal of attention, there are at least five dimensions in which we assess perceived value. These dimensions are economic, safety, social, experiential, and belief-driven. Products can have perceived value in one or more of these dimensions depending on the product.

This "jobs-to-be-done" perspective is an economic view.[55] This view of quality is one that values the ability of the product to perform the job when it is needed. This is an economic perspective because it takes into consideration the resources required to acquire the product. For the occasional home repair, a screwdriver made of the toughest metal known to man that costs $1,000 has no more quality than a standard steel one costing $10. As a consequence, the occasional home repairer will not spend more than $10 to buy a screwdriver.

Specification quality, while important as discussed below, often is the focal point in quality discussions. My argument for considering perceived value as a focal point for quality involves the possibly apocryphal story of the

Yugo.[56] It may be that the Yugo was a quality car by normal manufacturing quality control definitions. By normal quality control definitions, I mean that the Yugo met the specifications that were laid out for the vehicle. However, there hardly would be anyone who would argue that the Yugo was a quality car. Meeting the specifications of the product is not enough to make a quality product. Yet, that has been a substantial focus of a great number of organizations' quality efforts.

Perceived value drives the understanding of what constitutes a quality product. The issue for all product producers is to both understand the dimensions that are involved and produce a product that fulfils the expectations of the product acquirer.

Requirements

The next stage of PLQ is defining the requirements that the product will need to meet in order to produce the perceived value. The mapping of the list of requirements to perceived value is not an easy task. In some cases, the perceived value is not fully formed until the product is put to actual use. In other cases, the product developers confuse the number of functions that can be crammed into a product as perceived value.[57] In a great deal of cases, the requirements to meet the ideal perceived value are contradictory and need to be traded off.

The requirements, for say, an airplane are that it can fly from point A to point B using a specified amount of fuel and carrying a certain number of passengers safely, with comfort being an option depending on the airline involved. The better that an airplane can do this, the better quality that we perceive the airplane has up to a certain point. An airplane that only sometimes can go from point A to B because a great deal of the time it is down for repairs is not considered a quality airplane.

An airplane that was available all the time to go from Point A to Point B, but once in a great while could not sustain cabin pressure causing the passengers to die en route would also not be considered a quality airplane. The trick with this level of quality is to be able to match the requirements of the product with what it is that people perceive as value. For example, a child's toy with aerospace-like tolerances has no more quality than that same toy with normal toy-like tolerances.

Designs

Designs are the manifestations of requirements in physical form. At this phase of PLQ, the task is to map the requirements to physical shapes and components. There may be multiple physical manifestations that can produce the requirements. The term "design" at this stage not only includes form but the mechanisms by which this form produces the desired results, which is often referred to as engineering.

Decisions at this stage are critical to obtaining the perceived value. There are a number of issues that arise at this stage that complicate the goal of delivering the perceived value that the user of the product desires.

Invariably there need to be trade-offs in the requirements. Cars that weigh more are safer but less fuel-efficient. Planes that go faster have higher operating costs. Heart pacemaker leads that are thinner for easier insertion may not be as long lasting as thicker leads.

While designers and engineers are amazingly creative at developing new materials, technologies, and techniques for reducing the need for trade-offs, the need for trade-offs always exist. The task is to understand and evaluate how these requirements link to perceived value. In many instances, this will not be fully known until the product is actually used, and product users determine what it is that they actually value.

Another major issue at this stage is that what may appear to be a great design cannot actually be realized when individual instances of the product are manufactured. For a product to have perceived value, it has to have perceived value in all instances of the product. The overall perception of product quality can be negatively impacted if even a small number of products do not perform as expected.

Specifications

Designs are realized in specifications. Specifications are quantifiable descriptions of the material and the operations on and in the material to create the product. The goal of specifications is to realize individual physical products, the instances, from a virtual product, the design.

Specifications have historically been thought of as having four categories, although a fifth has been added in the last quarter of the 20th century. The four categories are Bill of Materials (BOM), geometric designs, characteristics, and Bill of Process (BOP). The fifth category is computer code, which is increasingly important in today's products. The quality of the product, that is the ability of the product to produce the required perceived value, depends on all five categories.

The Bill of Materials is an abstract of the product. It defines the list of components and the hierarchical structure in which those components are arranged. It is an exhaustive list of all the materials that make up a product, including those that do not have geometric shape, such as oils and powders.

The geometric designs are the dimensional structure that the product will take in space. Historically, these have been two-dimensional (2-D) views. However, three dimensional (3-D) models are emerging as the dominant organizing view for product information.

Characteristics are a material-specific description of the required attributes of that material. Steel needs to have a certain hardness and chemical composition. Oil needs to be of a certain viscosity. Plastic needs to be of a certain malleability and rheology. Characteristics are often not a stand-alone category, but are contained in the BOM or as call outs on the geometric designs.

The Bill of Process is the procedure by which material, labor, and equipment are sequenced and utilized to produce the completed product. The BOP is intended to be a repeatable procedure that results in identical instances of the product.

Computer code is a relatively new dimension of products that can have a major impact on how products perform and therefore the quality of the product. The issue of Configuration Management is both a new and thorny problem for modern products.

Specifications are the virtual representations of a to-be physical product. However, the physical world is not nearly as precise as the virtual world. As a result, specifications have tolerances associated with them. The theory is that if all the instances of the product have specifications within the tolerances allowed, then all these product instances would be equivalent, i.e., possess the same perceived value.

Specifications are the representation of the ideal product. The assumption for quality at this stage is that the specifications implement the design that represents the value requirements of the product user. These value requirements reflect what the product user requires, They are not simply functional or utilitarian. They also include the other values such as safety, social, experiential, and belief-driven.

Instances

This is the phase where products move from the virtual to the physical. This phase may be divided into three stages: making the first one, ramp up, and making the rest. While making the first product and ramp-up have substantial issues pertaining to quality, the focus here will be the steady state production of instances of the product that will be acquired and put to use.

The assumption at this stage of manufacturing the product is that the Bill of Process can produce products that meet the specifications. Much of the discussion around product quality has focused on the issue of producing products en masse that meet the required specifications. A great deal of the focus is on collecting data, analyzing it, and controlling manufacturing processes.[58]

Even though this aspect of quality is extremely important, we should view quality on a much broader and comprehensive basis. What is called Quality Control, but which may more accurately be referred to as Specification Control, is critical to producing instances of the product that conform to the specifications. That may or may not translate into a product actually being a quality product to the product user.

For example, some organizations, including the Department of Defense, require First Article Inspection of a 100% of the geometric features for some products. This means that manufacturers can spend a great deal of resources in dealing with issues that are not relevant to producing the perceived value of the product. Equating meeting all characteristics instead of key characteristics with product quality is consistent with the view that specifications equate to quality. The more specifications met, the better the quality. However, that may not be the case. Better quality, that is product performance that better meets or exceeds user expectations, may be better accomplished by focusing on fewer key characteristics.

From a PLQ perspective, the quality of the product is dependent on the product meeting the perceived value test of the product user. The problem with focusing only on specifications is that there may be new information being obtained from the usage of the product that indicates that the product created to the current specifications does not produce the requirements desired by the product user.

In actual use, the product may have performance, reliability, or durability problems. Too often, under today's siloed approach, there is little visibility of this issue in the manufacturing phase. Manufacturing is busy producing product that by their standards is of the highest quality, but in reality is simply expensive scrap. PLQ can at least alert manufacturing to the issue that there is a problem with the product so that manufacturing can make better decisions about whether to continue production or at least identify problem products.

Another potential issue is that producing instances of the product in high volumes also produces data about the ability of the manufacturing processes to meet the specifications within tolerances. By collecting Longitudinal Quality Data (LQD), this phase can provide valuable information to the design and specification phases that may require engineers to design for greater tolerances due to tool and die wear over the life of creating product instances. The last product produced needs to conform to the specifications in order to provide the user of that product with perceived value.

Performance

As stated before, the product performance in actual use is the true measure of whether a product is a quality product. If the product performs the perceived value for the product user, it is a quality product. If it does not, it is not a quality product.

The issue is that it is much easier to assess whether a product meets specifications than it is assessing whether or not the product performs. Warranty and survey information can be inherently flawed and collecting that information can even negatively affect the perception of quality by annoying the product owner.[59] Products need to be instrumented to collect in-use information.

However, it is not enough that the product delivers certain performance at the beginning of its life. It needs to continue to deliver the same level of performance throughout its life. If properly conceptualized and used, PLQ can collect and assess in-use performance data to spot problems early so that preventative measures can be taken. Prognostics, that is identifying potential problems before they occur, is an area with the possibility to insure products continuously provide perceived value to its users.

Performance not only refers to functional performance, but to the other dimensions of performance: social, safety, experiential, and belief driven. For example, if the perceived value involves social perceptions, companies need to be mindful of not cheapening their product. While it may perform the same economic function, it may not perform the same social function. This is much harder to assess.

Impact

While certainly by no means a universally accepted characteristic of quality, the trend is in the direction of considering products that have less impact on the environment at the end of their life to be of higher perceived value than those that do not. This trend is both economic and social.

On the economic dimension, governments are mandating disposal and recycling requirements. The European Union has mandated requirements for both vehicles and electronics. Over time, products that do not conform will have higher costs than products that do conform. Products that have less impact on the environment will eventually be perceived as being better quality because the perceived value of those products will be higher.

On the social side, there is more awareness of the environmental impact of products. Society, in general, is more aware of the external impacts of product disposal. Companies are becoming more aware of this issue with such initiatives as Design for the Environment (DfE). The issue of environmental impact was the theme of a 2007 Toyota commercial.[60]

PRODUCT QUALITY HIERARCHY

While Figure 11.1 shows that there is a sequential aspect to obtaining quality, the sequential aspect is also a hierarchical aspect. Although the term quality control has been almost the exclusive domain of manufacturing, quality control needs to be implemented throughout the product lifecycle. As Figure 11.2 shows, this quality control goes by different names depending on the phase of the lifecycle that the product is in. However, in order to have true quality, the focus on quality control needs to exist in this hierarchical fashion.

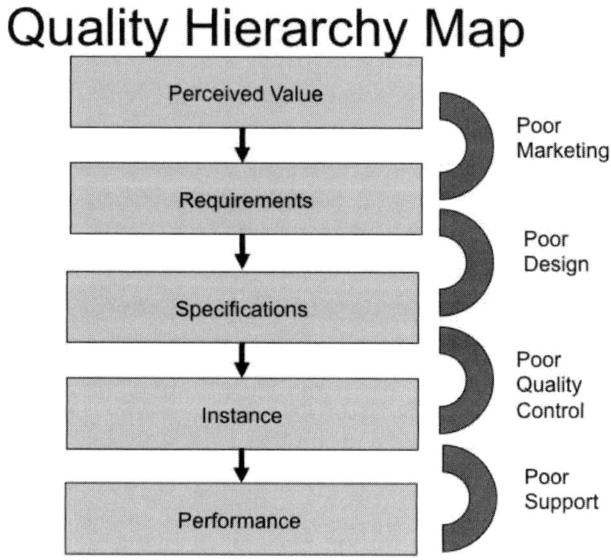

Figure 11.2

Perceived Value – Requirements

Even though quality can be translated into apparent objective metrics, many aspects of quality have been socially constructed and are implicitly well understood throughout our society. However, at the end of the day, the sole arbiter of quality is the perceived value by the product user. Translating that perceived value into next level, the product requirements, is a critical step in producing a product that has the attributes that will be perceived as having value by product user. These attributes need to be translated into requirements that the product must have. Historically, it is the marketing group who attempts to understand what customers want in a particular product. The marketing group then defines the requirements they believe are necessary to meet that perceived value.

This is often referred to as the "voice of the customer." This phrase almost takes on religious overtones with a preponderance of marketing people. Listening to the customer as to what he or she perceives as value is important. However, product organizations need to be careful about being slaves to this premise. Often times customers do not know what they want until they see it. As Bob Lutz, the famed automotive executive, said during a panel discussion, "if we had listened to the customer about the Chrysler PT Cruiser, we would've never built it." Marketing research at the time showed that customers did not like the PT Cruiser design. It was only by executives using their judgment about what customers would value that the PT Cruiser was built and became a success.

A failure in quality in this area is often referred to as poor marketing. Virtual products could greatly assist in mapping perceived value to requirements by creating prototype products in digital form that could be evaluated by potential customers. The time and cost of developing physical prototypes that can be truly evaluated by the potential customer takes way too long and is way too expensive. Putting a digital product into place that potential customers could try and evaluate could mean the difference between product success and product failure.

Requirements – Specifications

The next mapping that takes place is between requirements and specifications. Having a good understanding of the requirements that potential customers will perceive as having great value, but not being able to translate them into specifications of the product that produces those requirements is generally considered a design problem. In reality however, it is indeed a quality problem.

Mapping requirements to specifications is a prime task of engineering. It is also a task that engineering does reasonably well given the fuzziness that exists in performing this function. As I will discuss later in the chapter on systems engineering, the task is simply not to get a list of requirements to be mapped to specifications, but it is to obtain a system that performs all the requirements that will meet users' perceived value. Failure to get the requirements to specifications mappings right has been called poor engineering.

Virtual products can again assist here, because as shown previously, simulating the product is key to understanding whether the actual product will meet the requirements. It is extremely expensive and time-consuming to build a product physically only to find out that it will not perform as anticipated. Using virtual products, we can decrease the time and cost in developing this linkage between requirements and specifications.

Requirements – Instances

Creating actual physical instances of the product that meet the design specifications is something that quality control has been associated with for a long period of time. It has received a great deal of attention. The practice in this area has evolved so that producing quality products, as defined by the instance of the product meeting the specifications, is well advanced.

While this has been called quality control, I would contend it's more about specification control. The term "quality control" has been used for so long within the manufacturing environment that a change in terminology is unrealistic. However, it is important to keep in mind that quality control in this instance does not really mean that we have a quality product. The aspects of quality that precedes mapping an instance of the product to the specifications needs to take place in order to obtain true quality.

Virtual products again have a role here. Virtual products can be used in planning for the manufacturing that will produce products that meet their specifications. They can also be used in obtaining the information and data about how the product instances are being built in order to ascertain whether or not they are meeting the specifications.

Instances – Performance

Finally if the product does not perform reliably during the life of the product, then it will not be considered a quality product. Given that all the other linkages above are performed properly and given that the product leaves the factory with the perceived value that the user requires, the product will not be considered a quality product if it does not sustain that performance over its life. Too often product manufacturers lose sight of this particular aspect of quality.

The failure in this critical area is often called poor support, but the issues may have been generated long before this phase of the lifecycle. While a good product may be the victim of poor service and support, often the issues that caused the product to fail were generated back in the create and the build phases.

Virtual products can assist in this aspect of the lifecycle. Virtual products can reflect the operation of the product so that the product manufacturer can maintain the product to its required level. Virtual products can simulate the performance of the product over a period of time, so that product manufacturers can have a high level of assurance that this product will perform at the appropriate performance level over the product's life.

It is important as part of PLM to think about quality in a much more expanded way from what has commonly been called quality control or what I call specification management. Maintaining this hierarchy of quality and making sure that the mapping is done appropriately at each step of the lifecycle is critical to producing products with true quality. Product lifecycle quality is about quality in all of the product's lifecycle and not simply in a single phase, such as manufacturing.

GENERATING DUAL PRODUCTS FOR QUALITY

Delivering Product Lifecycle Quality throughout the product lifecycle requires that we be able to generate both manifestations of the product — the physical product and the virtual product. Clearly, we need to generate a physical product. Our physical world requires that we move atoms if we are to accomplish any real action. However, we can use the virtual product to create and maintain quality in the physical product.

Create

As discussed before, in the create phase the virtual product precedes the physical product. Before we start moving atoms, we need to develop the information that describes the form and functionality that will perform the job we expect our new product to perform.

It is not out of the realm of possibility that we could go out to a machine shop and start cutting, bending, and molding material to realize something that would perform our functions. At best, this approach is hugely wasteful in terms of consuming resources: time, energy, and material. More likely than not, we would not obtain anything that came close to realizing the functionality we desired. Taking a lump of material and carving out a design may work for sculptors who let the material "talk to them." It is not so good for purposeful product design.

So, product creation begins with a virtual product. In the past, that virtual product was fairly vague, consisting of sketches and rough drawings.

Because our ability to manage information was limited, we moved from a very rudimentary virtual product to an equally rudimentary physical product. While we refined our design by creating better and better physical prototypes, this was a costly and time-consuming method. In addition, only a certain amount of testing that the product possessed the characteristics that would make it a quality product to its users could be accomplished with physical-based products.

The use of virtual products allows for products that are closer to "virtually perfect." Product creators can afford to spend more time on their product and analyze and test it in more ways than they could with a physical product. The intent is to do as much work as they can in the virtual world before they have to physically realize the product. While they may not be able to limit physical prototypes entirely, simply reducing the number of prototypes will reduce the amount of resources and the amount of time it takes to bring a product to fruition.

Quality for a product starts in the create phase. If the product creators cannot develop the requirements that will be valued by the product user, then no matter how carefully they manufacture the product, it will not be perceived as a quality product. Getting the requirements right and then ensuring that the requirements are met by the product design are key elements in producing product quality.

Build

The next step in producing quality products is to produce instances of the product that conform to the product design. If we could control our manufacturing processes so that each product instance was identical to both the original design and to every other product instance and that product users would only want one configuration of the product, then we could stop here with virtual products. However, since individual products will differ not only in configuration, but also in actual dimensions, we need to consider creating virtual products that reflect each of the physical instances.

This is an absolute requirement for very expensive products like spacecraft, jet fighters, and nuclear reactors, but it may also be highly useful for products like automobiles, earthmoving equipment, and medical devices. Having virtual "as-builts" allows us to use information in the place of being in possession of the actual product. It also allows us to be assured that the characteristics that we perceive to be quality are present in each and every instance.

Product Specification Management (PSM)

What I call Product Specification Management (PSM) is the key to product quality in the manufacturing phase of the product lifecycle. Once a virtual product has been created that is validated as meeting the requirements that the product should possess, it is defined as the "Controlling" Virtual Product (CVP). The CVP is the virtual product that is to serve as the template for all the physical products to be manufactured. The next step is to then build a physical product that meets the specifications of this CVP.

As discussed earlier, to create this physical product, a Bill of Process (BOP) is developed. A BOP is a step-by-step list of operations that is to be performed on material by labor and equipment in order to create a physical product that meets or "mirrors" the specifications of the virtual product.

The physical product is of a different nature from the virtual product in that it exists in many instances, each with its own characteristics, slightly different from each other and from the controlling virtual product. Each of these product instances will be produced at a particular point in time and in a particular geographical location. Each instance may be close to each other in specification, but will never be identical.

As the physical product is manufactured, information about each instance — its shape, its dimensions, the torque applied to its fasteners, etc — is also created. The task of PSM is to capture this information for each product instance individually and for the collection of instances across time and geographical regions. This "as-built" virtual product can then be compared from various useful perspectives against the controlling "as-designed" virtual product to determine if it meets the necessary specifications.

This is Product Specification Management (PSM). The difference between PSM and spot quality control inspections or even statistical process control (SPC) is that PSM involves creating a comprehensive, product-centric view of the manufactured product across time and geography and is not simply a data point or a small set of points viewed from the narrow perspective of a work cell or inspection station.

In various ways, traditional inspection is limited in that it makes use of relatively small sets of data points in isolation from other data points that might be useful if viewed from an integrated perspective. For instance, under traditional inspection methods, only a very small set of features on a given product instance may be inspected, or only a very small sample size of the collection of instances may be inspected, or only a very small portion of the manufacturing process may be inspected for the purposes of a particular functional area of an organization (fabrication, assembly, final inspection, etc.).

The key innovation of PSM is that it consolidates information from all the available data points for use in any way necessary within an organization — across time, geography, and stages of the manufacturing process.

While PSM information can still be used to pass or fail an individual instance of the product or to determine the trend line using SPC techniques, the information becomes part of an "as-built" virtual product. This virtual product can be used within the manufacturing phase and also in other phases of the product's lifecycle.

This PSM as-built information can be directly used in the manufacturing process itself. A major issue for automobile manufacturers is the requirement that doors fit well within their frames. To that end, there are people at the end of the assembly line with rubber mallets in order to adjust the doors so they do fit well. The problem is that if people are stationed with rubber mallets, then they are going to want to pound on something — whether it needs it or not. This can cause as many quality problems as it corrects.

The solution is to measure and adjust as the door is being fitted earlier in the assembly process and produce what is called gap-and-flush data. This as-built information will then be collected and made available for each individual vehicle at the end of the assembly line. If this is done correctly, the people with mallets will not be needed or, at a minimum, they will only be directed to those vehicles where the as-built measurement shows an adjustment is needed.

The Value of As-Built Virtual Products

There are a myriad number of uses that can be made of the virtual product created through PSM. In the manufacturing or build phase, the "as-built" virtual product is immediately available and can be transmitted to customers and other parties in the supply chain who need the information about the product to assure themselves that the product is actually being created to the required specifications.

Unlike the physical product itself, the virtual product can be sent over large geographic areas instantaneously and can be sent to multiple locations simultaneously. As described in a later chapter, the new slogan of "transmit us the virtual product and we will then tell you whether or not to ship the physical product" may define a new paradigm in purchasing and manufacturing.

One automotive manufacturer has created a collaborative virtual space with its suppliers where the inspection of component parts at the supplier and later at the automotive firm is correlated down to the inspection point — though each may use different inspection methods and devices. The introduction of this collaborative model contributed to an 85% reduction in build issues in the subsequent model year.

In the create phase the as-built virtual product can be used to validate the design of new, similar products. The data collected on actual results compared against specifications is invaluable in assessing the manufacturing validity of new designs. By providing a feedback loop, the engineering / manufacturing divide can be bridged, reducing the slow iterative process of trial-and-error typically performed by manufacturing companies.

For instance, while a specification and its associated tolerances may be manufacturable at the beginning of a production run, it may be that tool and die wear over a much larger run does not allow for those specifications to be met. Having the sequence of as-built virtual products allows designers to understand either the requirement for different specifications or understand when new tool and/or die replacement is required.

At another automotive manufacturer, historical process capability information contained in the as-built virtual product of current and previous product models is being utilized in the early design of new product models. This is in the form of dimensional tolerances that can realistically be expected to hold using similar manufacturing methods. In the absence of PSM technology, proper tolerancing in design for manufacturability is a notoriously uncertain and difficult exercise, where the risk is that improperly assigned tolerances will lead to costly rework in design and tooling.

Components of PSM

In order to create the as-built virtual product of an individual physical product, there are four main components that need to exist. These components are: the Virtual Controlling Product, physical measuring tools, an as-built data collection and organizing system, and an as-built virtual product repository. These components are in varying states of progression. However, they are rapidly evolving.

Taking the VCP first (the right side of Figure 11.3), this component already exists in a fairly mature form. Product specifications in the form of CAD definitions fully and with great accuracy define the dimensions of the virtual product. Defining other characteristics such as force application (e.g., bolt torque force) and material specification other than dimensional (e.g., tensile strength, plasticity, etc.) are at varying stages of being integrated into virtual product representations. General Dimensioning and Tolerancing (GD&T) are also being integrated into these representations.

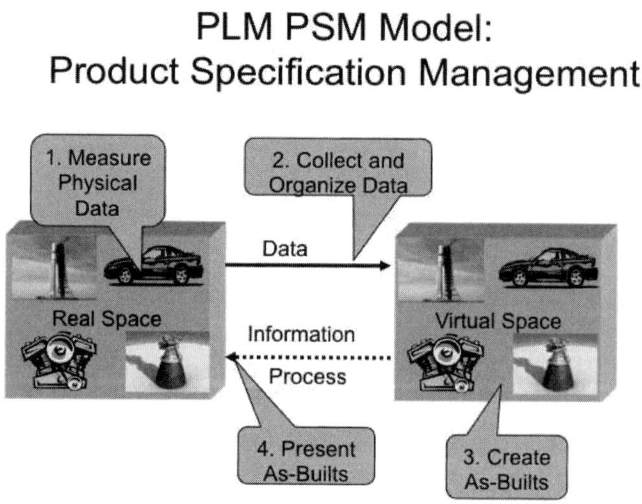

Figure 11.3

On the left side of Figure 11.3 the physical or real product, numerous hardware measuring systems exist that are being introduced on to the factory floor. Coordinate Measuring Machines (CMM's), laser measuring systems, gap-and-flush devices, and white light systems are just some of the hardware tools that are measuring the physical product in order to provide the data necessary to create an as-built virtual product.

The line in Figure 11.3 that connects the physical data collection to the virtual representation is a very critical aspect of this model. While the hardware measurement tools collect data on specific areas of interest, this data needs to be collected and organized in a comprehensive fashion. This PSM software needs to collect the input from disparate physical data collection tools in different formats and organize that data into an as-built virtual product.

The final component, the repository of the as-built virtual product, is the means by which all this as-built information is aggregated, stored, and made available for future purposes. I have previously proposed that Manufacturing Execution Systems (MES), which are part of the PLM framework, are the candidates for such a role. MES has access to the required detail in order to perform this activity.[61]

Without PSM, the physical data collection is simply individual data points whose usefulness is limited to assessing the quality of a single machine or work cell. PSM software is rapidly evolving to meet the requirements of creating virtual products from the physical products. True product quality requires that the entire product meet its manufacturing requirements.

Support

The role of the support function in Product Lifecycle Quality is to maintain the functionality of the product in the same condition as it left the factory. This of course assumes that the product design provides the functionality that the user values and that the product manufacturing produces a product that met the design and engineering specifications. The poor Yugo could have never been rehabilitated in terms of quality no matter how sterling the support of its dealers.

In order of desirability, we would like products that: A) never failed; B) predicted their failure so that they could be repaired before they actually failed; C) were repaired quickly. Condition A is unrealistic for anything but the simplest product.

Condition C has been one that organizations have spent a great deal of effort on. Virtual products can clearly add value in the support function. By knowing the configuration of the product and its history, the groups responsible for product support can understand what is in the product and what its history of repairs has been. Their opportunity to effectively and efficiently diagnose the product and put it back into service rapidly is enhanced. In addition, by linking the virtual product to its Bill of Service, individuals will have the appropriate knowledge as to how the product was designed to be repaired.

Condition B, predicting the failure of the product before it fails will constitute true product quality. If done correctly, this would mean that the product would only be out of service on a pre-scheduled basis. Product failures in use would diminish to the point of almost nothing.

This does require not only virtual products, but also reflective virtual products. By reflective, we mean that as the product goes about its life, we are collecting information on its changes in state. By aggregating the information and analyzing it, we can correlate state changes with subsequent failures of the product. This is actually done with complex products in a major way, such as jet airplane engines, or in a minor way, such as the check engine light in our automobiles. It could be done with more mundane products such as furnaces, garbage disposals, or garage door openers. No matter the level of the product, nothing is more frustrating for a product user or more detrimental to the perception of quality in a product than one that does not work when we go to use it.

The issue of occasional product failure for products that are in continuous operations has long been experienced and tolerated. While as described above, virtual products could go along way in even eliminating this kind of outage, historically people have been conditioned to expect product outages if they occur relatively infrequently and have minimal impact. However, there is a class of product where the product is only called for when there is a problem and a failure of any kind can cause a range of problems from major to catastrophic.

When I was a data center manager of a major computer center, the thing that drove me the craziest was when we had a power failure and the backup power generator failed to kick in. The only reason to have this backup power system was to be able to rely on it when we needed it. Even though we ran regular tests, there were a couple times that this backup system failed. Any failure of a product of this type is intolerable.

While my failures were relatively minor, they caused a substantial amount of lost productivity in computer downtime and wasted effort in restarting large mainframes. However, they pale in comparison with the current failure of BP's Blowout Preventer in the Deepwater Horizon disaster. This "failsafe" system failed to stop the oil leak when the oil well went out of control in the

Louisiana gulf. This product had one purpose and one purpose alone, and it failed miserably.

Whether or not there are other issues that led to this disaster is irrelevant to the discussion about the Blowout Preventer. The Blowout Preventer was designed to work in just this kind of catastrophic situation. It failed. While there may have been a hierarchy of failures, for example a failure in design because the cutting tool was insufficient to shear the pipe, there were also clearly sustainment issues. A battery in a key control module was dead.[62] While other products may not need the reflectivity of their operating condition, it is this type of product that absolutely needs to be instrumented to understand the state of operation at all times.

These products need to be instrumented so that the virtual product displays exactly the operational state of the physical product. If there is any deviation from what the physical state should be versus what the virtual product is showing the physical state to be, then the virtual product needs to immediately alert the necessary individuals. This disaster alone should justify any number of product manufacturers to better instrument and create a virtual product that reflects the operational state of the physical product at all times.

In the support phase, the issue of product liability often hinges on proving whether or not the individual product was manufactured to the required specifications. Without the ability to present data about the manufacture of a specific product, companies are at the mercy of plaintiff attorneys who raise doubt about the manufacturing process by asking, "Isn't it possible that the bolts holding my client's seat were not tightened properly?" Having the as-built virtual product, especially after the physical product may have been destroyed in an accident, gives the manufacturer protection against such an accusation.

Currently, the US government has legislated detailed traceability at the level of individual product instances as a requirement on the F-35 JSF aircraft program, necessitating the implementation of PSM technology by the prime defense contractor and its suppliers.

Dispose

While I have said many times before that disposal receives more lip service than actual attention, the issue of quality has relevance to the disposal phase.

In this respect, the quality concerns not how the product performs, but how effectively with respect to environmental impact it can be disposed of. Ideally, disposal should be weighted toward reuse and recycling. That clearly would have the least environmental impact. Absent that, disposing of the product with minimal environmental impact is desired.

The quality of performing that function will be directly related to having the information about how the product was designed and manufactured. Having the virtual product available at the disposal phase will allow for the most efficient disposal of the physical product. Absent that information, whoever is responsible for the product disposal will be making their best guess as to the decomposability and disposability of the product. In the worst-case situation, it will simply be dumped in a landfill because the cost of recreating the information necessary to dispose of the product properly will be too expensive. While quality has a different meaning in this phase, the idea of quality as it pertains to disposal is valid nonetheless.

QUALITY FEEDBACK LOOPS

While Figure 11.1 showed the create, build, service, and dispose phases as following one another in the product lifecycle quality loop, what should take place is a series of feedback loops within this quality circle. This is implied by the central core of information that each of these phases either populates or consumes, but we need to be much more explicit in defining the feedback loops that should occur within an organization.

Figure 11.4 presents this idea more explicitly. Each of the phases are followed by an evaluation of the effectiveness of that phase and the information learned from that is then fed back to the create phase where the product originates.

In the initial phase, the create phase, tests are done in order to ascertain whether or not the created product meets the requirements that have been defined for it. Because this takes place at the beginning of the product lifecycle, it is a fast iteration phase, compared to the other phases. However, how fast this phase will be will depend on whether the testing is done on physical products or on virtual products. If it is done on physical products, i.e., prototypes, this loop may not be so fast and may be fairly expensive. If it is done with virtual products, then it can very well be both fast and inexpensive.

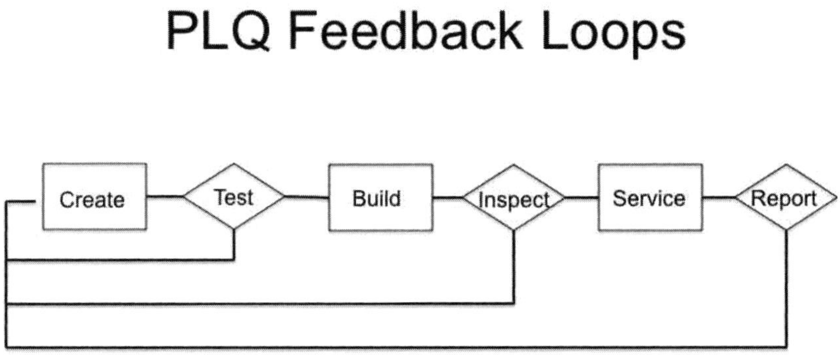

Figure 11.4

This feedback loop has always been relatively successful, since the engineers that are creating the product are generally in close proximity with the testing process. However, the cost of physical prototypes does not lend itself to exhaustive testing. The usual suspects are generally tested, but as I have mentioned before it is the unusual suspects that can cause the most problems. With virtual testing we can test many more conditions than we can with physical testing.

In the build phase, products are inspected and that information also needs to be fed back to the creation phase. In the past, this has not always been done well. Organizations have used the pass/fail inspection process to weed out nonconforming products. But oftentimes, the magnitude of scrap and rework in the factory was isolated in that factory setting. This obviously added to cumulative costs, without the design/engineering team being aware that the product that they created had either issues with the way it was designed or with the manufacturing processes that built it. Adding a feedback loop from the inspection process back to the creation phase provides valuable feedback that the design not only passes functional tests of potential performance, but also is able to be built with the requisite quality.

Often the issue is that the first few can be built to the requisite quality, but over time there are issues with the defined tolerances. Longitudinal Quality Management is about not only feeding back inspection data from the first few builds, but also is about creating a repository of the longitudinal data that the creation phase can use to simulate the manufacturing processes. This is so as to ensure that not only the first one can be built to specifications, but that as many as are required can also be built as well.

The third area, the area of service, has historically been underserved with respect to quality feedback loops. Unless the service issues were dramatic, meaning that they caused loss of life and/or media exposure about the defective products, the reporting as to product function and service deficiencies was generally slow to make it back into the creation phase of product development.

Since my definition of quality is a product that meets or exceeds the expectations of its customers as they use it, I view this link as probably the most important in terms of feeding back quality information. If designers in the create phase do not have visibility of the problems that their product has, chances are quite good that their future products will exhibit the same flaws in quality.

As I have mentioned in my previous book, warranty information is often fatally flawed. At worst, especially when the servicing organization is a different entity that is being paid by the product organization, the opportunity for servicers to maximize their revenue by, putting it delicately, "over servicing" the product is rampant. In the best of cases, the information gleaned from warranty reports can be almost unintelligible. I have recently gone through a series of warranty reports that originated from automobile dealerships. The descriptions as to what they found were fairly close to unintelligible. Between cryptic comments, abbreviated words, and liberties with the English language that preschoolers would not have taken, it was almost impossible to tell what the problem was and what was done.

The importance of this reporting that the product generates itself is not to be underestimated. Creating products that generate in-use data as to what their problems are in performance is of paramount importance if this feedback loop is going to be effective.

Figure 11.4 really does not illustrate anything more than Figure 11.1 does. However it does lay out in more detail and more explicitly that feedback loops need to exist from each of these phases. A major issue with most organizations is that each of these areas, the create, build, and service areas, are siloed. Information may flow within these areas, but oftentimes does not flow between these different areas.

I have not mentioned the need to create a feedback loop from the disposal phase, although Figure 11.1 implies that. That is the feedback loop that probably least exists. If organizations are going to be successful in recycling and disposing of their product, then this feedback will also need to exist. I have not dwelt on this, not because it is unimportant, but because organizations will focus on these first three areas before they focus on disposal.

Quality is one of the most important aspects of every phase of a product's lifecycle, yet most of the focus has been on manufacturing quality. True product quality relies on the perceived value of the product user. This chapter introduces the idea of Product Lifecycle Quality (PLQ) that defines quality for each of the product lifecycle phases.

Product Lifecycle Management defines the different aspects of quality throughout the product lifecycle as perceived value, requirements, designs, specifications, instances, and performance. PLQ also deals with the issue of quality as it pertains to product disposal by equating quality to environmental impact.

The chapter describes a product quality hierarchy where the implications of quality in one phase affect the implications of quality in the next phase. While these are all technically, "quality control" issues, they have different descriptions to indicate quality failures. The perceived value to requirements mapping failure has been called poor marketing. The failure of requirements to specifications mapping has been referred to as poor engineering. The requirements to instances mapping of the product has in the past received the most attention and has been referred to as quality control, although it might more accurately be called specification control. Finally instances of the product to their lifelong performance mapping has been defined as support issues when failures occur.

The key to generating true product quality throughout its life is to create both a physical and a virtual product. Product Specification Management (PSM) is instrumental in creating as-built products as they are physically being created. PSM consists of four parts: a Virtual Controlling Product, equipment to measure and capture physical characteristics, software to organize these physical characteristics in a product-centric fashion, and a system for retrieval and use of that information.

Creating true product quality requires a more comprehensive and holistic look of the product as it moves through its various lifecycle phases.

Notes

54 I introduced the concept of Product Lifecycle Quality (PLQ) in a paper entitled: Product Lifecycle Quality (PLQ): A Framework within Product Lifecycle Management (PLM) for Achieving Product Quality (See Grieves, M. (2010). Product Lifecycle Quality (PLQ): A Framework within Product Lifecycle Management (PLM) for Achieving Product Quality. *Int. J. Manufacturing Technology and Management, 19*(3/4), 180-190.) This chapter relies on some of the material from that paper.

55 See Christensen, C. M. and M. E. Raynor (2003). *The innovator's solution: creating and sustaining successful growth.* Boston, Mass., Harvard Business School Press.

56 Amazingly enough, the Yugo was marketed as a quality automobile. The American company that imported the Yugo made a significant effort to improve the quality of the factory in Yugoslavia that manufactured the car. So this example may not be so apocryphal. See Vuic, J. (2009). *The Yugo: the rise and fall of the worst car in history* (1st ed.). New York: Hill and Wang.

57 For an article on function creep, see Rust, R. T., D. V. Thompson, et al. (2006). "Defeating Feature Fatigue." *Harvard Business Review* **84**(2): 98-107.

58 For references on Quality Control, see Juran, J. M. (1995). *A history of managing for quality: the evolution, trends, and future directions of managing for quality.* Milwaukee, Wis., ASQC Quality Press, and also Juran, J. M. and A. B. Godfrey (1999). *Juran's quality handbook.* New York, McGraw Hill

59 See Meyer, C. and A. Schwager (2007). "Understanding Customer Experience." *Harvard Business Review* **85**(2): 116-126.

60 See *"Toyota Harmony TV Commercial." Retrieved 7/30/10, from* http://www.youtube.com/watch?v=qu6IcBnEfNM

61 See Grieves, M. (2007) "Multiplying MES Value with PLM Integration," http://www.apriso.com/library/white_papers.php.

62 See Mufson, S. and Fahrenthold (2010, May 13). Oil spill investigators find critical problems in blowout preventer. *The Washington Post.* Washington.

12

VIRTUALLY CONNECTED

For the most part, the discussion about product producers or manufacturers has ignored suppliers. The product producer has been assumed to be a single organization. However, the reality is that most products, especially complex products, are the result of the activities of a number of organizations. In fact in numerous situations, there are more people who deal with the information about the product outside of the product producer than within the product producer's own organization.

This was not an issue in the past. Companies that were involved in the production of products clustered together in geographical areas. The flow of information between individuals of different companies was relatively easy. It might have entailed travel of a few miles or so, but that was all.

This was certainly true during the build phase, as these production facilities were clustered together in order to reduce logistics and transportation expenses. When Just-in -Time manufacturing became popular, it was a requirement to locate supplier factories in close geographic proximity to the customer.

This was not as critical during the create phase, although most suppliers were on the same continent as their customers. They moved paper designs by mail or sometimes even by truck if they were voluminous enough. A lag of a few days was not considered critical. Since suppliers and customers were all on the same continent and since development times were relatively long, scheduling face-to-face meetings at periodic intervals sufficed.

At the end of the 20th century and at the beginning of the 21st century, the drivers began to emerge that required dramatic changes to the customer-supplier model. Two of the drivers that I discussed in my first book that changed this model are cycle times and globalization.

During the last quarter of the 20th century, cycle times of product creation and manufacturing began to shrink dramatically. With that shrinkage went the luxury of waiting days for the transfer of information and the ability to schedule periodic meetings to resolve issues. Information about the product, both in its creation and its manufacturing phases, was needed immediately. Collaboration on issues that arose needed immediate attention and resolution. The coordination of customer and supplier went from independent activities with periodic checkpoints to integrated efforts with constant movement of information.

At the same time that long cycle times with their slack that allowed for slow and periodic communications began rapid contraction, globalization began to accelerate quickly. No longer were customers and their suppliers within the proverbial stone's throw of each other. They were now, literally, spread out across the world. The ability for the customer to gather up its plans and walk across the street to a supplier or for that customer to walk out on the suppliers' factory floor in order to resolve issues vanished almost overnight.

It is still unclear whether this globalization occurred because of the search for cheaper locales in order to create and produce products and that information technology scrambled to provide tools in order to make this possible or whether information technology enabled companies to engage in this globalization. In any event, it happened. The issue is that it happened so fast that we have not thought through the conceptual implications of this momentous change. Given that this globalization has occurred, we need to think differently about how we think of products, their information, and the customer-supplier relationship.

SUPPLY CHAINS AND SUPPLY NETS

The common term in referring to a collection of organizations that are engaged in creating, manufacturing, and supporting the product that is sold by the product producer is a "supply chain."[63] However, with this new way of thinking about product information that is contained in the PLM concept, we need a new term to describe this collection of organizations that create and share information. My proposal is that we call them "supply nets." Figure 12.1 is a graphic representation of the two concepts.

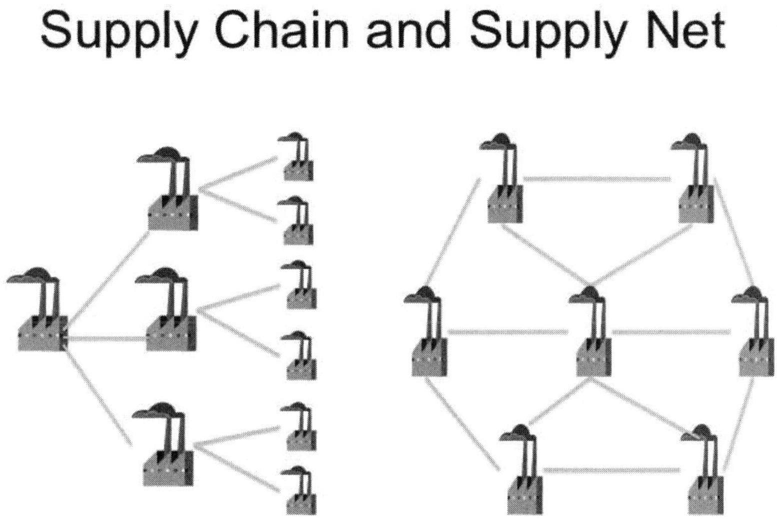

Figure 12.1

The reason that we need the new term, *supply net*, is that what we call things has a substantial influence about how we think of things. Metaphors are a powerful mechanism that we humans use to convey a substantial amount of tacit information. While there are some that would argue that metaphors such as "supply chain" are dead metaphors, i.e., they really do not invoke any other meaning beyond their dictionary definition. I, among others, have argued in previous research that this is not the case.[64]

The term, *supply chain*, does structure our way of thinking about products and the various organizations that cooperate in making these products possible. Before product manufacturers adopted PLM concepts, thinking about their suppliers as a *chain* did have merit. The concept of a supply chain was an apt description of how these participants were organized and how they moved about the necessary components that were combined to form the final product.

Chains are by their very nature atom-based and invoke the idea of sequential activity. If we were to examine a chain, we would see the links organized in a sequential fashion with each link separate and distinct. If we were to run the chain through our fingers, we would handle each link from the beginning to the end of the chain, and our fingers would only be on one link at a time.

The reason that we picked a *chain* as a metaphor is that it reflects how we think about the activities that go into producing a complete product. As components are made, they move up the chain of organizations that are involved in producing the products. Since these components are physical, they only reside in one organization or link at a time. Each organization or link performs its processes on the components and, upon completion, move these components up the chain to the next organization or link.

If there is a problem with the component, it is moved back down the chain until it reaches the organization that dealt with it originally. That supplier resolves the issue and ships the component back up the chain. Rarely, if ever, does one supplier who is only linked to the supplier above and below have any visibility of a supplier and its activities that is farther than that link above and below.

This metaphor of a chain was appropriate when all that moves from supplier to supplier in a sequential fashion was the actual part or component itself. With the advent of a virtual product, we need a new metaphor that reflects this new concept. This metaphor is that of a *supply net.*

Nets are different than chains because they are interconnected and not sequential. Even when we think of physical nets, we think in terms of interconnected nodes, which are nonlinear in nature. If we think of a basketball net or butterfly net, we think of interwoven strands that combine together in a collaborative fashion. We pull a chain, but we don't pull a net.

But when we think of a "net," we more often think of it in terms that are virtual rather than physical. When we think of a net, we more likely than not to think of the Internet, a phone network, or a network of friends. While the Internet and the phone network are implemented with actual equipment, we think of them in conceptual terms. They are virtual networks. So, not only does the idea of a net invoke thoughts of something that is integrated, collaborative, and non-sequential, but the idea of a net also invokes the idea of working in a virtual rather physical environment.

The idea of a chain invokes thoughts of a linear movement over a period of time. If I pull on a chain, I handle one link at a time and the link off in the distance takes time to get to me. On the other hand, the idea of a net invokes thoughts of simultaneous and instantaneous action. If I think of the Internet, my access to information and other nodes of the Internet are instantaneous. In addition, many of us can access that information simultaneously.

While the idea of a supply chain was appropriate to a world in which there was only one product, the physical product, we need a new metaphor where we now have two products, a physical one and a virtual one. As this book has consistently pointed out, in keeping with our desire to use bits instead of atoms wherever possible, we can use virtual products to make critical and important decisions. We can use the information that the virtual product makes available to us in a simultaneous and instantaneous fashion.

If we relied on possession of the physical product for information, as we have had to do in the past, we used up valuable time in transferring the physical product from one geographical location to another. In addition, only one participant in the supply chain had physical possession of that physical product at any point in time. Physical products traveled up and down the supply chain at a waste of valuable time and at a substantial cost of resources to physically move the products.

PRODUCTS REQUIRE BOTH SUPPLY CHAINS AND NETS

Supply nets do not replace supply chains. Supply nets augment supply chains. When product information was only contained as an intrinsic part of the physical product, then supply chains were not only a mechanism for moving around the physical product, but they also served as a mechanism for moving around the virtual product, i.e., the information about the product.

As we developed the ability to strip that information from the product and create virtual products, we are now able to move around that virtual product without also having to move the physical product. However, since we still live in the physical world, there is still the requirement to move physical products. The research into and experience with physical supply chains continues to be and will continue to be extremely relevant. Supply chain organization, process management, logistics, and cost management are extremely important in decreasing the use of scarce physical resources in moving physical products across the globe in a timely fashion.

Where supply nets come into play is our interest in trading off bits for atoms and replacing atoms with bits wherever possible. Supply nets augment supply chains by effecting the movement of the virtual product in place of moving the physical product whenever and wherever possible.

While we can have supply chains and not have supply nets, the converse is not true. We will always need to move the physical product, and, as we have done in the past, we can move the information about that product in physical form as either a part of the product or as pieces of paper that accompany the product.

The issue is that supply nets can decrease the consumption of valuable resources, especially elapsed time, as compared to supply chains. If we are looking to use only the information about the product to make decisions, then requiring the movement of that physical product in order to obtain that information is wasteful.

Using supply nets to move information about the product wherever possible and employing supply chains to move the physical product conserves physical resources, reduces elapsed time, and improves the quality of decisions. Supply nets are not a replacement for supply chains, but are major enhancements to productivity. Supply chains continue to move the physical product, while supply nets take on the responsibility for moving the virtual product.

HIERARCHY OF SUPPLIER PART QUALITY CONFIDENCE

As Figure 12.2 illustrates, the hierarchy of quality confidence is as follows: acceptance, certification, inspection, testing, and visibility. As we progress up through this hierarchy, our confidence that the product is of the quality we specify increases.

At the acceptance level, we merely accept the parts as they arrives at a loading dock. At this level, we are simply assuming that the parts fully meet our specifications. This may or may not be the case. If we have a long history of dealing with the supplier who has provided the same parts over the years, we may have an extremely high level of trust and confidence that this supplier will only deliver to us parts that fully meet our specifications.

However, as pointed out before, if it is a new supplier and/or it is a part that we have little history with, this may pose a potential, serious problem.

The issue with the acceptance approach is that finding out that this part is not up to the appropriate quality standards means that we will find this out only as we are attempting to use the part in production or, worse, we find out when the finished product fails in customer use because of this part.

Hierarchy of Supplier Part Quality Confidence

Visibility
Testing
Inspection
Certification
Acceptance

Figure 12.2

Certification is our reliance on the supplier certifying that the part meets the required specifications. This is very common in the aerospace industry where suppliers certify material, processes, and testing and produce certification documents that attest that they have tested or inspected the part such that they can make such certifications. These certifications carry legal ramifications with them, so that they are not insignificant. However, relying on someone else's certification is a second-best solution. If a product fails because of a defective but certified part, the product producer is still responsible for that product.

At the next level, we perform inspection processes as a element of receiving the part. Most commonly, we are performing an inspection of a sample, where we can use probability theory in order to determine whether or not the entire population of parts meets our requirements. However, inspections require us to commit resources, so that the cost of our quality inspections can range from minimal to substantial. At this level, we do have some assurance that we can find problems before they make their way onto the factory floor and into actual products.

At the next level, we are not only inspecting the product, but we are testing it for certain characteristics. Testing will be more expensive than simply an inspection, but it will take us a step further in our confidence that the part meets our quality demands. In addition to the issue that testing is a more expensive proposition, the required testing that we need to do may involve weakening or destroying the product. If this is the case, then we can only do this for a limited sample of the parts because we will not be able to use the tested parts in production.

The top level is visibility. What this means is that we have visibility into the production of the part as it occurs at the supplier facilities. We are receiving the data as the part goes through its various operations in order to understand that the part indeed was produced to the requisite specifications. This gives us the highest level of confidence, because we have information that the part went through the operations specified in the Bill of Process.

We also have the results from all inspection and quality control checks that go into creating the as-builts. While not a guarantee of part performance, having this information should give us great confidence that the part went through the processes it was required to go through and that the resulting key measurements on the part met our specifications. If this information is not available, it also tells use something important, namely that the supplier is not doing what is necessary to produce a quality part.

This visibility might appear more expensive, but in reality we are simply piggybacking on the work done by our supplier. Each previous level in this hierarchy increased our costs because we were recreating information that had previously been created at the supplier. If we can segregate out the information for our particular part as the supplier produces parts, a not unreasonable thing to do with today's information systems, we then can have great confidence without having to incur our own use of resources in assuring the quality of the product. Again, we use information as a substitute for wasted resources. In this case, the wasted resources are the costs of recreating information that will be available at the supplier if they are doing the required quality inspections.

SUPPLY CHAINS VERSUS SUPPLY NETS CHARACTERISTICS

Table 12.1 outlines the characteristic differences between supply chains and supply nets. Supply chains are material based while supply nets are digital based. Physical products transferred by supply chains are indivisible, while supply nets can adjust the granularity of the virtual product they transfer. Supply chains are sequential, while supply nets are integrative.

Suppliers: Chain vs. Net

Chain	Net
Materials based	Digital based
Low visibility	High visibility
Sequential	Integrative
Product precedes info	Info precedes product
IS int – None to low	IS int – med to high

Table 12.1

In supply chains, there is low visibility of a product's information except for the individual supplier that is in physical possession of that product. With supply nets, the virtual product provides all participants of the supply net with near simultaneous and instantaneous information about the product. Supply nets require information systems integration between participants that supply chains do not. In supply chains, the physical product precedes the information about the product. The opposite is true in supply nets. These characteristics are expanded on below.

Physical-based versus Digital-based

As should be clear at this point, supply chains are about physical resources while supply nets are about digital ones. Supply chains deal with warehouses, loading docks, trucks, railroads, planes, boxes and pallets. Supply nets deal with computers, communication lines, RFID, barcodes, and software.

While we have a pretty good understanding of the physical components of supply chains, we are in the initial phase of defining supply nets. While the physical pieces of supply nets are pretty well established, e.g. computers and the Internet, the digital makeup of the virtual product is still undefined and constitutes a very wide spectrum.

For low value, commodity products, the virtual product that is transmitted could be as simple as the part number and quantity. For high-value, precisely engineered products such as the common bulkhead in NASA's next launch vehicle, the virtual product could be as complicated as a complete point cloud from a white light scanner. Obviously, the amount and structure of virtual product information is dramatically different between these two examples.

Defining the transmission structure of virtual products throughout the supply net should be relatively straightforward. Defining the content of the virtual product will evolve over time and will be context and use case dependent.

Indivisible Material versus Granular Information

All participants of the supply net potentially have the same informational access as all other participants. However, there is even an additional benefit in the supply net versus the supply chain. In a supply chain, only one participant could have physical possession. In addition, when a participant had physical possession, they had full physical possession. It is an all or nothing access. The product is there in its entirety or it is not there at all. If the supplier wants to inspect and analyze it, short of sending someone to guard the product at all times, there is nothing to stop them.

However, with virtual products, there can be granularity in access to that virtual product. While the advantage of a supply net is that all participants could have instantaneous and simultaneous access to the virtual product, this access could also be granulated, so that all participants might not have full access to the product, but only to those aspects of the product to which they were entitled. If the product owner wants a particular participant to only have access to the outer shape and not to any inner structures, then that is easily accomplished.

This is the best of both worlds. Participants in supply net have simultaneous and instantaneous access to the virtual product in order to use that information to better integrate the components of an individual product. But the owner of that virtual product can control which aspects of that virtual product that they choose to share.

Sequential versus Integrative

As illustrated above, supply chains are sequential in nature. Only one participant at a time can possess the physical product. To move that product from participant to participant requires consuming physical resources. Elapsed time is often the most important of these resources. In addition, it would be one thing if we could count on a sequential process being efficient in that there was only one move of the physical product in a forward linear fashion from participant to participant.

However, as often is the case, the physical product moves up and down the supply chain because there are problems with the product that needs to be resolved. Supplier A moves physical product to Supplier B, only to have Supplier B determine that the product is substandard, which requires that the product to be shipped back to Supplier A.

Supply nets, on the other hand are integrative. If supply nets are implemented according to this concept, all suppliers in the network have visibility of the virtual product at the same time. Rather than Supplier B receiving products that are substandard from Supplier A, Supplier B can inspect the virtual product and determine whether it meets the requirements that have been agreed upon prior to Supplier A shipping any physical products.

Low Visibility versus High Visibility

Supply chains provide low visibility of products, while supply nets provide high visibility. In physical supply chains, only one supplier at a time can have possession of the physical product. This is not entirely true, as multiple suppliers can have physical access to the product, but only if the multiple suppliers travel to the location of the physical product. The issue is still the same issue: the waste of physical resources including time.

With virtual products, there is theoretically high visibility in that a number of suppliers can have access to the virtual product or product information simultaneously. Assuming the right technologies are in place and the right permissions are given, all the members of the supply net who are involved with the product can have access to the latest information about the product.

This visibility also applies to products that don't exist but should. Too often, suppliers integrating their product with others are caught off guard when the product fails to show up at the prescribed time. Human nature is such that suppliers often give false assurances to their partners that commitments will be met, even when the manufacturing activities that need to take place in order for this to occur are not happening. However, for those suppliers with access to the virtual product, when the appropriate information is not being created, they know that the product is not going to show up at the required time. This gives them valuable time that they would not have had in the past to take mitigating actions.

In some cases, the inability to admit to failure is baked into the culture. In a recent situation, an Asian supplier of aerospace parts kept giving reassurances to their customer that the parts were on schedule and would arrive on time. This did not occur. Had the customer visibility into the supplier's product information, they would have known that the production did not take place and could have taken steps to compensate for that. As it was, the failure of the product to show up caught the customer unaware and caused substantial delays in their production.

Product Precedes Info versus Info Precedes Product

In supply chains, the product precedes information about the product. What this means is that the receiving supplier must have physically received the product before they can begin to inspect it. In the best case, the product and the product information arrive at the same time, as in the case where the receiving supplier rolls up the door to the semi trailer to see that everything inside is broken. But what usually occurs is that the receiving supplier is not aware that the parts or components are substandard until after an inspection and/or testing process. By then, substantial costs have been incurred and valuable time has been lost.

The dirty little secret about supply chains is often this: suppliers attempt to calculate what is the most substandard part or component that their customer will accept. The shipping supplier knows that, especially in this era of Just-in-Time provisioning, the customer must try to accept all of the products in order to meet its obligations up the supply chain. By the time the physical product arrives at the receiving dock of this customer, it may be too late to do anything else other than to accept that product. If that sort of thing occurs up the supply chain, the final product would clearly be deficient or, at best, substandard.

The slogan of supply nets is, "Transmit us the virtual product and we will tell you whether or not to ship the physical product." By having the information about the part or component well in advance of the time that the physical part or component would have been received, supply participants have much better options than to *have* to accept the physical product. While this is important in the case of receiving substandard products, it is also important in the case where there is no physical product to receive.

Many times, receiving suppliers only realize that there is a problem with the product that they expect to receive when a product fails to show up on their receiving dock at the agreed upon time. By the time that occurs, the problem of not having the product has been seriously compounded. The receiving supplier is required to readjust manufacturing schedules, try and find replacement parts or components, or simply shut down its manufacturing line.

By requiring participants of the supply net to create and transmit virtual products, receiving suppliers have forewarning that a problem is in the works. Much like the Sherlock Holmes story where the dog did not bark, if the shipping supplier fails to transmit the virtual product at the required time, then the customer knows that there is a problem and reacts then, rather than waiting for the product not to show up at the receiving dock at a later time.

Low IS Integration versus High IS Integration

However, as the last element in the Supplier Chain versus Net table shows, supply nets require much more information systems integration than supply chains. For supply chains, there may be little to no information systems integration. The information that the shipping supplier might provide may be paper-based in nature. In this case, there is no electronic information flow from the shipping supplier to the receiving supplier. Even in cases today where members of the supply chain transmit information, it is often more useful for accounting than for the purposes of creating products.

Supply nets require a medium to high level of information systems integration. Both shipping supplier and receiving supplier must implement the concept of virtual products. They must be able to share this information about virtual products between them instantaneously and simultaneously. While the level of the abstraction of the virtual product may differ, and differ dramatically, between shipping supplier and receiving supplier, enough information about the virtual product must flow from the shipping supplier to the receiving supplier in order for the receiving supplier to make definitive decisions about the suitability of the product they are about to receive. Ideally, the receiving supplier can make use of this information as it adds its value to the product so that participants who deal with the product later can aggregate information from all the participants in the supply net that previously worked with the product.

As I have stated many times before, information is not free and there is a cost to developing, transmitting, and coordinating this product information. In order for information to be worth its cost, information needs to be able to replace the wasted resources and the cost of that information needs to be less than the cost of the wasted resources. We will look at the benefits to both product producer and their suppliers. While the savings in wasted resources are dependent on the specific situation, there are enough categories of potential savings that most organizations would benefit from investing in supply net capability.

SUPPLY NET BENEFITS

Unlike the early use of the Internet to connect product providers and their suppliers, supply nets can benefit both. The early use of the Internet in this area was Material Exchanges where product providers reverse auctioned their potential purchases to a pool of suppliers. The primary intent was to drive down the cost of product acquisition, which benefited the buyer but only drove down profit margins for the suppliers.

My early work in PLM proposed that if the product producer and its suppliers could collaborate and share information, then the win-lose proposition of Material Exchanges could be replaced with a win-win proposition of Information Exchanges. Sharing information could remove wasted costs from both parties and not simply from the product producer as Material Exchanges were intended to do. These Informational Exchanges, as I called them, were a better use of the Internet for product provider to supplier connections. Supply nets are a maturation of those ideas.

Product Provider Supply Net Benefits

The most valuable benefit of supply nets may be in savings of time. Time savings have two connotations. One is the savings of labor hours. The other is a savings of elapsed time or what I refer to as clock time. Clock time is a resource that cannot be compensated for once it is gone. As such, it may be humans' most valuable resource.

With visibility of the virtual products as the suppliers are producing them, product producers can gain valuable clock time in order to mitigate problems. The chances are that we can better compensate for an issue that we found out about four weeks ago than an issue we find out about today. If we know that a supplier's product is drifting out of tolerance, we can notify them that this is not acceptable and that they need to rerun the production.

If we find out today that we have an issue, when the product shows up at our shipping dock, and, if we need that product to keep our assembly lines moving, then our options are very limited. If four weeks ago, we did not receive the virtual product, then we have a pretty good idea that the physical product is not going to show up at our loading dock on time. We now have four weeks to address that issue, rather than dealing with it today, when the product simply does not show up.

Product providers also save the more traditional types of resources, such as labor time, material, and energy. By using virtual products, product providers can reduce the use of resources in physically moving products up and down the supply chain. The cost of moving atoms is far more expensive than moving bits. As the last link in the supply chain, the product provider will ultimately also be the recipient of all the costs in moving components up and down the supply chain. Product providers can reduce those costs by moving virtual products instead of physical products.

Supply nets also foster a more integrative approach with their suppliers. Through the use of virtual products, suppliers can participate and work closely with the product provider in resolving issues both during design and in the manufacture phase. In the past, once a supplier shipped the product, it was up to the product producer to resolve any issues because only they had possession of the physical product. Virtual products remain available for all in the supply net to have visibility of and work on. Problems can be identified and resolved much more quickly.

Finally, having the virtual product allows the product producer to have much more visibility and traceability of the product that they are ultimately responsible for. This allows the product producer to better support the product because they have information on all parts and components of that product.

Supplier Supply Net Benefits

While it may seem that suppliers would not benefit from fully disclosing the information on their products, that is not the case, or rather that is not the case for high-quality suppliers. If suppliers are trying to hide deficient products, then this is not to their advantage. For suppliers who do not have a good understanding of what happens in their manufacturing processes and are simply hoping that their products meet their customer's requirements, then supply nets are also not to their advantage.

However, for quality suppliers who are collecting the appropriate information on the factory floor that allows them to ensure that they are producing quality products, this is a major differentiator from those suppliers who cannot or will not do the same. The quality suppliers will have a competitive advantage if they are prepared to show their customer that their products meet the customer's requirements. They can do this by creating virtual products and transmitting it to their customers in advance of the physical products.

Since supply nets are much more integrative than supply chains, the suppliers will have a much closer connection to their customer, the product provider. The value of what suppliers will deliver to their customer increases and becomes a factor that will mitigate against a price-only mentality. The virtual product, even though it is bits and not atoms, has a value of its own.

The supplier who participates in the supply net will reduce their cost of production because they now have this information about what happens on the factory floor. By using the virtual product, they can reduce the waste of producing products that do not meet their customer requirements. They can reduce ramp up time by using simulation to determine the processes and methods that reduce their costs. While virtual products produce additional value, they also lead to reduced costs. That gives the suppliers substantial competitive advantages over suppliers who cannot do this.

SUPPLY NETS THROUGHOUT THE PRODUCT LIFECYCLE

The value in thinking about supply nets permeates throughout the whole product lifecycle. The ability of suppliers to have simultaneous and instantaneous access to a common virtual product allows them to better collaborate and conserve physical resources. The ability to have visibility of the virtual product allows suppliers to trade that information for wasted resources: time, energy, and material.

While the idea of supply chains and supply nets would generally encompass the time until the product was in the end users' hands, the focus here will be with the product producer who takes responsibility for the creation, manufacturing, and support of the product. This entity can go by a few terms such as product manufacturer, original equipment manufacturer (OEM), or product producer. However, while there are some differences in these terms, I will use product producer to represent the entity that takes responsibility for creating, building, supporting, and, in all probability in the future, disposing of the product.

Create

The creation phase of a product is where classical thinking about supply chains falls short, and thinking in terms of supply nets has great merit. In the create phase, product information and the virtual product takes center stage. In this phase, the physical product does not yet exist. There is only information about the product, and the purpose of this phase is to create a physical product. Within a single entity, there are always questions about who has responsibility and control of product information. When you bring other suppliers from other organizational entities into the picture, issues of responsibility and control are compounded.

Table 12.2 portrays the different combinations of product control between the suppliers and product producer. The range of product control is separated into low, medium, and high for each of these participants. The entries in each of the quadrants indicate the characteristic of the product relationship.

Producer-Supplier Info Flow

Supplier Control \ Producer Control	Low	Medium	High
High	III Low-Medium Supplier Engineered	VI High Custom Spec	IX High Collaborative Development
Medium	II Low Generic	V Med – High Configured	VIII High Producer Driven
Low	I Low Commodity	IV Low-High Producer Spec	VII High Producer Engineered

Table12.2

In Quadrant I, where supplier and producer product control are both low, neither supplier nor product producer has control of the virtual product. Instead, there are strong conventions or standards that define the products. These products are things like nuts, bolts, screws, hoses, wire, and similar commodity items. The nomenclature for these items is firmly established and all participants have the same virtual product in mind when there is a reference to that product. The virtual product will generally be in a library of common products that both suppliers and producer have access to. There is little information flow required and generally a part number or common description will be all that is necessary to convey product information between supplier and producer.

In Quadrant II, supplier control is medium while product producer control is low. In this case, the supplier has a catalog of parts that the product producer can select from. While there may be some uniqueness to the supplier, generally there are equivalent parts and components available from multiple suppliers in that these parts are generic. The supplier controls the virtual part and makes that virtual part available to the producer. Comparable virtual parts may vary from supplier to supplier, but this is probably more along the lines of specific characteristics rather than geometric design. There is relatively little information flow once the product producer has selected the part or component that meets their needs, and the supplier has sent over the corresponding virtual part information.

In Quadrant III, the supplier control is high while the product producer control is low. This is what would be called a supplier-engineered product. The supplier would view this virtual product as proprietary, at least in part. The supplier would be cautious about how much product information they shared with the producer. The supplier might provide external geometric shape information so that the producer could package this part or component in the overall product, but the supplier might do that in a lightweight form or model so that the producer did not have access to proprietary information. Information flow would be low to medium, depending on whether the supplier was constrained by dimensional requirements from the product producer and needed to provide iterations of the product information.

In Quadrant IV, supplier control is low, while product producer control is medium. In this situation, the product producer would be providing specifications of the particular component that it required. The supplier would be required to match the specifications against its product library to determine if they had a product acceptable to meet the specifications. Depending on the complexity of the specifications, the information flow could be low to high. The supplier would be required to convey the virtual product to the producer in order to convince the product producer that the part or component met the specifications. Once the product producer had the virtual product, the suppliers control over the virtual product would be greatly diminished.

In Quadrant V, both product producer and supplier control is medium. This is often the case in configurable products. The producer wants a configuration that the product supplier can provide that will meet its requirements.

The supplier has a little more control over its virtual product, in that the product producer would view that the configuration of the supplier would be relatively unique. There is a fair amount of information flow back and forth between the supplier and product producer until a configuration that the product producer is satisfied with is reached.

In Quadrant VI, the product producer control is medium while the supplier control is high. This is generally case where the producer gives the supplier a list of functional requirements that it requires. While the producer may do this for a part or component, this most often happens for a complete assembly, such as an engine, fuel pump, or even an entire automobile interior. The supplier then engineers a product that will meet those requirements.

The information flow is generally relatively high as the supplier creates the required virtual product. There may be a number of iterations of the virtual product before it is deemed sufficient by the product producer. While the positioning on the grid indicates that the supplier control is high, the supplier needs to take sufficient precautions to protect its virtual product. There was a notable situation a number of years back when the head of purchasing at General Motors shared the designs of the originating supplier with other suppliers. Since these other suppliers did not have to go to the cost of producing these designs, they could charge less for the product. Needless to say this caused a huge uproar in the supplier industry and damaged GM's relationship with its suppliers.

Quadrant VII is the case where supplier control is low and producer control is high. This is the case when the producer does the engineering work and the supplier is contracting to produce those parts or components. In this case, information flow can be high since there may be multiple iterations as a product producer and supplier agree to what can be built and at what cost.

The information flow is mostly one way. The supplier is generally constrained to use the same digital tools that the product producer uses. This generally means that suppliers who deal with a number of product producers are required to have multiple tools, increasing the costs.

Quadrant VIII is the case where supplier control is medium and product producer control is high. This is a situation where the product producer is the major developer of the product plans, but needs a considerable amount of supplier involvement. Information flows are high in that there needs to be a high level of collaboration between supplier and producer. The virtual

product that is arrived at, although under control of the producer, has major inputs from the supplier.

High information flows occur both ways. In addition, the supplier may have issues with protecting their intellectual property. They may have a difficult time in balancing out their wish for business at the expense of providing their designs to the product producer.

Quadrant IX is the case where supplier control and customer control are both high. This is effectively a partnership between supplier and producer. Neither can produce the product on their own, and close collaboration is required. Information flows of this quadrant are very high. There most likely will be many iterations before a virtual product can be decided upon. Generally, all the requirements are not attainable, and there needs to be trade-offs between some of the requirements. Not only are the information flows high, but also the possibility of conflict is also high. This means that there may be a great deal of arguments over what the prevailing virtual product should be. In fact, there may be a few virtual products that compete until the very end of the process.

Who winds up owning the virtual product may also be a source of contention. This issue should be discussed and specified ahead of time. In addition, the outcome may hinge on how sophisticated the product producer's procurement organization is. Most procurement organizations only have familiarity with acquiring physical products. As a result, there are a significant number of situations where product producer organizations have funded the development of products, only to discover that they have only acquired the physical product. They find this out when they go to make a change to the product, only to find that they have to purchase the information to do this from the supplier. In one particular Department of Defense case, the cost of the physical change was dwarfed by the cost of having to buy (again) the information necessary to make the change.

Lean and innovative

What the Producer-Supplier Info Flow table illustrates is that in the create phase of a product's life, the most prevalent manifestation of the product is the virtual product. As a result, the flow of information is high, while the flow of physical material is low. In fact, in order to be lean, the flow of physical resources needs to be low.

This was not always the case and still may be true for those organizations that have not adopted PLM. In environments that still have not adopted virtual products, the flow and ensuing costs of moving physical resources through the supply chain in the create phase is high. Companies that are still using actual blueprints and prototypes must expend costly physical resources in order to move them through their supply chain.

Prior to using virtual products, automotive companies literally used forklifts to move mountains of blueprints that were then shipped at significant expense to suppliers in order to allow those suppliers to quote on producing parts and components. Now, the same automotive companies package up their virtual designs and ship them via the Internet to their potential suppliers. This is done at a fraction of the cost and at a significant reduction in time.

Without virtual products, two-dimensional blueprints could only take designers so far. Sooner rather than later, these blueprints had to be turned into physical prototypes. Again, physical prototypes are for the most part a very expensive form of storing and working with information. In the absence of virtual products, the only way of creating information about how parts fit together and perform is to produce physical representations of those parts in order to perform fitting and performance tests. These physical parts, with their atom-based make up, would then be modified and the ensuing information that was learned from working with them would be extracted from these physical prototypes and transferred back into the blueprints.

This is a very expensive and time-consuming process. Manipulating bits versus atoms is potentially orders of magnitudes cheaper and less time-consuming. For companies to be truly lean in the create phase, they must replace the use of physical resources with virtual products wherever possible. Blueprints are rapidly disappearing from modern organizations and physical prototypes are probably not far behind.

In the past, companies produced finished prototypes of their products. Airplane manufacturers produced airplanes that served as their test articles, but were then scrapped or mothballed. Automobile manufacturers created a large number of test vehicles both for engineering testing and manufacturing feasibility. Today, airplane manufacturers sell the first airplane that they finish.

The first Boeing 787 was to be sold to an airline.[65] Automobile manufacturers are not yet in that position, but they have significantly decreased the number of vehicles that they have to build for test and feasibility purposes.

These companies are substituting virtual products in place of physical products. Their goal is to do their development on the virtual product, and, only when they get the virtual product perfected, do they create a physical one.

However, especially in the create phase, it is not enough to be lean. Organizations must also be innovative. Luckily, these two principles are not contradictory. Before PLM with its virtual products, the use of physical blueprints and prototypes made changes in information very costly. As the table shows, except for the lower left-hand quadrants, information flows are high. Constraining those information flows means that there will be very little change in information.

However, innovation is all about information change. No product concept comes into being fully formed. As new things are learned, the envisioned product needs to change so as to incorporate this new information. In the past, with the cost of information changes being so high, innovative products were hugely expensive and time-consuming. What usually happened is that products underwent incremental changes over long periods of time rather than innovative changes over short periods of time. The move to virtual products has allowed organizations to be much more innovative than they have been in the past.

This has had a major impact and has enabled changing supply chains into supply nets. In the past, the product producer more often than not used a supply chain as simply a contract manufacturer. The cost of physical information flows, i.e., blueprints and prototypes, was expensive enough within an organization. The cost of moving those physical artifacts within the supply chain was prohibitive. As a result, the idea of collaboration within the supply chain was for the most part nonexistent.

The arrival of virtual products and PLM has changed that. As the table shows, there are numerous quadrants where the supplier either collaborates with the product producer partly or fully in control of the virtual product. Without virtual products, the table shrinks down to only a couple of quadrants.

Build

I have previously divided up the build phase into three parts: make the first one, ramp up, and make the rest of them. With respect to supply nets, the flow of information between product producer and product supplier will generally be relevant to the first and third parts of manufacturing. Information flows during ramp up are generally contained within the supplier organization. For purposes of this discussion, we will assume that the supplier organization is only involved with ramping up a defined product, and that it is not dealing with product changes. That being the case, ramp-up becomes an internal function of the supplier organization and does not have an impact on either the product producer or other members of the supply net.

Building the first one

I have detailed the problems of the engineering - manufacturing interface in my previous book. Needless to say, the problems do not get any easier when the engineering is done in one organization and the manufacturing is done in another. In some cases it may simplify the problems, if the engineering group from the product producer has to pay for manufacturing services from the product supplier. If the product producer has to incur the costs of multiple iterations to get the product right, the engineering group might be driven to be much more careful that their engineering designs can actually be manufactured.

Regardless of this cost issue, making the first product can be difficult in those quadrants where the product producer has control over the virtual product. The issue here is to produce a Bill of Process, which is a step-by-step manufacturing procedure that will result in a virtual product being realized in physical form.

I recently sat through a meeting with a PLM software provider. They contended that manufacturing was a function of engineering, i.e., M=f(E). This is not an unusual position given that PLM software providers focus on CAD or geometric design. However, I would contend that the opposite is true. The desired engineering design is a function of the manufacturing process, i.e., E=f(M). What companies attempt to do is to take material, equipment, and labor and combine them in a series of operations that result in the engineering design. Way too often, engineering designs are a combination of wishful thinking and pretty pictures, since these designs cannot be built.

The key with respect to supply nets is to produce a Bill of Process that will result in a physical product that mirrors the virtual product. If that can't be done, then the product producer and the supplier need to collaborate in adjusting the engineering design and/or the Bill of Process until they do get a physical product that mirrors the virtual product.

Making the rest of them

From the product suppliers' point of view, their job is to make each instance of the product identical to each other and identical to the virtual product. That is the ideal. In reality, the products deviate from each other and from the virtual product. During the manufacturing process, material varies, machines have deviations, and humans rarely if never do exactly the same thing over and over again.

Since products will differ, it is not safe to rely on the virtual product that was used as the ideal for manufacturing each instance of the product as an indication of what was actually built. Instead, suppliers need to create as-builts of the actual manufactured instance of the product. This means that the supplier needs to collect the data that describes the dimensions and other characteristics of the manufactured product. In essence, the supplier is creating a new virtual product for each physical product that they manufacture.

As discussed above, this virtual product can be made available to the product producer and other members of the supply net simultaneously and instantaneously. Again, these virtual products can be examined well in advance of the shipment of the physical product in order to ascertain their suitability.

A core but contentious issue is, and will continue to be, having the supplier agree that the information about the production of a product should be given to the customer. I have gotten the objection any number of times that this information is proprietary. However, I have yet to get a satisfactory explanation as to why information about measuring the physical characteristics of the product are proprietary. The customer has purchased the physical product with which these characteristics are part of. Why the customer is not entitled to that information separate and apart from it being embedded into the product is not only mysterious but also highly inconsistent with the idea of purchasing a product. It becomes clear when we start to think about dual products — physical *and* virtual.

A recent example that I ran into at NASA was a situation in which a contractor was engaged to manufacture components that NASA engineered. NASA owns the facility, owns the equipment that the components are manufactured on, and buys the material that the components are manufactured out of. The contractor performs the work, which NASA pays them to do. However, the contractor also claims that they own manufacturing data from this work. This makes no sense, but more often than not that seems to be the currently held conventional practice. That needs to change.

Customers should be entitled to the virtual product as well as the physical product. It certainly may be that customers are not entitled to information about proprietary processes that the supplier uses to manufacturer products. However, they should always be entitled to manufacturing measurement and testing information. If the customer has bought a pipe, then they're entitled to the data that measures the inner and outer diameter of the pipe. And they are entitled to that data well in advance of being required to take possession of that pipe. The customer is entitled to make a decision about whether to take delivery of that pipe because it does not meet specifications well in advance of that pipe showing up at the delivery loading dock.

Support

The support phase has not been something that has been the focus of supply chains, nor have they been very good at it. This is because that, in supply chains, physical products must move up and down the chain during the support phase. This movement of physical products is generally a relatively expensive proposition.

Usually, suppliers washed their hands of any support responsibility once the product arrived at the loading dock of the product producer and was accepted by them. Supply chain participants generally do not support the products. The product producer undertook this responsibility for product support. The product producer would train their own people to support the entire product and would negotiate a certain percentage of additional products from the product supplier to cover failures.

This works reasonably well when the product producers have enough profit margin to allow for sloppiness in the support and warranty side of the business. However, over last few years, profit pressures on product companies have shown the inefficiency in this way of doing business. In addition, customers' expectations have increased as to the level of performance of the products that they acquire.

At the same time, the supply chains are turning into global supply chains, and the ability to move products up and down that supply chain is becoming more costly and time-consuming. It is one thing for the product producer to ship a component or part to a supplier a few miles away. It is quite another thing when that supplier is located on another continent, like Asia.

Being able to deal with the virtual product means that companies can become lean in their support processes. Product producers do not have to ship the physical product up and down the supply chain. Instead, they can collect information about the defective part or component and transmit that information to the supplier. In fact, under the supply net model, multiple suppliers can receive information about the product in order to assess whether it affects their parts and components.

Suppliers who have captured as-built data and have built a virtual representation of the products that they have manufactured can use that as-built virtual representation to identify and correct problems with their part or component. As part of the supply net, they can collaborate with the product producer and the other supply net participants in order to get to the root cause of a support issue.

But the supply net is also about innovation. By receiving feedback from the product producer about how their parts and components performed as a customer uses them, supply net participants can understand how their products were used and what areas that they need to concentrate on to make them better. Supply net participants can add sensors and intelligence to their parts and components in order to collect better data on their usage and provide updates and enhancements to their part of the product.

This can be done for all quadrants in our tables. Even commodity products can be instrumented for feedback and customization. Whether it is a supplier-controlled virtual product or producer-controlled virtual product, there is opportunity for the suppliers to use those virtual products to provide superior performance to the customer as they use it.

The support phase may be when the lack of a virtual product really makes itself felt to the product producer. Up till now, the product producer may have been satisfied with simply receiving the physical product. After all, that was all that they were used to receiving in the past. The product producer contracted for a physical part or component, and that part or component eventually showed up at its loading dock. Ignoring the issue that acquisition may have been more expensive and more time-consuming than if it had the advantages of a virtual product, the product producer may have been reasonably satisfied to have only the physical product.

However, now they have to support that product. If they are not supporting it directly by doing the actual repairs, they are financially responsible for warranty and service. If this product is for their own use, the product producer may want to modify it as they get experience with how the product performs in actual usage.

It is at this stage that one of two things may happen, both of them unsatisfactory to the product producer. The first is that without the virtual product, the physical product is more expensive to maintain. Product producer may be entirely dependent on the supplier to supply replacement parts. The supplier often uses this as an opportunity to make up profit margin that they may have lost in the negotiation to provide the original product. In the case of making modifications, the supplier may charge an extraordinary amount to make those modifications.

This is a problem currently being wrestled with by the Department of Defense. When they have gone back to the supplier for modifications of one of the weapons systems, they have been quoted extraordinary amounts to make modifications. When the Department of Defense objected, the supplier informed them that the government had only bought the physical product. The government did not buy the virtual product, i.e., the plans that created the physical product. In addition, the government has also found that they may have the right to bid out replacement parts, but because they never acquired the virtual product as part of the procurement package, it is infeasible for them to do so.

While organizations might make do, as they have in the past, with only acquiring the physical product, the lack of a virtual product makes itself known in the support phase. Because the second unsatisfactory thing that happens is that products are scrapped before the end of their useful life. This is because there is no ability or information to enable support of that product. This is clearly wasteful and inefficient. For companies to be truly lean, the waste in the support phase needs to be eliminated through the use of virtual products.

Dispose

The supply chain participants have been nonexistent in this phase of the product life. However, the ability to successfully dispose of a product that maximizes recycling begins at the supplier level. While the product producer may have overall responsibility for the disposal phase, this will be pretty meaningless without supplier involvement.

The disposer of the product at the end of the product life will need to have not only the overall information about the product, but will also need to have information about the individual components. In some cases, the product producer will have collected this as-built information. However, in other cases, they will have relied on the supplier to have collected and maintained that information.

By the time long-lived products will have reached their disposal stage, some of the supply chain participants may no longer exist. However, because supply nets are virtual, information about the product can be maintained indefinitely. For products that last decades if not longer, there are technological issues such as data format and data medium that will need to be addressed. These are solvable issues. However, there needs to be some consideration, at least to the issue of a plan for the evolving this data as the technology evolves. If we wait for the 50 years for the product to come out of service, we will probably not be able to find the appropriate data in a readable form to understand how we are to access it.

COUNTERFEIT PARTS

The assumption up until this point is that the members of the supply chain were legitimate providers of product. They may have attempted to push the boundary of what their customer would accept as a product that conformed to the requirements. However, they did not commit fraudulent or illegal acts in representing the product.

However, there are members of supply chains that do commit fraudulent or illegal acts in representing their products. They produce products that are counterfeit products. There are two basic classes of counterfeit products. The first class consists of those products that represent that they are produced by a specific organization by looking like and carrying the brand name of a well-established product. These products also are the same or equivalent quality as the legitimate products

In this case, the customer does not suffer any loss in usage value. As in the case of some counterfeit or "knockoff" luxury goods, the products may have been produced in the same factory. The counterfeit products simply went out the back door. While the product producer and owner of the brand may have legitimate legal issues with the seller of this product, the product purchaser obtains the same value that he or she would have gotten from the legitimate product.

The second category of counterfeit products is different. These products also represent that they are made by a certain manufacturer and carry markings that so indicate that. However, they are not of the same quality and intentionally so. In order to make undeserved profits, counterfeiters produce these products with cheaper and inferior materials and processes.

These counterfeit products present major reliability and safety issues. Counterfeit products have shown up in auto parts, military equipment, aerospace parts, and even spacecraft parts.[66] As organizations have gone global, this issue has gotten worse because supply chains have gotten longer, and organizations have lost the visibility they previously had by being geographically close to their suppliers.

Supply nets can greatly reduce the issue of counterfeit parts. While it is one thing to form the shape of a component and stamp a label on it, it is quite another to produce all the data that a legitimate component would have. At a minimum, it raises the cost of counterfeiting. At a maximum, the counterfeiter does not have the knowledge necessary to fabricate the correct data to make the virtual part that will need to accompany the physical part.

Traceability is a key characteristic of PLM. Virtual parts implement traceability that will make counterfeit parts that much harder to pass as legitimate ones. Organizations that capture and make available to their customers production information with PLM can differentiate themselves from organizations that cannot.

This chapter explored the idea of using virtual products in order to implement supply nets. Supply nets are not a replacement for supply chains, but augment them. What supply chains are to the physical product, supply nets are to the virtual product.

The chapter discussed the different characteristics of supply chains versus supply nets. Supply chains are physically based, while supply nets are digitally based. Supplying chains have indivisible material, while supply nets can have granular information. Supply chains are sequential in their approach to moving product, while supplies nets are integrative. Products in supply nets can be available instantaneously and simultaneously to all members. Products in supply chains are available to only a single participant.

Supply chains have low visibility, while supply nets have high visibility. In a supply chain, the product precedes information. In supply nets, information precedes the product. There are low Information System integration requirements in the supply chain, while supply nets require much higher Information Systems integration.

The chapter also discussed that while Internet material exchanges between product producer and suppliers were to the benefit of the product producers, both product producers and suppliers benefit from supply nets. Using supply nets, both product producer and product supplier are able to reduce wasted physical resources. One of the scarcest resources is that of clock time, which supply nets seek to conserve.

The chapter presented the idea of supply nets throughout the product lifecycle. It provided a matrix of information flow volume between product producer and supplier based on who was in control of the virtual product. It discussed the build cycle in terms of building the first one and making the rest of the products. It also discussed supply net opportunities in the support and dispose phase.

The chapter finished with a discussion on the problem of counterfeit parts. It discussed the idea that supply nets would reduce this issue through requiring virtual parts along with physical ones.

Notes

63 The area of supply chain management has been well developed. Professor Don Bowersox of Michigan State University has been a major contributor to the field. For earlier and later versions of his work, see Bowersox, D. J., Cooper, M. B., Lambert, D., & Taylor, D. A. (1980). *Management in marketing channels.* New York: McGraw-Hill. and Bowersox, D. J., Cooper, M. B., Lambert, D., & Taylor, D. A. (1980). *Management in marketing channels.* New York: McGraw-Hill.

65 My contribution was my doctoral dissertation, Grieves, M. W. (2000). *Business is war: An investigation into metaphor use in Internet and non-Internet IPOs.* Unpublished EDM diss., Case Western Reserve University, Cleveland. For other, more well-known research, see Lakoff, G., & Johnson, M. (1980). *Metaphors we live by.* Chicago: University of Chicago Press, Lakoff, G., & Johnson, M. (1999). *Philosophy in the flesh: the embodied mind and its challenge to Western thought.* New York: Basic Books, and, with one of my favorite titles, Lakoff, G. (1987). *Women, fire, and dangerous things: what categories reveal about the mind.* Chicago: University of Chicago Press.

65 But that did not quite work out. While selling the first Boeing 787 was the goal, it was not to be with this airplane. See Lunsford, J. L. (2007, December 7). Boeing Scrambles to Repair Problems With New Plane. *Wall Street Journal.* New York.

66 Counterfeit parts have been found on military planes, helicopters, and even aircraft carriers (See: Grow, B., Tschang, C.-C., Edwards, C., Burnsed, B., & Epstein, K. (2008, Oct. 13). DANGEROUS FAKES; How counterfeit, defective computer components from China are getting into U.S. warplanes and ships. *Business week.*) NASA discovered titanium parts that had been fraudulently certified in the Kepler spacecraft searching for habitable planets (See: Kim, E. K. (March 6, 2009). Suspect parts pester NASA. *Florida Today.*) Interestingly, the issue of counterfeit components is non-existent in the academic literature on supply chains, even though it is a serious and growing problem.

13

VIRTUALLY INDISTINGUISHABLE

Systems Engineering (SE) and Product Lifecycle Management (PLM) look to have a great deal in common. What serves to distinguish PLM from SE is the utilization of virtual products and virtual environments. However, System Engineering, as a concept, is indistinguishable from PLM in a great many ways. This chapter is a preliminary effort to connect PLM with SE and explore what they have in common and where they differ. Both PLM and SE should substantially benefit from this connection.

PLM AND SYSTEMS ENGINEERING

Previously I had stated that Product Lifecycle Management was literally a 21st century concept. However, PLM did not burst on the scene fully formed. Instead, it had its technological predecessors. I had proposed that the threads that made up Product Lifecycle Management were: Computer-Aided Design (CAD), Engineering Data Management (EDM), Product Data Management (PDM), and Computer Integrated Manufacturing (CIM). In retrospect, I realize that this perspective was one of an information systems perspective and that that there was a major conceptual thread that I had ignored. That conceptual thread is Systems Engineering (SE).

Having minored in Systems Engineering as an undergraduate, I have long felt that there was commonality between Systems Engineering and Product Lifecycle Management. My work with NASA, where the scale and complexity of systems do not come much bigger, allowed me to think through the connections between SE and PLM.[67] I suspect that Systems Engineering and PLM will get closer over time as PLM begins to manage product information that was previously "managed" as documents. A major example of this is the requirements of a system whose management consisted of engineers keeping in mind a series of "shall" statements contained in a systems requirements document.

At the risk of overreaching, I can make a fairly good argument that PLM extends Systems Engineering and that PLM needs to incorporate Systems Engineering as a major methodological component. PLM adds a dimension of virtuality to Systems Engineering in order to trade off information for wasted physical resources.

Systems Engineering is a rich and robust concept, with mathematical underpinnings.[68] It has been crucial in organizing major engineering projects. The description of it here will be by necessity cursory, keying in on elements that will be relevant to the discussion of Product Lifecycle Management. Rather than getting buried in the details of Systems Engineering, my purpose here is to focus on the major aspects that will highlight the linkages to Product Lifecycle Management.

Defining Systems

While I have used the system model in my discussion of processes and practices, it might be useful to define a little more clearly what a system is[69] and how it compares to what I have been calling a product. The system model that I have used as shown in Figure 13.1 is one where an input or inputs are acted on by routines and operations to produce an output or outputs. This was useful for the discussion on processes and practices, but needs to be tailored to systems made up of tangible components and to be expanded.

The idea of systems is that they are not monolithic things, but consist of components that are connected together to produce results that the individual components could not produce by themselves. This means that there is more than one component within the system rectangle that operates on the inputs and that are linked together. One such representation is shown in Figure 13.2.

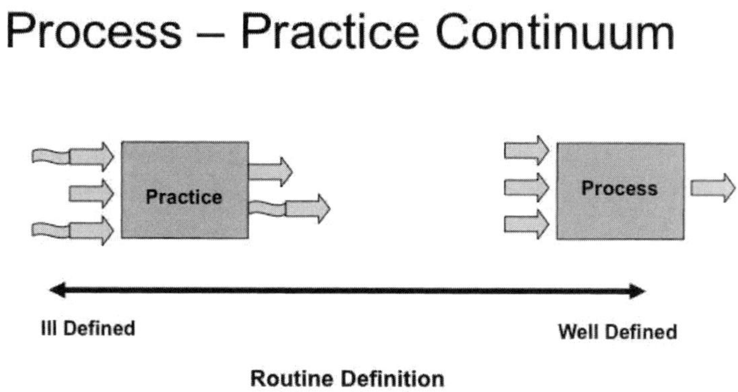

Figure 13.1

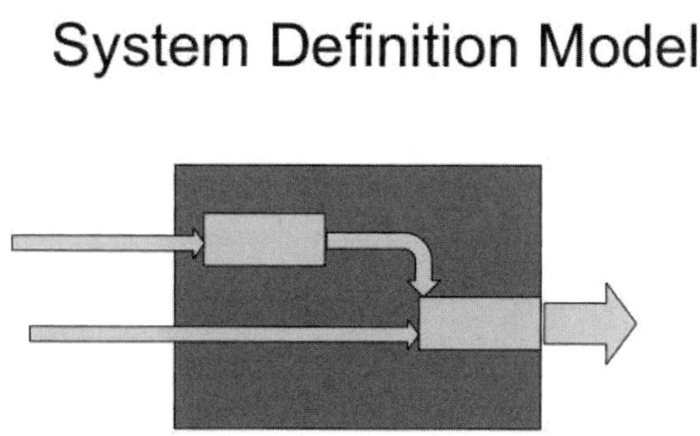

Figure 13.2

There are numerous definitions of systems, both tangible and intangible. I would like to propose the following definition of a system for the purposes of this discussion on Systems Engineering and PLM:

A system is two or more components that combine together to produce one or more results from one or more inputs.

Products such as airplanes, power plants, and medical scanners fulfill this definition. However, these are systems within a system. Airplanes are in themselves fantastic systems, but they are also part of a larger system that consists of airports, air traffic control, refueling trucks, and other systems that make up our air transport system.

PLM originally dealt with only the isolated product. PLM was concerned with the makeup and changes in the product itself. The mental view of PLM was of a series of the isolated product suspended in virtual space, reflecting the changes as it progressed throughout its life. However, as PLM rapidly evolved, it began concerning itself with simulating the product in its environment. PLM now can be said to involve the interaction of the product and the environment that the product operates in.

This makes PLM not only about the isolated product. It makes PLM also about the environment it finds itself in. PLM concerns itself with how inputs affect the product and what effects the product has on its environment. In other words, PLM is about product systems.

Defining Systems Engineering

The NASA Systems Engineering Handbook[70] defines Systems Engineering as "a methodical, disciplined approach for the design, realization, technical management, operations, and retirement of the system." This definition has a great deal in common with the definition of Product Lifecycle Management. These two definitions move even closer when I update my definition of Product Lifecycle Management, as I did in this book, that PLM is involved not only with the product but also with its environment. A product and its environment can certainly classify as a system.

The NASA handbook goes on to describe a system as a collection of different elements that deliver functionality that could not be gotten from the individual elements by themselves. Much like Product Lifecycle Management, Systems Engineering also views that the system is not simply the physical product or artifact, but that it is also composed of the surrounding environmental aspects including people, facilities, and processes that produce the functionality that the system intends to deliver.

Systems Engineering looks at the parts of a system in a holistic, integrative way as opposed to looking at each of the parts individually. Systems Engineering primarily concerns itself with two major elements. First, Systems Engineering concerns itself with the system that needs to be created to provide a desired functionality. Second, Systems Engineering concerns itself with the development lifecycle phases that enable the creation of this system. While Systems Engineering professes to be concerned with the entire lifecycle of the system, the reality is that it primarily focuses on the development phase of the system.

Systems Engineering starts with a view that a system needs to produce certain functionality. As shown in Figure 13.2, the view of a system is that of having inputs, actions, and outputs. The outputs are the functionality of the system, and they are defined as the requirements that the system must meet. The task of Systems Engineering is to determine what inputs are available and what types of devices it can create that will use those inputs in order to produce the actions that will create the required outputs.

For example, if we want to move an airframe through the air, we have earth's atmosphere as an input. Therefore, we can drive this airplane with either a propeller that creates the action of pulling the airplane through the air or a jet engine that creates the action of pushing the airplane through the air. However, if we want to travel in outer space, we no longer have air as an input, so therefore we have to create a different kind of mechanism, a rocket, in order to create the action that we need.

The premise behind Systems Engineering is that a system can be deconstructed into its components and that these components have to interact interdependently in order to produce the requirements that we desire. Systems Engineering deconstructs the overall system into smaller and smaller units until it gets to individual items called parts that then must come together in order to produce the desired requirements results. A sample nomenclature of these different divisions is contained in Figure 13.3.

Hierarchical System Terminology

- System
  - Segment
    - Element
      - Subsystem
        - Assembly
          - Subassembly
            - Part

Figure 13.3

Systems Engineering therefore is about breaking down systems such as a pacemaker, automobile, or space shuttle into more and more discrete levels, and at each of these levels duplicating the system of inputs, actions, and outputs. In addition to simply cascading these system diagrams as the system components get more granular, Systems Engineering has created a number of different representations to reflect this drilling down of system behavior.

The two-fold problem that Systems Engineering wrestles with is that in order to obtain specific individual requirements the system has to be decomposed into finer and finer components. At the same time these components have to be coordinated with each other in order to produce the overall system behavior that the Systems Engineering people desire. I will discuss how Systems Engineering and PLM models compare and contrast a little later.

In a similar fashion to the system being broken down into its componentry, the development of the system is also broken down into various lifecycle phases. In essence what is happening is that the system is moving from a conceptual idea to specific, concrete components that, combined together, will produce the requirements that the system is designed for.

A common way of looking at this is that there are three phases to this lifecycle: formulation, approval, and implementation. These areas are then broken down further in order to provide stages for this development to go through in order to determine whether or not progress is being made. These decision points allow for a determination as to whether the project should go ahead because it is deemed feasible or whether the requirements that have been set out to obtain are not obtainable.

In the formulation stage, this is divided into three stages: concept studies, concept and technology development, and preliminary design. The concept studies stage is meant to create a wide variety of possible solutions to the desired requirements. The concept stage is the preliminary stage in which both the framework of requirements are decided upon and a broad spectrum of ideas and technologies are surveyed as to their suitability for meeting these broad requirements.

In the concept and development stage, core technologies, such as a propeller-based engine or a jet-based engine are determined as the most suitable to meet the framework of requirements. In addition once the technology is settled upon, the requirements are further refined in order to both take advantage of and recognize the constraints of the core technology. The system-level requirements and the general breakdown of what subsystems will make up the system are defined at this point.

In the third phase, preliminary design and technology definition, the individual components are defined in the product structure that will make up the system. These components are both defined and fully fleshed out. The preliminary design is the baseline of what the system will completely look like. The analyses of the components as to the feasibility of being able to manufacture these individual components and to sustain and support them are also done at this particular point in time.

In the fourth phase, final design and realization, the actual components are built. At the end of this phase, the building of the first one is completed. Systems Engineering allows for an iterative process in terms of defining the final design in determining whether it could be actually manufactured. This has been an issue in that Systems Engineering, while cognizant of the need to actually manufacture the design, has not always taken into account manufacturability. As a result, the final design can take a great deal of time and resources in order to actually finalize as it moves from engineering to manufacturing to testing in order to determine whether or not the physical artifact that is being built can actually meet the defined requirements.

The assembly and manufacturing phase is when multiple instances of the system are built. While this is ostensibly part of the Systems Engineering purview, the reality is that as the system gets farther and farther away from final design, Systems Engineering has tended to be less and less involved. The general assumption has been that if the final product is produced, i.e. the first one that meets the requirements that have been set out, then the Systems Engineering's role is pretty much complete. As a result, Systems Engineering lacks significant interest in future lifecycle phases. At this point, Systems Engineering has done its job of verifying that its system meets the requirements. It is now an "implementation problem."

The farther from the system verification that a phase is, the less apparent interest there is from Systems Engineering. The operations and sustainment phase receives even less attention. System engineering really does not like to get pulled into operations problems. They would prefer that their theoretical operational phase not being sullied by actual performance issues.

Requirements to Verification and Validation

Systems Engineering begins with a list of requirements that the system must meet. These requirements are generally expressed as a series of "shall" statements, as in "the system shall exhibit this particular behavior." Matching up to these "shall" statements are validation and verifications[71] that sufficiently demonstrate that the designed system meets these requirements.

This issue always is that the only way to be completely comfortable that the requirements of the system are really met is to observe how the system performs throughout its entire life. That, obviously, is not feasible, so preparing validations and verifications that will test for the behaviors that are the outcome of our requirements is our proxy for observing the system over its life.

In order to adequately define and perform these validation and verification tests, the requirements must be defined with enough specificity to judge whether or not the system met its requirements. Requirements that an automobile be safe or an airplane be fuel efficient is inadequate. There must be measurable specificity to requirements.

There are a number of common issues that arise. The major issue is that the verifications and validations are either not appropriate or not exhaustive enough to demonstrate that the actual system will meet its requirements in use. That has been a flaw in classical Systems Engineering. While Systems Engineering brought a much more systematic approach to design and engineering, the document-based nature of SE meant that verification and validation was often confined to the usual suspects and siloed within sub-systems. As discussed below, PLM can make this richer and much more robust through simulation.

In addition, the lessons learned from the performance of the system in actual use were not fed back into the requirements and/or validation and verifications. As a result, system engineers made preventable errors over and over again, wrongly believing that their requirements translated into actual performance.

As a final note, there are constraints on requirements that must be taken into consideration. It is rare that system engineers have a completely blank sheet of paper on which they can start to set out their requirements. System engineers are generally constrained in the design phase by the technology, subsystem, or platform they select or are required to use. The manufacturing systems that they have available may constrain what they can actually build. The support network may constrain how the product can be sustained. This is not necessarily bad in that there is a history that the requirements can be met with the corresponding verification and validation tests.

Systems Engineers as Accountants

At its worst, Systems Engineering degenerates into an audit function and system engineers degenerate into auditors. However, instead of auditing costs, they are auditing requirements. The requirements that Systems Engineering deals with are translated into "shall" statements, as in "the engine shall deliver x pounds of thrust." There may be thousands of these requirements in a complex product.

Systems Engineering then needs to audit and verify whether those "shall" statements are met. In some organizations, this has degenerated into an audit function, with systems engineers simply acting as auditors of the system rather than working to make the system better. Especially in the cases where this has been reduced to a pure process, the check by systems engineers of requirements makes little difference to the system's efficiency or effectiveness. In this audit role, they can work through their requirements without digging too deep so that the system meets the letter of the requirements but this does not do one thing to make for a better system.

MODELS, SYSTEM ENGINEERING, AND PLM

The term model has at least two meanings that are in play with Systems Engineering and PLM. First, a model is an abstract representation that helps us visualize and understand something that we cannot directly observe, such as a process for doing product design or something we want to distill down to key aspects, such as a product's behavior. These are two types of models that we will look at: things that we do to realize products, process models, and things that products do, behavior models. Second, a model may be a rich description and not be something abstract. A model can also mean a mathematical representation of a physical object, such as a CAD model. This type of model is a spatial model. Systems Engineering uses models in the first way, while PLM uses the word in both meanings.

Given the era that Systems Engineering was developed in, it did not require a reliance on computing technology in order to enable it. Thus, Systems Engineering models are of the atom-based, two-dimensional, static kind. More informally, Systems Engineering models consist of documents, blueprints, and flow charts. When Systems Engineering requires three-dimensional, dynamic models, it relies on building physical prototypes.

Process Models

Figure 13.4 shows the different System Engineering model representations, which are referred to as a Waterfall representation, Vee representation, and a Spiral representation. These representations are all reflective about the idea that the system is deconstructed into ever more discreet components until it reaches the most basic component which is then designed. These basic components are then assembled up the hierarchy until they become the entire system.

There are both similarities and differences between the Systems Engineering model and the Product Lifecycle Management models. On the similarity side, the Waterfall model of Systems Engineering does deal with the entire product lifecycle, even though the Vee model and the Spiral model do not. While the PLM model does deal with the product development phase, the Vee model and the Spiral model deal more extensively with product development, as illustrated by the activities their models describe.

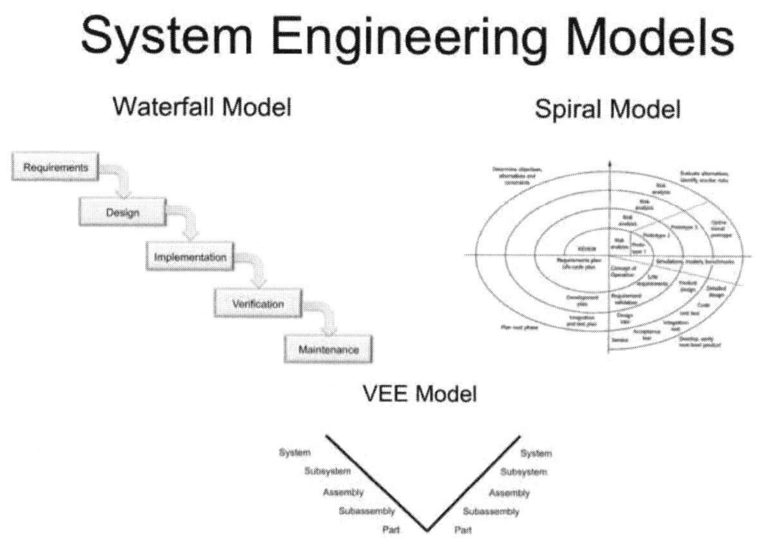

Figure 13.4

The primary differences in models are that the Systems Engineering models are sequential models. Even though this is not what usually happens in Systems Engineering, the conceptual premise of the models is that things happen in sequence during Systems Engineering. In the Spiral model the sequential nature of the model still exists, but with an iterative nature to it.

The PLM model clearly is an integrated model. The functional areas are arrayed around an inner core of information about the product that the functional areas either populate or consume. There is also a natural sequence to the create, build, support, and dispose nature of the product lifecycle. However, also implicit in the circular arrangement is the idea that functions can occur concurrently with each other as the information becomes available. Manufacturing, for example, can begin to design its build processes as the design of the product takes shape.

Systems Engineering, in spite of what might be its actual messy practices, has a logical, sequential flow about it models. Product Lifecycle Management, on the other hand, has a concurrency in terms of activities that take place surrounding the product.

Behavior and Spatial Models

I have elected to cover the behavioral and spatial models together. The reason for this is that the function and form of the product are closely interrelated. As the old adage goes, "form follows function."

Figure 13.5 divides spatial form information into two categories two-dimensional and three-dimensional. It also divides behavioral information into two aspects, static and dynamic. If we lay these out in a matrix, we can see where both Systems Engineering and Product Lifecycle Management fall in dealing with both form and functional product information.

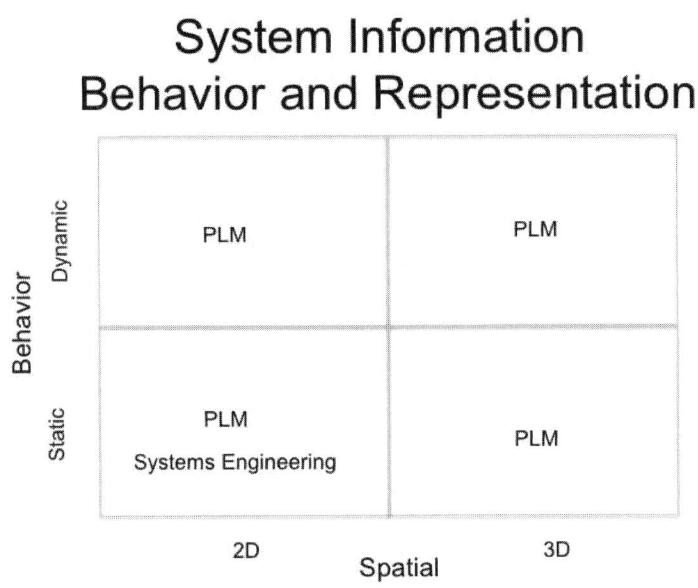

Figure 13.5

If we look at the quadrant for two-dimensional product information and static behavioral analysis, we see that both Systems Engineering and PLM deal with this information. This information is primarily document based. Two-dimensional spatial information is realized as drawings. Static behavioral information can be thought of as documents that deal with the results of analysis. The behavioral aspects of the product in static mode would be set out in requirements of formulas, analyses, and test results as captured in documents.

The line between static and dynamic behavior can be a little fuzzy. The analysis of a change in material deformation versus pressure applied over time would be dynamic in the sense that it would show changes over time. However, the Systems Engineering has typically dealt with this analysis as a series of computed points. PLM extends this with a continuous simulation that could stop and examine any point in time or any interval. Systems Engineering's analysis would be classified as static, while PLM's analysis is dynamic. Systems Engineering can be thought of dealing with a series of snapshots, while PLM deals with both snapshots and film.

Some in Systems Engineering will argue that they are now dealing with dynamic simulations. I would agree that this is the case since the advent of computers. However, Systems Engineering has a methodology that does not depend on it being enabled by technology. Because of that, I categorize Systems Engineering as being concerned with static analysis and PLM as being concerned with both static and dynamic analyses.

When it comes to dealing with three-dimensional spatial information, Product Lifecycle Management concerns itself with spatial models, while Systems Engineering does not. Again this may be a matter of definitional issues, in that System Engineering techniques and methodology may be applied to evaluating three-dimensional models. However, if we think of Product Lifecycle Management as extending Systems Engineering, then the Systems Engineering methodology becomes Product Lifecycle Management methodology.

The final quadrant, three-dimensional spatial models and dynamic behavioral models, is clearly the area of Product Lifecycle Management. As has been discussed extensively in this book, the use of simulation and virtual models in dynamic settings sets Product Lifecycle Management apart from its predecessors. It is in this quadrant that virtual products operate in independent virtual space.

Not only can the spatial elements of the product replace the use of expensive physical prototypes for visual purposes, virtual products can be put through extensive testing and simulation in order to determine what characteristics that the physical product will have. Again Product Lifecycle Management is not something entirely new. It takes the methodology of System Engineering in order to extend static, document-based information and analysis into three-dimensional dynamic virtual simulation of products.

Model-Based Systems Engineering

This focus on the system as an abstract, logical model from a behavioral perspective developed into a sub-branch of Systems Engineering called Model-based Systems Engineering (MBSE).[72] MBSE has as its premise that a system that meets its defined requirements can be mathematically modeled. This is done by breaking down the system into its logical components and defining the behavior of these components and their relationship to other components.

Modeling languages were then created to do just that. One such modeling languages, called SysML,[73] was developed in order to provide a standard for the system modeling that Systems Engineering concerns itself with. Modeling languages for MBSE are not simply languages like computer languages, but they also incorporate diagrams to show the flow of the system.

The system modeling language is basically a much more sophisticated version of the system models shown in figure 13.2. The intent of this modeling language is to model inputs, actions, and outputs of the discrete elements of the system and link these discrete elements together in order to have an accurate, albeit abstract, view of the system.

While subsequently, computer tools have been developed in order to automate this systems method, it still remains an abstract version of the system. While this is a useful representation of the system, there generally is a major leap between this abstract version of the system and the three-dimensional parts and components that need to be created in order to produce the system behaviors. An assumption with Systems Engineering was that physical prototypes would need to be built in order to provide the rich detail that would be required in order to actually test out the system assumptions.

PLM Models

Product Lifecycle Management, on the other hand, has much richer system representations. Given the technology that enables it, PLM not only models abstract systems behavior and characteristics, but it can also model the actual geometric representation that will provide these characteristics and behaviors. The Systems Engineering model might show a box that represents the wing control surface. This control surface has as its inputs its current angle and the pilot's command to change that angle. The output is a number that represents the new angle of the surface.

Product Lifecycle Management's simulation shows a representation of the actual wing and control surface. It will simulate in a visual fashion the actual movement of the surface as a pilot issues his commands. In addition, the simulation can incorporate external variations such as horizontal and vertical airflows in order to show how the wing surface will actually react in its natural environment. While Systems Engineering models are relatively static, Product Lifecycle Management models are dynamic.

Systems Engineering does not deal with spatial models, except as two-dimensional documents, i.e., drawings. Product Lifecycle Management does deal with spatial models. It is these two different uses of the term "models" that is often confusing. Systems Engineering in MBSE uses "models" as an abstract, logical representation. Product Lifecycle Management uses the term to represent spatial models that incorporate the behavioral characteristics.

Systems Engineering produces numerical or logical representations as its reflection of systems performance. Product Lifecycle Management produces those same numerical or logical representations, but then transforms them into spatial representation of systems performance. However, because computing enables it, PLM produces its representation of systems performance in a much richer, more granular fashion. Using the example above, Systems Engineering might give the angle of the control surface as a specific number. A PLM simulation can show the entire length of the control surface and show that some areas of the surface might have a different angle than other areas because of material deformation, weight distribution, or other factors.

Figure 13.5 illustrates how Systems Engineering and Product Lifecycle Management would map out in a quadrant with spatial models and behavioral models. As illustrated here, Systems Engineering provides some complexity of behavioral models and little or no complexity of spatial models. Product Lifecycle Management, on the other hand, provides fairly high levels of both visual and behavioral models. This is not to say that Product Lifecycle Management replaces Systems Engineering, but is to say that Systems Engineering is the methodology that creates the complex models that Product Lifecycle Management maintains and uses.

Product Information Feedback Loops

While technically systems can operate perfectly well by taking required inputs, performing routines and operations on them, and delivering an output, most systems operate with what is called a feedback control loop. The feedback control loop is the idea that the output is looked at with respect to a desired goal, and then the inputs and/or routines are modified in order to change the output to close the gap between what the output is producing and what is desired. Sometimes the feedback control loop is internal to the system, such as the governor on a motor. At other times, the feedback control loop will be external to the system, like a driver who looks at the speed that the automobile is traveling at and adjusts his pressure on the gas pedal or brake. In either case the output is compared against the desired output and adjustments are made to either the inputs or the routines that the system is running.

While this idea of a feedback control loop is usually implicit in systems that Systems Engineering deals with, it is also an aspect of the Systems Engineering process itself. A set of requirements is set out for the system. An evaluation or test is defined to see if the system being designed meets those requirements. If it does, then the design is approved. If it doesn't, either the system design is modified or the requirements are modified.

The issue with Systems Engineering is that the assumption is made that once the system passes these evaluations or tests, then the system will actually perform in its usage so as to meet those requirements. Often times, Systems Engineering feels that they have done their job if the system passes the test, irrespective of whether the product can be actually manufactured, or if the product performs to those requirements in actual usage.

Figure 13.6, which was introduced in a previous chapter, illustrates the difference between the Systems Engineering feedback loop and the PLM feedback loop. On left hand side, both Systems Engineering and PLM are in agreement that products are designed that meet requirements. Those designed products undergo verification and validation processes to insure that the designs indeed meet the desired requirements.

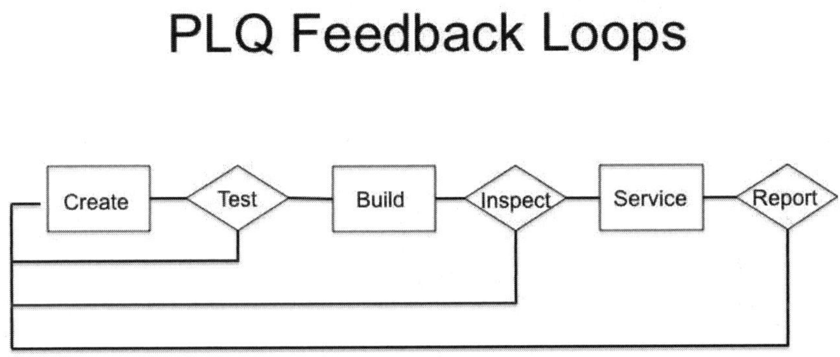

Figure 13.6

However, PLM goes on to do the same sort of feedback for the manufacturing and usage phases. In the manufacturing phase, the product is checked to see whether or not its physical form can meet the requirements set out for it. If it cannot, then that information is sent back to engineering in order to either adjust the requirements and/or develop a new methodology or manufacturing process in order to produce a product that meets those requirements.

In the support phase, the issue of meeting requirements goes from evaluations or tests that are a proxy for those requirements in the development phase to looking at the performance of the product in actual use in determining whether or not the product indeed met its design requirements. Again, if the product does not meet its design requirements in actual usage, that information is then sent back to engineering. At that point in time, it may be too late to do much with the current product, but this should be fed back into a base of knowledge so that engineering can understand the gap between the requirements they thought could be fulfilled and what actually occurred. They then can adjust the requirements for future versions of the product.

Comparing Systems Engineering and PLM

There are currently some differences between Systems Engineering and PLM. Those differences are:

- Systems Engineering is product realization focused while PLM is product lifecycle focused;
- Systems Engineering is functionally based versus Product Lifecycle Management which is lifecycle based;
- Systems Engineering concerns itself primarily with physical products where PLM concern itself with both physical and virtual products;
- Systems Engineering is document based, while PLM is digital based;
- Systems Engineering is a much deeper discipline versus PLM, which is much broader.

Product development focused versus product lifecycle focused

Systems Engineering has primarily focused on the development phase of defining and creating the system or product. It breaks down the product development phase into a number of divisions, such as: Concept Studies, Concept and Technology Development, Preliminary Design and Prototyping, Testing, and Final Design. It then often lumps manufacturing, support, and disposal into an aggregate category.

The implicit assumption is that the system engineering work is pretty much done once the system is designed and meets the testing requirements. The rest of the lifecycle is simply an exercise in execution. System Engineering believes it has done the hard part of factoring the build, support, and dispose phases into its system view. The messy part of actually making those phases work is someone else's responsibility.

Systems Engineering's view of the product lifecycle is much like the famous cartoon in the New Yorker Magazine that showed a detailed view of Manhattan with the farther away from Manhattan the view was, the smaller and more insignificant the world was. With System's Engineering, the create phase is the dominant view, with the other lifecycle phases being small and insignificant.

Product Lifecycle Management takes a more balanced view of the importance of the lifecycle phases, with primacy given to the usage phase. The ability of the system design to pass the required tests is not its definition of a product's success. The ability of the product to perform to the user's expectations over the time the product is in service determines whether a product is successful or not.

This is not to invalidate the system engineering perspective. On the contrary, the likelihood of the product to perform well in service is dependent on whether or not rigorous system engineering methodology is employed. However, the feedback loops between manufacturing and engineering and support and engineering need to occur for system engineering to have an accurate understanding of how well their system performed.

Systems Engineering is critical to getting the product lifecycle off to a strong start. However, under PLM, it needs to have more connection to the build, support, and dispose phases. It needs to collaborate in the development process more with those build and sustain phase experts in order to create a system that can actually be built and supported. Systems Engineers need feedback from those phases in order to validate that the system design actually performed to expectations.

Functional based versus lifecycle based

Systems Engineering, as even its name implies, is more about the engineering function than it is about the rest of the lifecycle. While system engineering does profess to concern itself with the rest of the product lifecycle, the build, sustain, and dispose phases, the reality is that Systems Engineering is more about getting a product that meets the defined requirements than it is about following that product through its lifecycle or to see if that it indeed fulfilled its functions in actual use.

In that respect Systems Engineering appears to be a bit siloed. The systems engineer finishes with a product that he or she deems has met the defined requirements, and then throws it over the wall to manufacturing. While Systems Engineering professes to concern itself with the support and sustainment phase, the reality is that the support and sustainment people are generally on their own when it comes to maintaining the product. If there is a major problem, the Systems Engineering staff gets dragged back in, but as a general rule they are done with the product when they hand it over to manufacturing.

Product Lifecycle Management on the other hand takes a broader view of the product. In fact, the product is not deemed to be successful unless it performs in the sustainment phase to the user's expectations. In addition, information from both the manufacturing and the sustainment phase are fed back into engineering to close the loop between what was theoretically possible with the product and what it actually did.

Physical product versus physical and virtual product

Systems Engineering generally concerns itself with the functioning of the product. It creates a set of requirements, and, if the product meets those requirements, the product is deemed to be successful. Systems Engineering does not concern itself with operations manuals, marketing collateral, repair manuals, or repair diagnostics.

Product Lifecycle Management does concern itself with these things and views them to be as important to the product as the actual functioning of the product itself. If a product can perform its requirements flawlessly, but the user does not know how to go about obtaining that functionality, then the product is not a successful or useful one.

Document-based versus Digital-based

At first glance, it might appear that the elements of PLM are people, process/practice, and technology, while Systems Engineering has as its elements only people and processes/practices. However, paper, pencil, binders, and blueprints are also technology.

The difference is that Systems Engineering is document based, while PLM is digital based. However, the difference is not simply the difference between information being represented in atoms or bits. Moving to digital technology represents a quantum jump in not only the representation of information, but in its handling.

Document-based technology is static, while digital technology is dynamic. If we wish to have a different view of a drawing, then we have to make a new drawing. If we wish a different view of a digital representation, then all we have to do is request it and the computer will rearrange the information.

Document-based technology requires that people follow the steps laid out in a process and methodology. If they choose not to follow those steps, only the active oversight of other people enforces those steps. Digital technology can enforce process and methodology steps, both directly by requesting that people comply before allowing them to proceed or indirectly by inspecting the digital information to see if it complies with the process requirements. While people can and often do try to circumvent digital enforcement, it adds a layer of difficulty that simply ignoring documents does not have. In addition, digital oversight does not have to be active. The digital technology can simply produce alerts when there is a lack of compliance, allowing humans to take the appropriate action.

The dynamic aspect of PLM also means that product behavior can be simulated and not simply analyzed as with document-based, static information. Systems Engineering requires that products go to prototypes much earlier and at increased costs.

Deeper versus broader

Systems Engineering is more mature and has had the time to develop into a deeper concept. Systems Engineering has well developed procedures and methodologies concerning how we should go about creating products. Systems Engineering methodologies have evolved over time and have been built upon as issues have arisen and have been tackled.

Product Lifecycle Management is much broader, as has been pointed out above. PLM is not only about making the product but is also about sustaining that product. PLM is not only about providing a detailed prescription in how to go about making the product. It is about what information about that product that needs to be captured, organized, and maintained.

SUGGESTIONS FOR FUTURE DIRECTION

I would like to close out this chapter by making some suggestions for future direction. In addition to the obvious suggestion that there needs to be more collaboration between the people working on Systems Engineering and Product Lifecycle Management, and that the intersection between the two disciplines needs further fleshing out and investigation, I would like to make three suggestions as to the actions needed in order to meld Product Lifecycle Management with Systems Engineering. These prescriptive suggestions are:

- Organizations should deal with Systems Engineering and PLM together rather than separately,
- Systems Engineering should be engaged across the entire lifecycle,
- PLM should more rigorously adopt Systems Engineering methodology.

Integrate dealings with Systems Engineering and Product Lifecycle Management

Even though Product Lifecycle Management generally starts as a design and engineering initiative, organizations deal with Product Lifecycle Management and Systems Engineering as two distinct disciplines. Systems Engineering standards and PLM processes are dealt with as two distinct things, when they should be considered from an integrated perspective. It is not uncommon to find organizations have two distinct policies and procedures for PLM and Systems Engineering, even as they overlap.

Systems Engineering spends a great deal of time and effort in developing "bluebooks." These bluebooks are the standards for addressing engineering practices and processes. Far too often, these bluebooks are developed at great expense, only to sit on the shelf of the engineer's cubicle. These bluebooks need to be made actionable, so that they are not simply a standard procedure that it is static, but are incorporated in the PLM design and development tools. This is but one example of combining Systems Engineering and Product Lifecycle Management.

Engage Systems Engineering across the lifecycle

As noted above, Systems Engineering often simply fades out in the phases beyond the product development phase. Part of that issue was that systems engineers have very little visibility of the product once it has left their siloed area in the engineering department. With Product Lifecycle Management, systems engineers can remain engaged with the product throughout the product lifecycle. As noted above, the feedback loops from manufacturing, support, and even disposal need to be enabled in order to provide Systems Engineering with the necessary visibility of further product lifecycle phases.

Systems engineers need to follow the product throughout its life in order to ascertain whether the work that they've done on the front end really did produce a system that performed as required and expected. Simply testing the requirements in the development phase is no longer acceptable. If the system engineers are to be truly involved with the entire system, then they will have to stop limiting their engagement to the design and development phase.

Adopt Systems Engineering methodology within PLM

In a number of organizations, the information systems group provides the PLM processes and procedures. While that may be acceptable from an information systems standpoint, it often does not address the problems that systems engineers actually have. Information systems needs to be the enabler of this capability, but the Systems Engineering methodology should drive it.

As I noted above, making the engineering bluebook standards actionable is an example of incorporating Systems Engineering methodology within Product Lifecycle Management. PLM has done an excellent job in capturing and organizing product information. It has also addressed workflow issues. It will provide real value when it can enable the Systems Engineering methodology, which up till now has been involved with more static information such as documents and reports.

There are going to be many other opportunities for Product Lifecycle Management and Systems Engineering to integrate and provide additional value to its users. The above suggestions are but an initial list of some obvious areas where this should occur. This area has been under-investigated by both Product Lifecycle Management and Systems Engineering researchers. I would hope that would change in the future.

This chapter proposed that Systems Engineering and Product Lifecycle Management are closely related. In fact, one of the threads of Product Lifecycle Management is Systems Engineering. Product Lifecycle Management extends Systems Engineering and uses many of its methodologies and processes.

The chapter went on to define systems, Systems Engineering, and the multiple use of the term "models." Models were further defined as being abstract models of things we do to realize products, process models, and things products do, behavioral models. Models are also rich descriptions, as in spatial models. Systems Engineering deals with abstract models, while PLM deals with both abstract and concrete models.

The chapter presented Systems Engineering and Product Lifecycle Management as to how they compare in looking at product information as static and dynamic and two-dimensional and three-dimensional. The chapter also discussed that, from a system engineering perspective, product information feedback loops need to extend from its current focus on product creation into the build and support phases.

In comparing Systems Engineering and PLM, it was proposed that Systems Engineering is product realization focused while PLM is product lifecycle focused; Systems Engineering is functionally based versus Product Lifecycle Management which is lifecycle based; Systems Engineering concerns itself primarily with physical products where PLM concerns itself with both physical and virtual products; Systems Engineering is document based, while PLM is digital based; Systems Engineering is a much deeper discipline versus PLM, which is much broader..

Suggestions for future direction were that there be more integration of Systems Engineering and Product Lifecycle Management, that we need to engage Systems Engineering across the product lifecycle, and that we need to adopt Systems Engineering methodology within PLM.

Notes

67 The first paper produced and presented highlighting this connection was for the American Institute of Aeronautics and Astronautics SPACE 2010 Conference. See Caruso, P., Dumbacher, D., & Grieves, M. (2010). Product Lifecycle Management and the Quest for Sustainable Space Explorations, *AIAA SPACE 2010 Conference & Exposition* Anaheim, CA.

68 One of the earliest and influential works on Systems Engineering is Wymore, A. W. (1967). *A mathematical theory of systems engineering: the elements. New York, Wiley.*

69 Underlying it all, mathematics are the means to describe the behavior of systems. The output of systems, i.e. their behaviors, is the result of the interactions of the system components as they process the system inputs. Predicting that output is done by simultaneously solving the equations that represent those interactions. For an early and seminal paper on general systems theory, see Bertalanffy, L. v. (1950). An Outline of General System Theory. *The British Journal for the Philosophy of Science, 1*(2), 134-165.

70 NASA Systems Engineering Handbook, Special Publication (SP) 6105, December 2007.

71 As pointed out by Grady, there is not universal agreement of what validation and verification mean. (See Grady, J. O. (1998). *System validation and verification.* Boca Raton: CRC Press.) Whatever the definition and distinction, there needs to be reliable tests to demonstrate that requirements have been met that serve as a proxy for actual in-use performance.

72 For a NASA-funded survey of MBSE methodologies and descriptions, see Estefan, J. A. (2008). *Survey of Model-Based Systems Engineering (MBSE) Methodologies:* INCOSE. It is available at: http://www.incose.org/productspubs/pdf/techdata/MTTC/MBSE_Methodology_Survey_2008-0610_RevB-JAE2.pdf last accessed 8/18/10.

73 For an excellent reference to this modeling language, see Friedenthal, S., Moore, A., & Steiner, R. (2008). *A practical guide to SysML: Systems Model Language.* Burlington, Mass.: Elsevier/ Morgan Kaufmann.

14

VIRTUALLY SUCCESSFUL

The interpretation of "virtually successful" as it applies to Product Lifecycle Management varies depending on the organization. For some organizations, their success is only virtual and not real. They convince themselves that they are adopting new concepts in order to be lean and innovative. The reality is that they may have acquired some new technologies, but they are simply doing what they have done in the past. The people and their processes and practices have not changed or changed only minimally.

For other organizations, they are "virtually successful" in the sense that, while it may not be a complete success as yet, they are making good progress in changing the way they are approaching product creation, manufacturing, sustainment, and disposal. They also are acquiring technology, but that technology is not simply a tool employed at the edges but an enabler of change in people's understanding of products and in the processes and practices that people perform to realize those products. These organizations' virtual successes include a transformation from thinking about products as only physical objects. They now view products as dual objects: a physical product and a virtual product.

For those organizations that want to be "virtually successful" in the second sense as it pertains to PLM, what are the issues that they must address in order for that to happen? For PLM as an approach, it requires that these organizations address the three components of PLM: people, practices/processes, and technology.

PEOPLE

The key to any hope of success in moving organizations to embrace virtual products is people. We can buy all the technology we like, and we can promulgate new processes and practices. However, if we do not get people to adopt and internalize this new way of thinking and dealing with product information, we may only obtain "virtual" success, which is simply people paying lip service to this new paradigm. We will not obtain real success.

I have seen organizations where this is the case. These organizations have bought new software and installed new processes and practices, but the people of the organization are still wedded to atoms rather than bits. The designs are done in 3D CAD models, but then are printed out on 2D drawings that are the accepted, if unofficial, authoritative designs.

CAE analysis is done, but no one is convinced until they build prototypes that they can physically analyze and test. Digital mockups are created, but plywood models are also built so the "old-timers" can see if things will "really fit." Manufacturing is simulated, but processes on the factory floor are adjusted to the way "they have always done things." There is much discussion about developing sensors to collect in-use information, but it never makes it anywhere because that is a downstream problem.

These organizations are not dissatisfied with PLM because, in spite of themselves, they have gotten some incremental benefit. However, they do not see the game changing nature of PLM. It is no wonder. They really have not embraced PLM as an approach. They have only added some PLM tools.

Engage Executive Leadership

The primary reason for this is that the executives of this organization do not fully understand PLM themselves. Because of this, they are not committed to having their people understand the new approach to products and have not really made much attempt to enable the change their people must undergo in order to fully incorporate PLM into their organizations.

For organizations that I have seen do well with PLM, there is executive leadership and sponsorship. These executives understand the concepts of PLM and actively move their people to embed it into their processes and practices. These executives are not technology junkies. They understand what the technology enables, but only want it if it supports use cases that cross functional barriers.

Organizations that are only getting marginal value have executives that view PLM as a tool, not a concept. They view it as something that their engineers use in place of a drafting board. They place a low value on information and cross-functional activities.

Educate

Organizations need to educate people on PLM itself. While, as discussed below, they need to determine whether to educate or train depending on the tasks people perform, they need to educate all their people on what PLM is and why it is important for them to apply its concepts.

It is all too common for organizations to acquire PLM technology and tools, train their people on how to use it, and let people figure out the larger concepts and implications for themselves. Surprisingly, this approach enjoys some degree of success, because motivated people are pretty good at working out the opportunities themselves and sharing them with their colleagues who pick these new capabilities up because they prove successful.

However, relying on education by osmosis is pretty inefficient. Organizations that get the best returns the quickest have an education plan in place. Creating a shared understanding and, driving that shared understanding, a shared language concerning PLM, leads to adoption that is deeper and more value producing than parachuting in technology and processes and hoping PLM will evolve.

Cross-Pollinate

Because PLM is so wide reaching and over-arching, one organization simply will not have a corner on the PLM use cases. PLM is also so new that there is not an organization that serves as the repository of all things PLM, such as one might find for project management.

When recently asked where their organization could go to understand what others are doing in PLM, I suggested some possibilities: research firms that specialize in PLM, such as AMR/Gartner and CIMdata; PLM conferences, both industry and user organized, and leading edge users. Of the three, leading edge users are my preference because of the depth of knowledge. However, they require personal contacts.

Focus

Organizations do not change people. People change themselves, but only if they are encouraged and channeled to devote sufficient energy and focus to "rewire" themselves. Organizations need to provide the educational environment to allow people to understand what PLM is and why the organization is embracing PLM.

While the education proposed above is necessary to condition people in thinking about PLM in the right way, it is only by focusing on PLM with their own tasks and situations will people internalize it. Education, without learning by doing, will not provide the necessary environment for them to make the new and required mental connections. People need to be put in situations where they can have their "Ah ha!" moment and have the concepts of PLM click into place.

PROCESSES/PRACTICE

I can only hope by this time, I have made the case for understanding and including practices (and even art) in the things that organizations do. Describing everything in terms of processes is at best fuzzy, even if we implicitly understand that some of these tasks that we do are not "really processes." At worst, it shoehorns us into deterministic behavior that is incompatible with innovation. Language, i.e., the words we use to describe things, matters and drives behavior.

Distinguish between process and practice

If organizations want to be both lean and innovative, they will need to make the distinction between process and practice. The concern is not so much with process, because that has been the focus of most modern organizational efforts. While this focus on process will allow organizations to meet their goals of becoming lean, it will not do much to foster their achievement of innovation.

Organizations should continue their focus on producing lean activities and in reducing waste from activities that are clearly processes. For tasks that are done over and over again, whose inputs and routines are well defined, organizations should strive to eliminate any wasted efforts. Once they have processes that work well and are optimized for performance, these processes should be adopted throughout the organization. Even though organizations are global, the processes that have proven to produce superior results should be universal and should be done throughout the organization no matter where those operations are located geographically.

However for those efforts in which the goal is to produce something new or innovative, organizations should empower their people to engage in true practices. This means allowing for a clash of ideas, noisy arguments, and negotiations that trade off competing objectives. Organizations that are trying to obtain a unique and innovative result should not try to close down the collaborative discussions in the interest of simply conforming to a process. They need to understand that their objective is to produce this innovative result and not simply to combine inputs and run routines the same way that they do with processes.

But that is not to say that this practice does not occur within a process. Without a process that moves people along a path to a goal, practice takes on a life of its own and is never completed. Organizations need to understand how to strike a balance between engaging people in a process that moves to a conclusion, yet allows them to produce new and different results without constraining them with rules, regulations, and processes that produce just the opposite.

Re-engineer processes for a digital environment

A common issue with many organizations is that they have defined their processes around an older paper environment. They have simply implemented technology to duplicate what used to be done with pieces of paper. This is both inefficient and does not allow the technology to produce efficiencies that it could otherwise produce.

Examples of this are sequential routing of information, because that is how it had to happen when there was only a single sheet of paper. Requiring physical signatures is also a holdover from an earlier era, because pieces of paper used to have to be physically signed. Digital signatures are clearly possible and are much more efficient than requiring tracking down an individual for a physical signature.

Approval processes should be reviewed. Review processes often existed because there were no dynamic alert processes available with pieces of paper. Pieces of paper simply sat there until they were looked at. The solution was to route the information through everyone who potentially would need to review the information for unacceptable deviations.

Digital systems can alert people when information is outside of predefined parameters. It can also alert different people under different conditions. Rote processes can be eliminated, with processes being triggered by the specific conditions of the information.

Match instruction with the type of process or practice

If we intend for our people to engage in a process, then we need to train them about what that process requires. We then should allow them the experience of performing those processes until they become ingrained in how to effectively do those processes. Processes are something that organizations should train their people on.

Practices on the other hand require education. We need to tell people why they are doing something, not simply tell them what to do. For those things that are practices, we need to not simply train our people in performing specific actions, but educate them on why they are performing those practices and what implications this has for the rest of the organization.

If we expect people to take on additional work, because this additional work will benefit the entire organization especially those functions that are later on in the product lifecycle, we need to be prepared to explain to people why this is the case. People do not take on additional responsibilities lightly. In the absence of a good explanation, people want to tend to do less work rather than more work. If we expect them to participate in producing efficiencies for the entire organization, then we need to educate them on the reasons and the impact that their work will have.

Match the amount of information according to the type of process or practice

The major differentiation in terms of information between process and practice is the amount of information that either requires. For processes we only require the minimal amount of information to move from one state of the process to the next state. Contextual information is for the most part irrelevant, especially in true processes. In practices the situation is much different. We need to make available a wide range of information. We need to provide people with this wide range of information, because we do not necessarily know what information that they will need in order to produce an innovative result.

We need to provide them with contextual information that allows them to make better decisions about the context in which their practices are operating. We need to provide them with samples, policies, exemplars, things that were approved, things that were rejected, so that they can have a full understanding of what it is that they're dealing with.

Processes can be defined and driven by applications that provide people with simply the information that they need to complete their process. For practice we need a vast amount of information that people can access. People see patterns in pools of information that computer analysis cannot see. To the extent that we can help them organize this information into knowledge management categories and make the access easier and more efficient, we can improve practices.

As technology continues to evolve, we would like to implement cued availability. We would like the knowledge of the organization to be presented to people based on the situation that they are working on. We are seeing the beginnings of this in new search technology. Search technology will transform searching from an explicit task to an implicit one that occurs whenever people engage in a task.

Capture practice activities

Processes are the application of an organization's knowledge base, while practices are the generator of that knowledge base. The ability for an organization to capture the knowledge that is generated during practice is, and will continue to be, key to their future success. The organization that can best capture knowledge creation and reuse it will be far superior in terms of resource usage than organizations that continue to create the same knowledge over and over again without capturing it.

In the past when the only possibility of knowledge capture was in physical form, i.e., paper and pencil, this capture of knowledge was both slow and expensive. Oftentimes it was quicker and cheaper to re-create information than it was to capture and organize information. As we continue to move into the realm of the digital world, the capture of information as it takes place in webinars, video meetings, e-mails, and other digital media means that we have the ability to capture, save this information, and retrieve it when needed.

As mentioned earlier, processes are the result of practices. Processes are the selection of inputs and their combination and manipulation in a specific way that gives the desired output. However, which inputs to select and how to combine them in order to get the desired result had to be discovered. That discovery process is a practice.

While I will be the first to admit that the capture, organization, and substantive retrieval on a cued availability basis is nowhere near where it needs to be, I have great confidence that the technology will continue to improve and improve rapidly. If slightly over only a decade ago, we were to suggest to people that for any information they wished to find that they could go on the Internet and, with a few key search words, obtain that information, we would have been viewed incredulously.

It is not a huge stretch to think that in the next few years we will be able to have knowledge management systems that automatically capture, tag, and present in a contextual form the information about certain activities that we are interested in. The idea of a Virtual Collaboration Room, where information about how products get created and the assumptions that drive their requirements and subsequent specifications, is a mechanism by which we could capture this information. The knowledge capture mechanisms to "understand" the material that we are discussing and how it relates to other aspects of a product that we are working on now or in the future will evolve over time. This is a much more difficult problem than dealing with structured information, but as the search engines of today show with unstructured information, we have come a very long way in a very short period of time.

Organizations that can capture, organize, and retrieve knowledge that they create in the course of their product creation, manufacture, and support will have a tremendous advantage over those organizations that do not do this. In addition this information presents them the opportunity to create processes out of those current practices. By analyzing the information that they have captured, organizations can correlate inputs to outputs and can create defined routines that produce the required results. This will prove a key differentiator of success for organizations in the future.

TECHNOLOGY

In my first book I covered the key PLM technology characteristics: adequate infrastructure; open, harmonized applications; configurable not customizable software; applications that were embedded and usable; and utility-like performance. These are all still important technological characteristics for the success of Product Lifecycle Management and for creating and using virtual products. I would like to add a few more technological characteristics necessary for success based on my observations in working with organizations over the past few years.

Match technology to use cases

Technology should always support the use cases of an organization as opposed to simply being acquired because it is the technology of Product Lifecycle Management. Too often organizations are caught up in the evaluation of technology in which they compare the features and capabilities of different offerings. They get caught up in the chase for the best technology offering and forget that the technology is only useful if it supports the use cases of their organization.

I have often been asked which technology provider do I favor for a particular organization. My response is always is to inquire what use cases that the organization intends the technology for. In a good number of cases, the use cases have not been thought out and articulated. The organization is buying technology because they've been told they need it.

Sometimes this does not hurt them because the technologies that currently exist are all fairly good and generally cover the most common use cases. However, it does put the cart before the horse. Organizations that buy technology without understanding fully their use cases are lucky if they get the maximum benefit from the technology. What organizations should be doing is creating use cases and then determining what technology best addresses those use cases.

Do not customize — ever

Okay, I know I am repeating a characteristic that I covered in my first book. However, the biggest technology issue that I see with organizations is the fact that they have customized their technology software and as a result have huge problems when new releases come along. The velocity of technology advancement continues to increase. This means that new releases of the software are bound to occur on a fairly rapid basis.

Organizations that have customized their software face substantial time delays and in some cases dramatic costs in re-customizing the next release of their software. The advantage that they thought they would get by customizing the software to the needs of their organization are totally outweighed by both the delays in implementing new releases that have important new capabilities and the extensive costs in porting the customization to the new release.

Organizations need to think long and hard about customization. If they decide to customize, then they need to go think about it even harder. If they really need specific capabilities that their software cannot provide, then rather than customization, they should develop modules that are outside the basic system itself in order to provide those functions. Customizing core packages always imposes a tremendous cost and a tremendous time delay in adopting new versions of software.

Continue to evaluate other technology offerings

The tendency for most organizations is that once they select a software offering they stay with that offering indefinitely. Obviously there are good reasons for that. Switching costs are extremely high and the training and education costs associated with changing to a different software offering certainly can be daunting.

However, there are compelling reasons to continue to look at other offerings from different solution providers. In some cases, being locked into a particular software system means that the company cannot go beyond a certain point in their approach to virtual products. Organizations need to not view switching costs as an insurmountable hurdle, although it often looks like that. Incurring those switching costs may be far superior to the alternative of crippling the future of the business.

In addition, this keeps the current solution provider honest if the organization has an understanding of what is possible with other solution providers. The answer, "it just can't be done," loses its effectiveness if the organization knows that the other solution providers can provide that capability.

We should not confound PLM with what software applications a PLM solutions provider offers. The concept of PLM is much larger than the offerings of even the most dominant PLM solutions providers. Organizations need to be continually looking at gaps in their needs that are not being fulfilled by their current suite of software and evaluate offering that fill those gaps. That may sometimes cause friction with the current solutions provider, but that should not stop organizations from engaging in this effort.

ELEMENTS FOR SUCCESS

In order to be successful in transitioning from their current physical product model to a dual physical-virtual model, there are a number of elements that an organization will need to have in place. These elements are: a vision of the future, an assessment of their current position, a plan to bridge the gap, the necessary resources, communications and acceptance, and leadership for the journey.

Vision of the Future

The first thing we need to have is a vision of future. Without that, we will simply get what we get with our current activities. Absent any change in environment, if we do what we did yesterday, we will get the same results. Some organizations operate in this fashion. They are reasonably happy with the current results, so they keep doing the same things over and over again.

The problem with this approach is the phrase "absent any change in environment." The environment is changing as competitors and customers understand what technology has to offer and look to acquire those capabilities. For most organizations, not having a vision of the future is equivalent to deciding to go out of business.

The vision of the future does not need to be cast in concrete. It needs to be directionally sound, but certainly can be conceptual in nature. It can be a framework with pieces to be filled in as technology changes and as we gain experience.

If organizations are to become "virtually perfect," then they will need a vision of the future in order to accomplish this. While there may be many successful variations, the concept of dual products, the old physical product with a new virtual product, provides both the concept and the potential framework. In order be successful in the future, organizations will need to realize that their true value is in their virtual assets and not simply in their physical plant, equipment, and tools. Some of today's top organizations are already thinking in this vein.

The vision of the future should not be so vague as to be little more than platitudes. It should also not be so specifically defined as to prevent adaptation and evolution to the environment as technology changes. It should challenge people to be innovative as opposed to simply being incremental.

Visions are always a little fuzzy, so organizations need to ensure that their people understand the difference between a vision and objectives. Objectives are way stations on the path to the vision. If we don't have objectives, we will never get close to our vision. However, if we don't have a vision, setting objectives will never take us anywhere new or novel.

In predicting a vision of the future, one thing is certain. The future will be different from what we envision. The key is to both being directionally correct and adaptive in our approach, with a willingness to change as the situation changes. What we can be relatively certain of is that this is a unique era of change. We are moving from dealing with physical-only products to physical and virtual products. Organizations that remain wedded to physical-only products will be at a substantial disadvantage to companies with a dual approach. The distinction between products and services will become blurrier and blurrier. Organizations with only a physical product will not be able to provide the services that future product users will value.

This will be a substantial change in many if not most organizations. Defining what their vision of the future will be in providing their customers with new capabilities will be the key to their success and even survival. Again, organizations do not need to have a completely defined vision, but they need to have a vision that will challenge them to think differently than they have in the past.

Assessment of Current Position

In order to have any hope of obtaining their vision of the future, organizations need to have an assessment of their current reality. If we know where we want to go, but do not know where we are, then the chances of getting there are pretty slim. Organizations need to really understand their current situations in order to understand what they will need to do in order to move toward their vision of the future. All too often organizations fail in their efforts because they lack real understanding of their current situation.

I see organizations all the time where this is the situation. I visit with senior managers where I ask them about gaps that I see in their organization. Invariably, they will tell me that they have them handled and/or dismiss any notion that they have any issues. In numerous situations, I have seen problems play out that are a result of these gaps. Senior management always seems surprised when this occurs.

Sometimes the reason for this blindness is arrogance. The organization could not have had this gap because the brilliant senior executives would have seen it. More often, the issue is one of denial. If the gap does exist, then senior managers are going to have to spend time and resources to resolve it. This gets in the way of their current plans, and they would rather believe that the problem does not exist.

Life is much simpler if that is the case, right up until the time the problem arising from this gap surfaces and bites them. One indication that I see when this is the situation is that senior management becomes defensive when asked about these gaps. There is no reason to become defensive if the gaps do not truly exist. Being defensive means that at some level the senior executives know they have an issue. They just do not want to have to address it.

Understanding the current situation is essential. Organizations need to have an assessment of their people, their process and practices, and their technology. The Airbus 380 is a cautionary tale in not understanding an organization's current situation. Airbus had a vision of the future, their new plane. However, they had a lack of understanding of where they were with their virtual technology. Their inability to have wiring designs on one CAD system fit into the plane that was designed on a different version of that CAD system led to a $6 billion profit problem. An inability to have a realistic assessment of the current situation can have disastrous consequences.

A common assessment tool is the SWOT analysis. SWOT stands for strengths, weaknesses, opportunities, and threats. This assessment tool has been taught to business students for decades. It is a good framework for assessing where we are.

We will have already addressed the opportunity aspect of this framework in our vision for the future. The purpose of this book has been to argue for the opportunities implicit in the idea of virtual products. There are numerous opportunities for organizations to use virtual products and PLM to create value for their customers. The vision of the future described above will hopefully have been crafted to incorporate many of the opportunities that virtual products can create.

Strengths are those things in our organization that we will want to build upon and exploit in obtaining our vision. As it relates to PLM, strengths can include such things as a workforce well acquainted with digital tools, a robust and extensive computer and communications infrastructure, or the use of cross functional teams to create, build, and support products. Again, we need to be honest in our assessment. Hoping we have certain strengths and having certain strengths are two different things entirely. Hope not grounded in reality is fantasy. If we're going to build upon a strength, then we need to make very sure that it really exists.

Weaknesses are issues internal to us that we need to substantially lessen or eliminate entirely. Weaknesses are elements about ourselves that will prevent us from realizing our vision. In the context of PLM, weaknesses can include a highly siloed organization where information is rarely shared, a supply chain that is paper driven and not digital, a dominant IT organization that makes decisions about how the functional units should do their jobs, or a workforce that has not been educated but simply trained.

Threats are those things external to the organization that potentially could cause us not to reach our goals. Threats need to be countered or eliminated in order for us to accomplish our vision. Threats can include competitors who are farther along in developing virtual products that create new value for our customers. A threat can be having customers who do not as yet understand the new value of digital products. A threat could also be an organization who in the past has provided support services for our product and who will not take lightly to our extending our reach by virtual products into their revenue area.[74]

Unlike strengths and weaknesses, we are not in control of threats. In addition, threats are not static. They can come at any time and from any direction. While we may be able to assess our strengths and weaknesses and feel comfortable that we understand them, we must continually scan the environment for new threats.

Strengths, weaknesses, and threats are the keys to capitalizing on our opportunities. Assessing them realistically and honestly is critical for us to understand where we are positioned.

Plan to Bridge the Gap

The next thing organizations need to have is the plan to bridge the gap between the current situation and the vision of the future. It is important to realize two things. First, there is not one right plan. The most important thing is to have a plan. A plan is simply a construct around which we can organize. As I often say, "any plan will do."

The second issue is that plans need to be adaptive. Nothing ever goes according to plan. While it is good to have a plan to organize around, slavish obedience to a plan will never get us to where we want to go. We need to be adaptive. That does not mean loose or sloppy, but it does mean that as we get information we make adjustments. No one can ever predict the state of the future, therefore we can never have a plan that works no matter what happens.

While there is plenty of literature on creating business plans, I would like to make a couple of points as it relates to virtual products and PLM. The first is that PLM is a new paradigm that many people will have to be convinced of its value. It is important that there be some quick wins in order to convince people that PLM is the right approach.

Unlike Enterprise Resource Planning (ERP), PLM is not an all or nothing proposition. Organizations do not need to go virtual in one fell swoop. Chances are good that organizations that approach this with a Big Bang philosophy will be disappointed, frustrated, and lose credibility with their people. PLM proponents should pick from the laundry list of PLM use cases and select one or two initially that they have great confidence can be successful.

In keeping with that, plans need to have checkpoints, and the success criteria needs to be evaluated early and often. Not only is PLM a relatively new concept, but the technology is also rapidly changing. As I mentioned before, we need to move directionally toward our vision of the future, but we need to be adaptive in both our vision and in the means to get there. Stepping back and taking stock on a frequent basis is highly advisable. Even stopping and reassessing is preferable to continuing to follow a plan that is not working. As I will discuss below, this requires real leadership as we transition from a physical-only world to one that is both physical and virtual.

Necessary Resources

The ability to marshal the necessary resources in order to carry out a plan to bridge the gap between where the organization is today and the vision of the future is a critical piece that is often overlooked in otherwise excellent works on strategic planning. It is clear that the academic writers of these papers and books never had to obtain the necessary resources to actually execute a plan. The general assumption, even in those works that deal with resources, is that the resources are available and that is a matter of identifying and marshaling those resources.

In smaller entrepreneurial companies, finding the cash to fund receivables and make payroll, let alone fund investment that the new virtual world requires, is a constant struggle. In difficult economic times, such as we have experienced at the end of the 2000's decade, even major corporations have had issues with obtaining resources. Who would have possibly thought that General Motors would run out of cash? But it did.

The fact of the matter is that we can have the right vision of the future, a realistic assessment of where we are today, and a great plan for bridging the gap. However, if we do not have adequate resources to execute our plan, it is all for naught. Having necessary resources is critical to accomplishing our vision of the future.

In addition, while the lack of resources is clearly an issue, having too many resources is also an issue. Too many organizations and too many managers think that throwing resources at an issue is the answer. The abundance of resources can lead organizations to confuse activities with accomplishments.

Having too much budget can lead to putting up too many mediocre projects rather than concentrating on a few outstanding ones. Money does not automatically translate into the specific resources that we require. Throwing money, instead of the right resources, at a project more often than not leads to poor result.

The development people at universities have a phrase of "treasure, talent, and time" to describe what they would like to get from their donors. I think it is a good description of the way that we should think of resources for our projects. Clearly, the treasure aspect of resources is important, but, as I have described above, it is not the only resource. The abundance of it can often be counterproductive.

As important, if not more important, is availability of talent. As I have repeatedly said, people are the most important element of PLM. Having the right people with the right capabilities and attitudes trump the amount of treasure that an organization has available. To see an example of this, we only have to look at the entrepreneurial activity in Silicon Valley, which has driven the major technology advances of the last part of the 20th century.

While treasure in the form of budget is critical to our being able to implement a vision of the virtual future, who we spend our budget on will be the difference between success and failure. We need individuals working on our plan who are bright, focused, and share an understanding of the digital future.

The last resource we have is time. Time is the scarcest resource we possess. Once a minute ticks away, it is gone for good. We need to make sure that we allocate enough time for our plan. Again, it needs to be the right amount of time. Too little time and we will not accomplish our goals. Too much time and our competitors will beat us to the market.

One resource that the university development people do not mention, but I have emphasized time and time again is the resource of information. Information is a substitute for wasting resources, something in this day and age no organization can afford to do. If we are to effectively use the resources that we have access to, then we need to create and maintain the information that we need in order not to waste valuable resources.

In the past, we may have had the luxury of treasure, talent, and time in excess of what we needed. As I pointed out in my previous book, the drivers of PLM are increasing scale in size of the organization, increasing product complexity, decreasing cycle times, globalization, and increasing regulation. These drivers are reducing or eliminating the excess resources that we once enjoyed. We need to employ information in order to effectively use the resources that we have access to.

Having the necessary resources in order to implement our plan is a key element. We need to understand what those resources are and how we are going to obtain them in order to be successful. Moving to a virtual world will require the right amount and kind of resources, deployed effectively.

Communication and Acceptance

The mistake that organizations often make is to underestimate the role that communications plays in having people understand and accept what they need to do in order to be successful. This is partly due to the misconception that organizations are all about process. They think if they define the processes appropriately, then they will get behavior from people that they want.

I was once asked by a leading aerospace company to help them with just-in-time training on PLM. They viewed people the same way they viewed their robots on the factory floor. If they could just "program" their employees the right way, then they could get the results they were looking for.

But as I described in an earlier chapter, we have very different hardware than factory robots have. Our brains are very different from computers. We are not programmed. We program ourselves.

In order to be successful in moving to our vision of the future, we need to both train and educate our people. For well-controlled processes, we can use training. However, for practices, we need to educate. If we are simply striving to be lean, then we may be able to use training and processes to do that. However, if what we require is innovation, then we'll need to educate and engage in practices.

Education requires that we communicate all three elements: our vision of the future, our current assessment, and our plan for bridging the gap. We need to make sure that our people not only know what they need to do but why they are doing it. Too often, organizations believe it is enough to tell people what to do. They may even get short-term results from doing that. However, people respond better and accept their roles and responsibilities better when they understand why they are doing things. In fact, when people understand the "why," because they are often much more knowledgeable about the tasks they perform, they have ideas for improvements that we, as management, had not thought about.

Organizations often think about communication with employees as a perfunctory matter. It is often done in conjunction with their other work. However, if we want people to change themselves, we need to give them the time and the environment to provide the necessary focus to do so. As organizations, we need to do a much better job in educating people as to why they need to embrace our vision of the future along with how they need to do so. It is only by doing this that we will get the acceptance that we need.

Leadership for the Journey

The last element we need is leadership for the journey between where we are and where we want to be. There is a big difference between managership and leadership. Too often we confuse the first with the second. While we may be able to get away with managing, when all we want to accomplish is the status quo, we need leadership wherever there is substantial change involved between where we are today and our vision of the future.

As I said above, our vision of the future is one of direction and not of an exact state. This means that we will need to make adjustments along the way. If we don't have leadership to be able to assess and modify our direction, we most likely may meet the goal that we set out to reach, but is not the goal that we really need to reach.

The leadership that we need is not simply the executive who is in charge, but we need shared leadership throughout the organization. Everyone can be a leader in their own way, if they understand what we are trying to achieve and why.

This is the other reason to educate rather than train. We want our most important resource, our people, to be constantly thinking about how we can best achieve the goals we have articulated. This virtual environment that we want to exploit is very different from the physical environment that we have worked with for thousands of years. We do not know nor understand all the characteristics that we will need in order to take full advantage of this new environment. We do know that we will need to be both lean and innovative.

This final chapter provided suggestions on how organizations can be successful using virtual products. The chapter discussed the three elements that make up PLM: people, process/practice, and technology. It also discussed the elements that are needed for success in the area of virtual products and Product Lifecycle Management.

With respect to people, the suggestions for success included engaging executive leadership, educating people on Product Lifecycle Management and virtual products, cross pollinating the organization with other organizations that are working with and having success in Product Lifecycle Management, and, finally, providing the capability for people to focus on making the necessary changes.

In the area of process/practice, the suggestions included distinguishing between process and practice, reengineering processes for the digital environment, matching instructions with the type of process or practice, matching the amount of information according to the type of process or practice, and being able to capture the information that was the result of practice activities. In the technology area, the suggestions were to match technology to the organizations' use cases, to refrain from customizing, and to continue to evaluate other technology offerings.

The chapter finished up with a discussion of the elements necessary for success. While the discussion concerns virtual products and Product Lifecycle Management, these are elements that would be necessary for any strategic plan. These elements for success include: a vision of the future, assessment of an organization's current position, a plan to bridge the gap between the current position and the vision of the future, marshaling the necessary resources to implement that plan, communications of the plan and vision and acceptance by the organization, and leadership for the journey toward the vision.

While Product Lifecycle Management is still in its early stage, many organizations have reaped tremendous advantages from focusing on and adopting PLM. For organizations that want to be both lean and innovative, a focus on Product Lifecycle Management is a requirement. While organizations will never be "perfect," they can become "virtually perfect" by adopting the concept of Product Lifecycle Management with this duality of the physical product and the virtual product.

Notes

74 From a conceptual perspective, these categories are all "competition." For the definitive book on this topic, see Porter, M. E. (2008). On competition (Updated and expanded ed.). Boston, MA: Harvard Business School Pub.

15

VIRTUALLY UNFINISHED

In opening this book, I described two issues that made second books difficult. These two issues are remaining consistent with the first book and yet covering new and informative material. There is a third issue with respect to the topic of Product Lifecycle Management. That issue is completing a book with the topic of discussion still evolving. Waiting until the area of Product Lifecycle Management stopped progressing would mean that this book would never be finished, at least not in the foreseeable future.

With that in mind, I realize that there are important areas that have been left unexamined. However, I would at least like to directionally indicate where I think advances will be made and barriers yet to be overcome.

I will divide my discussions among the three primary components of Product Lifecycle Management, namely technology, processes/practices, and people. Intentionally, this order is the reversal of what I believe to be the most important.

TECHNOLOGY

This is the area where I am most confident of evolution. Moore's Law is alive and well and shows no signs of abatement. The exponential growth of computing, communications, and storage capabilities will continue at an exponential pace. We have reached an inflection point of this exponential curve, so progress will be virtually unlimited, in both senses of the term. We passed 1 billion transistors on a chip in 2007. We are projected to pass an astounding trillion transistors on a chip by the year 2020. This is merely taking into account transistor density and does not take into account the power increases due to such things as multicore processors. If quantum computing or biological computing becomes more than a lab experiment, we would not be able to even imagine the kind of capability we could have.

The impacts of these technology increases will be felt in two areas. The first is in expansion of virtual capabilities. We will continue to get closer and closer to passing my tests of virtuality, where we can simulate the real world with computers. We will move from point solutions to more integrated capabilities. We will cross domain boundaries and pursue multi-domain capabilities, such as combining mechanical with electrical. Computer-aided engineering solvers will be integrated with each other and with the geometric design.

The second impact will be in the computing capabilities of the products themselves. We will go from millions of lines of code in products to tens of millions of lines of code to hundreds of millions of lines of code. Products will become much more "intelligent" and, as a result, more autonomous. It will be imperative that we virtually mirror these products, so that not only can we know how they are changing, but that also we can control them. Without this virtual mirroring, we could find our products outside of our control like Skynet of the Terminator movies.

We will have the capabilities of having very granular information about our products and the means to communicate that information to us. This will allow us to have a better understanding of product behavior and a subsequent increase in quality, because we will have information as to whether the product was successful in its intended use.

The issue of ownership and usage rights to information is as much of a people issue as it is a technical issue. We have well-established understandings, embodied in usage, policies, and even laws, to deal with ownership and usage of physical products. We are evolving and will continue to evolve these elements for virtual products. I look at this issue to be one that gets much attention in the coming years.

PROCESSES/PRACTICES

The four strategic drivers or goals of PLM that I have identified are productivity, innovation, quality, and collaboration. Processes and practices are the means to obtain these characteristics.

Processes are the means to obtain productivity or efficiencies. As more and more processes can be automated because we have better computing capability, our organizations can become more productive, efficient, and lean. The resources we free up will allow us more time to focus on practices, which has impacts on both innovation and quality. However, the issue is whether or not we will recognize that there is something else that goes on in our organization besides processes and not simply become a slave to processes at the expense of innovation.

As I have discussed, informational requirements for processes and practices differ. The issue will be how we take the wealth of information that will be available and present it to the individual who needs it. The idea of cued availability, where information will be presented depending on the individual and the context of their problem, will determine whether or not we can take a giant leap in creating new and innovative products.

Collaboration is not a direct goal, but is an enabler of the other three, quality, innovation, and productivity. The premise is that the better we collaborate with those within our organization, our supply chain, and our customers, the better we can break down the silos these groups are in and unlock productivity, innovation, and quality. The rise of information-based social networking is connecting people together as never before irrespective of past time/place physical constraints. How organizations will harness this enabling technology for productive and not simply trivial interactions is still evolving.

PEOPLE

This is the most important aspect of Product Lifecycle Management and the least under our control. Whether we'll be able to take full advantage of the technology and new processes and practices will depend on whether or not people will change and adapt to new ways of doing things. As I have discussed previously, the status quo is energy-efficient. As a general rule, people do not like to change.

How rapidly we will be able to take advantage of new capabilities will depend on how well an organization's leadership can and will change. If the leadership retains its attachments to the old ways of doing things, then progress will be slow.

Eventually, as always happens, progress wins out. Competitors who move to more efficient and effective ways of doing things drive their less efficient competitors from the marketplace. While the issue of technology is not wholly a generational one, later generations are more receptive to technology that they grew up with than the older generations who were not exposed to these technologies earlier in life. While the senior leadership of some organizations are highly receptive to digital and virtual technologies, there are other organizations with senior leadership who cannot put aside 2-D drawings and physical prototypes. The evolution to digital capabilities will eventually occur. The question will be how long it will take, not if it will occur.

For these reasons, Product Lifecycle Management is virtually unfinished. In fact in keeping with this theme, I might say that Product Lifecycle Management is only virtually starting. PLM is not in its infancy anymore, but with some of the issues of people, processes/practices, and technology there certainly is a feeling of adolescence. However, I am confident that because of the advantages of these concepts, we will see continued progress being made in the area of PLM.

Organizations that are adopting the concept of PLM in its entirety are "virtually successful" in the sense that, while it may not be a complete success as yet, they are making good progress in changing the way they are approaching product creation, manufacturing, sustaining, and disposal. They also are acquiring technology, but that technology is not simply a tool employed at the edges, but is an enabler of change in people's understanding of products and in the processes and practices that people employ to realize those products. These organizations' virtual successes include a transformation from thinking about products as only physical objects. They now view products as dual objects: a physical product and a virtual product.

Products that are "Virtually Perfect" are in our not-too-distant future.

ABOUT THE AUTHOR

Dr. Michael Grieves splits his time between the business and academic worlds. He is the author of the seminal book on PLM, *Product Lifecycle Management: Driving the Next Generation of Lean Thinking* (McGraw-Hill, 2006). He has authored numerous papers and articles for both industry and academic publications.

Dr. Grieves consults with a select number of international manufacturers, governmental organizations such as NASA and DoD, and information technology providers on PLM-related issues and has given speeches world-wide at PLM, engineering, and manufacturing conferences.

Dr. Grieves has been a Co-Director of the Purdue PLM Center of Excellence and served as a Visiting Professor at the Purdue University College of Technology. Dr. Grieves has also had positions with the Engineering College at the University of Michigan, the MIS Department at the University of Arizona, and the business school at the University of Kansas.

Dr. Grieves is Chairman Emeritus of Oakland University's School of Business Board of Visitors. He has taught in the United States, China, and Europe at the university senior undergraduate, and graduate school levels and has authored and taught executive education courses. Dr. Grieves is currently a Professor at CIMBA University, Asolo, Italy with an appointment at the University of Iowa.

Dr. Grieves is a founder and board member of Interactive Frontiers, Inc. the world leader in golf and sport instructional software, Dr. Grieves has over thirty-five years experience in the computer and data communications industry. He has been a senior executive at both Fortune 1000 companies and entrepreneurial organizations during his career. He founded and took public a $100 million systems integration company and subsequently served as its audit and compensation committee chair after recruiting a new CEO. Dr. Grieves has substantial board experience, including serving on a subsidiary company of NTT Communications of Japan.

Dr. Grieves has a Bachelor of Science, Computer Engineering (B.S.C.E) from Michigan State University, an M.B.A. from Oakland University, and an E.D.M. doctorate from Case Western Reserve University Weatherhead School of Management.

INDEX